THE COMPLETE WORKS

OF

ANDREW MARVELL

IN FOUR VOLUMES.

Vol. III. Prose.

AMS PRESS, INC.
New York
1966

AMS PRESS, INC.
New York, N.Y. 10003
1966

Manufactured in the United States of America

The Fuller Worthies' Library.

THE

COMPLETE WORKS OF ANDREW MARVELL
M.P.

Vol. III.

I. THE REHEARSAL TRANSPROSED. PART I. . . . . pp. 1—228
II. THE REHEARSAL TRANSPROSED. PART II. . . pp. 229—524
III. NOTES AND ILLUSTRATIONS . . . . pp. 525—580

𝔗𝔥𝔢 𝔉𝔲𝔩𝔩𝔢𝔯 𝔚𝔬𝔯𝔱𝔥𝔦𝔢𝔰' 𝔏𝔦𝔟𝔯𝔞𝔯𝔶.

THE COMPLETE PROSE WORKS

OF

ANDREW MARVELL

M.P.

FOR THE FIRST TIME FULLY COLLECTED AND COLLATED
WITH THE ORIGINAL AND EARLY EDITIONS, AND CONSIDERABLY
ENLARGED WITH HITHERTO INEDITED PROSE AND POEMS,
AND A TRANSLATION OF THE GREEK AND LATIN: AND
IN THE QUARTO FORM AN ORIGINAL PORTRAIT ON STEEL, AND OTHER
PORTRAITS, FACSIMILES, AND ILLUSTRATIONS.

EDITED, WITH MEMORIAL-INTRODUCTION, ESSAY, AND NOTES,

BY THE

REV. ALEXANDER B. GROSART,
ST. GEORGE'S, BLACKBURN, LANCASHIRE.

VOL. I.

PRINTED FOR PRIVATE CIRCULATION.
1873.

106 *copies only.*

THE REHEARSAL TRANSPROSED:

BOTH PARTS:

1672–1673.

NOTE.

NAMES, quotations, allusions, manners and customs, sayings, out-of-the-way words, and the like, in 'The Rehearsal Transprosed,' will be found elucidated and illustrated in Notes and Illustrations at end of this Volume; arranged according to the pages in which they occur. G.

THE

REHEARSAL

TRANSPROS'D;

Or,

Animadversions

Upon a late Book, Intituled,

A PREFACE

SHEWING

*What Grounds there are
of Fears and Jealousies
of* Popery.

The second Impression, with Additions
and Amendments.

London, Printed by *J. D.* for the Assigns of
John Calvin and *Theodore Beza*, at the sign
of the *King's Indulgence*, on the South-side
the Lake-*Lemane;* and sold by *N. Ponder* in
Chancery-Lane, 1672.

AN
ADVERTISEMENT FROM THE BOOKSELLER.

THIS Book having wrought it self thorow many difficulties, it hath newly incountred with that of a Counterfeit Impression in 12° under the Title and pretence of *the 2d Edition Corrected.* Whereas in truth that Impression is so far from having been Corrected, that it doth grosly and frequently corrupt both the Sence and Words of the Coppy.

N. P.

ANIMADVERSIONS UPON THE PREFACE TO BISHOP BRAMHALL'S VINDICATION,
ETC.

THE Author of this Preface had first writ *A Discourse of Ecclesiastical Policy;* after that, *A Defence and Continuation of the Ecclesiastical Policy;* and there he concludes his Epistle to the Reader in these words: 'But if this be the penance I must undergo for the wantonness of my pen, to answer the impertinent and slender exceptions of every peevish and disingenuous caviller; Reader, I am reformed from my incontinency of scribling, and do here heartily bid thee an eternal farewell.' Now this expression lyes open to his own dilemma against the Nonconformists confessing in their prayers to God such heinous enormities. For if he will not accept his own charge, his modesty is all impudent and counterfeit; or, if he will acknowledge it, why then he had been before, and did still remain upon record, the same wanton and incontinent Scribler.

But, however, I hop'd he had been a clergyman of

honour, and that when herein the world and he himself were now so fully agreed in the censure of his Writings, he would have kept his word; or at least that his pen would not so soon have created us a disturbance of the same nature, and so far manifested how indifferent he is as to the business either of Truth or Eternity. But the Author, alas, instead of his own, was fallen now into Amaryllis's dilemma.—I perceive the gentleman hath travelled by his remembring *Chi lava la testa al asino perde il sapone;* and therefore hope I may without pedantry quote the words in her own whining Italian:

> *S' il peccar è sì dolce e 'l non peccar sì necessario,*
> *O troppo imperfetta natura che ripugni a la legge!*
> *O troppo dura legge che natura offendi!*

> If to scrible be so sweet, and not to scrible be so necessary;
> O too frail inclination, that contradicteth obligation!
> O too severe obligation, that offendeth inclination!

For all his promise to write no more, I durst alwaies have laid ten pound to a crown on Nature's side. And accordingly he hath now blessed us with, as he calls it, *A Preface, shewing what Grounds there are of Fears and Jealousies of Popery.*

It will not be unpleasant to hear him begin his story: 'The ensuing treatise of Bishop Bramhall's being somewhat superannuated, the Bookseller was very sollicitous to have it set off with some Preface that might recommend it to the genius of the Age, and reconcile it to the present juncture of affairs.' A pretty task indeed! That is as much as to say, to trick-up the good old Bishop in a yellow coif and a bull's head, that he may be fit for the publick, and appear in fashion. In the mean time, 'tis what I always presaged: from a writer of books, our Author is already dwinled to a preface-monger, and from prefaces I am confident he may in a short time be improved to endite tickets for the Bear-garden. But the Bookseller I see was a cunning fellow, and knew his man. For who so proper as a young priest to sacrifice to the genius of the Age; yea, though his conscience were the offering? And none more ready to nick a juncture of affairs than a malapert chaplain; though not one indeed of a hundred but dislocates them in the handling. And yet our Author is very maidenly, and condescends to his Bookseller not without some reluctance, as being, forsooth, first of all 'none of the most zealous patrons of the press.'

Though he hath so lately forfeited his credit, yet herein I dare believe him: for the Press hath ought him a shame a long time, and is but now beginning to pay-off the debt. The Press (that villanous engine) invented much about the same time with the Reformation, that hath done more mischief to the discipline of our Church than all the doctrine can make amends for; 'twas an happy time when all learning was in manuscript, and some little officer, like our Author, did keep the keys of the Library. When the clergy needed no more knowledg than to read the Liturgy, and the laiety no more clerkship than to save them from hanging. But now, since Printing came into the world, such is the mischief, that a man cannot write a Book but presently he is answered. Could the Press but once be conjured to obey only an *Imprimatur*, our Author might not disdain perhaps to be one of its most zealous patrons. There have been wayes found out to banish ministers, to find not only the people, but even the grounds and fields where they assembled in conventicles; but no Art yet could prevent these seditious meetings of letters. Two or three brawny fellows in a corner, with meer ink and elbow-grease, do more harm than 'an hundred systematical divines' with their 'sweaty preaching.' And, which is a strange thing, the very spunges, which one would think should rather deface and blot-out the whole Book, and were antiently used to that purpose, are become now the instruments to make things legible. Their ugly printing-letters, that look but like so many rotten-teeth, how oft have they been pull'd out by B. and L. the publick-tooth-drawers! and yet these rascally operators of the Press have got a trick to fasten them again in a few minutes, that they grow as firm a set and as biting and talkative as ever. O Printing, how hast thou disturb'd the peace of mankind! that lead, when moulded into bullets, is not so mortal as when founded into letters! There was a mistake sure in the story of Cadmus; and the serpent's teeth which he sowed were nothing else but the letters which he invented. The first essay that was made towards this Art was in single characters upon iron, wherewith of old they stigmatized slaves and remarkable offenders; and it was of good use sometimes to brand a schismatick. But a bulky Dutchman diverted it quite from its first institution, and contriving those innumerable *syntagmes* of alphabets,- hath pestred the world ever since with ' the gross bodies of their German divinity.' One would have thought in reason that a Dutchman at least might have contented himself only with the winepress.

But, next of all, our Author, beside his aversion from the press, alledges, that ' he is as much concerned as De Wit, or any of the high and mighty Burgomasters, in matters of a closer and more comfortable importance to himself and his own affairs.' And yet whoever shall take the pains to read over his Preface, will find that it intermeddles with the King, the Succession, the Privy-council, Popery, Atheism, Bishops, Ecclesiastical Government, and above all with Nonconformity, and J. O. A man would wonder what this thing should be of a 'closer importance;' but being ' more comfortable' too, I conclude it must be one of these three things; either his salvation, or a benefice, or a female. Now as to Salvation, he could not be so much concern'd, for that care was over; there hath been a course taken to insure all that are on his bottom. And he is yet surer of a benefice; or else his patrons must be very ungrateful. He cannot have deserved less than a Prebend for his first book, a sinecure for his second, and for his third a rectorship, although it were that of Malmsbury. Why, then, of necessity it must be a female. For that, I confess, might have been a sufficient excuse from writing of Prefaces, and against the importunity of the Bookseller. 'Twas fit that all business should have given place to the work of propagation. Nor was there any thing that could more closely import him, than that the race and family of the Railers should be perpetuated among mankind. Who could in reason expect that a man should in the same moments undertake the labour of an Author and a father? 'Nevertheless,' he saith, ' he could not but yield so far as to improve every fragment of time that he could get into his own disposal, to gratify the importunity of the Bookseller.' Was ever civility graduated up and inhanc'd to such a value! His mistris herself could not have endeared a favour so nicely, nor granted it with more sweetness.

Was the Bookseller more importunate, or the Author more courteous?

The Author was the pink of courtesie, the Bookseller the bur of importunity.

And so, not being able to shake him off, 'this,' he saith, ' hath brought forth this Preface, such an one as it is ; for how it will prove, he himself neither is, nor (till 'tis too late) ever shall be a competent judge, in that it must be ravish'd out of his hands before his thoughts can possibly be cool enough to revive or correct the indecencies either of its stile or contrivance.' He is now growing a very enthusiast himself. No Nonconformist minister, as it seems, could have spoken more *extempore*. I see he is not so civil to his readers as he was to his Bookseller : and so A. C. and James Collins be gratified, he cares not how much the rest of the world be disobliged. Some man, that had less right to be fastidious and confident, would, before he exposed himself in publick, both have cool'd his thoughts, and corrected his indecencies; or would have considered whether it were necessary or wholsome that he should write at all. Forasmuch as one of the ancient Sophists (they were a kind of orators of his form) kill'd himself with declaming while he had a bone in his throat, and J. O. was still in being. ' Put up your trumpery, good noble marquess.' But there was no holding him. Thus it must be and no better, when a man's phancy is up, and his breeches are down; when the mind and the body make contrary assignations, and he hath both a Bookseller at once and a mistriss to satisfie; like Archimedes, into the street he runs out naked with his invention. And truly, if at any time, we might now pardon this extravagance and rapture of our Author, when he was perch'd upon the highest pinnacle of ecclesiastical felicity, being ready at once to asswage his concupiscence, and wreck [=wreak] his malice.

But yet he ' knows not which way his mind will work it self and its thoughts.' This is Bayes the second.—'Tis no matter for the plot—the intrigo was out of his head.—But you'l apprehend it better when you see't.' Or rather, he is like Bayes his actors, 'that could not guess what humour they were to be in: whether angry, melancholly, merry, or in love.' Nay, insomuch that he saith, 'he is neither prophet nor astrologer enough to foretell.' Never man certainly was so unacquainted with himself. And, indeed, 'tis part of his discretion to avoid his acquaintance and tell him as little of his mind as may be: for he is a dangerous fellow. But I must ask pardon if I treat him too homely. It is his own fault that misled me at first by concealing his quality under such vulgar comparisons as De Wit and the Burgomasters. I now see it all along: This can be no less a man than Prince Volscius himself, in dispute betwixt his boots which way his mind will 'work itself;' whether Love shall detain him with his 'closer importance, Parthenope, whose mother, sir, sells ale by the town wall:' or Honour shall carry him 'to head the army that lies concealed for him at Knightssbridge,' and to encounter J. O.

> ' Go on, cryes Honour: tender Love saith Nay.
> Honour aloud commands, Pluck both boots on.
> But safer Love doth whisper, Put on none.'

And so now, when it comes that he is 'not prophet nor astrologer enough to foretell' what he will do, 'tis just

> ' For as bright Day, with black approach of Night,
> Contending, makes a doubtful puzzling light;
> So does my honour and my love together
> Puzzle me so, I am resolv'd on neither.'

Yet no Astrologer could possibly have more advantage and opportunity to make a judgment. For he knew the very minute of the conception of his Preface, which was immediately upon his Majestie's issuing his Declaration of Indulgence to tender consciences. Nor could he be ignorant of the moment when it was brought forth. And I can so far refresh his memory, that it came out in the dog-dayes:

> '... the season hot, and she too near:
> O mighty Love, J. O. will be undone;'

according to the rule in Davenant's Ephemerides: ' But the heads which at this moment, and under the present schemes and aspects of the Heavens he intends to treat of (pure Sidrophel) are these two: first, something of the treatise it self; secondly, of the seasonableness of its publication: and this, unless his humour jade him ('tis come to a dog-trot already), will lead him further into the argument as it relates to the present state of things, and from thence 'tis odds but he shall take occasion to bestow some animadversions upon one J. O.' There's no trusting him: he doubtless knew from the beginning what he intended. And so too all his story of the Bookseller, and all the 'volo nolo's,' and 'shall I, shall I's' betwixt them, was nothing but fooling; and he now all along owns himself to be the Publisher, and alledges the slighter and the main reasons that induced him. Would he had told us so at first; for then he had saved me thus much of my labour; though as it chances it lights not amiss on our Author, whose delicate stomach could not brook that J. O. should say, 'he had prevailed with himself, much against his inclination, to bestow a few (and those idle) hours upon examining his Book:' and yet he himself stumbles so notoriously upon the very same fault at his own threshold.

But now from this Preamble he falls into his Preface to Bishop Bramhall: though indeed like Bayes, his prologue, that would have serv'd as well for an epilogue, I do not see but the Preface might have past as well for a postscript, or the headstall for a crooper. And our Author's divinity might have gone to pushpin with the Bishop, which of their two treatises was the 'procatarctical cause' of both their editions. For, as they are coupled together, to say the truth, 'tis not discernable, as in some animals, whether their motion begin at the head or tail; whether the author made his preface for 'Bishop Bramhall's dear sake,' or whether he published the Bishop's treatise for sake of his 'own dear Preface.' For my own part, I think it reasonable that the Bishop and our Author should (like fair gamsters at leap-frog) stand and skip in their turns; and however our Author got it for once, yet if the Bookseller should ever be sollicitous for a second edition, that then the Bishop's book should have the precedence.

But before I commit myself to the dangerous depths of his Discourse, which I am now upon the brink of, I would, with his leave, make a motion; that, instead of Author, I may henceforth indifferently call him Mr. Bayes as oft as I shall see occasion. And that first, because he hath no name, or at least will not own it, though he himself writes under the greatest security, and gives us the first letters of other men's names before he be asked them. Secondly, because he is, I perceive, a lover of elegancy of stile, and can endure no man's tautologies but his own; and therefore I would not distaste him with too frequent repetition of one word. But chiefly, because Mr. Bayes and he do very much symbolize, in their understandings, in their expressions, in their humour, in their contempt and quarrelling of all others, though of their own profession. Because our divine, the Author, manages his contest with the same prudence and civility which the Players and Poets have practised of late in their several divisions. And lastly, because both their talents do peculiarly lie in exposing and personating the Nonconformists. I would therefore give our Author a name, the memory of which may perpetually excite him to the exercise and highest improvement of that virtue. For, our Cicero doth not yet equal our Roscius, and one turn of Lacy's face hath more 'Ecclesiastical Policy' in it than all the books of our Author put together. Besides, to say Mr. Bayes is more civil than to say villain and caitiff, though these indeed are more tuant. And to conclude, the Irrefragable Doctor of School-divinity, page 460 of his 'Defence,' determining concerning symbolical ceremonies, hath warranted me 'that not only governors, but any thing else may have power to appropriate new names to things, without having absolute authority over the things themselves.' And therefore henceforward, seeing I am on such sure ground, Author, or Mr. Bayes, whether I please. Now, having 'had our dance, let us advance to our more serious counsels.'

And first: Our Author begins with a panegyrick upon Bishop Bramhall; a person whom my age had not given me leave to be acquainted with, nor my good fortune led me to converse with his Writings: but for whom I had collected a deep reverence from the general reputation he carried, beside the veneration due to the place he filled in the Church of England. So that our Author having a mind to shew us some proof of his good nature, and that his eloquence lay'd not all in satyr and invectives, could not, in my opinion, have fixed upon a fitter subject of commendation. And therefore I could have wished for my own sake that I had missed this occasion of being more fully informed of some of the Bishop's principles, whereby I have lost part of that pleasure which I had so long enjoyed in thinking well of so considerable a person. But, however, I recreate my self with believing that my simple judgment cannot, beyond my intention, abate any thing of his just value with others. And seeing he is long since dead, which I knew but lately, and now learn it with regret, I am the more obliged to repair in myself whatsoever breaches of his credit, by that additional civility which consecrates the ashes of the deceased. But by this means I am come to discern how it was possible for our Author to speak a good word for any man. The Bishop was expired, and his Writings jump much with our Author. So that if you have a mind to die, or to be of his Party (there are but these two conditions), you may perhaps be rendered capable of his charity. And then write what you will, he will make you a 'Preface that shall recommend you and it to the genius of the Age, and reconcile it to the juncture of affairs.' But truly he hath acquitted himself herein so ill-favourdly to the Bishop, that I do not think it so much worth to gain his approbation; and I had rather live and enjoy mine own opinion than be so treated.

For, beside his reflection on the Bishop, and the whole age he lived in, that 'he was, as far as the prejudice of the age would permit him, an acute philosopher' (which is a sufficient taste of Mr. Bayes his arrogance, that no man, no age can be so perfect but must abide his censure, and of the officious virulence of his humour, which infuses it self, by a malignant remark, that, but for this acuter philosopher, no man else would have thought of, into the praises of him whom he most intended to celebrate); if, I say, beside this, you consider the most elaborate and studious periods of his commendation, you find it at best very ridiculous. By the language he seems to transcribe out of the 'Grand Cyrus' and 'Cassandra,' but the exploits to have borrowed out of the 'Knight of the Sun' and 'King Arthur.' For in a luscious and effeminate stile he gives him such a termagant character, as must either fright or turn the stomach of any Reader: 'Being of a brave and enterprising temper, of an active and sprightly mind, he was always busied either in contriving or performing great designs.' Well, Mr. Bayes, I suppose by this, that he might have been an overmatch to the Bishop of Cullen [Cologne] and the Bishop of Strasburg. In another place, 'He finished all the glorious designs that he undertook.' This might have become the Bishop of Munster before he had rais'd the siege from Groningen. 'As he was able to accomplish the most gallant attempts, so he was always ready not only to justifie their innocence, but to make good their bravery.' I was too prodigal of my bishops at first, and now have never another left in the Gazette, which is too our Author's Magazin. ' His reputation and innocence were both armor of proof against Toryes and Presbyterians.' But methinks, Mr. Bayes, having to do with such dangerous enemies, you should have furnished him too with some weapon of offence, a good old fox, like that of another heroe, his contemporary in ' action upon the scene of Ireland,' of whom it was sung :

> ' Down by his side he wore a sword of price,
> Keen as a frost, glaz'd like a new-made ice:
> That cracks-men shell'd in steel in a less trice
> Than squirrel's nuts, or the Highlander's lice.'

Then he saith, ' 'Tis true the Church of Ireland was the largest scene of his actions; but yet there in a little time he wrought out such wonderous alterations, and so exceeding all belief, as may convince us that he had a mind large and active enough to have managed the Roman Empire at its greatest extent.' This indeed of our Author's is great; and yet it reacheth not a strain of his fellow-Pendets in the history of the Mogol, where he tells Dancehment Kan, ' That when he put his foot in the stirrop, and when he march'd upon horseback in the front of the cavalry, the earth trembles under his feet, the eight elephants that hold it on their heads not being able to support it.' But enough of this trash.

Beside that it is the highest indecorum for a divine to write in such a stile as this [part Play-book and part Romance] concerning a reverend Bishop: these improbable elogies too are of the greatest disservice to their own design, and do in effect diminish alwayes the person whom they pretend to magnifie. Any worthy man may pass through the world unquestion'd and safe with a moderate recommendation; but when he is thus set off, and bedawb'd with rhetorick, and embroyder'd so thick that you cannot discern the ground, it awakens naturally (and not altogether unjustly) interest, curiosity, and envy. For all men pretend a share in reputation, and love not to see it ingross'd and monopoliz'd, and are subject to enquire (as of great estates suddenly got) whether he came by all this honestly, or of what credit the person is that tells the story? And the same hath happened as to this Bishop, while our Author attributes to him such atchievements, which to one that could believe the legend of Captain Jones, might not be incredible. I have heard that there was indeed such a captain, an honest brave fellow; but a wag, that had a mind to be merry with him, hath quite spoil'd his history. Had our Author epitomiz'd the legend of sixty-six books *De Virtutibus Sancti Patricii* (I mean not the ingenious writer of the 'Friendly Debates,' but St. Patrick, the Irish Bishop), he could not have promis'd us greater. And 'tis well for him that he hath escaped the fate of Secundinus, who (as Josselin relates it) acquainting Patrick that he was inspired to compose something in his commendation, the Bishop foretold the Author should die as soon as it was perfected; which so done, so happened. I am sure our Author had died no other death but of this his own Preface, and a surfeit upon Bishop Bramhall, if the swelling of truth could have choak'd him. He tells us, I remember, somewhere, that this same Bishop of Derry said, 'the Scots had a civil expression for these improvers of verity, that they had good company;' and I shall say nothing severer, than that our Author speaks the language of a lover, and so may claim some pardon, if the habit and excess of his courtship do as yet give a tincture to his discourse upon more ordinary subjects. For I would not by any means be mistaken, as if I thought our Author so sharp set, or so necessitated that he should make a dead bishop his mistress; so far from that, that he hath taken such a course, that if the Bishop were alive, he would be out of love with himself. He hath, like those frightfull looking-glasses made for sport, represented him in such bloated lineaments, as, I am confident, if he could see his face in it, he would break the glass. For, hence it falls out too, that men seeing the Bishop furbish'd up in so martial accoutrements, like another Odo, bishop of Baieux, and having never before heard of his prowess, began to reflect what giants he defeated, and what damsells he rescued. Serious men consider whether he were ingaged in the conduct of the Irish army, and to have brought it over upon England, for the imputation of which the Earl of Strafford, his patron, so undeservedly suffered. But none knowes any thing of it. Others think it not to be taken literally, but the wonderfull and unheard-of alterations that he wrought out in Ireland are meant of some reformation that he made there in things of his own function. But then men ask again, how he comes to have all the honour of it, and whether all the while that great Bishop Usher, his metropolitan, were unconcerned? For even in ecclesiastical combates, how instrumental soever the Captain hath been, the General usually carries away the honour of the action. But the good Primate was engaged in designs of lesser moment, and was writing his *De Primordiis Ecclesiæ Britannicæ*, and the story of Pelagius our countryman. He, honest man, was deep gone in 'Grub-street and polemical divinity,' and troubled with fits of 'modern orthodoxy.' He satisfied himself with being 'admired by the blue and white aprons, and pointed at by the more judicious tankard-bearers.' Nay, which is worst of all, he undertook to abate of our episcopal grandeur, and condescended indeed to reduce the ceremonious discipline in these nations to the primitive simplicity. What, then, was this that Bishop Bramhall did? Did he, like a Protestant apostle, in one day convert thousands of the Irish Papists? The contrary is evident, by the Irish Rebellion and Massacre, which, notwithstanding his 'publick employment and great abilities,' happened in his time. So that, after all our Author's bombast, when we have search'd all over, we find ourselves bilk'd in our expectation; and he hath erected him, like a St. Christopher, in the Popish churches, as big as ten porters, and yet only imploy'd to sweat under the burden of an infant.

All that appears of him is, first, that he busied himself about a 'catholick agreement among the churches of Christendom.' But as to this, our Author himself saith, that he was not 'so vain, or so presuming as to hope to see it effected in his dayes.' And yet but two pages before, he told us that 'the Bishop finish'd all the glorious designes which he undertook.' But this design of his he draws out in such a circuit of words, that 'tis better taking it from the Bishop himself, who speaks more plainly always and much more to the purpose. And he saith, page 87 of his Vindication, 'My design is rather to reconcile the Popish party to the Church of England, than the Church of England to the Pope.' And how he manages it, I had rather any man would learn by reading over his own book, than that I should be thought to misrepresent him, which I might, unless I transcribed the whole. But in summe, it seems to me that he is upon his own single judgment too liberal of the publick, and that he retrenches both on our part more than he hath authority for, and grants more to the Popish than they can of right pretend to. It is, however, indeed a most glorious design, to reconcile all the churches to one doctrine and communion (though some that meddle in it do it chiefly in order to fetter men straiter under the formal bondage of fictitious discipline); but it is a thing rather to be wished and prayed for, than to be expected from these kind of endeavours. It is so large a field, that no man can see to the end of it : and all that have adventured to travel it have been bewildred. That man must have a vast opinion of his own sufficiency, that can think he may by his oratory or reason, either in his own time, or at any of our Author's ' more happy junctures of affairs,' so far perswade and fascinate the Roman Church, having by a regular contexture of continued Policy for so many ages interwoven itself with the secular interest, and made itself necessary to most princes, and having at last erected a throne of infallibility over their conscience, as to prevail with her to submit a power and empire so acquired and established in compromise to the arbitration of an humble Proposer. God only in His own time, and by the inscrutable methods of His providence, is able to effect that alteration : though I think too He hath signified in part by what means He intends to accomplish it, and to range so considerable a Church, and once so exemplary, into primitive unity and Christian order. In the mean time such projects are fit for pregnant scholars that have nothing else to do, to go big with for forty years, and may qualifie them to discourse with princes and statesmen at their leisure; but I never saw that they came to use or possibility: no more than that of Alexander's architect, who proposed to make him a statue of the mountain Athos (and that was no mole-hill); and among other things, that statue to carry in its hand a great habitable city. But the surveyor was gravell'd, being asked whence that city should be supplied with water. I would only have ask'd the Bishop, when he had carv'd and hammer'd the Romanists and Protestants into one Colossian church, how we should have done as to matter of Bibles. For the Bishop, p. 117, complains that 'unqualified people should have a promiscuous licence to read the Scriptures:' and you may guess thence, if he had moreover the Pope to friend, how the laity should have been used. There have been attempts in former ages to dig through the separating Isthmos of Peloponnesus, and another to make communication between the Red Sea and the Mediterranean; both more easie than to cut this ecclesiastick canal, and yet both laid by partly upon the difficulty of doing it, and partly upon the inconveniences if it had been effected. I must confess freely, yet I ask pardon for the presumption, that I cannot look upon these undertaking Churchmen, however otherwise of excellent prudence and learning, but as men struck with a notion, and craz'd on that side of their head. And so I think even the Bishop had much better have busied himself in preaching in his own diocess, and disarming the Papists of their arguments, instead of rebating our weapons, than in taking an œcumenical care upon him, which none called him to, and, as appears by the sequel, none conn'd him thanks for. But if he were so great a politician as I have heard, and indeed believe him to have been, methinks he should in the first place have contriv'd how we might live well with our Protestant neighbours, and to have united us in one body under the King of England, as head of the Protestant interest, which might have rendered us more considerable, and put us into a more likely posture to have reduced the church of Rome to reason. For the most leading party of the English clergy in his time retained such a pontifical stiffness towards the foreign divines, that it puts me in mind of Austin the monk, when he came into Kent, not deigning to rise up to the British or give them the hand, and could scarce afford their churches either communion or charity, or common civility. So that it is not to be wondred if they also on their parts looked upon our models of accommodation with the same jealousie that the British Christians had at Austin's design, to unite them first to (that is under) the Saxons, and then deliver them both over, bound, to the Papal government and ceremonies. But seeing hereby our hands were weakened, and there was no probability of arriving so near the end of the work as to a consent among Protestants abroad; had the Bishop but gone that step, to have reconciled the ecclesiastical differences in our own nations, and that we might have stood firm at home before we had taken such a jump beyond sea, it would have been a performance worthy of his wisdom. For at that time the ecclesiastical rigours here were in the highest ferment, and the Church in being, arrayed itself against the peaceable Dissenters only in some points of worship. And what great undertaking could we be ripe for abroad, while so divided at home? or what fruit expected from the labour of those mediating divines in weighty matters, who were not yet past the sucking-bottle; but seem'd to place all the business of Christianity in persecuting men for their consciences, differing from them in smaller matters? How ridiculous must we be to the Church of Rome to interpose in her affairs, and force our mediation upon her, when besides our ill correspondence with the foreign Protestants, she must observe our weakness within ourselves, that we could not, or would not step over a straw, though for the perpetual settlement and security of our Church and Nation! She might well look upon us as those that probably might be forced at some time by our folly to call her in to our assistance (for with no weapons or arguments but what are fetch'd out of her arsenals can the ceremonial-controversie be rightly defended), but never could she consider us as of such authority or wisdom as to give balance to her counsels. But this was far from Bishop Bramhall's thoughts; who, so he might (like Cæsar) 'manage the Roman empire at its utmost extent,' had quite forgot what would conduce to the peace of his own province and country; for, page 57, he settles this maxim as a truth, 'That second reformations are commonly like metal upon metal, which is false heraldry.' Where, by the way, it is a wonder that our Author, in enumerating the Bishop's perfections in divinity, law, history, and philosophy, neglected this peculiar gift he had in heraldry; and omitted to tell us that his mind was large enough to have animated the kingdoms of Garter and Clarencieux at their greatest dimensions. But, beside what I have said already in relation to this project upon Rome, there is this more, which I confess was below Bishop Bramhall's reflection, and was indeed fit only for some vulgar politician, or the commissioners of Scotland about the late Union: Whether it would not have succeeded as in the consolidation of kingdoms, where the greatest swallows down the less; so also in church-coalition, that though the Pope had condescended (which the Bishop owns to be his right) to be only a patriarch, yet he would have swoop'd up the patriarchate of Lambeth to his morning's-draught, like an egg in Muscadine. And then there is another danger always when things come once to a treaty, that beside the debates of reason, there is a better way of tampering to bring men over that have a power to conclude. And so who knows in such a treaty with Rome, if the Alps (as it is probable) would not have come over to England, as the Bishop design'd it, England might not have been obliged, lying so commodious for navigation, to undertake a voyage to Civita Vecchia? But what though we should have made all the advances imaginable, it would have been to no purpose; and nothing less than an entire and total resignation of the Protestant cause would have contented her. For the Church of Rome is so well satisfied of her own sufficiency, and hath so much more wit than we had in Bishop Bramhall's days, or seem to have yet learn'd, that it would have succeeded just as at the Council of Trent. For there, though many divines of the greatest sincerity and learning endeavoured a reformation, yet no more could be obtained of her than the Nonconformists got of those of the Church of England at the conference of Worcester-house. But, on the contrary, all her excesses and errors were further riveted and confirmed, and that great machine of her Ecclesiastical Policy there perfected.

So that this enterprise of Bishop Bramhall's, being so ill laid and so unseasonable, deserves rather an excuse than a commendation. And all that can be gathered besides out of our Author concerning him is of little better value; for he saith indeed, that 'he was a zealous and resolute assertor of the publick rites and ceremonies of the Church.' But those things, being only matters of external neatness, could never merit the trophies that our Author erects him. For neither can a justice of peace for his severity about dirt-baskets deserve a statue. And as for 'his expunging some dear and darling articles from the Protestant cause,' it is, as far as I can perceive, onely his substituting some Arminian tenets (which I name so, not for reproach, but for difference) instead of the Calvinian doctrines. But this too could not challenge all these triumphal ornaments in which he installs him: for, I suppose, these were but meer 'mistakes on either side, for want of being (as the Bishop saith, page 134) scholastically stated; and that he, with a distinction of school-theologie, could have smoothed over and plained away these knots, though they had been much harder.'

For the rest, which he leaves us to seek for, and I meet casually with in the Bishop's own book; I find him to have been doubtless a very good-natured gentleman. Page 160, 'He hath much respect for poor readers;' and page 161, he judges 'that if they come short of preachers in point of efficacy, yet they have advantage of preachers as to point of security.' And, page 163, he commends the care taken by 'the canons that the meanest cure of souls should have formal sermons at least four times every year.' Page 155, he 'maintains the publick sports on the Lord's day by the proclamation to that purpose, and the example of the Reformed Churches beyond sea;' and 'for the publick dances of our youth upon country greens on Sundayes, after the duties of the day, he sees nothing in them but innocent, and agreeable to that under-sort of people.' And page 117 (which I quoted before), he ' takes the promiscuous licence to unqualified persons to reade the Scriptures, far more prejudicial, nay, more pernitious, than the over-rigorous restraints of the Romanists.' And indeed, all along he complies much for peace-sake, and judiciously shows wherein our separation from the Church of Rome is not warrantable. But although I cannot warrant any man who hence took occasion to traduce him of Popery, the contrary of which is evident, yet neither is it to be wondred, if he did hereby lye under some imputation, which he might otherwise have avoided. Neither can I be so hardhearted as our Author in the Nonconformists' case of discipline, to think it were better that he, or a hundred more divines of his temper, should suffer, though innocent, in their reputation, than that we should come under a possibility of losing our religion.' For as they (the Bishop, and, I hope, most of his Party) did not intend it so, neither could they have effected it. But he could not expect to enjoy his imagination without the annoyances incident to such as dwell in the middle story—the pots from above, and the smoak from below. And those churches which are seated nearer upon the frontire of Popery did naturally and well if they took alarm at the march. For, in fact, that incomparable person, Grotius, did yet make a bridge for the enemy to come over; or at least laid some of our most considerable passes open to them and unguarded: a crime something like what his son De Groot (here's Gazette again for you) and his son-in-law Mombas have been charged with. And, as to the Bishop himself, his friend, an accusatory spirit, would desire no better play than he gives in his own vindication. But that's neither my business nor humour; and whatsoever may have glanced upon him was directed only to our Author, for publishing that Book, which the Bishop himself had thought fit to conceal, and for his impertinent efflorescence of rhetorick upon so mean topicks, in so choice and copious a subject as Bishop Bramhall.

Yet though the Bishop prudently undertook a design, which he hoped not to accomplish in his own dayes, our Author, however, was something wiser, and hath made sure to obtain his end. For the Bishop's honour was the farthest thing from his thoughts, and he hath managed that part so that I have accounted it a work of some piety to vindicate his memory from so scurvy a commendation. But the Author's end was only railing. He could never have induced himself to praise one man but in order to rail on another. He never oyls his hone but that he may whet his razor, and that not to shave, but to cut men's throats. And whoever will take the pains to compare, will find that, as it is his only end, so his best, nay, his only talent is railing.. So that he hath, while he pretends so much for the good Bishop, used him but for a stalking-horse till he might come within shot of the foreign divines and the Nonconformists. The other was only a copy of his countenance. But look to yourselves, my masters; for in so venomous a malice, courtesie is always fatal. Under colour of some men's having taxed the Bishop, he flyes out into a furious debauch and breaks the windows; if he could, would raze the foundations of all the Protestant churches beyond sea: but for all men at home of their perswasion, if he meets them in the dark, he runs them thorow. He usurps to himself the authority of the Church of England, who is so well-bred, that if he would have allowed her to speak, she would doubtless have treated more civilly those over whom she pretends no jurisdiction: and under the names of Germany and Geneva, he rallies and rails at the whole Protestancy of Europe. For you are mistaken in our Author (but I have worn him threadbare) if you think he designs to enter the lists where he hath but one man to combate. Mr. Bayes, ye know, 'prefers that one quality of fighting single with whole armies, before all the moral virtues put together.' And yet I assure you, he hath several times obliged 'moral Virtue' so highly, that she owes him a good turn whensoever she can meet him. But it is a brave thing to be the ecclesiastical Draw-can-sir; he kills whole nations, he kills friend and foe; Hungary, Transylvania, Bohemia, Poland, Savoy, France, the Netherlands, Denmark, Sweden, and a great part of the Church of England, and all Scotland (for these, beside many more, he mocks under the title of Germany and Geneva) may perhaps rouse our mastiff, and make up a danger worthy of his courage. A man would guess that this giant had promised his 'comfortable importance' a simarre of the beards of all the 'orthodox theologues' in Christendom. But I wonder how he comes to be prolocutor of the Church of England! For he talks at that rate as if he were a *synodical individuum;* nay, if he had a fifth council in his belly, he could not dictate more dogmatically. There had been indeed, as I have heard, about the dayes of Bishop Bramhall, a sort of divines here of that leaven, who being dead, I cover their names, if not for health's sake, yet for decency, who never could speak of the first Reformers with any patience; who pruned themselves in the peculiar virulency of their pens, and so they might say a tart thing concerning the foreign churches, cared not what obloquy they cast upon the history or the profession of Religion. And those men undertook likewise to vent their wit and their choler under the style of the Church of England; and were indeed so far owned by her, that what preferments were in her own disposal she rather conferr'd upon them. And now, when they were gone off the stage, there is risen up this spiritual

Mr. Bayes, who, having assumed to himself an incongruous plurality of ecclesiastical offices, one of the most severe, of penitentiary-universal to the Reformed Churches; the other most rediculous, of buffoon-general to the Church of England, may be henceforth capable of any other promotion. And not being content to enjoy his own folly, he has taken two others into partnership, as fit for his design as those two that clubb'd with Mahomet in making the Alchoran; who by perverse wit and representation might travesteere the Scripture, and render all the careful and serious part of Religion odious and contemptible. But, lest I might be mistaken as to the persons I mention, I will assure the reader that I intend not Huddibras; for he is a man of the other robe, and his excellent wit hath taken a flight far above these whiflers: that whoever dislikes the choice of his subject, cannot but commend his performance, and calculate if on so barren a theme he were so copious, what admirable sport he would have made with an Ecclesiastical Politician. But for a Daw-Divine not onely to foul his own nest in England, but to pull in peices the nests of those beyond sea, 'tis that which I think undecent and of very ill example. There is not indeed much danger (his book, his letter, and his Preface being writ in English), that they should pass abroad; but, if they be printed upon incombustible paper, or by reason of the many avocations of our Church, they may escape a censure, yet 'tis likely they may dye at home, the common fate of such treatises, amongst the more judicious oylmen and grocers. Unless Mr. Bayes be so far in love with his own whelp, that, as a modern lady, he will be at the charge of translating his works into Latin, transmitting them to the universities, and dedicating them in the Vaticane. But, should they unhappily get vent abroad (as I hear some are already sent over for curiosity), what scandal, what heart-burning and animosity must it raise against our Church; unless they chance to take it right at first, and limit the provocation within the Author. And then, what can he expect in return of his civility, but that the compliment which passed betwixt Arminius and Baudius should concenter upon him, that he is both *opprobrium academiæ* and *pestis Ecclesiæ?* For they will see at the first that his books come not out under publick authority or recommendation; but only as things of buffoonery do commonly, they carry with them their own *imprimatur;* (but I hope he hath considered Mr. L. in private, and payed his fees). Neither will the gravity therefore of their judgements take the measures I hope, either of the education at our universities, or of the spirit of our divines, or of the prudence, piety, and doctrine of the Church of England, from such an interloper. Those Gardens of ours use to bear much better fruit. There may happen sometimes an ill year, or there may be such a crabstock as cannot by all ingrafting be corrected. But generally it proves otherwise. Once perhaps in a hundred years there may arise such a prodigy in the University (where all men else learn better Arts and better manners), and from thence may creep into the Church (where the teachers at least ought to be well instructed in the knowledge and practice of Christianity); so prodigious a person, I say, may even there be hatch'd, as shal neither know or care how to behave himself to God or man; and who having never seen the receptacle of grace or conscience at an anatomical dissection, may conclude therefore that there is no such matter, or no such obligation among Christians; who shall persecute the Scripture it self, unless it will conform to his interpretation; who shall strive to put the world into blood, and animate princes to be the executioners of their own subjects for well-doing. All this is possible; but comes to pass as rarely and at as long periods in our climate as the birth of a false prophet. But unluckily, in this fatal year of seventy-two, among all the calamities that astrologers foretel, this also hath befaln us. I would not hereby confirm his vanity, as if I also believed that any scheme of heaven did influence his actions, or that he were so considerable as that the comet, under which they say we yet labour, had foreboded the appearance of his Preface. No, no: though he be a creature most noxious, yet he is more despicable. A comet is of far higher quality, and hath other kind of imployment. Although we call it an hairy-star, it affords no prognostick of what breeds there: but the astrologer that would discern our author and his business must lay-by his telescope, and use a microscope. You may find him still in Master Calvin's head. Poor Mr. Calvin and Bp. Bramhall, what crime did you dye guilty of, that you cannot lye quiet in your graves, but must be conjured up on the stage as oft as Mr. Bayes will ferret you? And which of you two are most unfortunate. I cannot determine : whether the Bishop in being alwayes courted, or the Presbyter in being alwayes rail'd at. But in good earnest I think Mr. Calvin hath the better of it. For, though an ill man cannot by praising confer honour, nor by reproaching fix an ignominy, and so they may seem on equal terms, yet there is more in it; for at the same time that we may imagine what is said by such an Author to be false, we conceive the contrary to be true. What he said of him indeed in this place did not come very well in; for Calvin writ nothing against Bishop Bramhall, and therefore here it amounts to no more than that his spirit forsooth had propagated an original waspishness and false orthodoxy amongst all his followers. But if you look in other pages of his book, and particularly page 663 of his Defence, you never saw such a scarecrow as he makes him : ' There sprang up a mighty bramble on the South side the Lake Lemane, that (such is the rankness of the soil) spread and flourished with such a sudden growth, that, partly by the industry of his agents abroad, and partly by its own indefatigable pains and pragmaticalness, it quite overran the whole Reformation.' You must conceive that Mr. Bayes was all this while in an extasy in Dodona's Grove; or else here is strange work, worse than 'explicating a post,' or 'examining a pillar.' A 'bramble' that had 'agents abroad,' and itself an 'indefatigable bramble.' But straight our bramble is transformed to a man, and he 'makes a chair of infallibility for himself' out of his own bramble-timber. Yet all this while we know not his name. One would suspect it might be a Bp. Bramble. But then 'he made himself both pope and emperor too of the greatest part of the reformed world.' How near does this come to his commendation of Bishop Bramhall before! For our Author seems copious, but is indeed very poor of expression; and, as smiling and frowning are performed in the face with the same muscles very little altered, so the changing of a line or two in Mr. Bayes at any time, will make the same thing serve for a panegyrick or a philippick. But what do you think of this man? Could Mistress Mopsa herself have furnished you with a more pleasant and worshipful tale? It wants nothing of perfection, but that it doth not begin with 'Once upon a time;' which Mr. Bayes, according to his accuracy, if he had thought on't, would never have omitted. Yet some critical people, who will exact truth in falshood, and tax up an old-wife's fable to the punctuality of

History, were blaming him t' other day for placing this 'bramble' on the 'south side' of Lake Lemane. I said, it was well and wisely done, that he chose a south sun for the better and more sudden growth of such a fruit-tree. Ay, said they, but he means Calvin by the bramble; and the 'rank soyl on the south side the Lake Lemane' is the city of Geneva, situate (as he would have it) on the south side of that Lake. Now it is strange that he, having travell'd so well, should not have observ'd that the Lake lies east and west, and that Geneva is built at the west end of it. Pish, said I, that's no such great matter; and, as Master Bayes hath it upon another occasion, 'Whether it be so or no, the fortunes of Cæsar and the Roman empire are not concerned in 't.' One of the company would not let that pass, but told us if we look'd in Cæsar's Commentaries, we should find their fortunes were concerned; for it was the Helvetian Passage, and many mistakes might have risen in the marching of the army. Why, then, replyed I again, whether it be east, west, north, or south, there is neither vice nor idolatry in it, and the Ecclesiastical Politician may command you to believe it, and you are bound to acquiesce in his judgment, whatsoever may be your 'private opinion.' Another, to continue the mirth, answered, That yet there might be some religious consideration in building a town east and west, or north and south, and 'twas not a thing so indifferent as men thought it; but because in the Church of England, where the table is set altarwise, the minister is nevertheless obliged to stand at the north side (though it be the north end of the table), it was fit to place the Geneva presbyter in diametrical opposition to him upon the 'South side of the Lake.' But this we all took for a cold conceit, and not enough matured. I, that was still upon the doubtful and excusing part, said, That to give the right situation of a town, it was necessary first to know in what position the gentleman's head then was when he made his observation, and that might cause a great diversity. Yes, replyed my next neighbour; or, perhaps some roguing boy that managed the puppets turned the city wrong, and so disoccidented our geographer. It was grown almost as good as a Play among us; and at last they all concluded that 'Geneva had sold Mr. Bayes a bargain, as the Moon serv'd the Earth in the Rehearsal,' and in good sooth had 'turn'd her breech on him.' But this, I doubt not, Mr. Bayes will bring himself off with honour; but that which sticks with me is, that our Author having undertaken to make Calvin and Geneva ridicule, hath not pursued it to so high a point as the subject would have afforded. First, he might have taken the name of the beast Calvinus, and of that have given the anagram, Lucianus. Next, I would have turned him inside outward, and have made him Usinulca. That was a good hobgoblin name to have frighted children with. Then he should have been a 'bramble' still, ay, an 'indefatigable bramble' too : but after that he should have continued (for in such a book a passage in a Play is clear gain, and a great loss if omitted), and upon that bramble 'reasons grew as plentiful as blackberries;' but both unwholesome, and they stain'd all the 'white aprons so,' that there was no getting of it out. And then, to make a fuller description of the place, he should have added, That near to the city of roaring lions there was a lake, and that lake was all of brimstone, but stored with overgrown trouts, which trouts spawned Presbyterians, and those spawned the Millecantons of all other fanaticks ; that this shoal of Presbyterians landed at Geneva, and devoured all the bishops of Geneva's capons, which are of the greatest size of any in the Reformed world. And ever since their mouths have been so in relish, that the Presbyterians are in all parts the very canibals of capons : insomuch that, if princes do not take care, the race of capons is in danger to be totally extinguished. But that the river Rhosne [Rhone] was so sober and intelligent that its waters would not mix with this Lake perillous, but ran sheer thorow, without ever touching it : nay, such is its apprehension lest the Lake should overtake it, that the river dives itself under ground, till the Lake hath lost the scent : and yet when it rises again, imagining that the Lake is still at its heels, it runs on so impetuously that it chuseth rather to pass through the roaring lions, and never thinks itself safe till it hath taken sanctuary at the Pope's town of Avinion [Avignon]. He might too have proved that Calvin made himself ' Pope and Emperour,' because the city of Geneva stamps upon its coyn the two-headed imperial eagle. And, to have given us the utmost terror, he might have considered the alliance and vicinity of Geneva to the Canton of Bern, the arms of which city is the Bear (and an argument in heraldry, even Bishop Bramhall himself being judge, might have also held in divinity), and therefore they keep under the town-house constantly a whole den of bears: so that there was never a more dangerous situation, nor any thing so carefully to be avoided by all travellers in their wits, as Geneva—the Lions on one side, and the Bears on the other. This story would have been nuts to Mother Midnight, and was fit to have been embellish'd with Mr. Bayes his allegorical eloquence. And all that he saith, either by fits and girds of Calvin, or in his justest narratives, hath less foundation in nature; and is indeed twice incredible, first in the matter related, and then because Mr. Bayes it comes from; or, to express it shorter, because of the tale and the tale's-man. He is not yet come to that authority, but that his dogmatical *ipse-dixits* may rather be a reason why we should not believe him. If Mr. Bayes will speak of controversy, let him enter into a regular disputation concerning these Calvinian tenets, and not write an History; or, if he will give us the history of Calvin, let him at the same time produce his authors. And whether History or Controversy, let him be pleas'd so long to abate of the exuberancy of his fancy and wit, to dispense with his ornaments and superfluencies of invention and satyre; and then a man may consider whether he may believe his story, and submit to his argument. But in the meantime (for all he pleads in page 97 of his Defence) it looks all so like subterfuge and inveigling; it is so nauseating and tedious a task, that no man thinks he owes the Author so much service as to find out the reason of his own categoricalness for him. One may beat the bush a whole day, but after so much labour shall, for all game, only spring a butterfly, or start an hedg-hog. Insomuch that I am ever and anon disputing with myself whether Mr. Bayes be indeed so ill-natured a person as some would have him, and do not rather innocently write things (as he professes page 4 of his Preface) so 'exceeding all belief' that he may make himself and the company merry. I sometimes could think that he intends no harm either to publick or private, but onely rails contentedly to himself and his Muses; that he seeks onely his own diversion, and chargeth his gun with wind but to shoot at the air; or that, like boyes, so he may make a great paper-kite of his own Letter of 850 pages, and his Preface of an hundred, he hath no further design upon the poultry of the village. But he takes care that I shall never be long deceived with that pleasing imagination: and though his hyperboles and impossibilities can have only a ridiculous effect, he will be sure to manifest that he had a felonious intention. He would take it ill if we should not value him as an enemy of mankind: and like a raging Indian (for in Europe it was never before practised), he runs a-mucke (as they call it there), stabbing every man he meets, till himself be knockt on the head. This here is the least pernicious of all his mischiefs: though it be no less in this and all his other books than to make the 'German Protestancy' a reproachful proverb, and to turn Geneva and Calvin into a common-place of railing. I had alwayes heard that Calvin was a good scholar and an honest divine. I have indeed read that he spoke something contemptuously of our Liturgy: *Sunt in illo libro quœdam tolerabiles ineptiœ*. But that was a sin which we may charitably suppose he repented of on his deathbed! And if Mr. Bayes had some just quarrel to him on that or other account, yet, for divinitye's sake, he needed not thus have made a constant pissing-place of his grave. And as for Geneva, I never perceiv'd before but that it was a very laudable city; that there grew an excellent grape 'on the south side of the Lake Lemane;' that a man might make good chear there; and there was a Pall-mall; and one might shoot wth the arbalet, or play at Courteboule on Sundaies. What was here to inrage our Author so, that he must raze the fort of St. Katherine, and attempt with the same success a second escalade? but the difficulty of the enterprize doubtless provoked his courage, and the honour he might win made the justice of his quarrel. He knew that not only the commonwealth of Switzerland, but the King of France, the King of Spain, and the Duke of Savoy would enter the lists for the common preservation of the place; and therefore though it be otherwise but a petty town, he disdain'd not, where the race was to be run by monarchs, to exercise his footmanship. But is it not a great pity to see a man in the flower of his age and the vigor of his studies, to fall into such a distraction, that his head runs upon nothing but 'Roman Empire' and 'Ecclesiastical Policy'? This happens by his growing too early acquainted with Don Quixot, and reading the Bible too late; so that the first impressions being most strong, and mixing with the last, as more novel, have made such a medly in his brain-pan that he is become a mad priest, which of all the sorts is the most incurable. Hence it is that you shall hear him anon instructing princes, like Sancho, how to govern his island: as he is busied at present in vanquishing the Calvinists of Germany and Geneva. Had he no friends to have given him good counsel before his understanding were quite unsettled? or if there was none near, why did not men call-in the neighbours, and send for the parson of the parish, to perswade with him in time, but let it run on thus till he is fit for nothing but Bedlam or Hogsdon? However, though it be a particular damage, it may tend to a general advantage; and young students will, I hope, by his example learn to beware henceforward of overweening presumption and preposterous ambition. For this gentleman, as I have heard, after he had read Don Quixot and the Bible, besides such school-books as were necessary for his age, was sent early to the University; and there studied hard, and in a short time became a competent rhetorician, and no ill disputant. He had learnt how to erect a thesis, and to defend it *pro* or *con* with a serviceable distinction; while the truth (as his camarade Mr. Bayes hath it on another occasion),

> ' Before a full pot of ale you can swallow,
> Was here with a whoop and gone with a holla.'

And so thinking himself now ripe and qualified for the greatest undertakings and highest fortune, he therefore exchanged the narrowness of the university for the town; but coming out of the confinement of the square-cap and the quadrangle into the open air, the world began to turn round with him, which he imagined, though it were his own giddiness, to be nothing less than the quadrature of the circle. This accident, concurring so happily to increase the good opinion which he naturally had of himself, he thenceforward applied to gain a like reputation with others. He follow'd the town life, haunted the best companies, and, to polish himself from any pedantick roughness, he read and saw the Plaies, with much care and more proficiency than most of the auditory. But all this while he forgot not the main chance, but hearing of a vacancy with a nobleman, he clap'd in, and easily obtain'd to be his chaplain. From that day you may take the date of his preferments and his ruine. For having soon wrought himself dexteriously into his patron's favour, by short graces and sermons, and a mimical way of drolling upon the Puritans, which he knew would take both at chappel and table; he gained a great authority likewise among all the domesticks. They all listened to him as an oracle; and they allow'd him by common consent to have not onely all the divinity, but more wit too than all the rest of the family put together. This thing alone elevated him exceedingly in his own conceit, and raised his hypochondria into the region of the brain, that his head swell'd like any bladder with wind and vapour. But after he was stretch'd to such an height in his own fancy, that he could not look down from top to toe but his eyes dazzled at the precipice of his stature, there fell out, or in, another natural chance which push'd him headlong; for being of an amorous complexion, and finding himself (as I told you) the cock-divine and the cock-wit of the family, he took the priviledge to walk among the hens: and thought it was not impolitick to establish his new acquired reputation upon the gentlewomen's side. And they that perceived he was a rising-man, and of plea-

sant conversation, dividing his day among them into
canonical hours, of reading now the Common Prayer,
and now the Romances, were very much taken with
him. The sympathy of silk began to stir and attract
the tippet to the pettycoat and the pettycoat toward
the tippet. The innocent ladies found a strange un-
quietness in their minds, and could not distinguish
whether it were love or devotion. Neither was he
wanting on his part to carry on the work; but shifted
himself every day with a clean surplice, and, as oft as
he had occasion to bow, he directed his reverence towards the gentlewomen's pew. Till, having before had
enough of the libertine, and undertaken his calling
only for preferment, he was transported now with the
sanctity of his office, even to extasy: and like the
Bishop over Maudlin College altar, or like *Maudlin de
la Croix*, he was seen in his prayers to be lifted up
sometimes in the air, and once particularly so high that
he crack'd his scull against the chappel ceiling. I do
not hear, for all this, that he had ever practised upon
the honour of the ladies, but that he preserved alwayes
the civility of a Platonick knight-errant. For all this
courtship had no other operation than to make him
stil more in love with himself; and if he frequented
their company, it was only to speculate his own baby
in their eyes. But being thus, without competitor or
rival, the darling of both sexes in the family, and his
own minion, he grew beyond all measure elated, and

that crack of his scull, as in broken looking-glasses, multiplied him in self-conceit and imagination.

Having fixed his center in this nobleman's house, he thought he could now move and govern the whole earth with the same facility. Nothing now would serve him but he must be a madman in print, and write a book of Ecclesiastical Policy. There he distributes all the 'territories of Conscience' into the Prince's province, and makes the Hierarchy to be but Bishops of the air: and talks at such an extravagant rate in things of higher concernment, that the Reader will avow that in the whole discourse he had not one lucid interval. This book he was so bent upon, that he sate up late at nights, and wanting sleep, and drinking sometimes wine to animate his fancy, it increas'd his distemper. Beside that too, he had the misfortune to have two friends, who being both also out of their wits, and of the same, though something a calmer, phrensy, spurr'd him on perpetually with commendation. And when his Book was once come out, and he saw himself an Author; that some of the gallants of the town layd by the new tune, and the 'tay, tay, tarree,' to quote some of his impertinencies; that his title-page was posted and pasted up at every avenue next under the Play for that afternoon at the King's or the Duke's house: the vain-glory of this totally confounded him. He lost all the little remains of his understanding, and his *cerebellum* was so dryed up that there was more brains in a walnut, and both their shells were alike thin and brittle. The King of France that lost his wits had not near so many unlucky circumstances to occasion it: and in the last of all there is some similitude. For, as a negligent page that rode behind and carried the King's lance, let it fall on his head, the King being in armour, and the day hot, which so disordered him that he never recovered it; so this gentleman in the dog-days, stragling by Temple-bar, in a massy cassock and surcingle, and taking the opportunity at once to piss and admire the title-page of his book; a tall servant of his, one J. O., that was not so carefull as he should be, or whether he did it of purpose, lets another book of four hundred leaves fall upon his head; which meeting with the former fracture in his *cranium*, and all the concurrent accidents already mentioned, has utterly undone him. And so, in conclusion, his madness hath formed itself into a perfect lycanthropy. He doth so severely believe himself to be a wolf, that his speech is all turn'd into howling, yelling, and barking; and if there were any sheep here, you should see him pull out their throats and suck the blood. Alas, that a sweet gentleman, and so hopeful, should miscarry! For want of cattel here, you find him raving now against all the Calvinists of England, and worrying the whole flock of them. For how can they hope to escape his chops and his paws better than those of Germany and Geneva; of which he is so hungry, that he hath scratch'd-up even their dead bodies out of their graves to prey upon? And yet this is nothing if you saw him in the height of his fits: but he hath so beaten and spent himself before, that he is out of breath at present; and though you may discover the same fury, yet it wants of the same vigour. But, however, you see enough of him, my masters, to make you beware, I hope, of valuing too high, and trusting too far to your own abilities.

It were a wild thing for me to squire it after this knight, and accompany him here through all his extravagancies against our Calvinists. You find nothing but ' orthodoxy, systems, and syntagms, polemical theology, subtilties, and distinctions: Demosthenes; tankard-bearers; pragmatical; controversial:' general terms without foundation or reason assigned. That they seem like words of Cabal, and have no significance till they be decipher'd; or, you would think he were playing at substantives and adjectives. All that rationally can be gathered from what he saith, is, that the man is mad. But if you would supply his meaning with your imagination, as if he spoke sense and to some determinate purpose; it is very strange that, conceiving himself to be the champion of the Church of England, he should bid such a general defiance to the Calvinists. For he knows, or perhaps I may better say he did know before this phrensy had subverted both his understanding and memory, that most of our ancient, and many of the later Bishops nearer our times, did both hold and maintain those doctrines which he traduces under that by-word. And the contrary opinions were even in Bishop Prideaux's time accounted so novel, that, being then publick professor of divinity, he thought fit to tax Doctor Heylin at the Commencement, for his new-fangled divinity: '*cujus*,' saith he, in the very words of promotion, '*te doctorem creo*.' He knew likewise that of our present Bishops, though one had leisure formerly to write a 'Rationale of the Ceremonies and Liturgie,' and another a Treatise of the 'Holiness of Lent;' yet that most of them, and 'tis to be supposed all, have studied other controversies, and at another rate than Mr. Bayes his lead can fathom. And as I know none of them that hath published any treatise against the Calvinian tenets, so I have the honour to be acquainted with some of them who are intirely of that judgment, and differ nothing but, as of good reason, in the point of Episcopacy. And as for that, Bishop Bramhall, page 61, hath proved that Calvin himself was of the Episcopal perswasion. So that I see no reason why Mr. Bayes should here and every where be such an enemy to 'controversial skill' or the Calvinists. But I perceive 'tis for Bishop Bramhall's sake here that all the tribe must suffer. This Bayes is not a good dog: for he runs at a whole flock of sheep, when Mr. B. was the deer whom he had in view from the beginning. However, having foil'd himself so long with every thing he meets, after him now he goes, and will never leave till he hath run him down. Poor Mr. B.! I find that when he was a boy he pluck'd Bishop Bramhall's sloes and ate his bullice; and now, when he is as superannuated as the Bishop's book, he must be whipt for't; there is no remedy. And yet I have heard, and Mr. Bayes himself seems to intimate as much, that however he might in his younger years have mistaken, yet that even as early as Bishop Bramhall's Discourse, he began to retract: and that as for all his sins against the Church of England, he hath in some late treatises cried *peccavi* with a witness. But, Mr. Bayes, doth not this now look like sorcery and extortion, which of all crimes you purge yourself from so often without an accuser? For first, whereas the old Bishop was at rest, and had under his last pillow laid-by all cares and contests of this lower world, you by your necromancy have disturb'd him, and rais'd his ghost to persecute and haunt Mr. B., whom doubtless at his death he had pardoned. But if you called him up to ask some questions too concerning your Ecclesiastical Policy, as I am apt to suppose, I doubt you had no better answer than in the song:

'Art thou forlorn of God, and com'st to me?
What can I tell thee, then, but miserie?'

And then as for extortion; who but such an Hebrew Jew as you would, after an honest man had made so full and voluntary restitution, not yet have been satisfied without so many pounds of his flesh over into the bargain? Though J. O. be in a desperate condition, yet methinks Mr. B., not 'being past grace,' should not neither 'have been past mercy.' Are there no terms of pardon, Mr. Bayes? is there no time for expiation? but, after so simple a confession as he hath made, must he now be hang'd too to make good the proverb? It puts me in mind of a story in the time of the Guelphs and Ghibilines, whom I perceive Mr. Bayes hath heard of. There were two factions in Italy, of which the Guelphs were for the Pope, and the Ghibilines for the Emperour; and these were for many years carried on and fomented with much animosity, to the great disturbance of Christendom. Which of these two were the Nonconformists in those days I can no more determine than which of our parties here at home is now schismatical. But so nonconformable they were to one another, that the Historian said they took care to differ in the least circumstances of any humane action: and as those that have the Mason's word, secretly discern one another, so in the peeling or cutting but of an onion, a Guelph, and *vice versa*, would at first sight have distinguished a Ghibiline. Now, one of this latter sort, coming at Rome to confession upon Ash-Wednesday, the Pope or the penitentiary sprinkling ashes on the man's head with the usual ceremony, instead of pronouncing *memento, homo, quod cinis es, et in cinerem reverteris*, changed it to *memento, homo, quod Ghibilinus es, &c.* And even thus it fares with Mr. B., who, though he should creep on his knees up the whole stairs of scholastick penitence, I am confident neither he, nor any of his party, shall by Mr. Bayes his good will ever be absolved. And therefore truly, if I were in Mr. B.'s case, if I could not have my confession back again, yet it should be a warning unto me not without better grounds to be so coming and so good-natured for the future. But whatever he do, I hope others will consider what usage they are like to find at Mr. Bayes's hand, and not suffer themselves by the touch of his penitential rod to be transformed into beasts, even into rats, as here he hath done with Mr. B. I have indeed wondred often at this Bayes his insolence, who summons-in all the world and preacheth-up only this repentance; and so frequently in his books he calls for 'testimonies, signal marks, publick acknowledgment, satisfaction, recantation,' and I know not what. He that hath made the passage to Heaven so easie that one may fly thither without grace (as Gonzales to the moon only by the help of his Gansa's); he that hath 'disintricated' its narrow paths from those 'labyrinths' which J. O. and Mr. B. have planted; this overseer of God's highwayes (if I may with reverence speak it), who hath paved a broad causway with moral virtue thorow His kingdom; he methinks should not have made the 'process of loyalty' more difficult than that of salvation. What 'signal marks,' what 'testimonies,' would he have of this conversion? Every man cannot, as he hath done, write an 'Ecclesiastical Policy,' a 'Defence,' a 'Preface;' and some, if they could, would not do it after his manner; lest in stead of obliging thereby the King and the Church, it should be a Testimony to the contrary. Neither, unless men have better principles of allegiance at home, are they likely to be reduced by Mr. Bayes his way of perswasion. He is the first minister of the Gospel that ever had it in his commission 'to rail at all nations.' And though it hath been long practised, I never observed any great success by reviling men into Conformity. I have heard that charms may even invite the moon out of heaven, but I never could see her moved by the rhetorick of barking. I think it ought to be highly penal for any man to impose other conditions upon his Majestie's good subjects than the King expects, or the Law requires. When you have done all, you must yet appear before Mr. Bayes his tribunal, and he hath a new test yet to put you to. I must confess, at this rate the Nonconformists deserve some compassion; that after they have done or suffered legally and to the utmost, they must still be subjected to the wand of a verger or to the wanton lash of every pedant; that they must run the ganteloop, or down with their breeches as oft as he wants the prospect of a more pleasing 'nudity.' But I think they may chuse whether they will submit or no to his jurisdiction. Let them but, as I hope they do, fear God, honour the King, preserve their consciences, follow their trades, and look to their chimnies, and they need not fear Mr. Bayes and all his malice. But after he hath sufficiently insulted over Mr. B.'s ignorance and vanity, with other compliments of the like nature, in recompense of that 'candor and civility' which he acknowledges 'him to have now learnt towards the Church of England,' Mr. Bayes (forgetting what had past long since betwixt him and the Bookseller) saith in excuse of his severity, that 'this treatise was not published to impair Mr. B.'s esteem in the least, but for a correction of his scribling humour, and to warn their rat-divines that are perpetually nibbling and gnawing other men's Writings.' Now I must confess, Mr. Bayes, this is a very handsome welcome to Mr. B., that was come so far to see you, and doubtless upon this encouragement he will visit you often. This is an admirable dexterity our Author hath (I wish I could learn it) 'to correct a man's scribling humour without impairing in the least his reputation.' He is as courteous as lightning, and can melt the sword without ever hurting the scabbard. But as for their 'rat-divines,' I wonder they are not all poysoned with nibbling at his writings, he hath strewn so much arsenick in every leaf. But, however, methinks he should not have grudged them so slender a sustenance. For though there was a sow in Arcadia so fat and insensible that she suffered a rat's nest in her buttock, and they had both dyet and lodging in the same gammon, yet it is not every rat's good fortune to be so well provided. And for 'push-pin divinity,' I confess it is a new term of Art, and I shall henceforward take notice of it; but I am afraid in general it doth not tend much to the reputation of the faculty.

And now, though he told us at the beginning that the Bookseller was the main reason of publishing this book of the Bishop and his own Preface, he tels us that the main reason of its publication was to give some check to their present disingenuity, that is to say, to that of J. O.; and J. O. be it at present. He is come so much nearer, however, to the truth, though we shall find ere we have done that there is still a mainer reason.

When I first took notice of this misunderstanding betwixt Mr. Bayes and J. O., I considered whether it were not execution-day with the Latine Alphabet; whether all the letters were not to suffer in the same manner, except C. only, which (having been the mark of condemnation) might have a pardon to serve for the executioner. I began to repent of my undertaking, being afraid that the quarrel was with the whole Cris-cros-row, and that we must fight it out through all the squadrons of the vowels, the mutes, the semi-vowels, and the liquids. I foresaw a sore and endless labour, and a battel the longest that ever was read of; being probable to continue as long as one letter was left alive, or there were any use of reading. Therefore, to spare mine own pains, and prevent ink-shed, I was advising the letters to go before Mr. Bales, or any other his Majestie's justices of peace, to swear that they were in danger of their lives, and desire that Mr. Bayes might be bound to the good behaviour. But after this I had another phancy, and that not altogether unreasonable; that Mr. Bayes had, onely for health and exercise sake, drawn J. O. by chance out of the number of the rest, to try how he could rail at a letter, and that he might be well in breath upon any occasion of greater consequence. For, how perfect soever a man may have been in any science, yet without continual practice he will find a sensible decay of his faculty. Hence also, and upon the same natural ground, it is the wisdome of cats to wet their claws against the chairs and hangings, in meditation of the next rat they are to encounter. And I am confident that Mr. Bayes by this way hath brought himself into so good railing-case, that pick what letter you will out of the alphabet, he is able to write an epistle upon it of 723 pages (I have now told them right) to the author of the 'Friendly Debates.'

Now though this had very much of probability, I had yet a further conjecture; that this J. O. was a talisman, signed under some peculiar influence of the heavenly bodies, and that the fate of Mr. Bayes was bound up within it. Whether it be so or no I know not: but this I am assured of, without the help either of syderal

magic or judicial astrologie, that when J and O are in
conjunction, they do more certainly than any of the
planets forbode that a great Ecclesiastical Politician shall
that year run mad. I confess after all this, when I was
come to the dregs of my phansie (for we all have our infirmities, and Mr. Bayes his Defence was but the blew-
John of his Ecclesiastical Policy, and this Preface the
tap-dropings of his Defence), I reflected whether Mr.
Bayes having no particular cause of indignation against
the letters, there might not have been a mistake of the
printer, and that they were to be read in one word Io,
that use to go before Pæan : that is in English a triumph
before the victory. Or whether it alluded to Io that
we read of at school, the daughter of Inachus; and that
as Juno persecuted the heifer, so this was an he-cow,
that is to say a bull, to be baited by Mr. Bayes the thun-
derer. But these being conceits too trivial, though a
ragoust fit enough for Mr. Bayes his palate, I was forced
moreover to quit them, remarking that it was an J consonant. And I plainly at last perceived that this J. O.
was a very man as any of us are, and had a head, and a
mouth with tongue and teeth in it, and hands with fingers and nails upon them : nay, that he could read and
write, and speak as well as I or Mr. Bayes, either of us.
When I once found this, the business appear'd more
serious, and I was willing to see what was the matter
that so much exasperated Mr. Bayes, who is 'a person,'
as he saith himself, 'of such a tame and softly humour,

and so cold a complexion, that he thinks himself scarce capable of hot and passionate impressions.' I concluded that necessarily there must be some extraordinary accident and occasion that could alter so good a nature. For I saw that he pursued J. O., if not from post to pillar, yet from pillar to post, and I discerned all along the footsteps of a most inveterate and implacable malice. As oft as he does but name those two first letters, he is, like the island of Fayal, on fire in threescore and ten places.

You see, Mr. Bayes, that I too have improved my wit with reading the Gazetts. Were you of that fellow's diet here about town, that epicurizes upon burning coals, drinks healths in scalding brimstone, scraunches the glasses for his dessert, and draws his breath through glowing tobacco-pipes; nay, to say a thing yet greater, had you never tasted other sustenance than the focus of burning-glasses, you could not show more flame than you do alwayes upon that subject. And yet one would think that even from the 'little sports,' with your 'comfortable importance' after supper, you should have learnt when J. O. came into play, to 'love your love' with an J, because he is judicious, though you 'hate your love with an J,' because he is 'jealous:' and then to 'love your love with an O,' because he is 'oraculous,' though you 'hate your love with an O,' because he is 'obscure.' Is it not strange that in those most benign minutes of a man's life, when the stars smile, the birds sing, the winds whisper, the fountains warble, the trees blossom, and universal nature seems to invite it selfe to the bridal ; when the lion pulls-in his claws and the aspick layes-by its poyson, and all the most noxious creatures grow amorously innocent ; that even then Mr. Bayes alone should not be able to refrain his malignity ? As you love yourself, madam, let him not come near you. He hath been fed all his life with vipers insteed of lampreys, and scorpions for cray-fish; and if at any time he eat chickens, they had been cramb'd with spiders, till he hath so invenomed his whole substance that 'tis much safer to bed with a mountebank before he hath taken his antidote. But it cannot be any vulgar furnace that hath chafed so cool a salamander. 'Tis not the strewing of cow-itch in his genial-bed that could thus disquiet him the first night. And therefore let's take the candle and see whether there be not somebody underneath that hath cut the bed-cords. There was a worthy divine, not many years dead, who in his younger time, being of a facetious and unlucky humour, was commonly known by the name of Tom Triplet : he was brought up at Paul's school, under a severe master, Dr. Gill, and from thence he went to the University. There he took liberty (as 'tis usual with those that are emancipated from school) to tel tales, and make the discipline ridiculous under which he was bred. But, not suspecting the doctor's intelligence, coming once to town, he went in full school to give him a visite, and expected no less than to get a play-day for his former acquaintances. But, instead of that, he found himself hors'd up in a trice; though he appeal'd in vain to the priviledges of the University, pleaded *adultus*, and invoked the mercy of the spectators. Nor was he let down till the master had planted a grove of birch in his back-side, for the terrour and publick example of all waggs that divulge the secrets of Priscian, and make merry with their teachers. This stuck so with Triplet, that all his life-time he never forgave the doctor, but sent him every New-year's-tide an anniversary ballad to a new tune, and so in his turn avenged himself of his jerking pedagogue.

Now when I observed that of late years Mr. Bayes had regularly spawned his books; in 1670 the Ecclesiastical Policy; in 1671 the Defence of the Ecclesiastical Policy; and now in 1672 this Preface to Bishop Bramhal; and that they were writ in a stile so vindictive and poynant, that they wanted nothing but rime to be right Tom Triplet, and that their edge bore alwayes upon J. O. either in broad meanings or in plain terms; I began to suspect that where there was so great a resemblance in the effects, there might be some parallel in their causes. For though the peeks of players among themselves, or of poet against poet, or of a Conformist divine against a Nonconformist, are dangerous, and of late times have caused great disturbance; yet I never remarked so irreconcileable a spirit as that of boyes against their schoolmasters or tutors. The quarrels of their education have an influence upon their memories and understandings for ever after. They cannot speak of their teachers with any patience or civility; and their discourse is never so flippant, nor their wits so fluent, as when you put them upon that theme. Nay, I have heard old men, otherwise sober, peaceable, and good-natured, who never could forgive Osbolston, as the younger are still inveighing against Dr. Busby. It were well that both old and young would reform this vice, and consider how easie a thing it is upon particular grudges, and as they conceived out of a just censure, to slip either into juvenile petulancy or inveterate uncharitableness. And had there not been something of this in his own case, I am confident Mr. Bayes in his Ecclesiastical Policy, in order to the publick peace and security of the Government, could not have failed to admonish princes to beware of this growing evil, and to brandish the publick rods, if not the axes, against the boyes, to teach them better manners. And he would have assured them that they might have done it with all safety, notwithstanding that there were in proportion an hundred boyes against one preceptor. But therefore is it not possible that J. O. and Mr. Bayes have known one another formerly in the University; and that (as in seniority there is a kind of magistracy) Bayes being yet young, J. O. conceiv'd himself in those dayes to be his superiour, and exercised an academical jurisdiction or dominion over him? Now whether J. O. might not be too severe upon him there (for all men are prone to be cogent and supercilious when they are in office), or whether Mr. Bayes might not make some little escapes and excursions there (as young men are apt to do when they are got together), that I know not, and rather believe the contrary. But that is certain, that the young wits in the Universities have always an animosity against the doctors, and take a peculiar felicity in having a lucky hit at any of them. I rather suppose that after Mr. Bayes had changed the place, and his condition, to be the nobleman's chaplain, that he might commit some exorbitance in J. O.'s opinion, or preach or write something to J. O.'s reproach, and published the secrets of the holy brotherhood: and that J. O. having got him within his reach, did therefore (figuratively speaking),

' Instead of maid Jillian,
Take up his Mallepillian,
And whipt him like a baggage—'

as Tom Triplet expresses it. This might well raise Mr. Bayes his choler, who, considering himself to be now in holy orders, and conceiving that he had been as safe as in a sanctuary under his patron's protection, must needs take it ill to be handled so irreverently.

If it were thus in fact, and that J. O. might presume too much upon his former authority to give him correction; yet it is the more excusable, if Mr. Bayes had on his part been guilty of so much disingenuity. For though a man may be allowed once in his life to change his Party, and the whole scene of his affairs, either for his safety or preferment; nay, though every man be obliged to change an hundred times backward and forward, if his judgement be so weak and variable; yet there are some drudgeries that no man of honour would put himself upon, and but few submit to if they were imposed. As, suppose one had thought fit to pass over from one perswasion of the Christian Religion unto another; he would not chuse to spit thrice at every article that he relinquished, to curse solemnly his father and mother for having educated him in those opinions, to animate his new acquaintances to the massacring of his former camarades. These are businesses that can only be expected from a renegade of Algier or Tunis; to overdoe in expiation, and gain better credence of being a sincere Mussulman. And truly, though I can scarcely believe that Mr. Bayes hath so mean and desperate intentions, which yet his words seem too often to manifest; the offices, however, which he undertakes are almost as dishonourable. For he hath so studied and improved their jargon, as he calls it, heard their sermons and prayers so attentively, searched the scriptures so narrowly, that a man may justly suspect he had formerly set up J. O.'s profession, and having the language so perfectly, hath upon 'this juncture of affairs' betaken himself to turn spy and intelligencer; and 'tis evident that he hath travelled the country for that purpose. So that I cannot resemble him better than to that politick engine who about two years ago was employed by some of Oxford as a missionary amongst the Nonconformists of the adjacent counties; and, upon design, either gathered a congregation of his own, or preach'd amongst others, till having got all their names, he threw-off the vizard, and appeared in his colours, an honest informer. But I would not have any man take Mr. Bayes his fanatical geography for authentick, lest he should be as far misled as in the situation of Geneva. It suffices that Mr. Bayes hath done therein as much as served to his purpose, and mixed probability enough for such as know not better, and whose ears are of a just bore for his fable.

But J. O. being of age and parts sufficient either to manage or to neglect this quarrel, I shall as far as possible decline the mentioning of him, seeing I have too, upon further intelligence and consideration, found that he was not the person whom Mr. Bayes principally intended. For, the truth of it is, the King was the person concern'd from the beginning.

His Majesty, before his most happy and miraculous Restauration, had sent over a Declaration of his Indulgence, to tender consciences in ecclesiastical matters. Which, as it was doubtless the real result of the last advice left him by his glorious father, and of his own consummate prudence and natural benignity; so at his Return he religiously observed and promoted it as far as the passions and influence of the contrary Party would give leave. For whereas among all the decent circumstances of his welcom Return, the providence of God had so cooperated with the duty of his subjects, that so glorious an action should neither be soiled with the blood of victory, nor lessened by any capitulations of Treaty, so, not to be wanting on his part in courtesy, as I may say, to so happy a conjuncture, he imposed upon himself an oblivion of former offences, and his indulgence in Ecclesiastical Affairs. And to royal and generous minds no stipulations are so binding as their own voluntary promises: nor is it to be wondred if they hold those conditions that they put upon themselves the most inviolable. He therefore carried the Act of Oblivion and Indemnity thorow; that Party who had suffered vastly in the late combustions not refusing to imitate his generosity, but throwing all their particular losses and resentments into the publick reckoning. But when it came to the ecclesiastical part, the accomplishment of which onely remained behind to have perfected his Majesty's felicity, the business I warrant you would not go so (as I shall have occasion to say more particularly). For, though

I am sorry to speak it, yet it is a sad truth, that the animosities and obstinacy of some of the clergy have in all ages been the greatest obstacle to the clemency, prudence, and good intentions of princes, and the establishment of their affairs. His Majesty therefore expected a better season, and having at last rid himself of a great minister of State who had headed this interest, he now proceeded plainly to recommend to his Parliament effectually, and with repeated instances, the consideration of tender consciences. After the King's last representing of this matter to the Parliament, Mr. Bayes took so much time as was necessary for the maturing of so accurate a book, which was to be the standard of Government for all future ages, and he was happily delivered in 1670 of his Ecclesiastical Policy. And, though he thought fit in this first Book to treat his Majesty more tenderly than in those that followed, yet even in this he doth all along use great liberty and presumption. Nor can what he objects, page 282, to weak consciences, take place so justly upon them as upon himself: 'who, while his prince might expect his compliance, doth give him council, advises him how to govern the kingdom, blames and corrects the laws, and tells him how this and the other might be mended.' But that I may not involve the thing in generals, but represent undeniably Mr. Bayes his performance in this undertaking, I shall without art write down his own words and his *quod scripsi scripsi*, as they ly naked to the view of every reader.

The grand thesis upon which he stakes not onely all his own divinity and policy, his reputation, preferment, and conscience (of most of which he hath no reason to be prodigal), but even the crowns and fate of princes, and the liberties, lives, and estates, and, which is more, the consciences of their subjects (which are too valuable to be trusted in his disposal), is this, page 10, 'That it is absolutely necessary to the peace and government of the world, that the supream magistrate of every Commonwealth should be vested with a power to govern and conduct the consciences of subjects in affairs of religion.' And page 12 he explains himself more fully, that 'unless princes have power to bind their subjects to that religion that they apprehend most advantageous to public peace and tranquillity, and restrain those religious mistakes that tend to its subversion, they are no better than statues and images of authority.' Page 13, 'A prince is endued with a power to conduct religion, and that must be subject to his dominion as well as all other affairs of State.' Page 27, ' If princes should forgoe their soveraignty over men's consciences in matter of religion, they leave themselves less power than is absolutely necessary.' And in brief, ' The supream government of every Commonwealth, wherever it is lodged, must of necessity be universal, absolute, and uncontroulable in all affairs whatsoever that concern the interests of mankind and the ends of government.' Page 32, 'He in whom the supream power resides, having authority to assign to every subject his proper function, and among others these of the priesthood; the exercise thereof as he has power to transfer upon others, so he may if he please reserve it to himself.' Page 33, 'Our Saviour came not to unsettle the foundations of government, but left the government of the world in the same condition he found it.' Page 34, 'The government of religion was vested in princes by an antecedent right to Christ.' This being the magisterial and main point that he maintains, the rest of his assertions may be reckoned as corollaries to this THESIS, and without which indeed such an unlimited maxime can never be justified. Therefore, to make a conscience fit for the nonse, he says, page 89, 'Men may think of things according to their own perswasions, and assert the freedom of their judgments against all the powers of the earth. This is the prerogative of the mind of man within its own dominions, its kingdom is intellectual, &c. Whilst conscience acts within its proper sphere, the civil power is so far from doing it violence, that it never can.' Page 92, 'Mankind have the same natural right to liberty of conscience in matters of religious worship as in affairs of justice and honesty; that is to say, a liberty of judgment, but not of practice.' And in the same page he determines christian liberty to be founded upon the reasonableness of this principle. Page 308, 'In cases and disputes of publick concernment, private men are not properly *sui juris;* they have no power over their own actions: they are not to be directed by their own judgments, or determined by their own wills, but by the commands and determinations of the publick conscience; and if there be any sin in the command, he that imposed it shall answer for it, and not I whose whole duty it is to obey. The commands of Authority will warrant my obedience, my obedience will hallow, or at least excuse my action, and so secure me from sin, if not from error; and in all doubtful and disputable cases 'tis better to err with Authority than to be in the right against it: not only because the danger of a little error (and so it is if it be disputable) is outweighed by the importance of the great duty of obedience, &c.'

Another of his corollaries is, 'That God hath appointed' (page 80) 'the magistrates to be His trustees upon earth, and His officials to act and determine in moral virtues and pious devotions according to all accidents and emergencies of affairs; to assign new particulars of the divine law; to declare new bounds of right and wrong, which the law of God neither doth nor can limit.' Page 69, 'Moral virtue being the most material and useful part of all religion, is also the utmost end of all its other duties.' Page 76, 'All religion must of necessity be resolved into enthusiasm or morality. The former is meer imposture, and therefore all that is true must be reduced to the latter.' Having thus enabled the prince, dispensed with conscience, and fitted up a moral religion for that conscience; to shew how much those moral virtues are to be valued, page 53 of the Preface to his Ecclesiastical Policy, he affirms that ''tis absolutely necessary to the peace and happiness of kingdoms that there be set up a more severe government over men's consciences and religious perswasions than over their vices and immoralities.' And page 55 of the same, 'that princes may with less hazard give liberty to men's vices and debaucheries than their consciences.' But for what belongs particularly to the use of their power in Religion, he first (page 56 of his Book) saith, 'that the Protestant Reformation hath not been able to resettle princes in their full and natural rights in reference to its concerns;' and page 58, 'most Protestant princes have been frighted, not to say hector'd, out of the exercise of their ecclesiastical jurisdiction.' Page 271, 'If princes will be resolute (and if they will govern, so they must be), they may easily make the most stubborn conscience bend to their resolutions.' Page 221, 'Princes must be sure to bind on at first their Ecclesiastical Laws with the straightest knot, and afterwards keep them in force by the severity of their execution.' Page 223, speaking of honest and well-meaning men, 'so easy is it for men to deserve to be punished for their consciences, that there is no nation in the world in which, were government rightly understood and duly managed, mistakes and abuses of religion would not supply the galleys with vastly greater numbers than villany.' Page 54 of the Preface to Ecclesiast. Policy: 'Of all villains the well-meaning zealot is the most dangerous.' Page 46, 'The fanatick party in country towns and villages ariseth not (to speak within compass) above the proportion of one to twenty. Whilst the publick peace and settlement is so unluckily defeated by quarrels and mutinies of Religion, to erect and create new trading combinations, is only to build so many nests of faction and sedition, &c. For it is notorious that there is not any sort of people so inclinable to seditious practices as the trading part of a nation.' And now, though many as material passages might be heap'd-up out of his Book on all those and other as tender subjects, I shall conclude this imperfect enumeration with one corollary more, to which indeed his grand Thesis and all the superstructures are subordinate and accommodated. Page 166, 'Princes cannot pluck a pin out of the Church, but the State immediately shakes and totters.' This is the syntagm of Mr. Bayes his divinity, and system of his Policy: the principles of which confine upon the territories of Malmsbury, and the stile, as far as his wit would give him leave, imitates that language: but the arrogance and dictature with which he imposes it on the world surpasses by far the presumption either of Gondibert or Leviathan. For he had indeed a very politick fetch or two that might have made a much wiser than he more confident. For he imagined, first of all, that he had perfectly secured himself from any man's answering him: not so much upon the true treason, that is, because indeed so paltry a Book did not deserve an Answer; as because he had so confounded the question with differing terms and contradictory expressions, that he might upon occasion affirm whatsoever he denied, or deny whatsoever he affirmed. And then besides, because he had so intangled the matter of conscience with the magistrates' power, that he supposed no man could handle it thorowly without bringing himself within the statute of treasonable words, and at least a *premunire*. But last of all, because he thought that whosoever answered him must for certain be of a contrary judgment, and he that was of a contrary judgment should be a fanatick; and if one of them presumed to be medling, then Mr. Bayes (as all divines have a *non-obstante* to the *jejunium Cecilianum*, and to the Act of Oblivion and Indempnity) would either burn that, or tear it in pieces. Being so well fortified on this side, upon the other he took himself to be impregnable. His Majesty must needs take it kindly that he gave him so great an accession of territory; and, lest he should not be thought rightly to understand government, nay, lest Mr. Bayes by virtue of page 271 should not think him fit to govern, he could not in prudence and safety but submit to his admonition and instructions. But if he would not, Mr. Bayes knew, ay that he did, how to be even with him, and would write another Book that should do his business. For the same power that had given the prince that authority could also revoke it.

But let us see therefore what success the whole contrivance met with, or what it deserved. For, after things have been laid with all the depth of humane Policy, there happens lightly some ugly little contrary accident from some quarter or other of heaven, that frustrates and renders all ridiculous.

And here, for brevity and distinction sake, I must make use of the same priviledge by which I call him Mr. Bayes, to denominate also his several aphorisms or hypotheses: and let him take care whether or no they be significant.

First, The Unlimitted Magistrate.
Secondly, The Publick Conscience.
Thirdly, Moral Grace.
Fourthly, Debauchery Tolerated.
Fifthly, Persecution Recommended.
And lastly, Push-pin Divinity.

And now, though I intend not to be longer than the nature of Animadversions requires (this also being but collateral to my work of examining the Preface, and having been so abundantly performed already), yet neither can I proceed well without some Preface. For, as I am obliged to ask pardon if I speak of serious things ridiculously, so I must now beg excuse if I should hap to discourse of ridiculous things seriously. But I shall, so far as possible, observe decorum, and, whatever I talk of, not commit such an absurdity as to be grave with a buffoon. But the principal cause of my Apology is, because I see I am drawn-in to mention kings and princes, and even our own; whom, as I think of with all duty and reverence, so I avoid speaking of either in jest or earnest, lest by reason of my private condition and breeding I should, though most unwillingly, trip in a word, or fail in the mannerliness of an expression. But Mr. Bayes, because princes sometimes hear men of his quality play their part, or preach a sermon, grows so insolent that he thinks himself fit to be their governour. So dangerous is it to let such creatures be too familiar. They know not their distance.; and like the ass in the fable, because they see the spaniel play with their master's leggs, they think themselves priviledged to paw and ramp upon his shoulders. Yet though I must follow his track now I am in, I hope I shall not write after his copy.

As for his first hypothesis of the UNLIMITTED MAGISTRATE, I must for this once do him right, that after I had read in his 12th page, 'that princes have power to bind their subjects to that religion they apprehend most advantageous to publick peace and tranquillity ;' a long time after, not, as I remember, till page 82, when he bethought himself better, he saith, 'No rites nor ceremonies can be esteemed unlawful in the worship of God, unless they tend to debauch men either in their practices or their conceptions of the Deity.' But no man is in ingenuity obliged to do him that service for the future; neither yet doth that limitation bind up or interpret what he before so loosely affirmed. However, take all along the power of the magistrate as he hath stated it; I am confident if Bishop Bramhall were alive (who could no more forbear Grotius than Mr. Bayes could the Bishop, notwithstanding their friendship), he would bestow the same censure upon him that he doth upon Grotius, page 18, 'When I read his book of the right of the sovereign magistrate in sacred things, he seem'd to me to come too near an Erastian, and to lessen the power of the keys too much, which Christ left as a legacy to His Church. It may be he did write that before he was come to full maturity of judgement: and some other things, I do not say after he was superannuated, but without that due deliberation which he useth at other times' (wherein a man may discern Mr. Bayes in Mr. Bayes); 'or, it may be, some things may be changed in his Book, as I have been told by one of his nearest friends, and that we shall shortly see a more authentick edition of all his works. This is certain, that some of those things which I dislike were not his own judgement after he was come to maturity in theological matter.' And had Mr.

Bayes (as he ought to have done) carryed his Book to any of the present Bishops or their chaplains, for a licence to print it, I cannot conceive that he could have obtained it in better terms than what I have collected out of the 108 page of his Answer: 'Notwithstanding the old pleas of the *jus divinum* of episcopacy, of example and direction apostolical, of a parity of reason between the condition of the Church whilst under extraordinary officers, and whilst under ordinary, of the power of the Church to appoint ceremonies for decency and order, of the patern of the churches of old' (all which, under Protestation, are reserved till the first opportunity). I have upon reading of this book found that it may be of use for 'the present juncture of affairs,' and therefore let it be printed. And as I think he hath disobliged the clergy of England in this matter, so I believe the favour that he doth his Majesty is not equivalent to that damage. For (that I may, with Mr. Bayes his leave, prophane Ben Johnson) 'though the gravest divines should be his flaterers;' he hath a very quick sense (shall I prophane Horace too in the same period?):

'Hunc male si palpere, recalcitrat undique tutus.'

If one stroke him ill-favouredly, he hath a terrible way of kicking, and will fling you to the stable-door, but is himself safe on every side. He knows it's all but that you may get into the saddle again; and that the priest may ride him, though it be to a precipice. He therefore contents himself with the power that he hath inherited from his royal progenitors kings and queens of England, and as it is declared by Parliament, and is not to be trepann'd into another kind of tenure of dominion to be held at Mr. Bayes his pleasure, and depend upon the strength only of his argument. But (that I may not offend in Latin too frequently) he considers that by not assuming a Deity to himself, he becomes secure and worthy of his government. There are lightly about the courts of princes a sort of projectors for concealed lands, to which they entitle the King, to begg them for themselves; and yet generally they get not much by it, but are exceedingly vexatious to the subject. And even such an one is this Mr. Bayes, with his project of 'concealed power,' that most princes, as he said, ' have not yet rightly understood;' but whereof the King is so little enamour'd, that I am confident, were it not for prolling and molesting the people, his Majesty would give Mr. Bayes the patent for it, and let him make his best on't, after he hath paid the fees to my Lord Keeper.

But one thing I must confess is very pleasant, and he hath past an high compliment upon his Majesty in it: that he may, if he please, reserve the priesthood and the exercise of it to himself. Now this indeed is surprising; but this onely troubles me, how his Majesty would look in all the sacerdotal habiliments, and the pontifical wardrobe. I am afraid the King would find himself incommoded with all that furniture upon his back, and would scarce reconcile himself to wear even the lawn sleeves and the surplice. But what? even Charles the Fifth, as I have read, was, at his inauguration by the Pope, content to be vested, according to the Roman ceremonial, in the habit of a deacon; and a man would not scruple too much the formality of the dress in order to empire.

But one thing I doubt Mr. Bayes did not well consider; that, if the King may discharge the function of the priesthood, he may too (and 'tis all the reason in the world) assume the revenue. It would be the best subsidy that ever was voluntarily given by the clergy. But truly, otherwise, I do not see but that the King does lead a more unblamable conversation, and takes more care of souls than many of them, and understands their office much better, and deserves something already for the pains he hath taken.

The next is PUBLICK CONSCIENCE: for as to men's private consciences, he hath made them very inconsiderable, and reading what he saith of them with some attention, I only found this new and important discovery and great priviledge of Christian liberty, that 'thought is free.' We are, however, obliged to him for that, seeing by consequence we think of him what we please. And this he saith a man may assert against all the powers of the earth. And, indeed, with much reason and to great purpose, seeing, as he also alledges, the civil power is so far from doing violence to that liberty, that it never can. But yet if the freedom of thoughts be in not lying open to discovery, there have been wayes of compelling men to discover them; or if the freedom consist in retaining their judgments when so manifested, that also hath been made penal. And I doubt not but, beside oaths and renunciations, and assents and consents, Mr. Bayes, if he were searched, hath twenty other tests and picklocks in his pocket. Would Mr. Bayes, then, perswade men to assert this against all the powers of the earth? I would ask, in what manner? To say the truth, I do not like him, and would wish the Nonconformists to be upon their guard, lest he trepan them, first by this means into a Plot, and then peach, and so hang them. If Mr. Bayes meant otherwise in this matter, I confess my stupidity, and the fault is most his own, who should have writ to the capacity of vulgar readers. He cuts, indeed, and faulters in this discourse, which is no good sign, perswading men that they may and ought to practise against their consciences, where the commands of the magistrate intervene. None of them denies that it is their duty, where their judgements or consciences cannot comply with what is injoyned, that they ought in obedience patiently to suffer, but further they have not learned. I dare say that the casual divinity of the Jesuits is all thorow as orthodox as this maxime of our

Author's: and as the opinion is brutish, so the consequences are devilish. To make it therefore go down more glibly, he saith, that ' 'tis better to err with Authority, than to be in the right against it in all doubtful and disputable cases; because the great duty of obedience outweighs the danger of a little error (and little it is if it be disputable).' I cannot understand the truth of this reasoning, that whatsoever is disputable is little; for even the most important matters are subject to controversie, and besides, things are little or great according to the eyes or understandings of several men; and however, a man would suffer something rather than commit that little error against his conscience, which must render him an hypocrite to God and a knave amongst men. ' The commands,' he saith, 'and determinations of the publick conscience ought to carry it; and if there be any sin in the command, he that imposed it shall answer for it, and not I, whose duty it is to obey.' And mark, 'the commands of Authority will warrant my obedience, my obedience will hallow, or at least excuse, my action, and so secure me from sin, if not from error;' and so you are welcome, gentlemen. Truly a very fair and conscionable reckoning! So far is this from hallowing the action, that I dare say it will, if followed home, lead only to all that 'sanctified villany' for the invention of which we are beholden to the Author. But let him have the honour of it, for he is the first Divine that ever taught Christians how another man's sin could confer an 'imputative righteousness' upon all mankind that shall follow and comply with it. Though the subject made me serious, yet I could not read the expression without laughter: 'My obedience will hallow, or at least excuse, my action.' So inconsiderable a difference he seems to make betwixt those terms, that if ever our Author come for his merits to be a Bishop, a man might almost adventure, instead of 'consecrated,' to say that he was 'excused.'

The third is MORAL GRACE. And whoever is not satisfied with those passages of his concerning it before quoted, may find enough where he discourseth it at large, even to surfeit. I cannot make either less or more of it than that he overturns the whole fabrick of Christianity and power of religion. For my part, if GRACE be resolved into morality, I think a man may almost as well make God too to be only a notional and moral existence.

And white-aproned Amaryllis was of that opinion:

> *Ma tu sanctissima honestà, che sola sei*
> *D' alma ben nata inviolabil nume.*

'But thou most holy honesty, that only art the inviolable Deity of the well-born soul.'

And so too was the moral poet; for why may not I too bring out my Latin shreds as well as he his?

> *Quaesitum ad fontem solos deducere verpos . . .*
> *Nullum numen abest, si sit prudentia—*

'There is no need of a Deity where there is prudence; or, if you will, where there is Ecclesiastical Policy.'

But so far I must do Mr. Bayes right, that, to my best observation, if prudence had been God, Bayes had been a most damnable atheist. Or, perhaps, only an idolater of their number, concerning whom he adds in the next line,

... *sed te*
Nos facimus, fortuna, deam, coeloque locamus.

'But we make thee, Fortune, a goddess, and place thee in heaven.'

However, I cannot but be sorry that he hath undertaken this desperate vocation, when there are twenty other honest and painful wayes wherein he might have got a '*living*,' and made Fortune propitious. But he cares not upon what argument or how dangerous he runns, to show his ambitious activity: whereas those that will dance upon ropes do lightly some time or other break their necks. And I have heard that even the Turk, every day he was to mount the high-rope, took leave of his '*comfortable importance*,' as if he should never see her more. But this is a matter foreign to my judicature, and therefore I leave him to be tryed by any jury of divines: and, that he may have all right done him, let half of them be school-divines and the other moiety systematical, and let him except against as many as the Law allows; and so God send him a good deliverance. But I am afraid he will never come off.

The fourth is DEBAUCHERY TOLERATED. For supposing, as he does, that 'tis better and 'safer to give a toleration to men's debaucheries than to their religious perswasions,' it amounts to the same reckoning. This is a very ill way of discoursing, and that a ' greater severity ought to be exercised over men's consciences than over their vices and immoralities.' For it argues too much indiscretion by avoiding one evil to run up into the contrary extream. And debauch'd persons will be ready hence to conclude, although it be a perverse way of reasoning, That where the severity ought to be less, the crime is less also; nay, even that the more they are debauch'd, it is just that the punishment should still abate in proportion; but, however, that it were very imprudent and unadvisable to reform and err on the religious hand, lest they should thereby incur the greater penalties. Mr. Bayes would have done much better had he singled out the theme of Religion. He might have loaded it with all the truth which that subject would bear. I would allow him that 'rebellion is as the sin of witchcraft' [1 Samuel xv. 23], though that text of Scripture will scarce admit his interpretation. He could not have declaimed more sharply than I, or any honest man else, would upon occasion against all those who under pretence of conscience raise war, or create publick disturbances. But comparisons of vice are dangerous, and though he should do this without design, yet, while he aggravates upon Religion, and

puts it in balance, he doth so far alleviate and encourage debauchery. And moreover (which, to be sure, is against his design) he doth hereby more confirm the austerer sort of sinners, and furnishes them with a more specious colour and stronger argument. It had been better policy to instruct the magistrate that there is no readier way to shame these out of their religious niceties than by improving men's morals. But, as he handles it, never was there any point more unseasonably exposed; at such a time, when there is so general a depravation of manners, that even those who contribute towards it do yet complain of it; and though they cannot reform their practice, yet feel the effects, and tremble under the apprehension of the consequences. It were easie here to shew a man's reading, and to discourse out of History the causes of the decay and ruine of Mr. Bayes his Roman empire, when, as the moralist has it,
. . . *saevior armis*
Luxuria incubuit, victumque ulciscitur orbem.

And descending to those times since Christianity was in the throne, 'tis demonstrable that for one War upon a fanatical or religious account, there have been an hundred occasioned by the thirst of glory and empire that hath inflamed some great prince to invade his neighbours. And more have sprung from the contentiousness and ambition of some of the clergy; but the most of all from the corruption of manners and alwayes fatal debauchery. It exhausts the estates of private persons, and makes them fit for nothing but the highway or an army. It debases the spirits and weakens the vigour of any nation; at once indisposing them for War, and rendring them uncapable of Peace. For if they escape intestine troubles, which would certainly follow when they had left themselves by their prodigality or intemperance no other means of subsistence but by preying upon one another; then must they either, to get a maintenance, pick a quarrel with some other Nation, wherein they are sure to be worsted; or else (which more frequently happens) some neighbouring prince that understands government takes them at the advantage, and if they do not like ripe fruit fall into his lap, 'tis but shaking the tree once or twice, and he is sure of them. Where the horses are, like those of the Sybarites, taught to dance, the enemy need only learn the tune and bring the fiddles. But therefore (as far as I understand) his Majesty, to obviate and prevent these inconveniences in his kingdoms, hath on the one hand never refused a just Warre; that so he might take down our grease and luxury, and keep the English courage in breath and exercise; and on the other (though himself most constantly addicted to the Church of England) hath thought fit to grant some liberty to all other sober people (and longer than they are so God forbid they should have it!), thereby to give more temper and allay to the common and notorious debauchery.

But Mr. Bayes nevertheless is for his fifth: PERSECUTION RECOMMENDED; and he does it to the purpose. Julian himself, who I think was first a Reader, and held forth in the Christian churches before he turned apostate and then persecutor, could not have outdone him either in irony or cruelty. Only it is God's mercy that Mr. Bayes is not emperour. You have seen how he inveighs against trade: 'That whilst men's consciences are actuated by such peevish and ungovernable principles, to erect trading combinations is but to build so many nests of faction and sedition.' Lay up your ships, my masters, set bills on your shop-doors, shut up the custom-house; and why not adjourn the Term, mure-up Westminster-hall, leave plowing and sowing, and keep a dismal holy-day through the Nation? for Mr. Bayes is out of humour. But I assure you it is no jesting matter. For he hath in one place taken a list of the fanatick ministers, whom he reckons to be but a hundred 'systematical divines;' though I believe the Bartlemew register or the March licenses would make them about an hundred and three or an hundred and four, or so: but this is but for rounder number, and breaks no square. And then for their people, either 'they live in greater societies of men' (he means the city of London and the other cities and towns corporate, but expresses it so to prevent some inconvenience that might betide him); 'but there their noise is greater than their number. Or else in country towns and villages, where they arise not above the proportion of one to twenty.' It were not unwisely done indeed if he could perswade the magistrate that all the fanaticks have but one neck, so that he might cut off Nonconformity at one blow. I suppose the Nonconformists value themselves, tho', upon their conscience, and not their numbers: but they would do well to be watchful, lest he have taken a list of their names as well as their number, and have set crosses upon all their doors against there should be occasion. But till that 'happy juncture,' when Mr. Bayes 'shall be fully avenged of his new enemies, the wealthy fanaticks' (which is soon done too, for he saith, 'there are but few of them men of estates or interest'), he is contented that they should only be exposed (they are his own expressions) to the 'pillories, whipping-posts, galleys, rods and axes;' and moreover and above, to all other punishments whatsoever, provided they be of a severer nature than those that are inflicted on men for their immoralities. O more than humane clemency! I suppose the division betwixt immoralities and conscience is universal; and whatsoever is wicked or penal is comprehended within their territories. So that although a man should be guilty of all those heinous enormities which are 'not to be named among Christians' [Ephesians v. 3], beside all lesser peccadillo's expressly against the Ten Commandments, or such other part of the divine Law as shall be of the magistrates' making, he shall be in a better condition, and more gently handled, than a 'well-meaning zealot;' for this is the man that Mr. Bayes saith 'is of all villains the most dangerous' (even more dangerous, it seems, than a malicious and ill-meaning Zelot): this is he whom in 'all kingdoms where government is rightly understood,' he would have condemned 'to the galleys for his mistakes and abuses of Religion.' Although the other punishments are more severe, yet this being more new and unacquainted, I cannot pass it by without some reflexion. For I considered what princes make use of gallyes. The first that occurred to me was the Turk, who, according to Bayes his maxim, hath established Mahometism among his subjects, as the 'Religion that he apprehends most advantageous to publick peace and settlement.' Now in his empire the Christians only are guilty of those 'religious mistakes that tend to the subversion of Mahometism;' so that he understands government rightly in chaining the Christians to the oar. But then in Christendom, all that I could think of were the king of France, the king of Spain, the Knights of Malta, the Pope, and the rest of the Italian princes. And these all have bound their subjects to the Romish Religion as most advantagious. But these people [fill] their galleys with immoral fellows and debauchees; whereas the Protestants, being their fanaticks and mistakers in Religion, should have been their *ciurma*. But it is to be hoped these princes will take advice and understand it better for the future. And then at last I remembred that his Majesty too hath one gally lately built, but I dare say it is not with that intention: and our fanaticks, though few, are so many, that one will not serve. But therefore, if Mr. Bayes and his partners would be at the charge to build the king a whole squadron for this use, I know not but it might do very well (for we delight in novelties), and it would be a singular obligation to Sir John Baptist Dutel, who might have some pretence to be general of his Majesty's gallies. But so much for that. Yet in the mean time I cannot but admire at Mr. Bayes his courage; who knowing how dangerous a villain a well meaning Zelot is, and having calculated to a man how many of them there are in the whole nation, yet dares thus openly stimulate the magistrate against them, and talk of nothing less, but much more, than 'pillories, whipping-posts, galleys, and axes,' in this manner. It is sure some sign (and if he knew not so much, he would scarce adventure) of the peaceableness of their principles, and of that restraint under which their tender consciences hold them, when nevertheless he may walk night and day in safety; though it were so easy a thing to deifie the divine after the ancient manner, and no man be the wiser. But that which I confess would vex me most, were I either an ill or a well meaning Zealot, would be, after all, to hear him (as he frequently does) sneering at me in an ironical harangue to persuade me, forsooth, to take all patiently for conscience-sake and the good example of mankind; nay, to wheedle one almost to make himself away, to save the hangman a labour. It was indeed near that pass in the primitive times, and the tired magistrates asked them, whether they had not altars and rivers and precipices, if they were so greedy of suffering? But, by the good leave of your insolence, we are not come to that yet. *Non tibi, sed Petro;* or rather, *sed Regi.* The Nonconformists have suffered as well as any men in the world, and could do so still if it were his Majesty's pleasure. Their duty to God hath hallowed, and their duty to the magistrate hath excused, both their pain and ignominy. To die by a noble hand is some satisfaction: but when his Majesty, for reasons best known to himself, hath been graciously pleased to abate of your rigors, I hope, Mr. Bayes, that we shall not see when you have a mind to junket with your 'comfortable importance,' that the entremets shall be of a fanatick's giblits, nor that a Nonconformist's head must be whipped off as oft as your nose drivels. It is sufficient, Sir, we know your inclination, we know your abilities, and we know your lodging; and when there is any further occasion, you will doubtless be sent for. For, to say the truth, this Bayes is an excellent tool, and more useful than ten other men. I will undertake that he shall, rather than fail, be the trepanner, the informer, the witness, the attorney, the judge; and, if the Nonconformist need the benefit of his book, he shall be ordinary too, and say he is an ignorant fellow, *non legit:* and then, to do him the last Christian office, he would be his hangman. In the mean time, let him enjoy it in speculation, secure of all the imployments when they shall fall. For I know no gentleman that will take any of them out of his hands, although it be in an Age wherein men cannot well support their quality without some accession from the publick : and for the ordinary sort of people, they are, I know not by what disaster, besotted and abandon'd to fanaticism. So that Mr. Bayes must either do it himself in person, or constitute the cheif magistrate to be his deputy. But princes do indeed understand themselves better most of 'em, and do neither think it so safe to intrust a clergyman with their authority, nor decent for themselves to do the drudgery of the clergy. That would have past in the dayes of Saint Dominick ; but when even the Inquisition hath lost its edge in the Popish countryes, there is little appearance it should be set up in England. It were a worthy spectacle—were it not?—to see his Majesty, like the governor in Synesius, busied in his cabinet among those engines whose very names are so hard that it is some torture to name them ; the Podostrabæ, the Dactylethreæ, the Otagræ, the Rhinolabides, the Cheilostrophia, devising, as they say there are particular diseases, so a peculiar rack for every limb and member of a Christian's body. Or, would he (with all reverence be it spoken) exchange his kingdom of England for that of Macassar? where the great *arcanum* of Government is the cultivating of a garden of venimous plants, and preparing thence a poyson, in which the prince dips a dart, that where it does but draw blood, rots the person immediately to pieces; and his office is with that to be the executioner of his subjects. God be praised, his Majesty is far of another temper; and he is wise, though some men be malicious.

But Mr. Bayes his sixt is that which I call his PUSH-PIN DIVINITY; for he would persuade princes that 'there cannot be a pin pull'd out of the Church but the State immediately totters.' That is strange. And yet I have seen many a pin pull'd out upon occasion, and yet not so much as the Church itself hath wagg'd. It is true indeed, and we have had sad experiments of it, that some clergymen have been so opiniastre that they have rather exposed the State to ruin than they would part with a pin, I will not say out of their Church, but out of their sleeve. There is nothing more natural than for the ivy to be of opinion that the oak cannot stand without its support; or, seeing we are got into ivy, that the Church cannot hold up longer than it underprops the walls; whereas it is a sneaking insinuating imp, scarce better than bindweed, that sucks the tree dry and moulders the building where it catches. But what, pray, Mr. Bayes, is this pinne in Pallas's buckler? Why, 'tis some ceremony or other that is 'indifferent in its own nature; that hath no antecedent necessity but only as commanded; that signifies nothing in it self but what the commander pleases; that even by the Church which commands it is declared to have nothing of Religion in it; and that is in it self of no great moment or consequence, only it is absolutely necessary that governours should enjoyn it, to avoid the evils that would follow if it were not determined.' Very well, Mr. Bayes. This I see will keep cold: anon, perhaps I may have a stomach. But I must take care lest I swallow your pin.

Here we had the titles, and some short rehearsal of Mr. Bayes his six Playes. Not but that, should we disvalise him, he hath to my knowledge a hundred more as good in his budget; but really I consult mine own repose. But now, among friends, was there ever any thing so monstrous? You see what a man may come to with divinity and high-feeding. There is a scurvy disease which, though some derive from America, others tell a story that the Genoueses in their Wars with Venice took some of their noblemen, whom they cut to pieces and barrel'd up like tunny, and so maliciously vented it to the Venetians, who, eating it ignorantly, broke out in those nasty botches and ugly symptoms that are not curable but by mercury. What I relate it for is out of no further intention, nor is there any more similitude, than that the mind too hath its nodes sometimes, and tho stile its buboes; and that

I doubt, before Mr. Bayes can be rid of 'em, he must pass through the grand cure and a dry diet.

And now it is high time that I resume the thread of my former history concerning Mr. Bayes his Books in relation to his Majesty. I do not find that the 'Ecclesiastical Policy' found more acceptance than could be expected from so judicious a prince; nor do I perceive that he was ever considered of at a promotion of Bishops, nor that he hath the reversion of the archbishoprick of Canterbury. But if he have not by marriage barr'd his way, and if it should ever fall to his lot, I am resolved, instead of his *Grace*, to call him alwayes his *Morality*. But as he got no preferment that I know of at Court (though his patron doubtless, having many things in his gift, did abundantly recompence him), so he mist no less of his aim as to the reformation of ecclesiastical government upon his principles. But still, what he complains of, page 20, 'the ecclesiastical laws were either weakened through want of execution, or in a manner cancell'd by the opposition of civil constitutions.' For, beside what in England, where all things went on at the same rate, in the neighbouring kingdom of Scotland there were I know not how many Mas Johns restored in one day to the work of their ministry, and a door opened whereby all the rest might come in for the future, and all this by his Majesty's Commission. Nay, I think there was (a thing of very ill example) an archbishop turn'd out of his See for some misdemeanor or other. I have not been curious of his name nor his crime, because as much as possible I would not expose the nakedness of any person so eminent formerly in the Church. But henceforward the King fell into disgrace with Mr. Bayes, and any one that had eyes might discern that our Author did not afford his Majesty that countenance and favour which he had formerly enjoy'd. So that a book too of J. O.'s happening mischievously to come out at the same season, upon pretence of answering that, he resolved to make his Majesty feel the effects of his displeasure. So that he set pen to paper again, and having kept his midwife of the 'Friendly Debate' by him all the time of his pregnancy for fear of miscarrying, he was at last happily delivered of his second child, the 'Defence of the Ecclesiastical Policy,' in the year 1671. It was a very lusty baby, and twice as big as the former, and (which some observed as an ill sign, and that if it lived it would prove a great tyrant) it had, when born, all the teeth, as perfect as ever you saw in any man's head. But I do not reckon much upon those ominous criticisms. For there was partly a natural cause in it, Mr. Bayes having gone so many months more than the Civil Law allows for the utmost term of legitimation, that it was no wonder if the brat were at its birth more forward than others usually are. And indeed, Mr. Bayes was so provident against abortion, and careful for some reasons that the child should cry, that the only question in town (though without much cause, for truly 'twas very like him) was whether it was not spurious or supposititious. But, allegories and raillery and hard words apart: in this his second Book, and what I quoted before out of Bishop Bramhal, page 18, with allusion to our Author, is here faln out as exactly true as if it had been expresly calculated for Bayes his meridian. He finds himself to have come too near, nay to have far outgone an Erastian; that he had writ his Ecclesiastical Policy before he was come to maturity of judgment; that one might desire Mr. Bays in Mr. Bays; that something had been changed in his Book; that a more authentick edition was necessary; that some things which he had said before were not his judgement after he was come to maturity in theological matters.

I will not herein too much insist upon his 'Reply,' where his Answerer asks him pertinently enough to his grand Thesis, what was then become of their old plea of *Jus Divinum?* Why, saith he, must you prescribe me what I shall write? Perhaps my next Book shall be of that subject. For, perhaps he said so only for evasion, being old, excellent at parrying and fencing. Though I have good reason to believe that we may shortly see some piece of his upon that theme, and in defence of an aphorism of a great prelate in the last king's time, 'That the king had no more to do in ecclesiastical matters than Jack that rubbed his horses' heels.' For Mr. Bayes is so interprising, you know, 'look too't, I'll doo't.' He has face enough to say or unsay any thing, and 'tis his priviledge, what the School-divines deny to be even within the power of the Almighty, to make contradictions true. An evidence of which (though I reserve the further instances to another occasion that draws near) does plainly appear in what I now principally urge, to show how dangerous a thing it is for his Majesty and all other princes to lose Mr. Bayes his favour. For whereas he had all along in his first Book treated them like a company of ignorants, and that did not understand government (but that is pardonable in Mr. Bayes), in this his second, now that they will not do as he would have them, when he had given them power and instructions how to be wiser for the future, he casts them quite off, like men that were desperate. He had, you know, page 35 of his first Book, and in other places, vested them with an universal and unlimited power, and uncontroulable in the government of Religion (that is, over men's consciences); but now in his second, to make them an example to all incorrigible and ungrateful persons, he strips and disrobes them again of all those regal ornaments that he had superinduced upon them, and leaves them good princes in *querpo* as he found 'em, to shift for themselves in the wide world as well as they can. Do but read his own words, page 237 of his 'Defence,' paragraph 5, and sure you will be of my mind. ' To vest the supreme magistrate in an unlimited and uncontroulable power, is clearly to defeat the efficacy and obligatory force of all his laws, that cannot possibly have any binding vertue upon the minds of men, when they have no other inducement to obedience but only to avoid the penalty. But if the supreme power be absolute and unlimited, it doth for that very reason remove and evacuate all other obligations, for otherwise it is restrained and conditional; and if men lye under no other impulsion than of the Law it self, they lye under no other obligation than that of prudence and self-interest, and it remains intirely in the choice of their own discretion whether they shall or shall not obey, and then there is neither government nor obligation to obedience; and the principle of men's complyance with the mind of their superiours is not the declaration of their will and pleasure, but purely the determination of their own judgments; and therefore 'tis necessary for the security of government, though for nothing else, to set bounds to its jurisdiction; otherwise, like the Roman empire, &c.' I know it would be difficult to quote twenty lines in Mr. Bayes but we should encounter with the Roman Empire. But observe how laboriously here he hath asserted and proved that all he had said in his first Book was a meer mistake, before he were come to years of discretion. For, as in law a man is not accounted so till he hath compleated twenty-one, and 'tis but the last minute of that time that makes him his own man (as to all things but conscience I mean, for as to that he saith men are never *sui juris*), so though the distance of Bayes his books was but betwixt 1670 and 1671, yet a year, nay an instant at any time of a man's life may make him wiser, and he hath, like all other fruits, his annual maturity. It was so long since as 1670, page 33, that this ' universal unlimited and uncontroulable power was the natural right of princes antecedent to Christ, firmly established by the unalterable dictates of natural reason, universal practice, and consent of Nations, that the Scripture rather supposes than asserts the Ecclesiastical (and so the Civil) jurisdiction of princes.' 'Twas in 1670, page 10, That it was 'absolutely necessary;' and page 12, ' that princes have that power to bind their subjects to that Religion that they apprehend most advantageous to publick peace, &c.' So that they derive their title from eternal necessity, which the Moralists say the gods themselves cannot impeach. His Majesty may lay-by his *Dieu*, and make use only of his *Mon Droit*. He hath a patent for his kingdom under the broad seal of Nature, and next under that, and immediately before Christ, is over all persons and in all causes as well Ecclesiastical as Civil (and over all men's consciences) within his Majesty's realms and dominions supream head and governour. 'Tis true, the Author sometimes for fashion-sake speaks in that Book of Religion and of a Deity ; but his principles do necessarily, if not in terms, make the prince's power paramount to both those, and if he may by his uncontroulable and unlimited universal authority introduce what religion he may, of consequence what Deity also he pleases. Or if there were no Deity, yet there must be some Religion, that being an engine most advantageous for publick peace and tranquillity. This was in 1670; but by 1671 you see the case is altered. Even one night hath made some men gray. And now page 238 of his second Book, he hath made princes accountable, ay and to so severe an auditor as God Himself. 'The thrones of princes are established upon the dominion of God.' And page 241, ''Tis no part of the prince's concernment to institute rules of moral good and evil; that is the care and the prerogative of a superiour Lawgiver.' And page 260, he owns, that if the subjects can plead a clear and undoubted preingagement to that higher authority, they have liberty to remonstrate to the equity of their laws. I do not like this remonstrating nor these remonstrants. I wish again that Mr. Bayes would tell us what he means by the term, and where it will end, whether he would have the fanaticks remonstrate: but they are wary, and asham'd of what they have done in former times of that nature: or whether he himself hath a mind to remonstrate, because the fanaticks are tolerated. That is the thing, that is the business of this whole Book; and knowing that there is a clear and undoubted preingagement to the higher authority of nature and necessity, if the king will persist in tolerating these people, who knows, after remonstrating, what Mr. Bayes will doe next? But now in sum, what shall we say of this man, and how had the King been served if he had followed Bayes's advice, and assumed the power of his first Book? He had run himself into a fine *premunire*, when now, after all, he comes to be made accountable to God, nay even to his subjects. And by this means it happens, though it were beyond Mr. Bayes his forecast, and I dare say he would rather have given the prince again a power antecedent to Christ, and to bring in what Religion he please: he hath obliged him to as tender a conscience as any of his Christian subjects, and then good night to 'Ecclesiastical Policy.' I have herein indeavoured the utmost ingenuity toward Mr. Bayes, for he hath laid himself open but to too many disadvantages already, so that I need not, I would not press him beyond measure, but to my best understanding, and if I faile, I even ask him pardon, I do him right. 'Tis true, that being distracted betwixt his desire that the consciences of men should be persecuted, and his anger at princes that will not be advised, he confounds himself every where in his reasonings, that you can hardly distinguish which is the whoop and which is the holla, and he makes indentures on each side of the way wheresoever he goes. But no man that is sober will follow him, lest some Justice of Peace should make him pay his five shillings, beside the scandal; and it is apparent to every one what he drives at. But were this otherwise, I can spare it, and 'tis sufficient to my purpose that I do thus historically deduce the reason of his setting forth his Books, and shew that it was plainly to remonstrate against the power of his prince, and the measures that he hath taken of governing; to set his Majesty at variance not only with his subjects, but with himself, and to raise a Civil War in his intellectual kingdom betwixt his controulable and his uncontroulable jurisdiction. And because, having to do with a wise man, as Mr. Bayes is, one may often gather more of his mind out of a word that drops casually, than out of his whole watchful and serious discourse, when he is talking of matters of Policy and that require caution,—I cannot slight one passage of Mr. Bayes, page 656, where, raging bitterly against all the Presbyterians and other sects, and as much against the allowing them any tenderness, liberty, toleration, or indulgence, he concludes thus: 'Tenderness and indulgence to such men were to nourish vipers in our own bowels, and the most sottish neglect of our own quiet and security, and we should deserve to perish with the dishonour of Sardanapalus.' Now this of Sardanapalus I remember some little thing ever since I read, I think it was my Justine; and I would not willingly be such a fool as to make a dangerous similitude that has no foundation. For if Mr. Bayes in the Preface of his Defence, to excuse his long-teeming before it were brought forth, places it partly upon his recreations, I know not why much more a prince should not 'be willing to enjoy the innocent comforts of this life, as well as to do the common drugeries.' But I am thinking what Mr. Bayes meant by it; for every similitude must have, though not all, yet some likeness. Now I am sure there were no Nonconformists and Presbyterians in Sardanapalus his dayes. I am sure also that Sardanapalus was no clergyman, that he was no subject; but he was one of the uncontroulable creatures that, instead of exercising his Ecclesiastical Power, delighted in spinning; till some body came in on the sudden, and catching him at it, cut his thread. Come, 'tis better we left this argument and the company too, for you see the crime, you see the sentence: and who ever it be, there is some prince or other whom Mr. Bayes will have to perish. That page 641 is indeed not so severe, but 'tis pretty well; where, on the same kind of subject, whetting the prince against those people, he saith, 'that prince that hath felt the pounces of these ravening vultures, if after that he shall be persuaded to regard their fair speeches at such time as they want power, without other evident and unquestionable tokens of their conversation, deserves to be king of the Night.' Now, for this matter, I believe Mr. Bayes knows that his Majesty hath received such evident and unquestionable tokens of loyalty from the Nonconformists; otherwise his own loyalty would have hindered him from daring to use that expression.

And now I should continue my history to his third Book in hand, the Preface to Bishop Bramhal. But having his second Book still before me, I could not but look a little further into it, to see how he hath left matters standing betwixt himself and his Answerer. And first I lighted on that place where he strives to disintangle himself from what he had said about Trade in his former Book. Here therefore he defies the whole fanatick world to discover one syllable that tends to its discouragement. Let us put it upon that issue, and by this one example take the pattern of his ingenuity in all his other contests. 'Whoop,' Mr. Bayes! page 49: 'With what conscience does the Answerer tell the people that I have represented all tradesmen as seditious, when 'tis so notorious I only suppose that some of them may be tainted with seditious principles? If I should affirm that when the nobility or clergy are possest with principles that incline to rebellion and disloyal practices, they are of all rebels the most dangerous, should I be thought to impeach them of treason and rebellion?' Holla, Mr. Bayes! but in the 49th page of your first Book you say expressly, 'For 'tis notorious that there is not any sort of people so inclinable to seditious practices as the trading part of a Nation.' Is this the same thing now? and how does this Defence take off the objection? And yet he tears and insults and declaims as if he had the truth on his side. At last he strives to bring himself off and salve the matter in the same page 49 with, 'In brief, it is not the rich citizen, but the wealthy fanatick that I have branded for an ungovernable beast, and that not as wealthy but as fanatick.' Subtle distinguisher! I see, if we give him but rope enough what he will come to. Mr. Bayes, many as proper a man as yourself hath marched up Holborn for distinguishing betwixt the wealthy and the fanatick; and moreover let me tell you, fanatick money hath no ear-mark.

So concerning the magistrate's power in Religion, wherein his Answerer had remarked some unsafe passages: Whoop, Mr. Bayes! page 12 of his first Book before quoted: 'Unless princes have power to bind their subjects to what religion they apprehend most advantageous, &c. they are no better than statues of authority.' Holla, Bayes! Page 467 of the second Book: 'this bold calumny I have already I hope competently enough discovered and detested. Yet he repeats this fundamental forgery in all places, so that his whole Book is but one huge lye four hundred pages long.' Judge now who is the forger; and yet he roars too here as if he would mix heaven and earth together. But you may spare your raving; you will never claw it off as long as your name is Bayes.

So his Answerer, it seems, having, p. 85, said that Bayes confines the whole duty of conscience to the inward thoughts and perswasions of the mind, over which the magistrate hath no power at all: Whoop, Bayes! Page 89 of his first Book: 'Let all matters of mere conscience, whether purely moral or religious, be subject to conscience only; *i.e.* let men think of things according to their own perswasions, and assert the freedom of their judgments against all the powers of the earth. This is the prerogative of the mind of man within its own dominions; its kingdom is intellectual, &c.' Page 91: 'Liberty of conscience is internal and invisible, and confined to the minds and judgements of men; and while conscience acts within its proper sphere, the civil power is so far from doing it violence, that it never can.' Holla, Bayes! Page 229 of his second Book: 'This in downright English is a shameless lye. Sir, you must pardon my rudeness, for I will assure you, after long meditation, I could not devise a more pertinent answer to so bold an one as this.' I believe you, Mr. Bayes: you meditated long, some twelve months at least; and you could not devise any other answer; and in good earnest he hath not attempted to give any other answer. 'I confess 'tis no extraordinary conceit; but 'tis the best repartee my barren fancy was able to suggest to me upon so rude an occasion.' Well, Mr. Bayes! I see it must come to a quarrel; for thus the Hectors use to do, and to give the lye at adventure, when they have a mind to try a man's courage. But I have often known them dye on the spot.

So his Answerer, page 134, having taxed him for his speaking against an expression in the act of parliament of 5to Eliz. concerning the Wednesday Fast: Whoop, Bayes! Page 59 of his first Book: 'The act for the Wednesday fast, the *Jejunium Caecilianum*' (our ecclesiastical politician is the better statesman of the two by far, and may make sport with Cecil when he pleases), 'was injoyned with this clause of exception, That if any person should affirm it to be imposed with an intention to bind the conscience, he should be punished as a spreader of false news.' So careful was the supreme magistrate in those days not to impose upon the conscience; and the wisdom of it is confirmed by the experience of our time: when so eminent a divine, as I mentioned before, thought fit to write a whole volume concerning the Holiness of Lent; though, if I be not deceived, this doctrine too is prohibited by Act of Parliament under the same penalty. But, saith Bayes there, 'The matter indeed of this law was not of any great moment, but this declaration annexed to it proved of a fatal and mischievous consequence.' 'Tis very well worth reading at large: but in short the consequence (or the occasion, 'tis no matter when I have to do with Bayes) was, that 'princes, how peremptory soever they have been in asserting the rights of their supreme power, in civil affairs they have been forced to seem modest and diffident in the exercise of their ecclesiastical supremacy.' Now, Holla, Bayes!

page 298 of his second Book: 'To what purpose does he so briskly taunt me for thwarting mine own principles, because I have censured the impertinency of a needless provision in an Act of Parliament?' Observe, these are not the Answerer's but Bayes his own words; whereby you may see with what reverence and duty he uses to speak of his superiors and their actions, when they are not so happy as to please him. 'I may obey the law, though I may be of a different perswasion from the lawgivers in an opinion remote and impertinent to the matter of the law itself: nay, I may condemn the wisdom of enacting it, and yet at the same time think my self to lie under an indispensable obligation to obey it: for the formal reason of its obligatory power (as any Casuist will inform him) is not the judgement and opinion of the lawgiver, but the declaration of his will and pleasure.' Very good and sound, Mr. Bayes: but here you have opened a passage; and this is as impertinent in you and more dangerous than what you blamed in that Act, that the Nonconformists may speak against your Ecclesiastical Laws; for their Casuists then tell them that, they lying under an indispensable obligation not to conform to some of them, do fulfil and satisfie their obedience in submitting to the penalty.

I looked further into what he saith in defence of the magistrate's assuming the priesthood; what for his scheme of moral grace; what to palliate his irreverent expressions concerning our Blessed Saviour and the

Holy Spirit; what of all other matters objected by his Answerer: and if you will believe me, but I had much rather the Reader would take the pains to examine all himself, there is scarce anything but slender trifling, unworthy of a logician, and beastly railing unbecoming any man, much more a divine. At last, having read it all through with some attention, I resolved, having failed so of anything material, to try my fortune whether it might be more lucky, and to open the book in several places as it chanced. But whereas they say that in the *Sortes Virgilianæ*, wheresoever you light you will find something that will hit and is proper to your intention; on the contrary here, there was not any leaf that I met with but had something impertinent, so that I resolved to give it over. This only I observed upon the whole, that he does treat his Answerer the most basely and ingratefully that ever man did. For, whereas in his whole first Book there was not one sound principle, and scarce anything in the second but what the Answerer had given him occasion to amend and rectifie if he had understanding,—after so great an obligation he handles him with more rudeness than is imaginable. I know it may be said in Mr. Bayes his defence, that in this his second Book he hath made his matters in many places much worse than they were before. But I say that was Bayes his want of understanding; and that he knew not how to take hold of so charitable an opportunity as was offered him, and 'twas none of the

Answerer's fault. There are amongst men some that do not study alwayes the true rules of wisdom and honesty, but delight in a perverse kind of cunning, which sometimes may take for a while and attain their design; but most usually it fails in the end and hath a foul farewel. And such are all Mr. Bayes his plots. In all his writings he doth so confound terms, he leaps cross, he hath more doubles (nay triples and quadruples) than any hare, so that he thinks himself secure of the hunters. And in this second Book, even the length of it was some Policy. For you must know it is all but an Epistle to the author of the 'Friendly Debate;' and thought he with himself, who hath so much leisure from his own affairs, that he will read a Letter of another man's business of eight hundred pages? But yet, thought he again (and I could be content they did read it), in all matters of argument I will so muddle my self in ink, that there shall be no catching, no finding me; and besides, I will speak always with so magisterial a confidence, that no modest man (and most ingenious persons are so) shall so much as quetch at me, but be beat out of countenance; and plain men shall think that I durst not talk at such a rate but that I have a commission. I will first, said he in his heart, like a stout vagrant, beg; and if that will not do, I will command the question, and as soon as I have got it, I will so alter the property and put on another periweg, that I defie them all for discovering me or ever finding it again. This, beside all the lock and advantage that I have the Nonconformists upon since the late times; and though they were born since, and have taken more sober principles, it shall be all one for that matter. And then for oratory and railing, let Bayes alone. This contrivance is indeed all the strength of Mr. Bayes his argument, and as he said (how properly let the Reader judge), page 69 before quoted, 'that moral virtue is not only the most material and useful part of all Religion, but the ultimate end of all its other duties:' so, railing is not onely the most material and useful part of his Religion, his reason, his oratory, and his practise, but the ultimate end of this and all his other Books. Otherwise he is neither so strongly fortified nor so well guarded but that, without any ceremony of trenches or approaches, you may at the very first march up to his counters-scrap without danger. He puts me in mind of the incorrigible scold, that though she was duck'd over head and ears under water, yet stretched up her hands with her two thumb-nails in the nit-cracking posture, or with two fingers 'devaricated,' to call the man still in that language lousy rascal and cuckold. But indeed, when I consider how miserable a wretch his Answerer has rendred him, and yet how he persists still and more to rail and revile him, I can liken it to nothing better betwixt them than to what I have seen with some pleasure, the hawking at the magpy. The poor bird understands very well the terrible pounces of that vulture; but therefore she chatters amain most rufully, and spreads and cocks her tail, so that one that first saw and heard the sport would think that she insulted over the hawk in that chatter, and she huff'd her train in token of courage and victory; when, alas, 'tis her fear all, and another way of crying the hawk mercy; and to the end that, the hawk finding nothing but tail and feather to strike at, she may so perhaps shelter her body.

Therefore I think there is nothing in my way that hinders me, but that I may now go on to the History of this Mr. Bayes his third Book, the Preface to Bishop Bramhall, and to what 'juncture of affairs' it was reconciled. His Majesty (perhaps upon Mr. Bayes his frequent admonitions, both in his first and second Book, that princes should be more attentive and confident in exercising their ecclesiastical jurisdiction, though I rather believe he never deigned to read a line in him, but what he did herein was only the result of his own good understanding) resolved to make some clear tryal how the Nonconformists could bear themselves under some liberty of conscience. And accordingly he issued on March the 15th, 1671, his gracious Declaration of Indulgence, of which I wish his Majesty and the kingdom much joy, and as far as my slender judgement can divine, dare augurate and presage mutual felicity, and that whatever humane accident may happen (I fear not what Bayes foresees), they will, they can never have cause to repent this action or its consequences. But hereupon Bayes finding that the King had so vigorously exerted his Ecclesiastical Power, but to a purpose quite contrary to what Mr. Bayes had always intended, he grew terribly angry at the King and his Privy Council; so that hereupon 'he started,' as himself says, 'into many warm and glowing meditations: his heart burnt and the fire kindled, and that heated him into all this wild and rambling talk (as some will be forward enough to call it), though he hopes it is not altogether idle, and whether it be or be not, he hath now neither leisure nor patience to examine.' This he confesses upon his best recollection, in the last page of this Preface: whereupon I cannot but animadvert, as in my first page, that this too lies open to his dilemma against the Nonconformists' prayers; for if he will not accept his own charge, his modesty is all impudent and counterfeit; if he does not acknowledge it, he is an hot-headed incendiary, and a wild rambling talker, and in part, if not altogether, an idle fellow. Really I cannot but pity him, and look upon him as under some great disturbance of mind—that this, with some other scattering passages here and there, argues him to be in as ill a case as Tiberius was in his distracted letter to the Senate: there wants nothing of it but the *Dii Deæque me perdant*, wishing, Let the Gods and Goddesses confound him worse than he finds himself to be every day confounded. But that I may not lose my thred. Upon occasion of this his Majesty's gracious Declaration, and against it, he writes this his third Book, the Preface to Bishop Bramhall, and accordingly was unhappily delivered of it in June (I have forgot) or July, in 1672. For he did not go his full time of it, but miscarried; partly by a fright from J. O., and partly by a fall he had upon a 'Closer Importance.' But of all his three bolts, this was the soonest shot, and therefore 'tis no wonder if he miss'd his mark, and took no care where his arrow glanced. But what he saith of his Majesty and his Council, being toward the latter end of his Discourse, I am forced to defer that a little, because, there being no method at all in his wild rambling talk, I must either tread just on in his footsteps, or else I shall be in a perpetual maze, and never know when I am come to my journey's end.

And here I cannot altogether escape the mentioning of J. O. again, whom (though I have shown that he was not the main cause of publishing Bayes his Books) yet he singles out, and on his pretence runs down all the Nonconformists; this being, as he imagined, the safest way by which he might proceed first to undermine, and then blow-up his Majestie's gracious Declaration. And this indeed is the least immethodical part in the whole Discourse. For first he undertakes to defend, that railing is not only lawful, but expedient. Secondly, that though he had railed, the person he spoke of ought not to have taken notice of it. And thirdly, that he did not rail. As to these things I do not much trouble myself, nor interest myself in the least in J. O.'s quarrel; no otherwise than if he were John a Nokes, and I heard him rail'd at by John a Styles. Nor yet would I concern myself unnecessarily in any man's behalf; knowing that it is better being at the beginning of a feast, than to come in at the latter end of a fray. For if so I should, as often it happens in such rencounters, not onely draw Mr. Bayes, but J. O. too, upon my back, I should have made a sweet business on't for myself.

Now as to the lawfulness and expedience of railing: were it not that I do really make conscience of using Scripture with such a drolling companion as Mr. Bayes, I could overload him thence both with authority and example. Nor is it worth one's while to teach him out of other Authors, and the best precedents of the kind, how he, being a Christian and a Divine, ought to have carried himself. But I cannot but remark his insolence, and how bold he makes upon this argument, p. 88 of his second Book, with the memories of those great persons there enumerated, several of whom, and particularly my Lord Verulam, I could quote to his confusion, upon a contrary and much better account. ' So far am I from repenting my severity towards them, that I am tempted rather to applaud it by the glorious examples of the greatest wits of our nation, King James, Archbishop Whitgift, Archbishop

Bancroft, Bishop Andrews, Bishop Bilson, Bishop Montague, Bishop Bramhall, Sir Walter Rawleigh, Lord Bacon, &c. ;' and he might have added Mr. Tarlton, with as good pretence to this honour as himself. The niches are yet empty in the Old Exchange; pray let us speak to the statuary, that, next to King James's, we may have Bayes his effigies; for such great wits are princes' fellows, at least when dead. At this rate there is not a scold at Billingsgate but may defend herself by the pattern of King James and Archbishop Whitgift, &c.; yet this is passable, if you consider our man. But that is most intolerable, page 17 of the Preface to his first Book, where he justifies his debauched way of writing by parallel to our blessed Saviour. And I cannot but with some awe reflect how near the punishment was to the offence; when, having undertaken so profane an argument, he was in the very instant so infatuated as to say that Christ was not onely ' in an hot fit of zeal, but in a seeming fury too, and transport of passion.' But however, seeing he hath brought us so good vouchers, let us suppose what is not to be suppos'd, that railing is lawful. Whether it be expedient or no, will yet be a new question. And I think Mr. Bayes, when he hath had time 'to cool his thoughts,' may be trusted yet with that consideration, and to compute whether the good that he hath done by railing do countervail the damage which both he in particular and the cause he labours have suffered by it. For in my observation, if we meet with an argument in the streets, both men, women, and boys, that are the auditory, do usually give it on the modester side, and conclude that she that rails most has the least reason.

For the second : where he would prove that though he had railed, yet his Answerer, J. O., ought not to have taken notice of it, nor those of the Party who are under the same condemnation ; but that he should have abstracted and kept close to the argument,—I must confess it is a very secure and wholesome way of railing. And allowing this, he hath good reason to find fault with his Answerer, as he does, for turning over his Book ; though without turning it over, I know not how he could have answered him, but with his hat, or with mum. But for ought I can see in that only answer which is to his first Book, he hath been obedient, and abstracted the argument sufficiently ; and if he hath been anywhere severe upon him, he hath done it more cleanly, and much more like a gentleman ; and it hath been only in showing the necessary inferences that must follow upon the Author's maximes and unsound principles. But as to any answer to Bayes his second Book or his third, for ought I can see, J. O. sleeps upon both ears.

To this third undertaking, to show that he hath not rail'd, I shall not say any thing more, but let it be judged by the company, and to them let it be refer'd.

But in my poor opinion, I never saw a man thorow all his three Books in so high a salivation.

And therefore, till I meet with something more serious, I will take a walk in the garden and gather some of Mr. Bayes his flowers; or I might more properly have said, I will go see Bedlam, and pick straws with our mad-man. First he saith, that some that pretend a great interest in the holy brotherhood, upon every slight accident are beating-up the drums against the Pope and Popish Plots; they descry Popery in every common and usual chance; and a chimney cannot take fire in the city or suburbs, but they are immediately crying, Jesuites and Firebals! I understand you, sir. This, Mr. Bayes, is your prologue, that is to be spoke by Thunder and Lightning: 'I am loud Thunder; brisk Lightning I. I strike men down. I fire the town. Look to't. Wee'll do't.' Mr. Bayes, it is something dangerous meddling with those matters. As innocent persons as your self have felt the fury of the wild multitude, when such a calamity hath disordered them; and after your late severity against tradesmen, it had been better you had not touched the fire. Take heed lest the reasons which sparkle, forsooth, in your discourse have not set their chimneys on fire. None accuses you, what you make sport with, of burning the ships at Chatham, much less of blowing-up the Thames. But you ought to be careful, lest having so newly distinguished betwixt the fanatick and his wealth, they should say that you are distinguishing now betwixt the fanaticks and their houses. These things are too edged to be jested with, if you did but consider that not onely the 'holy brotherhood,' but the 'sober and intelligent citizens,' are equally involved in these sad accidents. And in that lamentable Conflagration (which was so terrible, that, though so many years ago, it is yet fresh in men's memories; and besides, is yearly, by Act of Parliament, observed with due humiliation and solemnity) it was not Trade onely and merchandise suffered, which you call their Diana, and was not so much to be considered; but St. Paul's too was burnt, which the historians tell us was Diana's temple.

The next thing is more directly levell'd at J. O. for having in some later book used those words, 'We cannot conform to Arminianism or Socinianism on the one hand, or Popery on the other.' What the Answerer meant by those words, I concern not myself; onely I cannot but say that there is a very great neglect somewhere, wheresoever the inspection of books is lodged, that at least the Socinian books are tolerated and sell as openly as the Bible. But Bayes turns all into mirth: 'He might as well have added all the -isms in the Old Testament, Perizzitism, Hittitism, Jebusitism, Hivitism, &c.'

No, Mr. Bayes, that need not; and though this indeed is a very pretty conceit, and 'twere pity it should have been lost, yet I can tell you a better way. For, if rhyming be the business, and you are so good at 'tagging of points in a garret,' there is another word that will do it better, and for which, I know not how truly, you tax your Answerer too here, as if he said, 'The Church of England were desperately schismatical, because the Independents are resolved, one and all, to continue separate from her communion.' Therefore let schism, if you please, rhyme to -ism. And though no man is obliged to produce the authority of the greatest wits of the Nation to justifie a rhime, yet for your dear sake, Mr. Bayes, I will this once supererogate. The first shall be your good friend Bishop Bramhall; who, among many other memorable passages, which I believe were the reason that he never thought fit to print his own book, page 101 teacheth us, not absurdly, that 'It was not the erroneous opinions of the Church of Rome, but the obtruding them by laws upon other Churches, which warranted a separation.' But if this will not doe, *vous avez* Dr. Thorndike's deposition in print; for he, I hear, is lately dead. 'The Church of England in separating from the Church of Rome is guilty of schism before God.' I have not the Book by me, but I am sure 'tis candidly recited as I have read it. Then (to show too that there is a King on this side) his present Majesty's father, in his Declaration, 4to *Caroli*, 1628, affirms that a Book, entituled '*Appello Cæsarem*, or an Appeal to Cæsar, and published in the year 1625, by Richard Montague, then Batchelor of Divinity, and now Bishop of Chichester, had opened the way to these schisms and divisions which have since ensued in the Church; and that therefore, for the redress and remedy thereof, and for the satisfaction of the consciences of his good people, he had not onely by publick proclamation called-in that Book, which ministred matter of offence, but, to prevent the like danger for the future, reprinted the Articles of Religion established in the time of Queen Elizabeth, of famous memory; and by a Declaration, before those Articles, did restrain all opinions to the sense of those Articles, that nothing might be left for private fancies and innovations, &c.' And if this will not amount fully, I shall conclude with a villanous pamphlet that I met with t'other day, but of which a great wit indeed was the Author. And whereas Mr. Bayes is always defying the Nonconformists with Mr. Hooker's 'Ecclesiastical Polity,' and the 'Friendly Debate,' I am of opinion, though I have a great reverence for Mr. Hooker, who in some things did answer himself, that this little Book, of not full eight leaves, hath shut that 'Ecclesiastical Polity,' and Mr. Bayes's too, out of doors; but for the Friendly Debate, I must confess that is unanswerable. 'Tis one Mr. Hales, of Eaton; a most learned divine, and one of the Church of England, and most remarkable for his sufferings in the late times, and his Christian patience under them. And I reckon it not one of the least ignominies of that age, that so eminent a person should have been by the iniquity of the times reduced to those necessities under which he lived; as I account it no small honour to have grown up into some part of his acquaintance, and convers'd a while with the living remains of one of the clearest heads and best-prepared breasts in Christendom. That which I speak of is his little 'Treatise of Schism,' which, though I had read many years ago, was quite out of my mind, till I occasionally light[ed] upon't at a Bookseller's stall. I hope it will not be tedious, though I write of some few (and yet whatsoever I omit I shall have left behind more) material passages. 'Schism is one of those theological scare-crows with which they who use to uphold a party in religion, use to fright away such as, making inquiry into it, are ready to relinquish and oppose it, if it appear either erroneous or suspitious. Schism is, if we would define it, an unnecessary separation of Christians from that part of the Visible Church of which they were once members. Some, reverencing antiquity more than needs, have suffered themselves to be scared with imputation of schism more than needs. Nothing absolves men from the guilt of schism but true and unpretended conscience. But the judgements of the ancients many times (to speak most gently) are justly to be suspected. Where the cause of schism is necessary, there not he that separates, but he that is the cause of separation, is the schismatick. Where the occasion of separation is unnecessary, neither side can be excused from guilt of schism. But who shall be the judg? That is a point of great difficulty, because it carries fire in the tail of it; for it brings with it a piece of doctrine which is seldom pleasing to superiours. You shall find that all schisms have crept into the Church by one of these three waies—either upon matter of fact, or upon matter of opinion, or point of ambition. For the first, I call that matter of fact, when something is required to be done by us which either we know or strongly suspect to be unlawful.' Where he instances in the old great controversie about Easter. 'For it being upon error taken for necessary that an Easter must be kept, and upon worse than error (for it was no less than a point of Judaism forced upon the Church) thought further necessary that the ground of the time for the feast must be the rule left by Moses to the Jews: there arose a stout question, whether it was to be celebrated with the Jews on the fourteenth Moon, or the Sunday following. This caused as great a combustion as ever was; the West separating and refusing communion with the East for many years together. Here I cannot see but all the world were schismaticks, excepting onely that we charitably suppose to excuse them from it, that all parties did what they did out of conscience. A thing which befell them by the ignorance, for I will not say the malice, of their guides; and that through the just judgment of God, because, through sloth and blind obedience, men examined not the things they were taught, but like beasts of burthen patiently couched down, and indifferently underwent all whatsoever their superiors laid upon them. If the discretion of the chiefest guides of the Church did, in a point so trivial, so inconsiderable, so mainly fail them; can we, without the imputation of great grossness and folly, think so poor-spirited persons competent judges of the questions now on foot betwixt the Churches? Where, or among whom, or how many the Church shall be, it is a thing indifferent. What if those to whom the execution of the publick service is committed, do something either unseemly or suspitious, or peradventure unlawful; what if the garments they wear be censured, nay, indeed be suspitious; what if the gesture or adoration to be used to the altars, as now we have learned to speak? What if the Homilist have preached or delivered any doctrine, of the truth of which we are not well perswaded (a thing which very often falls out); yet, for all this, we may not separate, except we be constrained personally to bear a part in it ourselves. Nothing can be a just cause of refusing communion in schism that concerns fact, but only to require the execution of some unlawful or suspected act. For, not only in reason, but in religion too, that maxim admits of no release, *Cautissimi cujusque præceptum, quod dubitas, ne feceris:* That whatsoever you doubt of, that you in no case do.' He instances then in the second Council of Nice, where, saith he, 'the Synod itself was the schismatical party in the point of using the images, which,' saith he, 'all acknowledge unnecessary, most do suspect, and many hold utterly unlawful: can then the enjoyning of such a thing be ought else but an abuse? Can the refusal of communion here be thought any other thing than duty? Here, or upon the like occasion, to separate may peradventure bring personal trouble or danger, against which it concerns any honest man to have *pectus præparatum.*' Then of Schism from opinion: 'Prayer, confession, thanksgiving, reading of Scripture, administration of Sacraments in the plainest and simplest manner, were matter enough to furnish-out a sufficient Liturgy, though nothing either of private opinion or of Church-pomp, of garments, of prescribed gestures, of imagery, of musick, of matter concerning the dead, of many superfluities which creep into the Church under the name of order and decency, did interpose itself. To charge Churches and Liturgies with things unnecessary, was the first beginning of superstition. If the Fathers and special guides of the Church would be a little sparing in incumbring Churches with superfluities, or not over-rigid either in reviving obsolete customs or imposing new, there would be far less cause of Schism or Superstition; and all the inconvenience likely to ensue would be but this—they should in so doing yield a little to the imbecility of their inferiours;

a thing which Saint Paul would never have refused to do. It is alike unlawful to make profession of known or suspected falshood, as to put in practice unlawful or suspected actions. The third thing I named for matter of Schism was ambition, I mean episcopal ambition; one head of which is one bishop's claiming supremacy over another, which, as it hath been from time to time a great trespass against the Church's peace, so it is now the final ruin of it. For they do but abuse themselves and others, who would perswade us that Bishops by Christ's institution have any superiority over other men further than positive order agreed upon among Christians hath prescribed. Time hath taken leave, sometimes, to fix this name of CONVENTICLES upon good and honest meetings. Though open assemblies are required, yet at all times, while men are really pious, all meetings of men for mutual help of piety and devotion, wheresoever and by whomsoever celebrated, were permitted without exception. In times of manifest corruption and persecution, wherein religious assembling is dangerous, private meetings, howsoever besides publick order, are not onely lawful, but they are of necessity and duty. All pious assemblies, in times of persecution and corruption howsoever practised, are indeed, or rather alone, the lawful congregations; and publick assemblies, though according to form of law, are indeed nothing else but RIOTS and CONVENTICLES, if they be stained with corruption and superstition.'

Do you not see now, Mr. Bayes, that you needed not have gone so far for a word, when you might have had it in the neighbourhood? If there be any coherence left in your scull, you cannot but perceive that I brought you authority enough to prove that *schism* (for the reason we may discourse another time) do's at least rhime to *-ism*. But you have a peculiar delight and felicity (which no man envies you) in Scripture-drollery; nothing less will taste to your palate; whereas otherwise you have travelled so far in Italy, that you could not escape the titles of some books which would have served your turn as well, *cardinalism, nepotism, putanism,* if you were in a paroxism of the *-isms*.

When I had writ this, and undergone so grateful a penance for no less than that I had transcribed before out of our Author, I could not, upon comparing them both together, but reflect most seriously upon the difference of their two ways of discoursing. I could not but admire that majesty and beauty which sits upon the forehead of masculine Truth and generous Honesty; but no less detest the deformity of Falshood disguised in all its ornaments. How much another thing it is to hear him speak, that hath cleared himself from froth and growns [=groans], and who suffers neither sloth, nor fear, nor ambition, nor any other tempting spirit of that nature to abuse him, from one who, as Mr. Hales expresseth it, makes Christianity lacquey to ambition! How wretchedly, the one, to uphold his fiction, must incite princes to persecution and tyranny, degrade grace to morality, debauch conscience against its own principles, distort and mis-interpret the Scripture, fill the world with blood, execution, and massacre; while the other needs and requires no more but a peaceable and unprejudicat soul, and the native simplicity of a Christian spirit! And methinks, if our Author had any spark of vertue unextinguished, he should, upon considering these together, retire into his closet, and there lament and pine away for his desperate folly; for the disgrace he hath, as far as in him is, brought upon the Church of England by such an undertaking, and for the eternal shame to which he has hereby condemned his own memory.

I ask you heartily pardon, Mr. Bayes, for treating you, against decorum here, with so much gravity. 'Tis possible I may not trouble you above once or twice more in the like nature; but so often at least, I hope, one may, in the writing of a whole Book, have leave to be serious. Your next flower, and that indeed is a sweet one, ' Dear heart, how could I hug and kiss thee for all this love and sweetness !' Fy, fy, Mr. Bayes! Is this the language of a divine, and to be used, as you sometimes express it, in the face of the sun? Who can escape from thinking that you are adream'd of your ' comfortable importance'? These are (as the moral Satyrist calls them in the cleanliest manner the thing would bear) ' words left betwixt the sheets.' Somebody might take it ill that you should misapply your courtship to an enemy. But in the Roman Empire it was the privilege of the hangman to deflour a virgin before execution. But, sweet Mr. Bayes (for I know you do nothing without a precedent of some of the greatest wits of the Nation), whose example had you for this seeming transport of a gentler passion?

Then comes 'Well fare poor Macedo for a modest fool.' This I know is matter of Gazette, which is as canonical as 'Ecclesiastical Policy.' Therefore I have the less to say to't. Onely, I could wish that there were some severer laws against such villains who raise so false and scandalous reports of worthy gentlemen, and that those laws were put in execution; and that men might not be suffered to walk the streets in so confident a garb, who commit those assassinats upon the reputation of deserving persons.

Here follows a sore charge: that the Answerer had 'without any provocation, in a publick and solemn way, undertaken the defence of the fanatick cause.' Here indeed, Mr. Bayes, you have reason, and you might have had as just a quarrel against whosoever had undertaken it. For your design and hope was from the beginning, that no man would have answered you in a publick and solemn way; and nothing would vex a wise man, as you are, more than to have his intention and counsel frustrated. When you have rang'd all your forces in battel, when you have plac'd your cannon, when you have founded a charge, and given the word to fall upon the whole Party,—if you could then perswade every particular person of 'em, that you gave him no provocation, I confess, Mr. Bayes, this were an excellent and a new way of your inventing, to conquer single ('tis your moral vertue) whole armies. And so the 'admiring drove' might stand gaping, till, one by one, you had cut all their throats. But, Mr. Bayes, I cannot discern but that you gave him as much provocation in your first Book as he has you in his 'Evangelical Love,' 'Church Peace and Unity,' which is the pretence of your issuing this preface.

For, having for your 'dear sake' (beside many other troubles that I have undertaken, without your giving me any provocation) sought out and perused that Book too, I do not find you any where personally concern'd, but as you have, it seems upon some conviction, assumed to yourself some vices or errours against which he speaks in general, and with some modesty. But for the rest, you say upon full perusal, 'you find not one syllable to the purpose beside a perpetual repetition of the old out-worn story of unscriptural ceremonies, and some frequent whinings, and sometimes ravings, &c.' Now to see the dulness of some men's capacities above others! I, upon this occasion, begun, I know not how it came, at page 127, and thence read on to the end of his Book. And from thence I turned to the beginning and continued to page 127, and could not, all along, observe any thing but what was very pertinent to the matter in hand. But this is your way of excusing yourself from replying to things that yet you will be medling with and nibling at; and 'tis besides a pretty knack (the Nonconformists have it not alone) of frighting or discouraging sober people from reading those dangerous treatises, which might contribute to their better information. I cannot but observe, Mr. Bayes, this admirable way (like fat Sir John Falstaffe's singular dexterity in sinking) that you have of answering whole Books or Discourses, how pithy and knotty soever, in a line or two, nay sometimes with a word. So it fares with this Book of the Answerer's. So with a Book or Discourse of his, I know not, of the 'Morality of the Lord's Day;' which is answered by a 'Septenary Portion' in the 'Hebdomadal Revolution.' So, whether Book or Discourse, I also know not of the 'self-evidencing light of the Scripture,' where Bayes offers (and it seems strange) to produce as good proofs for it out of the Alcoran. So I show'd you where he answers demonstration with the lye. And one thing more comes into my mind; where, after he has blunder'd a great while to bring himself off the magistrate's exercising the priesthood in his own person, he concludes with an irresistable defence against his Answerer: 'this is suitable to the genius of his ingenuity, and betraies him as much as the word INTANGLEMENT, which is the Shiboleth of all his Writings.' So he defeats all the 'gross bodies of orthodoxy' with calling them 'systemes and syntagmes.' So you know he answers all the controversial books of the Calvinists that ever had been written, with the tale of Robin Hood, and the 'mighty bramble on the south side of the lake Leman.' Mr. Bayes, you cannot enough esteem and cherish this faculty. For, next to your single beating whole armies, I do not know any virtue that you have need of so often, or that will upon tryal be found more useful.

And to this succeeds another flower, I am sure, though I can scarce smell-out the sence of it. But it is printed in a distinct character, and that is always a certain sign of a flower. For our Booksellers have many arts to make us 'yield to their importunity;' and among the rest, they promise us, that it shall be printed on fine paper, and in a very fair and large letter; that it shall be very well examined, that there be no errata; that wheresoever there shall be a pretty conceit, it shall be marked out in another character; that the sentences shall be boxed-up in several paragraphs and more drawers than in any cabinet; that the books shall all be bound-up in calves' leather. But my greatest care was, that when I quoted any sentence or word of our Author's, it might be so discernable, lest I should go for a plagiary. And I am much offended to see that in several places he hath not kept touch with me. The word of Mr. Bayes's that he has here made notorious is '*categoricalness:*' and I observe that wheresoever there comes a word of that termination he shows it the same honour, as if he had a mind to make Bayes a collar of -*nesses*. What the mystery is, I cannot so easily imagine; no more than of '*shiboleth*' and '*intanglement*.' But I doubt Mr. Bayes is sick of many complicated diseases; or, to keep to our rhime, *sicknesses*. He is troubled not onely with the -*ismes* but the -*nesses*. He might, if he had pleased, here too to have showed his wit, as he did in the others, and have told us of Sheerness, Dongioness, Innerness, and Cathness. But he omitted it perhaps in this place, knowing how well he had acquitted himself in another, and out of the Scripture too, which gives his wit the highest relish. 'Tis page 72 of his first Book, where, to prove that the fruits of the Spirit are no more than morality, he quotes Saint Paul, Gal. v. 22, where the Apostle enumerates them: 'love, joy, peace, patience, gentleness, goodness, faith, meekness, and temperance:' but our Author translates '*joy*' to '*chearfulness*,' '*peace*' to '*peaceableness*,' and '*faith*' to '*faithfulness*.' What ignorance, or rather what forgery, is this of Scripture and Religion! Who is there of the 'systematical German, Geneva, orthodox Divines' but could have taught him better? Who is there of the 'sober, intelligent, Episcopal Divines of the Church of England' but would abhor this interpretation? Yet when his Answerer, I see, objects this to him, page 200, Bayes, like a dextrous scholastical disputant, it being told him that joy is not cheerfulness, but that 'spiritual joy which is unspeakable;' that peace is not peaceableness in his sense, but 'that peace of God which through Jesus Christ is wrought in the hearts of believers by the Holy Ghost;' and that faith in God is there intended, not 'faithfulness in our duties, trusts, or offices:' what does he doe? Page 337, he very ingenuously and wisely, when he is to answer, quite forgets that faith was once named; and having suppress that, as to the rest he wipes his mouth, and rubs his forehead, and saith the 'cavil is but a little one, and the fortune of Cæsar and the Roman Empire depend not upon it, and therefore he will not trouble the reader with a critical account of the reason of his translation.' No, don't, Mr. Bayes. 'Tis very well; let it alone. But, though not the fortunes of Cæsar and the Roman Empire, I doubt there is something more depends upon it, if it be matter of salvation. And I am afraid besides, that there may a curse too belong to him who shall knowingly 'add or diminish in the Scripture' [Rev. xxii. 18-19]. Do you think Bishop Bramhal himself, if he had seen this, could have abstained (page 117 before quoted) from telling our Author, 'That the promiscuous licence given to people qualified or unqualified, not onely to read but to interpret the Scriptures according to their private spirits or particular fancies, without regard either to the analogy of faith, which they understand not, or to the interpretation of the doctors of former ages, is more prejudicial, I might better say pernicious, both to particular Christians and to whole societies, than the over-rigorous restraints of the Romanists'?

The next is a piece of mirth, on occasion of some discourse of the Answerer's about the 'Morality of the Lord's-day;' where it seems he useth some hard words, which I am naturally an enemy to; but might be done of purpose to keep the controversy from the white-aprons, within the white-surplices, to be more learnedly debated. But this fares no better than all the rest. There is no kind of morality, I see, but Bayes will try to debauch it. 'O what edifying doctrine,' saith he, 'is this to the white-aprons! and doubtless they would, with the Jews, sooner roast themselves than a small joint of mutton upon the sacred day of rest.' Now I do not, neither, I believe, does Bayes himself, know any of them that are thus superstitious. So that Mr. Bayes might, if he had pleased, have spared his gibing at that day, which hath more sacredness in it by far than many, nay than any of those things he pleaded for. But when men are once *adepti*, and have attained Bayes his height, and 'divinity' at least is 'rightly understood,' they have a priviledge, it seems, not only to play and make merry *on* the Sabbath day, but *with* it.

After this I walked a great way through bushes and brambles before I could find another flower; but then I met with two upon one stalk, on occasion of his Answerer's having said something of the day of judgment, when men should be accountable. 'Oh,' saith he, ' we shall be sure to be accounted with at that day of judgment;' and again, 'Ah sweet day! when these people of God shall once for all, to their unspeakable comfort and support, wreak their eternal revenge upon their reprobat enemies.' This puts me in mind of another expression of our Author's alluding too this way: ' 'Tis an easie matter by this dancing and capering humour to perpetuate all the controversies in the world, how plainly soever determinable, to the coming of Elias; and after this rate shall the barber's bason remain Mambrino's helmet, and the ass's pannel a furniture for the great horse, till the day of judgement.' Now, good Mr. Bayes, I am one that desire to be very well resolved in these things; and though not much indeed, yet I attribute something to your judgment. Pray tell us in good earnest, what you think of these things, that we may know how to take our measure of living accordingly. For if indeed there be no judgment, no account for what is done here below, I have lost a great deal of precious time, that I might have injoyed in one of the fruits of your spirit, that is '*chearfulness.*' How many good jests have I balk'd, even in writing this book, lest I should be brought to answer for every profane and idle word! How frequent opportunities have I mist in my life of geniality and pleasure, and fulfilling nature in all its ends! How have you frighted the magistrate in vain from exercising his uncontroulable ecclesiastical power, with the fear of an after-reckoning to God Almighty! And how have you, page 238, defeated the obligatory force of all his laws, and set his subjects at liberty from all obligations to the duty of obedience! for they lie under no obligation, you say then, but of prudence and self-interest. But unless there hath been some error in the education, and we have been seasoned with ill books at first, so that we can never lose the impression, there is some such matter, and the governor had reason when he trembled to hear Saint Paul discoursing of that subject. The fanatical book of martyrs (for we will not with some call the Bible so) tells us some old stories of persons that have been cited by some of them to appear at such a day, and that by dying at the time prefixed, they have saved their reconnoissances [=recognisances]. And in the Scotch history we read of a great cardinal that was so summoned by poor Mr. Guichard, and yet could not help it, but he must take that long and sad journey of death to answer at the Grand Assizes. If therefore there be such a thing, I would not for fear, and if there be not, yet I would not for good-luck' sake, set that terrible day at defiance, or make too merry with it. 'Tis possible that the Nonconformists many of them may be too censorious of others, and too confident of their own integrity. Others of them are more temperate, and perhaps destitute of all humane redress against their sufferings. Some of those make rash challenges, and the other just appeals to appear at that dreadful tribunal. In the mean time, 'tis not for you to be both the enemy and their judge. Much less do's it befit you, because perhaps they speak too sillily or demurely of it, or too braving and confidently, therefore to make a meer mockery of the whole business of that Supreme Judge and judicature. And one thing I will say more, though slighter: that, though I am not so far gone as Campanella was in the efficacy of words, and the magick of the face, and pronunciation, yet I marked how your Answerer look'd when he spoke of the day of judgment. Very gravely, I assure you, and yet without any dressing or adorning his superciliums; and I have most often observed that serious words have produced serious effects.

I have by this time, methinks, gather'd enow: nor are there many more left, unless I should go for a flower to the dunghil, which he saith 'is his only magazin.' And this being an expression which he has several times used (for no Nonconformist repeats so often), I cannot but remark, that besides his natural talent, Mr. Bayes hath been very industrious, and neglected no opportunity of acquiring a perfection of railing. For this is a phrase borrowed from a modern author lately dead, and I suppose Bayes had given him a bond for repayment at the day that he spoke of so lately.

There are, indeed, several others at which I am forced to stop my nose. For by the smell, any man may discern they grew upon a ranker soil than that on 'the south-side of the Lake Lemane,' even upon the bank of the Thames in the meadow of Billinsgate: as that of the lye, which, he saith, no gentleman, much less a divine, ought to put up. Now if this were to be tryed by a court-martial of the brothers of the blade, 'tis to be considered whether it were the down-right lye, or whether it were only the lye by interpretation. For in the disputes of the Schools there is nothing more usual than *hoc est verum, hoc est falsum*. But this passes without any blemish of honour on either side, and so far it is from any obligation to a challenge or a duel, that it never comes to be decided so much as by the study-door key. But *quod restat probandum* does the business without demanding other satisfaction. Then, if it were the down-right lye, it is to be examined who gave the lye first; for that alters the case. And last of all (but which is indeed upon a quarrel the least material point, yet, too, it comes under some consideration), which of the two was in the right, and which of them spoke truth, and which lyed. These are all things to be discussed in their proper places. For I do not observe that the Answerer gave Bayes the down-right lye. But I find that Bayes gave him the lye first in terms. And as to the truth of the things controverted and alledg'd, there needs no more than the depositions that I formerly transcribed concerning Bayes his own words. But all this is only a scene out of Bayes his rehearsal.

> Villain, thou liest!
> Arm, arm, Valerio, arm!
> The lie no flesh can bear, I trow.

And then as to the success of the combate,

> ... They fly, they fly,
> Who first did give the lye.

For that of 'caitife,' and other provocations that are proper for the same Court, I will not meddle further. And for the being '*past grace, and so past mercy,*' I shall only observe that the Church of England is much obliged to Mr. Bayes for having proved that Nonconformity is the sin against the Holy Ghost.

There remains but one flower more that I have a mind to. But that indeed is a rapper. 'Tis a 'flower of the sun,' and might alone serve both for a staff and a nosegay for any nobleman's porter. 'Symbolicalness is the very essence of paganism, superstition, and idolatry. They will and ought sooner to broil in Smithfield than submit to such abominations of the Strumpet and the Beast. 'Tis the very potion wherewith the scarlet Whore made drunk the kings of the earth. Heliogabalus and Bishop Bonner lov'd it like clary and eggs, and always made it their morning's draught upon burning-days; and it is not to be doubted but the seven vials of wrath that were to be poured-out upon the nations of the Earth under the reign of Antichrist, were filled with symbolical extracts and spirits.' This I confess a pretty posy for the nose of such a divine. Doctor Baily's romance of the Wall-flower had nothing comparable to't. And I question whether, as well as Mr. Bayes loves preferment, yet though he had lived in the primitive Church, he would not, as Heliodorus Bishop of Trissa, I take it, that renounced his bishoprick rather than his title to the History of Theagenes and Chariclea, have done in like manner; nay, and have delivered up his Bible too into the bargain, before he would quit the honour of so excellent a piece of drollery. This is surely the bill-of-fare, not at the Ordination-dinner at the Nag's-head, but at the Cock; and never did divine make so good chear of Owen's peas-porridge and Scripture. I know no dainty wanting, or that could have pleased his tooth so well, except the leg of a pheasant at the Dog and Partridge; for he is of Thomas a-Becket's dyet, who eat, he said, phaesianum sicut alii muluellum, and can mortifie himself upon pheasant as well as others with salt-fish. Good Mr. Bayes, or Mr. Thunder, or Mr. Cartwright (not the Nonconformist Cartwright that was, you say—as some others too of your acquaintance—converted; but the Player, in the Rehearsal), this Divinity I doubt was the Bacchus of your thigh, and not the Pallas of your brain.

Here it is that, after so great an excess of wit, he

thinks fit to take a julep and re-settle his brain and the government. He grows as serious as 'tis possible for a madman, and pretends to sum-up the whole state of the controversie with the Nonconformists. And to be sure he will make the story as plausible for himself as he may; but therefore it was that I have before so particularly quoted and bound him up with his own words as fast as such a Proteus could be pinion'd. For he is as waxen as the first matter, and no form comes amiss to him. Every change of posture does either alter his opinion or vary the expression by which we should judge of it; and sitting he is of one mind, and standing of another. Therefore I take myself the less concern'd to fight with a windmill like Quixote; or to whip a gig as boyes do; or with the lacqueys at Charing-Cross or Lincoln's-Inn-Fields to play at the Wheel of Fortune; lest I should fall into the hands of my Lord Chief-Justice, or Sir Edmond Godfrey. The truth is, in short, and let Bayes make more or less of it if he can, Bayes had at first built-up such a stupendous magistrate as never was of God's making. He had put all princes upon the rack to stretch them to his dimension. And as a straight line continued grows a circle, he had given them so infinite a power, that it was extended unto impotency. For though he found it not till it was too late in the cause, yet he felt it all along (which is the understanding of brutes) in the effect. For hence it is that he so often complains that princes knew not aright that supremacy over consciences, to which they were so lately, since their deserting the Church of Rome, restored; that in most Nations government was not rightly understood, and many expressions of that nature: whereas indeed the matter is, that princes have alwayes found that uncontroulable government over CONSCIENCE to be both unsafe and impracticable. He had run himself here to a stand, and perceived that there was a God, there was Scripture; the magistrate himself had a conscience, and must 'take care that he did not enjoyn things apparently evil.' Being at a stop here, he would therefore try how he could play the broker on the subjects' side: and no pimp did ever enter into a more serious disputation to vitiate an innocent virgin than he to debauch their consciences. And to harden their unpractis'd modesty, he imboldens them by his own example, shewing them the experiment upon his own conscience first. But after all, he finds himself again at the same stand here, and is run up to the wall by an angel. God, and Scripture, and conscience will not let him go further; but he owns, that if the magistrate enjoyns things apparently evil, the subject may have liberty to remonstrate. What shall he do, then? for it is too glorious an enterprize to be abandoned at the first rebuffe. Why, he gives us a new translation of the Bible, and a new commentary! He saith, that tenderness of conscience might be allowed in a Church to be constituted, not in a Church constituted already. That tenderness of conscience and scandal are ignorance, pride, and obstinacy. He saith, the Nonconformists should communicate with him till they have clear evidence that it is evil. This is a civil way indeed of gaining the question, to perswade men that are unsatisfied, to be satisfied till they be dissatisfied. He threatens, he rails, he jeers them, if it were possible, out of all their consciences and honesty; and finding that will not do, he calls out the magistrate, tells him these men are not fit to live; there can be no security of government while they are in being. Bring out the pillories, whipping-posts, gallies [=galleys], rods, and axes (which are *ratio ultima cleri*, a clergyman's last argument, ay and his first too), and pull in pieces all the Trading Corporations, those nests of Faction and Sedition. This is a faithful account of the summ and intention of all his undertaking, for which, I confess, he was as pick'd a man as could have been employed or found out in a whole kingdome; but it is so much too hard a task for any man to atchieve, that no goose but would grow giddy with it.

For whereas he reduces the whole controversy to a matter of two or three symbolical ceremonies (and if there be nothing else, more the shame of those that keep such a pudder for them), it is very well worth observing how he hath behaved himself, and how come off in this dispute. It seems that the Conformists define a sacrament to be 'an outward visible sign of an inward spiritual grace.' It seems the sacraments are usually called in the Greek Symbola. It seems further that some of the Nonconformists, under the name therefore of symbolical ceremonies, dispute the lawfulness of those that are by our Church enjoyned, whereby the Nonconformists can only intend that these ceremonies are so applyed as if they were of a sacramental nature and institution, and that therefore they are unlawful. Our Author's Answerer, handling this argument, does among other things make use of a pertinent passage in Saint Austin, 'Signa cum ad res divinas pertinent Sacramenta appellantur.' What does Mr. Bayes in this case? for it went hard with him. Why, as good luck would have it, not being willing that so great a politician, to the irreparable damage of the Church, should yet be destroyed, J. O. had forgot to quote the book and the page. Now though you send a man the length of your weapon, and name your second, yet Mr. Bayes, being, as you see often, admirably read in the laws of duelling, knew that unless the time and place be appointed, there is no danger. He saith therefore, page 452 of his second book, that he 'should have advantage on his side, if he should lay odds with him that there is no such passage in all the volumes of Saint Austin.' But however, that is neither civil nor ingenuous to trouble him with such objections, as he cannot answer without reading over eight or ten large volumes in folio. It was too much to expect from one of so much business, good Augustulus:

> 'Quum tot sustineas et tanta negotia solus,
> Res sacras armis tuteris, moribus ornes,
> Legibus emendes.' . . .

Which may be thus translated: When you alone have the ceremonies to defend with whipping-posts, rods, and axes; when you have grace to turn into morality; when you have the Act of Oblivion and Indemnity and the Ecclesiastical Declaration of March to tear in pieces; it were unreasonable and too much to the dammage of the publick to put you in such an imployment. I ask your pardon, Mr. Bayes, for this paraphrase and digression; for I perceive I am even hardned in my Latine, and am prone to use it without fear or reverence. But, Mr. Bayes, there might have been a remedy for this, had you pleased. Where, then, were all your leaf-turners? a sort of poor readers 'you as well as Bishop Bramhall ought to have some reverence for,' having made so much use of them to gather materials for your structures and superstructures. I cannot be persuaded, for all this, but that he knows it well enough, the passage being so remarkable in itself, and so dirtyed with the Nonconformists' thumbs, that he could not possibly miss it; and I doubt he does but laugh at me now, when, to save him a labour, I tell him, in the simplicity of my heart, that even I myself met with it in *Ep. 5ta ad Marcellinum,* and the words these, 'Nimis autem longum est convenienter disputare de varietate signorum, quae cum ad res divinas pertinent Sacramenta appellantur.' But, whether there be such a place or no, he hath no mind that his Answerer should make use of it; nor of the Schoolmen, whom before he had owned for the Authors of the Church of England's divinity; but would bind-up the Answerer to the Law only and the Gospel. And now Mr. Bayes saith he will be of the Schoolmen's opinion '*as long as they speak sense*,' and no longer (and so I believe of Saint Austin's), that is to say, so long as they will serve his turn; for all politicians shake men off when they have no more use of 'em, or find them to thwart the[ir] design. But, Mr. Bayes, why may not your Answerer or any man else quote Saint Austin, as well as you may the Scriptures? I am sure there is less danger of perverting the place, or of misinterpretation. And though perhaps a Nonconformist may value the authority of the Bible above that of the Fathers, yet the Welch have a proverb, that the Bible and a stone do well together; meaning, perhaps, that if one miss, the other will hit. You, that are a duellist, know how great a bravery 'tis to gain an enemie's sword, and that there is no more home-thrust in disputation than the *argumentum ad hominem*. So that if your adversary fell upon you with one of your own Fathers, it was gallantly done on his part; and no less wisely on yours to fence in this manner, and use all your shifts to put it by. For you too, Mr. Bayes, do know—no man better—that it is not at all times safe nor honourable to be of a Father's opinion.

Having escaped this danger, he grows, nor can I blame him, exceeding merry; and insults heavily over '*symbolical*' wheresoever he meets with it; for in his Answerer I find it not. But wheresoever 'twas, it serves to good purpose. For no man would imagin that he could have received so universal a defeat, and appear in so good humour. A terrible disputant he is, when he has set up an hard word to be his opponent. 'Tis a very wholesome thing he knows, and prolongs life; for all the while he can keep up this ball he may decline the question. But the poor word is sure to be mumbled and mowsled to purpose, and to be made an example. But let us, with Mr. Bayes his leave, examine the thing for once a little closer. The Nonconformists, as I took notice before, do object to some of the rites of the Church of England, under the name of 'symbolical or significant ceremonies.' They observe the Church of England does, in the discourse of ceremonies printed before the Common Prayer-book, declare that the retaining of those ceremonies is not onely ' as they serve for decent order and godly discipline, but as they are apt to stir up the dull mind of man to the remembrance of his duty to God, by some special and notable significancy, whereby he may be edified.' They further observe the Church of England's definition of a sacrament: that it is 'an outward visible sign of an inward spiritual grace.' They find these ceremonies, so constituted, impos'd upon them by authority; and moreover, according to our author's principle, made a new part of the divine law. They therefore quarrel and except against these under the notion of sacraments, and insist that the Church is not impowered to institute such ceremonies under such obligations and penalties as they are imposed. Or, if you will, instead of Church you may say rather the magistrate; forasmuch as our Author hath *pro hac vice* delivered the keys and the whole power of the house into his hands.

Now the Author having got them at this lock, cries victory. Nothing less will serve him than a three dayes' triumph, as if he had conquered Europe, Asia, and Africa, and let him have a fourth day added, if he please, over the *Terra Incognita* of Geneva. There is no end of his ostentation and pageantry; and the dejected Nonconformists follow the wheels of his chariot, to be led afterwards to the prison and there executed. He had said, page 446 of his second Book, ' Here Cartwright begun his objection, and here he was immediately checked in his career by Whitgift' (you might, Mr. Author, for respect sake, have called him at least Mr. if not Archbishop Whitgift), ' who told him plainly, he could not be ignorant that to the making of a sacrament, besides the external element, there is required a commandment of God in His Word that it should be done, and a promise annexed to it, whereof the sacrament is a seal.' And in pursuance hereof, page 447, our Author saith, 'Here then I fix my foot, and dare him to his teeth to prove that any thing can be capable of the nature or office of sacraments that is not established by divine institution and upon promise of divine acceptance.' Upon the confidence of this argument 'tis that he Hectors and Achillizes all the Nonconformists out of the pit in this Preface. This is the sword that was consecrated first upon the altar, and thence presented to the champions of the Church in all ages. This is that with which Archbishop Whitgift gave 'Cartwright his death's wound; and laid the Puritan reformation a-gasping.' This is the weapon wherewith Master Hooker 'gained those lasting and eternal trophies over that baffled cause.' This is that with which Bishop Bramhal ' wrought those wonderful things that exceeded all belief.' This hath been transmitted successively to the writer of the 'Friendly Debate,' and to this our Author. It is, in conclusion, the *curtana* of our Church. 'Tis Sir Salomon's sword; cock of as many men as it hath been drawn against. Wo worth the man that comes in the way of so dead-doing a tool, and when wielded with the arm of such a Scanderbag as our Author! The Nonconformists had need desire a truce to bury their dead. Nay, there are none left alive to desire it; but they are slain, every mother's son of them. Yet perhaps they are but stounded, and may revive again. For I do not see, all this while, that any of them have written, as a great Prelate of ours, a book of 'Seven Sacraments,' or attempted to prove that these symbolical ceremonies are indeed sacraments. Nothing less. 'Tis that which they most labour against, and they complain that these things should be imposed on them with so high penalty, as want nothing of a sacramental nature but divine institution. And because an humane institution is herein made of equal force to a divine institution, therefore it is that they are agrieved. All that they mean, or could mean, as far as I or any man can perceive, is onely that these ceremonies are a kind of anti-sacraments, and so obtruded upon the Church, that without condescending to these additional inventions, no man is to be admitted to partake of the true sacraments which were of Christ's appointing. For, without the sign of the cross our Church will not receive any one to Baptism; as also without kneeling no man is suffered to come to the Communion. So that, methinks, our Author and his partners have wounded themselves only with this argument; and have had as little occasion here to sing their *Te-Deums* as the Roman Emperour had to triumph over the ocean, because he had gathered periwinkles and scallop-shells on the beach. For the Author may transform their reasonings as oft as he pleases (even as oft as he doth his own, or the Scriptures): but this is indeed their fort, out of which

I do not see they are likely to be beat with all our Author's cannon: that no such new conditions ought to be imposed upon Christians by a less than divine authority, and unto which if they do not submit, though against their consciences, they shall therefore be deprived of communion with the Church. And I wonder that our Author 'could not observe any thing in the discourse of Evangelical Love, that was to the purpose, beside a perpetual repetition' of the out-worn story of unscriptural ceremonies, and a peculiar uncouthness and obscurity of stile; when as this Plea is there for so many pages distinctly and vigorously insisted on. For it is a childish thing (how high soever our Author magnifies himself in this way of reasoning) either to demand from the Nonconformists a pattern of their worship from the Scripture, who affect therein a simplicity free from all exterior circumstances but such as are natural or customary; or else to require of them some particular command against the cross, or kneeling, and such-like ceremonies, which in the time of the Apostles, and many ages after, were not thought of. But therefore general and applicable rules of Scripture they urge as directions to the conscience; unto which our Author gives no satisfactory solution, but by superseding and extinguishing the conscience, or exposing it to the severest penalties. But here I say, then, is their main exception: that things indifferent, and that have no proper signature or significancy to that purpose, should by command be made necessary conditions of Church-communion. I have many times wished, for peaceableness-sake, that they had a greater latitude; but if, unless they should stretch their consciences till they tear again, they cannot conform, what remedy? For I must confess that Christians have a better right and title to the Church, and to the ordinances of God there, than the Author hath to his surplice. And that right is so undoubted and ancient, that it is not to be innovated upon by humane restrictions and capitulations.

Bishop Bramhall, page 141, saith, 'I do profess to all the world, that the transforming of indifferent opinions into necessary articles of faith hath been that *insana laurus*, or cursed bay-tree, the cause of all our brawling and contention.' That which he saw in matter of doctrine he would not discern in discipline; whereas this among us—the transforming of things at best indifferent into necessary points of practice—hath been of as ill consequence. And (to reform a little my seriousness) I shall not let this pass without taking notice that you, Mr. Bayes, being the most extravagant person in this matter that ever I heard of, as I have shown you are mad, and so the *insana laurus;* so I wish you may not prove 'that cursed bay-tree, too,' as the Bishop translates it. If you had thought of this, perhaps we might have missed both the Bishop's book and your Preface; for you see that sometimes no man hath a worse friend than he brings from home.

It is true, and very piously done, that our Church does declare that the kneeling at the Lord's Supper is not injoyned for adoration of those elements, and concerning the other ceremonies as before. But the Romanists (from whom we have them, and who said of old we would come to feed on their meat as well as eat of their porridge) do offer us here many a fair declaration, and destinction in very weighty matters, to which nevertheless the conscience of our Church hath not complyed. But in this particular matter of kneeling, which came in first with the doctrine of transubstantiation, the Romish Church do reproach us with flat idolatry, in that we, not believing the real presence in the bread and wine, do yet pay to something or other the same adoration. Suppose the ancient Pagans had declared to the primitive Christians that the offering of some grains of incense was only to perfume the room, or that the delivering up of their Bibles was but for preserving the book more carefully; do you think the Christians would have palliated so far, and colluded with their consciences? Men are too prone to erre on that hand. In the last king's time, some eminent persons of our clergy made an open defection to the Church of Rome. One, and he yet certainly a Protestant, and that hath deserved well of that cause, writ the book of Seven Sacraments. One in the Church at present, though certainly no less a Protestant, could not abstain from arguing the 'Holiness of Lent:' Doctor Thorndike, lately dead, left for his epitaph, 'Hic jacet corpus Herberti Thorndike Præbendarii hujus Ecclesiæ, qui vivus veram Reformatæ Ecclesiæ rationem et modum precibus studiisq. prosequebatur;' and nevertheless he adds, 'Tu, Lector, requiem ei et beatam in Christo resurrectionem precare.' Which thing I do thus sparingly set down, onely to shew the danger of inventive piety; and if men come once to add new devices to the Scripture, how easily they slide on into superstition. Therefore, although the Church do consider herself so much as not to alter her mode unto the fancy of others, yet I cannot see why she ought to exclude those from communion whose weaker consciences cannot for fear of scandal step further. For the Nonconformists, as to these Declarations of our Church against the reverence to the creatures of bread and wine, and concerning the other ceremonies as before, will be ready to think they have as good a plea as that so much commended by our Author against the clause, 'That whosoever should affirm the Wednesday Fast to be imposed with an intention to bind the conscience,' should be punished 'like the spreaders of false news;' which is, saith a learned Prelate, 'plainly to them that understand it, to evacuate the whole law. For all humane power being derived from God, and bound upon our consciences by His power, not by man, he that saith it shall not bind the conscience saith it shall be no law, it shall have no authority from God, and then it hath none at all; and if it be not tyed upon the conscience, then to break it is no sin, and then to keep it is no duty. So that a law without such an intention is a contradiction. It is a law onely which binds if we please, and we may obey when we have a mind to it, and to so much we are tyed before the constitution. But then if by such a Declaration it was meant, that to keep such fasting-days was no part of a direct commandment from God, that is, God had not required them by Himself immediately, and so it was abstracting from that law no duty evangelical, it had been below the wisdom of the contrivers of it; no man pretends it, no man saith it, no man thinks it; and they might as well have declared that that law was none of the Ten Commandments.' Page 59 of his first Book.

So much pains does that learned Prelate of his take (whoever he was) to prove a whole parliament of England coxcombs. Now I say that those Ecclesiastical Laws, with such declarations concerning the ceremonies by them injoined, might, *mutatis mutandis*, be taxed upon the same topick. But I love not that task, and shall rather leave it to Mr. Bayes to paraphrase his learned Prelate; for he is very good at correcting the impertinence of laws and lawgivers; and though this work, indeed, be not for his turn at present, yet it may be for the future. And I have heard a good engineer say, that he never fortified any place so, but that he reserv'd a feeble point, by which he knew how to take it, if there were occasion.

I know a medicine for Mr. Bayes his hiccough (it is but naming J. O.), but I cannot tell certainly, though I have a shrewd guess, what is the cause of it. For indeed all his arguments are so abrupt and short, that I cannot liken them better, considering too that frequent and perpetual repetition. Such as this, 'Why may not the sovereign power bestow this priviledge upon ceremony and custom, by vertue of its prerogative? What greater immorality is there in them when determined by the command and institution of the prince than when by the consent and institution of the people?' This the tap-lash of what he said, page 110: 'When the civil magistrate takes upon him to determine any particular forms of outward worship, 'tis of no worse consequence than if he should go about to define the signification of all words used in the worship of God.' And page 108 of his first Book: 'So that all the magistrate's power of instituting significant ceremonies &c. can be no more usurpation upon the CONSCIENCES of men than if the sovereign authority should take upon itself, as some princes have done, to define the signification of words.' And afterwards: 'The same gesture and actions are indifferently capable of signifying either honour or contumely, and so words; and therefore 'tis necessary their signification should be determined, &c.' 'Tis all very well worth reading. Page 441 of his second Book : ' It is no other usurpation upon their subjects' consciences than if he should take upon him to refine their language and determine the proper signification of all phrases imployed in divine worship, as well as in trades, arts, and sciences.' Page 461 of the same : ' Once we will so far gratifie the tenderness of their consciences and curiosity of their fancies, as to promise never to ascribe any other significancy to things than what himself is here content to bestow upon words.' And 462 of the same : ' So that you see my comparison between the signification of words and ceremonies stands firm as the pillars of the earth and the foundations of our faith.' Mr. Bayes might, I see, have spared Sir Salomon's sword of the divine institution of the sacraments. Here is the terriblest weapon in all his armory ; and therefore, I perceive, reserved by our duellist for the last onset. And I, who am a great well-wisher to the pillars of the earth, or the eight elephants, lest we should have an earthquake ; and much more a servant to the king's prerogative, lest we should all fall into confusion ; and perfectly devoted to the foundations of our faith, lest we should run out into Popery or Paganism,—have no heart to this incounter, lest, if I should prove that the magistrate's absolute, unlimited, and uncontroulable power doth not extend to define the signification of all words, I should thereby not only be the occasion of all those mischiefs mentioned, but, which is of far more dismal importance, the loss of two or three so significant ceremonies. But, though I therefore will not dispute against that flower of the prince's crown, yet I hope that, without doing much harm, I may observe that, for the most part, they left it to the people, and seldom themselves exercised it. And even Augustus Cæsar, though he was so great an emperour and so valiant a man in his own person, was used to fly from a new word, though it were single, as studiously as a mariner would avoid a rock for fear of splitting. The difference of one syllable in the same word hath made as considerable a controversy as most have been in the church, betwixt the *homousians* and the *homœiousians*. One letter in the name of *beans* in Languedoc, one party calling them *faves* and the other *haves;* as the transposition only of a letter another time in the name of a goat, by some call'd *crabe*, and by others *cabre*, was the loss of more men's lives than the distinguishing but by an aspiration in *shiboleth* upon the like occasion [Judges xii. 6]. So that if a man would be learnedly impertinent, he might enlarge here, to show that 'tis as dangerous to take a man by the tongue as a bear by the tooth. And had I a mind to play the politician, like Mr. Bayes, upon so pleasant and copious a subject, I would demonstrate that though the imposition of ceremonies hath bred much mischief in the world, yet (shall I not venture too on a word once for tryal?) such a penetration or transubstantiation of language would throw all into rebellion and anarchy, would shake the crowns of all princes, and reduce the world into a second Babel. Therefore, Mr. Bayes, I doubt you were not well advised to make so close an anology betwixt imposing of significant words and significant ceremonies; for I fear the argument may be improved against you, and that princes, finding that of words so impracticable and of ill consequence, will conclude that of ceremonies to be no less pernicious. And the Nonconformists (who are great traders, you know, in Scripture) will be certainly on your back; for they will appropriate your pregnant text of 'Let all things be done decently and in order' [1 Cor. xiv. 40] to preaching or praying in an unknown tongue, which such an imposition of words would be; and then, to keep you to your similitude, they will say too that yours are all Latine ceremonies, and the congregation does not understand them. But were not this dominion of words so dangerous (for how many millions of men did it cost your Roman Empire to attain it!), yet it was very unmannerly in you to assign to princes, who have enough beside, so mean a trouble. When you gave them leave to exercise the priesthood in person, that was something to the purpose; that was both honourable, and something belongs to it that would have helped to bear the charge. But this mint of words will never quit cost, nor pay for the coynage.

This is such a drudgery, that rather than undergo it, I dare say there is no prince but would resign to you so pedantical a soveraignty. I cannot but think how full that prince's head must be of proclamations; for if he published but once a proclamation to that purpose, he must forthwith set out another to stamp and declare the signification of all the words contained in it, and then another to appoint the meaning of all the words in this, and so on—that here is work cut out in one Paper of State for the whole Privy Council, both Secretaries of State, and all the clerks of the Council, for one king's reign, and *in infinitum*. But I cannot but wonder, knowing how ambitious Mr. Bayes is of the power over words, and jealous of his own prerogative of refining language, how he came to be so liberal of it to the prince; why, the same thing that induced him to give the prince a power antecedent and independent to Christ, and to establish what religion he pleased, &c. Nothing but his spight against the Nonconformists. I know not that thing in the world, except a jest, that he would not part with to be satisfied in that particular. He hoped, doubtless, by holding up this maxim, to obtain that the words of the Declaration of March 15th should be understood by contraries. You may well think he expected no less an equivalent; he would never else have permitted the prince even to define the signification of all words used in the worship of God, and to determine the proper signification of all phrases imploy'd in divine worship. Nay, Mr. Bayes, if it be come to that, and you will surrender your Liturgy to the prince, I know not what you mean, for 'tis bound up with your Bible. Was it ever heard that the Book so sacred, and in which there could not one error be found by all the Presbyterians at the Worster-House conference, should, upon so uncertain a prospect, be now abandon'd so far as that every word and phrase in it may receive a new and contrary signification? But the king, for ought I see, likes it well as it is, and therefore I do so too. Yet in case his Majesty should ever think fit to reform it, and because such kind of work is usually referred back to some of the clergy, I would gladly put in a caveat, that our Author may in no case be one of them. For 'tis known that Mr. Bayes is subject to a distemper; and who knows but when he is in a fit, as he made such mad alterations of the 'fruit of the Spirit,' in the Epistle for the day, he may as well insert in some other part of the service, 'Well fare poor Macedo for a modest fool;' and then, 'Oh how I hug thee, dear heart, for this!' and pretend that the supreme magistrate should stamp upon it a signification sacred and serious? I would not have spoken so severely of him, but that his 'more laboured periods,' as he calls them, are so often fill'd with much bolder and more unwholesome translations. But however, that he may not at his better intervals be wholly unemploy'd in the work of uniformity, I should recommend to him rather to turn the Liturgy and the 'Rationale' into the universal language, and so in time the whole world might come to be of his parish.

When he was drawn thus low, did not he, think you, stand in need of tilting? He had done much more service to the cause had he laid by all those cheating argumentations, and dealt candidly, like the good Archdeacon, not long since dead; who went about both court and country, preaching upon the 'cloke left at Troas, and the books, but especially the parchments' [2 Timothy iv. 13]. The honest man had found out there the whole Liturgy, the canonical habits, and all the equipage of a Conformist. This was something to the matter in hand, to produce apostolical example and authority, and much more to the purpose than that beaten text of ' doing all things decently and in order.'

One argument, I confess, remains still behind, and that will justifie any thing. 'Tis that which I called lately *rationem ultimam cleri;* force, law, execution, or what you will have it. I would not be mistaken, as though I hereby meant the body of the English clergy, who have been ever since the Reformation (I say it without disparagement to the foraign Churches) of the most eminent for divinity and piety in all Christendom. And as far am I from censuring, under this title, the Bishops of England, for whose function, their learning, their persons I have too deep a veneration to speak anything of them irreverently. But those that I intend onely are a particular bran of persons, who will, in spight of fate, be accounted the Church of England, and to shew they are pluralists, never write in a modester stile than *we, we ;* nay, even these, several of them, are men of parts sufficient to deserve rank among the teachers and governors of the Church. Only what Bishop Bramhall saith of Grotius his defect in school-divinity,

' Unum hoc maceror et doleo tibi deesse,'

I may apply to their excess and rigour in matter of Discipline. They want all consideration, all moderation in those things; and I never heard of any of them at any time, who, if they got into power or office, did ever make the least experiment or overture towards the peace of the Church and Nation they lived in. They are the 'politick Would-be's' of the clergy. Not Bishops, but men that have a mind to be Bishops, and that will do any thing in the world to compass it. And though princes have always a particular mark upon these men, and value them no more than they deserve, yet I know not very well, or perhaps I do not know, how it oftentimes happens that they come to be advanced. They are men of a fiery nature, that must always be uppermost; and, so they may increase their own splendor, care not though they set all on flame about them. You would think the same day that they took up divinity they divested themselves of humanity, and, so they may procure and execute a law against the Nonconformists, that they had forgot the Gospel. They cannot endure that humility, that meekness, that strictness of manners and conversation, which is the true way of gaining reputation and authority to the clergy; much less can they content themselves with the ordinary and comfortable provision that is made for the ministry; but having wholy calculated themselves for preferment and grandeur, know or practise no other means to make themselves venerable but by ceremony and severity. Whereas the highest advantage of promotion is the opportunity of condescention, and the greatest dignity in our Church can but raise them to the title of Your Grace, which is in the Latine *vestra clementia*. But of all these, none are so eager and virulent, as some who, having had relation to the late times, have got access to 'Ecclesiastical Fortune,' and are resolved to make their best of her. For so, of all beasts, none are so fierce and cruel as those that have been taught once by hunger to prey upon their own kind; as, of all men, none are so inhuman as the canibals. But whether this be the true way of ingratiating themselves with a generous and discerning prince, I meddle not; nor whether it be an ingenuous practice towards those whom they have been formerly acquainted with: but whatsoever they think themselves obliged to for the approving of their new loyalty, I rather commend. That which astonishes me, and onely raises my indignation, is, that of all sorts of men this kind of clergy should always be, and have been, for the most precipitate, brutish, and sanguinary counsels. The former Civil War cannot make them wise, nor his Majestie's happy return good-natured; but they are still for running things up unto the same extreams. The softness of the Universities where they have been bred, the gentleness of Christianity in which they have been nurtured, hath but exasperated their nature; and they seem to have contracted no idea of wisdom but what they learnt at School, the pedantry of whipping. They take themselves qualified to preach the Gospel, and no less to intermeddle in affairs of State; though the reach of their divinity is but to persecution, and an inquisition is the height of their Policy.

And you, Mr. Bayes, had you lived in the dayes of Augustus Cæsar (be not scandalized; for why may you not bring sixteen hundred years, as well as five hours, into one of your Playes?), would not you have made, think you, an excellent privy-counsellour? His father too was murdered. Or (to come nearer both to our times and your resemblance of the late War, which you trumpet alwaies in the ear of his Majesty) had you hapen'd in the time of Henry the Fourth of France, should you not have done well in the cabinet? His predecessor too was assassinated. No, Mr. Bayes, you would not have been for their purpose: they took other measures of government, and accordingly it succeeded with them. And his Majesty, whose genius hath much of both those princes, and who derives half of the blood in his veins from the latter, will in all probability not be so forward to hearken to your advice as to follow their example. For these Kings, Mr. Bayes, how negligent soever or ignorant you take 'em to be, have, I doubt, a shrewd understanding with them. 'Tis a trade that, God be thanked, neither you nor I are of; and therefore we are not so competent judges of their actions. I my self have oftentimes seen them, some of them, do strange things, and unreasonable in my opinion; and yet a little while, or sometimes many years after, I have found that all the men in the world could not have contrived any thing better. 'Tis not with them as with you. You have but one cure of souls, or perhaps two, as being a nobleman's chaplain, to look after; and if you make conscience of discharging them as you ought, you would find you had work sufficient without writing your 'Ecclesiastical Policies.' But they are the incumbents of whole kingdoms, and the rectorship of the common people, the nobility, and even of the clergy, whom you are prone to ' affirm when possest with principles that incline to rebellion and disloyal practises, to be of all rebels the most dangerous,' page 49. The care, I say, of all these rests upon them. So that they are fain to condescend to many things for peace-sake, and the quiet of mankind, that your proud heart would break before it would bend to. They do not think fit to require any thing that is impossible, unnecessary, or wanton, of their people ; but are fain to consider the very temper of the climate in which they live, the constitution and laws under which they have been formerly bred; and upon all occasions to give them good words, and humour them like children. They reflect upon the histories of former times, and the present transactions, to regulate themselves by in every circumstance. They observe how the Parliament of Poland will be their King's taylor, and among other reasons, because he would not wear their mode, have suffered the Turk to enter, as coming nearer their fashion. Nay, that even Alexander the Great had almost lost all he had conquered, by forcing his subjects to conform to the Persian habit. That the King of Spain, when upon a Progress he enters Biscay, is pleased to ride with one leg naked; and above all, to take care that there be not a Bishop in his retinue. So their people will pay their taxes in good gold and silver, they demand no subsidy of so many bushels of fleas, lest they should receive the same answer with the tyrant, that the subject could not furnish that quantity; and besides, they would be leaping out still before they could be measured, and should they fine the people for nonpayment, they reckon there would be little got by distraining. They have been told that a certain Queen being desired to give a town-seal to one of her cities, lighting from her horse, sate down naked on the snow, and left them that impression; and though it caused no disturbance, but all the town-leases are letters-pattents, Kings do not approve the example. That the late Queen of Sweden did herself no good with saying, *Io non voglio governar le bestie*, but afterwards resigned. That the occasion of the revolt of Switzerland from the Emperour, and its turning Commonwealth, was only the imposing of a civil ceremony by a capricious governour, who set up a pole in the highway, with a cap upon the top of it, to which he would have all passengers be uncover'd, and do obeysance. One sturdy Swiss that would not conform, thereupon overturn'd the government, as 'tis at large in History. That the King of Spain lost Flanders chiefly upon introducing the Inquisition. And you now, Mr. Bayes, will think these, and a hundred more that I could tell you, but idle stories; and yet Kings can tell how to make use of 'em. And hence 'tis that in stead of assuming your unhoopable jurisdiction, they are so satisfied with the abundance of their power, that they rather think meet to abate of its exercise by their discretion. The greater their fortune is, they are content to use the less extravagancy. But because I see, Mr. Bayes, you are a little deaf on this ear, I will talk somewhat closer to you. In this very matter of ceremonies, which you are so bent upon, that your mind is alwayes running on 't, when you should be hearkning to the sermon,—do not you think that the King knows every word you said, although he never gave your Book the reading? That you say that the clause 50 Eliz. of the Wednesday-Fast has been the original of all the Puritan disorders? That the controversy is now reduced onely to two or three 'symbolical ceremonies'? That these ceremonies are things indifferent in their own nature, and have no antecedent necessity, but onely bind as they are commanded? That they signify nothing in themselves but what the commander pleases? That the Church it self declares that there is nothing of religion or adoration in them? That they are no parts of religious worship? That they are onely circumstances? That the imposing of a significant ceremony is no more than to impose significancy upon a word? That there is not a word of any of these ceremonies in the Scriptures? That they are in themselves of no great moment and consequence, but 'tis absolutely necessary that government should injoyn them, to avoid the evil that would follow if they were not determined; and that there cannot be 'a pin pulled out of the Church, but the State immediately totters'? Do not you think that the King has considered all these things? I believe he has; and perhaps, as you have minced the matter, he may well think the Nonconformists have very nice stomachs, that they cannot digest such chopp'd hay; but, on the other side, he must needs take you to be very strange men to cram these in spite down the throats of any Christian. If a man have an antipathy against anything, the company is generally so civil as [if not] to refrain the use of it, however, not to press it upon the person. If a man be sick or weak, the Pope grants a dispensation from Lent, or fasting-daies; ay and from many a thing that strikes deeper in his religion. If one have got a cold, their betters will force them to be covered. There is no end of similitudes; but I am led into them by your calling these ceremonies 'pins of the Church.' It would almost tempt a prince that is curious, and that is setled (God be praised!) pretty fast in his throne, to try for experiment whether the pulling out of one of these pins would make the State totter. But, Mr. Bayes, there is more in it. 'Tis matter of conscience; and if Kings do, out of discretion, connive at the other infirmities of their people; if great persons do out of civility condescend to their inferiours; and if all men out of common humanity do yield to the weaker; will your clergy only be the men who, in an affair of conscience, and where perhaps 'tis you are in the wrong, be the only hard-hearted and inflexible tyrants; and not only so, but instigate and provoke princes to be the ministers of your cruelty? But I say, princes, as far as I can take the height of things so far above me, must needs have other thoughts, and are past such boye's-play, to stake their crowns against your pins. They do not think fit to command things unnecessary, and where the profit cannot countervail the hazard. But above all, they consider that God has instated them in the government of mankind, with that incumbrance (if it may so be called) of reason, and that incumbrance upon reason of conscience. That He might have given them as large an extent of ground and other kind of cattle for their subjects; but it had been a melancholy empire to have been only supreme grasiers and soveraign shepherds. And therefore, though the laziness of that brutal magistracy might have been more secure, yet the difficulty of this does make it more honourable. That men therefore are to be dealt with reasonably, and conscientious men by conscience. That even law is force, and the execution of that law a greater violence; and therefore with rational creatures not to be used but upon the utmost extremity. That the body is in the power of the mind; so that corporal punishments do never reach the offender, but the innocent suffers for the guilty. That the mind is in the hand of God, and cannot correct those perswasions which upon the best of its natural capacity it hath collected; so that it too, though erroneous, is so far innocent. That the prince therefore, by how much God hath indued him with a clearer reason, and by consequence with a more enlightned judgment, ought the rather to take heed, lest by punishing conscience he violate not only his own, but the Divine Majesty. But as to that, Mr. Bayes, which you still inculcate of the late War, and its horrid catastrophe, which you will needs have to be upon a religious account: 'tis four-and-twenty years ago, and after an Act of Oblivion; and for ought I can see, it had been as seasonable to have shown Cæsar's bloody coat, or Thomas à-Becket's bloody rochet. The chief of the offenders have long since made satisfaction to justice; and the whole nation hath been swept sufficiently of late years by those terrible scourges of Heaven; so that methinks you might in all this while have satiated your mischievous appetite. Whatsoever you suffered in those times, his Majesty, who had much the greater loss, knowing that the memory of his glorious father will alwayes be preserved, is the best judge how long the revenge ought to be pursued. But if indeed, out of your superlative care of his Majesty and your '*living*,' you are afraid of some new disturbance of the same nature, let me so far satisfy you as I am satisfied. The Nonconformists say, that they are bound in conscience to act as far as they can, and for the rest to suffer to the utmost. But because though they do mean honestly, 'tis so hard a chapter for one that thinks himself in the right to suffer extremities patiently, that some think it impossible,—I say next, that it's very seldom seen that in the same age, a Civil War, after such an interval, has been raised again upon the same pretences: but men are also wary, that he would be knock'd on the head that should raise the first disturbance of the same nature. A new War must have, like a book that would sell, a new title.

I am asham'd, Mr. Bayes, that you put me on talking thus impertinently (for Policy in us is so). Therefore, to be short, the King hath so indulged and obliged the Nonconformists by his late mercy, that if there were any such knave, there can be no such fool among them that would ever lift up an ill thought against him. And for you, Mr. Bayes, he is assured of your loyalty; so that I think you may enjoy your '*living*' very peaceably, which I know is all your business. 'Twas well replyed of the Englishman in Edward the Fourth's time, to the Frenchman that ask'd him insulting, when they should see us there again? 'When your sins are greater than ours.' There are as many occasions of War as there are vices in a nation, and therefore it concerns a prince to be watchful on all hands. But should kings remember an injury as long as you implacable divines do, or should we take up arms upon your peaks [piques], because your 'Ecclesiastical Policy' is answered, to revenge your quarrel, the world would never be at quiet. Therefore, Mr. Bayes, let all those things of former times alone, and mind your own business; for kings, believe me, as they have royal understandings, so have gentlemen's memories.

And now, Master Bayes, I think it is time to take my leave, having troubled you with so long a visit. Only, before I quit this matter, because I do not love to be accounted singular in my opinion, I will add the judgment of one Author, and that as pertinent as I could pick out to our purpose. I have observed that not onely other princes, but Queen Elizabeth too, hath the misfortune to be much out of favour; but for what reason I cannot possibly imagine, for none ever deserved better as to the thing of Uniformity, unless it be the ill-luck she had to pass that 'impertinent clause in the Act of the fifth of Elizabeth, of the *Jejunium Cecilianum.*' You cannot, for her sake, indure the wit or learning of her times, but say, page 94 of your second Book, 'though this trifling artifice of sprinkling little fragments of wit and poetry might have passed for wit and learning in the daies of Queen Elizabeth, yet to men of learning, reading, and ingenuity, their vulgar use has sullied their lustre and abated their value.' This is indeed, Mr. Bayes, a very laboured period, and prepared by you, I believe, on purpose as a model of the wit and eloquence of your daies. But not only so, but page 483 of the same Book, I think you call her in derision, and most spitefully and unmanneredly, plain 'old Elisibeth.' And those that knew her humour, think you, could not have disobliged her more than in stiling her so; both as a woman, which sex never love to be thought old, and as a queen, who was jealous lest men should therefore talk of the succession. Besides the irreverent nick-name you give her, that you might as well have presumed to call her queen Bess, or Bold Betrice. Now, to the end that that queen of famous memory may have a little female revenge upon you, and to give you a taste of the wit and learning even of her times, I will 'sprinkle' here one 'fragment,' which not being a 'scholar-like saying of antient poet or philosopher,' but of a reverend divine, I hope, Mr. Bayes, may be less displeasing to you. The man is Parker; not Robert Parker, who writ another treatise of Ecclesiastical Policy, and the book *de Cruce*, for which, if they had catched him, he had possibly gone to the gallows, or at least the gallyes; for he was one of those 'well-meaning zealots that are, of all villains, the most dangerous;' but it is the Archbishop of Canterbury, Parker (for if I named him before without addition, 'twas what I learnt of you speaking of Whitgift). He, in his book *de Antiquitatibus Ecclesiæ Britannicæ*, page 47, speaking of the slaughter of the monks of Bangor, and so many Christians more, upon the instigation of Austin the monk, who stirred up Ethelbert, king of Kent, against them, because they would not receive the Romish ceremonies, useth these words: 'Et sane illa prima de Romanis ritibus inducendis per Augustinum tunc excitata contentio, quae non nisi clade et sanguine innocentium Britannorum poterat extingui; ad nostra recentiora tempora, cum simili pernicie caedeque Christianorum pervenit. Cum enim illis gloriosis ceremoniis a pura primitivae Ecclesiae simplicitate recesserunt, non de vitae sanctitate, de evangelii praedicatione, de Spiritus Sancti vi et consolatione multum laborabant; sed novas indies altercationes de novis ritibus per papas singulos additis, qui neminem tam excelso gradu dignum, qui aliquid, ceremoniosi non dicam, monstrosi, inauditi et inusitati non adjecisset, instituebant. Suggestaque et scholas fabulis rixisque suis implebant. Nam ecclesiae species simplicior et integro et interno Dei cultu, ab ipso verbo praescripto, nec vestibus splendidis, nec magnificis structuris decorata, nec auro, argento, gemmisque fulgens fuit: etsi liceat his exterioribus uti modo animum ab illo interiori et integro Dei cultu non abducant; curiosis et morosis ritibus ab illa primaeva et recta simplicitate evangelica degeneravit. Illa autem in Romana ecclesia rituum multitudo ad immensum illius magni Augustini Hipponensis Episcopi temporibus creverat: ut questus sit Christianorum in ceremoniis et ritibus duriorem tunc fuisse conditionem quam Judaeorum, qui etiamsi tempus libertatis non agnoverint, legalibus tamen sarcinis non humanis praesumptionibus subjiciebantur; nam paucioribus in divino cultu quam Christiani ceremoniis utebantur. Qui si sensisset quantus deinde per singulos papas coacervatus cumulus accessit, modum Christianum credo ipse statuisset; qui hoc malum tunc in ecclesia viderat. Videmus enim ab illa ceremoniarum contentione nedum ecclesiam esse vacuam; quin homines, alioquin docti atque pii de vestibus et hujusmodi nugis adhuc rixiso magis et militari, quam aut philosophico aut Christiano more inter se digladiantur.' These words do run direct against the genius of some men that contributed not a little to the late Rebellion, and, though so long since writ, do so exactly describe that evil spirit with which some men are even in these times possest, who seem desirous upon the same grounds to put all things in combustion, that I think them very well worth the labour of translating. 'And indeed, that first contention then raised by Augustine about the introducing of the Romish ceremonies, which could not be quenched but by the blood and slaughter of the innocent Brittains, hath been continued e'n to our later times, with the like mischief and murder of Christians. For when once by those glorious ceremonies they forsook the pure simplicity of the primitive Church, they did not much trouble themselves about holiness of life, the preaching of the Gospel, the efficacy and comfort of the Holy Spirit; but they fell every day into new squabbles about new-fangled ceremonies added by every Pope, who reckoned no man worthy of so high a degree but such as invented somewhat, I will not say ceremonious, but monstrous, unheard-of, and before unpractised; and they fill'd the schools and the pulpits with their fables and brawling of such matters. For the first beauty of the Church had more of simplicity and plainness, and was neither adorned with splendid vestments, nor magnificent structures, nor shin'd with gold, silver, and precious stones, but with the intire and inward worship of God, as it was by Christ Himself prescribed, although it may be lawful to use these external things, so they do not lead the mind astray from that more inward and entire worship of God, by those curious and crabbed rites it degenerated from that antient and right evangelical simplicity. But that multitude of rites in the Romish Church had unmeasurably increased in the times of that great Augustine, the Bishop of Hippo, in so much that he complained that the condition of Christians as to rites and ceremonies was then harder than that of the Jews; who, although they did not discern the time of their liberty, yet were onely subjected to legal burthens, instituted first by God Himself, not to humane presumptions, for they used fewer ceremonies in the worship of God than Christians. Who, if he could have foreseen how great a heap of them was afterwards piled up, and added by the several popes, he himself doubtless would have restrained it within Christian measure, having already perceived this growing evil in the Church; for we see that even yet the Church is not free from that contention: but men, otherwise learned and pious, do still cut and slash about vestments and such kind of trifles, rather in a swash-buckler and hectoring way, than either like philosophers or like Christians.'

Now, Mr. Bayes, I doubt you must be put to the trouble of writing another Preface against this Archbishop; for nothing in your Answerer's treatise of 'Evangelical Love' does so gird or aim at you, for ought I can see, or at those whom you call the Church of England, as this passage. But the last period does so plainly delineate you to the life, that what St. Austine did not presage, the Bishop seems to have foreseen most distinctly. 'Tis just your way of writing all along in this matter. You bring nothing sound or solid. Onely you think you have got the 'great secret,' or the 'philosopher's stone' of railing; and I believe it, you have so multiplied it in 'projection:' and as they into gold, so you turn every thing you meet with into railing. And yet the secret is not great, nor the process long or difficult, if a man would study it and make a trade on't. Every scold hath it naturally. It is but crying whore first, and having the last word, and whatsoever t'other sayes, cry, Oh, these are your Nonconformists' tricks; oh, you have learnt this of the Puritans in Grub-street; oh, you white-apron'd gossip! For indeed I never saw so provident a fetch: you have taken in before hand all the posts of railing, and so beset all the topicks of just crimination, foreseeing where you are feeble, that if this trick would pass, it were impossible to open one's mouth to find the least fault with you. For in your first chapter of your second Book, beside what you do alwayes in an hundred places when you are at a loss, you have spent almost an hundred pages upon 'a character of the fanatick deportment towards all adversaries.' And then, on the other side, you have so ingrossed and brought up all the ammunition of railing, searched every corner in the Bible and Don Quixot for powder, that you thought, not unreasonably, that there was not one shot left for a fanatick. But Truth, you see, cannot want words: and she laughs too sometimes when she speaks, and rather than all fail too,[will] be serious. But what wil you say to that of the Archbishop's, 'than either like philosophers or like Christians'? For the excellency of your logick, philosophy, and Christianity in all your books, is either, as in conscience, to take away the subject of the question; or as in the magistrate, having gotten one absurdity, to raise a thousand more from it. So that, except the manufacture and labour of your periods, you have done no more than any school-boy could have done on the same terms. And so, Mr. Bayes, good-night.

And now good-morrow, Mr. Bayes; for though it seems so little a time and that you are now gone to bed, it hath been a whole live-long night, and you have toss'd up and down in many a troublesome dream, and are but just now awaked at the title-page of your Book: 'A preface shewing what grounds there are of fears and jealousies of Popery.' It is something artificially couch'd, but looks as if it did allow that there are some grounds of fears and jealousies of that nature. But here he words it, 'A consideration what likelihood, or how much danger there is of the return of Popery into this Nation.' Had he not come to this at last, I should have thought I had been all this while reading a chapter in Mountagne's Essayes; where you find sometimes scarce one word in the discourse of the matter held forth in the title. But now indeed he takes up this argument and debates it to purpose. For I had before begun to shew that he had writ not only his two former Books, but especially too this Preface, with an evil eye and aim at his Majesty, and the measures he had taken of government. And whoever will take the pains to read here, will soon be of my mind. His Majesty had, I said, the 15th of March 1671, issued his Declaration of Indulgence to tender consciences. He, on the contrary, issues out thereupon, all in haste and as fast as he could write, this his Remonstrance or Manifesto against Indulgence to tender consciences; and to make his Majestie's proceedings more odious, stirs up this seditious matter, of what probability there is of Popery.

And this he discourses, to be sure, in his own imagination very cunningly. For he knows that there was an act of parliament in this king's reign with a greater penalty than that of 50 Eliz. of spreading false news, against reports of this nature. And therefore he resolves to handle it so warily, that he himself might escape, but might draw others that should answer him within the danger of that Act, and that he may lay the crime at their doors. But notwithstanding all his slights [=sleights] and legerdemain, it doth enough detect his malice and ill-intention to his Majestie's government, that he should take this occasion, altogether foreign and unseasonable, to raise a publick and solemn discourse through the whole Nation, concerning a matter the most odious and dangerous that could be exposed. So that now no man can look at the wall, no man can pass by a Bookseller's stall, but he must see ' A Preface shewing what grounds there are for FEARS and JEALOUSIES of POPERY.'

It had been something a safer and more dutiful way of writing a Preface shewing the CAUSELESNESS of the Fears and Jealousies of Popery. For I do not think it will excuse a witch, to say that she conjur'd up a spirit only that she might lay it; nor can there be a more dexterous and malicious way of calumny, than by making a needless Apology for another in a criminal subject. As, suppose I should write a Preface showing what grounds there are of fears and jealousies of Bayes his being an atheist. But this is exactly our Author's method and way of contrivance; whereby more effectually by far, than by any flying coffee-house tattle, he traduces the State, and by printing so pernicious a question fills all men's mouths and beats out all men's eyes with the probability of the return of POPERY. Had he heard any that malignly and officiously talk'd to such a purpose, it had been the part of one so prudent as he is, not to have continued the Discourse. Had he (as he hath a great gift that way) pick'd up out of any man's talk or writing, matter whereof to make an ill story, there was a better and more regular way of proceeding, had he meant honestly to his Majestie's government, to have prevented the evil, and to have brought the offender to punishment. He should have gone to one of the Secretaries of State, or to some other of his Majestie's Privy Council, and have given them information. But instead of that, I am afraid that in the survey of this business we shall find, that even some of them are either accused, or shrewdly marked out with a character of our Author's displeasure. Therefore, I will now come nearer to his matter in hand, although it concerns me to be careful of coming too near; nor shall I dwell too long upon so jealous and impertinent a subject.

'To consider what likelihood or how much danger there is of the return of Popery into this Nation.' The very first word is, 'for my part, I know none.' Very well considered. Why then, Mr. Bayes, I must tell you, that if I had printed a Book or Preface upon that argument, I should have thought myself at least a fool for my labour. The next considerer is mine enemy; I mean he is an enemy to the State, whoever shall foment such discourses without any likelihood or danger. Yet, Mr. Bayes, you know I have for a good while had no great opinion of your integrity; neither here. I doubt you prevaricate a little with somebody. For I suppose you cannot be ignorant that some of your superiors of your robe did, upon the publishing that Declaration, give the word, and deliver orders through their ecclesiastical camp, to beat up the pulpit drums against Popery. Nay, even so much that there was care taken too for arming the 'poor Readers, that though they came short of preachers in point of efficacy, yet they might be enabled to do something in point of common security.' So that, though for so many years those your superiors had forgot there was any such thing in the nation as a Popish recusant; though 'polemical and controversial divinity' had for so long been hung up in the halls, like the rusty obsolete armour of our ancestors, for monuments of antiquity, and for derision rather than service; all on a sudden (as if the 15th of March had been the 5th of November) happy was he that could climb up first to get down one of the old cuirasses or an habergeon that had been worn in the days of Queen Elizabeth. Great variety there was and heavy too. Some clapp'd it on all rusty as it was, others fell of oyling and furbishing their armour; some piss'd in their barrels, others spit in their pans, to scowr them. Here you might see one put on his helmet the wrong way; there one buckle on a back in place of a breast. Some by mistake catched up a Socinian-Arminian argument, and some a Popeish to fight a Papist. Here a dwarf lost in the accoutrements of a giant: there a Don Quixot in an equipage of differing pieces and of several parishes. Never was such incongruity and Nonconformity in their furniture. One ran to borrow a sword of Calvin; this man for a musket from Beza; that for a bandeleers even, from Keckerman. But when they came to seek match, and bullet, and powder, there was none to be had. The fanaticks had bought it all up, and made them pay for it most unconscionably and through the nose. And no less sport was it to see their leaders. Few could tell how to give the word of command, nor understood to drill a company: they were as unexpert as their souldiers aukward; and the whole was as pleasant a spectacle as the exercising of the trained bands in —shire. But, Mr. Bayes (for I believe you do nothing but upon common advice), either this was all intended but for a false alarum, and was onely for a pretence to take arms against the fanaticks (which you might have done without raising all this din and obloquy against the State and disquieting his Majestie's good subjects); or else you did really think (and who can help misapprehensions?) that you did know some likelihood or danger of the return of Popery. I crave you mercy, Mr. Bayes, I took you a little short. 'For my part, I know none,' you say, 'but the Nonconformists' boysterous and unreasonable opposition to the Church of England.'

This, I confess, hath some weight in it. For truly before 'I knew none' too. I was of your opinion, Mr. Bayes, and believed that Popery could never return into England again, but by some very sinister accident. This expression of mine is something uncouth; and therefore, because I love to give you satisfaction in all things, Mr. Bayes, I will acquaint you with my reason of using it. Henry the Fourth of France, his Majestie's Grandfather, lived (you know) in the days of Queen Elizabeth. Now the wit of France and England, as you may have observed, is much of the same mode, and hath at all times gone much after the same current rate and standard; only there hath been some little difference in the alloy, and advantage or disadvantage in the exchange, according to men's occasions. Now Henry the Fourth was (you know too) a prince, like Bishop Bramhall, 'of a brave and enterprising temper, and had a mind large and active enough to have managed the Roman Empire at its utmost extent; and particularly (as far as the prejudice of the age (Old Elisabeth's age) would permit him)' he was very wittie and facetious, and the courtiers strove to humour him alwayes in it, and increase the mirth. So one night after supper he gave a subject (which recreation did well enough in those times, but were now insipid), upon which, like boyes at Westminster, they should make French verse extempore. The subject was, *Un accident sinistre.* Straight answers, I know not whether 'twas Bassompierre or Abigné:

' Un sinistre accident et un accident sinistre,
De veoir un Père Capuchin chevaucher un Ministre.'

For when I said, to see Popery return here would

be a very sinister accident, I was just thinking upon that story; the verses, to humour them in translation, being only this:

> O what a trick unlucky, and how unlucky a trick,
> To see friend Doctor Patrick bestrid by Father Patrick!

Which seem'd to me, would be the most improbable and preposterous spectacle that ever was seen; and more ridiculous for a sight, than the 'Friendly Debate' is for a Book. And yet if Popery come in, this must be, and worse.

But now I see there is some danger by the Nonconformists' opposition to the Church of England. And now your business is all fixed. The fanaticks are ready at hand to bear the blame of all things. Many a good job have I seen done in my time upon pretence of the fanaticks. I do not think Mr. Bayes ever breaks his shins but it is by stumbling upon a fanatick. And how shall they bring in Popery? Why thus, three wayes. 'First, by creating disorders and disturbances in the State. Secondly, by the assistance of atheism and irreligion. Thirdly, by joining with crafty and sacrilegious statesmen in confederacy.' Now here I remark two things. One, that however you do not find that the fanaticks are inclinable to Popery, only they may accommodate it by creating disturbances in the State. Another is, that I see these gentlemen, the fanaticks, the atheists, and the sacrilegious statesmen are not yet acquainted; but you have appointed them a meeting (I believe it must be at your lodgings, or no where), and I hope you will treat them handsomly. But I think it was not so wisely done, nor very honestly, Mr. Bayes, to lay so dangerous a Plot as this, and instruct men that are strangers yet to one another, how to contrive together such a conspiracy. But first to your first.

The 'fanaticks,' you say, 'may probably raise disturbance in the State.' For they 'are so little friends to the present government, that their enmity to that is one of the main grounds of their quarrel to the Church.' But now, though I must confess it is very much to your purpose, if you could perswade men so, I think you are clear out, and misrepresent here the whole matter. For I know of no enmity they have to the Church itself, but what it was in her power always to have remedied; and so it is still. But such as you it is that have alwayes strove by your leasings to keep up a strangeness and misunderstanding betwixt the King and his people; and all the mischief that hath come on't does lye much at your door.

Whereas they, as all the rest of mankind, are men for their own ends too; and no sooner hath the King shown them this late favour, but you, Mr. Bayes, and your partners, reproach them for being too much friends to the prerogative. And no less would they be to the Church, had they ever at any age in any time found her in a treatable temper. I know nothing they demand, but what is so far from doing you any harm, that it would only make you better. But that indeed is the harm, that is the thing you are afraid of. Here our Author divides the discourse into a great elogy [eulogy] of the Church of England, that if he were making her funeral sermon he could not say more in her commendation; and a contrary invective against the Nonconformists, upon whom (as if all he had said before had been nothing) he unloads his whole leystal, and dresseth them up all in *sanbenitas*, painted with all the flames and devils in hell, to be led to the place of execution, and there burnt to ashes. Nevertheless, I find on either side only the natural effect of such hyperboles and oratory; that is, not to be believed. The Church of England (I mean as it is by law established, lest you should think I equivocate) hath such a stock of solid and deserved reputation, that it is more than you, Mr. Bayes, can spoil or deface by all the pedantry of your commendation. Only there is that partie of the clergy, that I not long ago described, and who will always presume to be the only Church of England, who have been a perpetual eye-sore, that I may not say a canker and gangreen, in so perfect a beauty. And as it joyes my heart to hear any thing well said of her, so, I must confess, it stirs my choler when I hear those men pride and boast themselves under the mask of her authority. Neither did I therefore approve of an expression you here use: 'the power of princes would be a very precarious thing without the assistance of ecclesiasticks, and all government do's and must owe its quiet and continuance to the Church's patronage.' That is as much as to say, that but for the assistance of your Ecclesiastical Policy, princes might go a-begging; and that the Church, that is you, have the *jus patronatus* of the kingdom, and may present whom you think fitting to the crown of England. This is indeed something like the return of Popery, and right

   Petra dedit Petro, Petrus diadema Rudolpho.

The crown were surely well help'd up, if it were to be held at your convenience, and the Emperour must lead the Patriarch's ass all his life-time. And little better do I like your 'We may rest satisfied in the present security of the Church of England, under the protection of a wise and gracious prince; especially when, besides the impregnable confidence that we have from his own inclination, it is so manifest that he never can forsake it either in honour or interest.' This is a pretty way of cokesing [=coaxing] indeed, while you are all this while cutting the grass under his feet, and animating the people against the exercise of his ecclesiastical supremacy. Men are not so plain-hearted but they can see through this oblique rhetorication and sophistry. If there be no danger in his time of taking 'a pin out of the Church' (for that it is you intend), why do you then speak of it in his time, but that you mean mischief? But here you do not only mow the grass under his feet, but you take the pillow from under his head. 'But should it ever happen that any King of England should be prevailed with to deliver up the Church, he had as good at the same time resign up his crown.' This is pretty plain dealing, and you have doubtless secur'd hereby that prince's favour. I should have thought it better courtship in a divine to have said, O King, live for ever! But I see, Mr. Bayes, that you and your partners are very necessary men, and it were dangerous disobliging you. But as in this imprudent and nauseous discourse you have all along appropriated or impropriated all the loyalty from the nobility, the gentry, and the commonalty, and dedicated it to the Church; so I doubt you are a little too immoderate against the body of the Nonconformists. You represent them, to a man, to be all of them of republican principles, most pestilent, and *eo nomine* enemies to monarchy, traytors and rebels; such miscreants as never were in the world before, and fit to be pack'd out of it with the first convenience. And I observe that all the argument of your Book is but very frivolous and trivial; only the memory of the late War serves for demonstration, and the detestable sentence and execution of his late Majesty is represented again upon the scaffold; and you having been, I suspect, better acquainted with Parliament Declarations formerly upon another account, do now apply and turn them all over to prove that the late War was wholly upon a fanatical cause, and the Dissenting Party do still go big with the same monster. I grew hereupon much displeased with my own ignorance of the occasion of those troubles so near our own times, and betook myself to get the best information concerning them, to the end that I might, if it appeared so, decline the dangerous acquaintance of the Nonconformists, some of whom I had taken for honest men, nor therefore avoided their company. But I took care, nevertheless, not to receive impressions from any of their Party; but to gather my lights from the most impartial authorities that I could meet with. And I think I am now partly prepared to give you, Mr. Bayes, some better satisfaction in this matter. And because you are a dangerous person, I shall, as little as possible, say any thing of my own, but speak too before good witnesses. First of all, therefore, I will, without farther ceremony, fall upon you with the but-end of another Archbishop. 'Tis the Archbishop of Canterbury, Abbot, in the Narrative under his own hand, concerning his disgrace at Court in the time of his late Majesty. I shall only in the way demand excuse, if, contrary to my fashion, the names of some eminent persons in our Church, long since dead, be revived here under no very good character; and most particularly that of Archbishop Laud, who, if for nothing else, yet for his learned book against Fisher deserved far another fate than he met with, and ought not now to be mentioned without due honour. But those names having so many years since escaped the press, it is not in my power to conceal them; and I believe Archbishop Abbot did not write but upon good consideration.

This I have premised for my own satisfaction; and I will add one thing more, Mr. Bayes, for yours—that whereas the things now to be alledged relate much to some impositions of money in the late King's time, that were carried on by the clergy, I know you will be ready to carp at that, as if the Nonconformists had, and would be always enemies to the King's supply. Whereas, Mr. Bayes, if I can do the Nonconformists no good, I am resolv'd I will do them no harm, nor desire that they should lye under any imputation on my account. For I write by my own advice, and what I shall alledge concerning the clergie's intermeddling with supplies, is upon a particular aversion that I have, upon good reason, against their disposing of our money. And, Mr. Bayes, I will acquaint you with the reason, which is this: 'Tis not very many years ago that I used to play at picket; and there was a gentleman of your robe, a dignitory of Lincoln, very well known and remembred in the ordinaries, but being not long since dead, I will save his name. Now, I used to play pieces, and this gentleman would alwayes go half-a-crown with me; and so all the while he sate on my hand he very honestly *'gave the sign;'* so that I was alwayes sure to lose. I afterwards discovered it; but of all the money that ever I was cheated of in my life, none ever vexed me so as what I lost by his occasion. And ever since I have borne a great grudge against their fingering of any thing that belongs to me. And I have been told, and showed the place where the man dwelt in the late King's time, near Hampton Court, that there was one that used to rob on the highway in the habit of a bishop, and all his fellows rid too in canonical coats. And I can but fancy how it madded those, that would have perhaps been content to relieve an honest gentleman in distress, or, however, would have been less grieved to be robbed by such an one, to see themselves so episcopally pillag'd. Neither must it be less displeasing alwaies to the gentry and commonalty of England, that the clergy (as you do, Mr. Bayes,) should tell them that they are never *sui juris*, not only as to their consciences, but even as to their purses; and you should pretend to have this power of the keys too, where they lock their money. Nay, I dare almost aver, upon my best observation, that there never was, nor ever will be, a Parliament in England that could or can refuse the King supplies proportionable to his occasions, without any need of recourse to extraordinary wayes, but for the pickthankness of the clergy, who will always presume to have the thanks and honour of it, nay, and are ready alwayes to obstruct the parliamentary aids, unless they may have their own little project pass too into the bargain, and they may be gratified with some new Ecclesiastical Power, or some new law against the fanaticks. This is the naked truth of the matter. Whereas Englishmen alwayes love to see how their money goes, and if there be any interest or profit to be got by it, to receive it themselves. Therefore, Mr. Bayes, I will go on with my business, not fearing all the mischief that you can make of it.

'There was,' saith he, 'one Sibthorp, who not being so much as Batchelor of Arts, by the means of Doctor Pierce, Vice-chancellor of Oxford, got to be confer'd upon him the title of Doctor. This man was Vicar of Brackley in Northamptonshire, and hath another benefice. This man preaching at Northampton, had taught that princes had power to put poll-money upon their subjects' heads. He, being a man of a low fortune, conceiv'd the putting his sermon in print might gain favour at Court, and raise his fortune higher. It was at the same time that the business of the loan was on foot.' In the same sermon ' he called that loan a tribute; taught that the King's duty is first to direct and make laws; that nothing may excuse the subject from active obedience, but what is against the law of God or nature, or impossible; that all antiquity was absolutely for absolute obedience in all civil and temporal things.' And the imposing of poll-money by princes he justified out of St. Matthew: and in the matter of the loan, ' What a speech is this!' saith the Bishop; 'he observes the forwardness of the Papists to offer double.' For this sermon was sent to the Bishop from Court, and he required to licence it, not under his chaplain, but his own hand. But he, not being satisfi'd of the doctrine delivered, sent back his reasons why he thought not fit to give his approbation; and unto these Bishop Laud, who was in this whole business, and a rising man at Court, undertook an answer. 'His life in Oxford,' saith Archbishop Abbot, 'was to pick quarrels in the lectures of Public Readers, and to advertise them to the Bishop of Durham, that he might fill the ears of King James with discontent against the honest men that took pains in their places, and setled the truth (which he called Puritanism) in their auditors. He made it his work to see what books were in the press, and to look over epistles dedicatory, and prefaces to the reader, to see what faults might be found. 'Twas an observation what a sweet man this was like to be, that the first observable act he did was the marrying of the Earl of D. to the Lady R. when she had another husband, a nobleman, and divers children by him.' Here he tells how, for this very cause, King James would not a great while endure him, till he yielded at last to Bishop Williams his importunity, whom notwithstanding he straight strove to undermine, and did at last to purpose: for, saith the Archbishop, 'Verily such is his undermining nature, that he will underwork any man in the world, so he may gain by it. He call'd in the

Bishop of Durham, Rochester, and Oxford, tryed men for such a purpose, to the answering of my reasons, and the whole stile of the speech runs We, We. In my memory, Doctor Harsnet, then Bishop of Chichester, and now of Norwich (as he came afterward to be Archbishop of York), preached at Whitehall upon *Give unto Cæsar the things that are Cæsar's;* a sermon that was afterwards burned, teaching that goods and money were Cæsar's, and so the King's: whereupon King James told the Lords and Commons, that he had failed in not adding, according to the laws and customs of the country wherein they did live. But Sibthorp was for absolutely absolute. So that if the King had sent to me for all my money and goods, and so to the clergy, I must, by Sibthorp's proportion, send him all. If the King should send to the City of London to command all their wealth, they were bound to do it. I know the King is so gracious he will attempt no such matter; but if he do it not, the defect is not in these flattering divines.' Then he saith, reflecting again upon the loan, which Sibthorp called a tribute, 'I am sorry at heart the King's gracious Majesty should rest so great a building on so weak a foundation, the treatise being so slender, and without substance, but that proceeded from an hungry man.' Then he speaks of his own case as to the licensing this book, in parallel to the Earl of Essex his divorce; which to give it more authority, 'was to be ratified judicially by the archbishop.' He concludes, how finally he refused his approbation to this sermon, and saith, 'it was thereupon carried to the Bishop of London, who gave a great and stately allowance of it, the good man not being willing that any thing should stick with him that came from Court, as appears by a book commonly called the Seven Sacraments, which was allowed by his lordship with all the errors, which have been since expunged.' And he adds a pretty story of one Doctor Woral, the Bishop of London's chaplain, 'scholar good enough, but a free-fellow-like man, and of no very tender conscience,' who before it was licensed by the Bishop, Sibthorp's sermon being brought to him, 'hand over head approved it, and subscribed his name:' but afterwards hearing more of it, went to a counsel at the Temple, who told him, that by that book 'there was no *meum* nor *tuum* left in England, and if ever the tide turn'd, he might come to be hang'd for it;' and thereupon 'Woral scraped out his name again,' and left it to his lord to license. Then the Archbishop takes notice of the instructions for that loan. 'Those that refused, to be sent for souldiers to the King of Denmark. Oaths to be administred with whom they had conference; and who disswaded them, such persons to be sent to prison, &c. He saith that he had complained thrice of Mountague's Arminian book, to no purpose: Cosins put out his book of "Seven Sacraments" (strange things), but I knew nothing of it; but as it pleased my Lord of Durham and the Bishop of Bath, so it went.' In conclusion, the good Archbishop, for refusing this license of Sibthorp's sermons, was, by the under-working of his adversaries, first commanded from Lambeth, and confined to his house in Kent, and afterwards sequestred, and a commission passed to exercise the Archiepiscopal Jurisdiction to the Bishops of London, Durham, Rochester, Oxford, and Bishop Laud (who from thence arose in time to be the Archbishop). If I had leisure, how easy a thing it were for me to extract out of the Narrative a just parallel of our Author, even almost upon all points! but I am now upon a more serious subject, and therefore shall leave the application to his own ingenuity and the good intelligence of the Reader.

About the same time (for I am speaking within the circle of 2°, 3°, and 4° Caroli) that this book of Sibthorp's called 'Apostolical Obedience' was printed, there came out another of the same stamp, intitled 'Religion and Allegiance,' by one Doctor Manwaring. It was the substance of two sermons preached by him at Whitehall, beside what of the same nature at his own parish of Saint Giles. Therein he delivered for truth, 'that the king is not bound to observe the laws of the realm concerning the subject's rights and liberties, but that his royal word and command, in imposing loans and taxes without common consent in Parliament, does oblige the subject's conscience upon pain of eternal damnation; that those who refused to pay this loan offended against the law of God and the king's supream authority, and became guilty of impiety, disloyalty, and rebellion; that the authority of Parliament was not necessary for raising of aids and subsidies, and the slow proceedings of such great Assemblies were not fitted for the supply of the State's urgent necessities, but would rather produce sundry impediments to the just designs of princes.' And after he had been questioned for this doctrine, nevertheless he preached again, 'that the king had right to order all as to him should seem good, without any man's consent; that the king might, in time of necessity, demand aid, and if the subject did not supply him, the king might justly avenge it; that the propriety [=property] of estate and goods was ordinarily in the subject, but extraordinarily in the king; that in case of the king's need he hath right to dispose them.' He had besides, entring into comparison, called the refusers of the loan 'temporal recusants, and said, the same disobedience that they (the Papists, as they then called them) practise in spirituals, that or worse some of our side, if ours they be, dare to practise in temporals.' And he aggravated further upon them under the resemblance of Turks, Jews, Corah, Dathan and Abiram [Numbers xvi.]; ' which last,' said he, ' might as well liken themselves to the three children; or Theudas and Judas [Acts v. 35, 36], the two incendiaries in the daies of Cæsar's tribute, might as well pretend their cause to be like that of the Maccabees, as what the refusers alledged in their own defence.'

I should not have been so large in these particulars, had they been only single and volatile Sermons; but because this was then the doctrine of those persons that pretended to be the Church of England. The whole quire sung that tune, and instead of the Common Law of England and the statutes of Parliament, that part of the clergy had invented these Ecclesiastical Laws, which, according to their predominancy, were sure to be put in execution. So that between their own revenue, which must be held *jure divino*, as every thing else that belong'd to them, and the prince's, that was *jure regio*, they had not left an inch of propriety for the subject. It seemed that they had granted themselves letters of reprisal against the laity for the losses of the Church under Henry the Eighth, and that they would make a greater havock upon their temporalities in retaliation. And indeed, having many times since pondred with my greatest and earnest impartiality, what could be the true reason of the spleen that they manifested in those daies, on the one hand against the Puritans, and on the other against the Gentry (for it was come, they tell me, to Jack Gentleman), I could not devise any cause, but that the Puritans had ever since the Reformation obstructed that laziness and splendor which they injoyed under the Pope's supremacy, and the Gentry had (sacrilegiously) divided the Abby-Lands, and other fat morsels of the Church at the Dissolution, and now was the time to be revenged on them.

While, therefore, the kingdome was turned into a prison upon occasion of this Ecclesiastical Loan, and many of the eminentest of the gentry of England were under restraint, they thought it seasonable to recover once again their ancient glory, and to magnificate the Church with triumphant pomp and ceremony. The three ceremonies that have the countenance of Law would not suffice ; but they were all upon new inventions ; and happy was he that was endued with that capacity, for he was sure before all others to be preferr'd. There was a second service, 'the table set *altarwise*,' and to be called the '*altar;*' '*candles, crucifixes, paintings, imagery, copes, bowing to the east, bowing to the altar,*' and so many several cringes and genuflexions, that a man unpractised stood in need to entertain both a dancing master and a Remembrancer. And though these things were very uncouth to English Protestants, who naturally affect a plainness of fashion, especially in sacred things ; yet if those gentlemen could have contented themselves with their own formalitie, the innovation had been more excusable. But many of these additions, and to be sure, all that had any colour of Law, were so imposed and prest upon others, that a great part of the Nation was even put to it as it were to fine and ransom upon this account. What censures, what excommunications, what deprivations, what imprisonments! I cannot represent the misery and desolation as it hath been represented to me. But wearied out at home, many thousand of his Majestie's subjects, to his and the Nation's great loss, thought themselves constrained to seek another habitation; and every country, even though it were among savages and caniballs, appeared more hospitable to them than their own.

And although I have been told by those that have seen both, that our Church did even then exceed the Romish in ceremonies and decorations — and indeed, several of our Church did thereby frequently mistake their way, and from a Popish kind of worship fell into the Romish religion—yet I cannot upon my best judgment believe that that Party had generally a design to alter the religion so far, but rather to set up a new kind of Papacy of their own here in England. And it seemed they had, to that purpose, provided themselves of a new religion in Holland. It was Arminianism, which, though it were the republican opinion there, and so odious to King James that it helped on the death of Barnevelt, yet now they undertook to accommodate it to monarchy and Episcopacy. And the choice seemed not imprudent. For, on the one hand, it was removed at so moderate a distance from Popery that they should not disoblige the Papists more than formerly, neither yet could the Puritans, with justice, reproach these men as Romish Catholicks; and yet, on the other hand, they knew it was so contrary to the ancient reformed doctrine of the Church of England, that the Puritans would never imbrace it, and so they should gain this pretence further to keep up that convenient and necessary quarrel against Nonconformity. And accordingly it happened; so that here again was a new shiboleth. And the Calvinists were all studiously discountenanced, and none but an Arminian was judged capable and qualified for imployment in the Church. And though the king did declare, as I have before mentioned, that Mountagne's (*Arminian*) book had been the occasion of the schisms in the Church, yet care was immediately taken, by those of the same robe and Party, that he should be the more rewarded and advanced. As also it was in Manwaring's case; who, though by censure in Parliament made incapable of any ecclesiastical preferment, was straight made rector of Stamford-Rivers in Essex, with a dispensation to hold too his living in St. Giles's. And all dexterity was practised to propagate the same opinions, and to suppress all writings or discourses to the contrary.

So that those who were of understanding in those dayes tell me that a man would wonder to have heard their kind of preaching. How, instead of the practical doctrine which tends to the reforming of men's lives and manners, all their sermons were a very mash of Arminian subtilties, of ceremonies and decency, and of Manwaring and Sibthorpianism brew'd together; besides that in their conversation they thought fit to take some more license, the better to *dis-Ghibeline* themselves from the Puritans. And though there needed nothing more to make them unacceptable to the sober part of the Nation, yet moreover they were so exceeding pragmatical, so intolerably ambitious, and so desperately proud, that scarce any gentleman might come near the tayle of their mules. And many things I perceive of that nature do even yet stick upon the stomachs of the old gentlemen of those times. For the English have been always very tender of their religion, their liberty, their propriety [=property], and (I was going to say) no less of their reputation. Neither yet do I speak of these things with passion, considering at more distance how natural it is for men to desire to be in office, and no less natural to grow proud and intractable in office; and the less a clergyman is so, the more he deserves to be commended. But these things before mentioned grew yet higher, after that Bishop Laud was once not only exalted to the See of Canterbury, but to be chief Minister. Happy had it been for the King, happy for the Nation, and happy for himself, had he never climbed that pinacle. For whether it be or no, that the clergy are not so well fitted by education as others for political affairs, I know not, though I should rather think they have advantage above others, and even, if they would but keep to their Bibles, might make the best ministers of State in the world; yet it is generally observed that things miscarry under their government. If there be any counsel more precipitate, more violent, more rigorous, more extreme than other, that is theirs. Truly, I think the reason that God does not bless them in affairs of State is, because He never intended them for that imployment. Or if government and the preaching of the gospel may well concur in the same person, God therefore frustrates him, because, though knowing better, he seeks and manages his greatness by the lesser and meaner maxims. I am confident the Bishop studied to do both God and his Majesty good service; but, alas, how utterly was he mistaken! Though so learned, so pious, so wise a man, he seem'd to know nothing beyond Ceremonies, Arminianism, and Manwaring. With that he begun, and with that ended; and thereby deform'd the whole reign of the best prince that ever wielded the English scepter.

For his late Majesty being a prince truly pious and religious, was thereby the more inclined to esteem and favour the clergy. And thence, though himself of a most exquisite understanding, yet he could not trust it better than in their keeping. Whereas every man is best in his own post, and so the preacher in the pulpit. But he that will do the clergie's drudgery must look for his reward in another world. For they having gained this ascendent upon him, resolv'd, whatever became on't, to make their best of him; and having made the whole business of State their Arminian jangles and the persecution for ceremonies, did for recompence assign him that imaginary absolute government, upon which rock we all ruined.

For now was come the last part of the Archbishop's indiscretion; who, having strained those strings so high here, and all at the same time, which no wise man ever did, he moreover had a mind to try the same dangerous experiment in Scotland, and sent thither the Book of the English Liturgy to be imposed upon them. What followed thereupon is yet within the compass of most men's memories. And how the War broke out, and then to be sure 'Hell's broke loose.' Whether it be a war of religion or of liberty, is not worth the labour to inquire. Whichsoever was at the top, the other was at the bottom; but upon considering all, I think the cause was too good to have been fought for. Men ought to have trusted God; they ought and might have trusted the King with that whole matter. 'The arms of the Church are prayers and tears;' the arms of the subjects are patience and petitions. The King himself, being of so accurate and piercing a judgment, would soon have felt where it stuck. For men may spare their pains where nature is at work, and the world will not go the faster for our driving. Even as his present Majestie's happy

Restauration did it self, so all things else happen in their best and proper time, without any need of our officiousness.

But after all the fatal consequences of that Rebellion, which can only serve as sea-marks unto wise princes to avoid the causes, shall this sort of men still vindicate themselves as the most zealous assertors of the rights of princes? They are but at the best 'well-meaning zealots.' Shall, to decline so pernicious counsels, and to provide better for the quiet of government, be traduced as the Author does here, under these odious terms of 'forsaking the Church, and delivering up the Church'? Shall these men always presume to usurp to themselves that venerable stile of the 'Church of England'? God forbid! The Independents at that rate would not have so many distinct congregations as they. There would be Sibthorp's church, and Manwaring's church, and Montague's church, and a whole bed-roll [=bead-roll] more, whom for decency's sake I abstain from naming. And every man that could invent a new opinion, or a new ceremony, or a new tax, should be a new Church of England.

Neither, as far as I can discern, have this sort of the clergy, since his Majestie's return, given him better encouragement to steer by their compass. I am told that preparatory to that, they had frequent meetings in the city, I know not whether in Grub-street, with the divines of the other Party, and that there, in their

Feasts of Love, they promised to forget all former offences, to lay-by all animosities; that there should be a new heaven and a new earth, all meekness, charity, and condescension. His Majesty, I am sure, sent over his gracious Declaration of liberty to tender consciences, and, upon his coming over, seconded it with his commission under the broad seal for a Conference betwixt the two parties, to prepare things for an Accommodation, that he might confirm it by his royal authority. Hereupon what do they? Notwithstanding this happy conjuncture of his Majestie's Restauration, which had put all men into so good a humour, that, upon a little moderation and temper of things, the Nonconformists could not have stuck out; some of these men so contriv'd it, that there should not be the least abatement to bring them off with conscience and (which insinuates into all men) some little reputation. But, to the contrary, several unnecessary additions were made, only because they knew they would be more ingrateful and stigmatical to the Nonconformists. I remember one in the Letany, where to 'false doctrine and heresie' they added 'schism,' though it were to spoil the musick and cadence of the period. But these things were the best. To show that they were men like others, even cunning men, revengeful men, they drill'd things on, till they might procure a law, wherein, besides all the Conformity that had been of former times enacted, there might be some new conditions imposed on those that should have or hold any churchlivings, such as they assur'd themselves that, rather than swallow, the Nonconformists would disgorge all their benefices. And accordingly it succeeded; several thousands of those ministers being upon one memorable day outed of their subsistence. His Majesty in the mean time, although they had thus far prevailed to frustrate his royal intentions, had reinstated the Church in all its former revenues, dignities, and advantages; so far from the Author's mischievous aspersion of ever thinking of converting them to his own use, that he restored them free from what was due to him by law upon their first admission. So careful was he, 'because all government must owe its quiet and continuance to the Churche's patronage,' to pay them even what they ought. But I have observed, that if a man be in the Church's debt once, 'tis very hard to get an acquittance: and these men never think they have their full rights, unless they reign. What would they have had more? They rowl'd on a flood of wealth, and yet in matter of a lease would make no difference betwixt a Nonconformist and one of their own fellow-sufferers, who had ventured his life and spent his estate for the king's service. They were restor'd to Parliament, and to take their places with the king and the nobility. They had a new Liturgy to their own hearts' desire; and to cumulate all this happiness, they had this new law against the Fanaticks. All they had that could be devised in the world to make a clergyman goodnatur'd.

Nevertheless, after all their former sufferings, and after all these new enjoyments and acquisitions, they have proceeded still in the same track. The matter of ceremonies, to be sure, hath not only exercised their ancient rigour and severity, but hath been a main ingredient of their publick discourses, of their sermons, of their writings. I could not (though I do not make it my work, after a great example, to look over Epistles Dedicatory) but observe by chance the title-page of a book t'other day, as an emblem how much some of them do neglect the Scripture in respect to their darling ceremonies. 'A Rationale upon the Book of Common-Prayer of the Church of England, by A. Sparrow, D.D. Bishop of Exon. With the Form of Consecration of a Church or Chapel, and of the place of Christian Burial. By Lancelot Andrews, late Lord Bishop of Winchester. Sold by Robert Pawlet at the sign of the Bible in Chancery Lane.' These surely are worthy cares for the Fathers of the Church.

But, to let these things alone, how have they of late years demean'd themselves to his Majesty, although our Author urges their immediate dependance on the King to be a great obligation he hath upon their loyalty and fidelity? I have heard that some of them, when a great minister of State grew burdensome to his Majesty and the Nation, stood almost in defiance of his Majestie's good pleasure, and fought it out to the uttermost in his defence. I have been told that some of them in a matter of divorce, wherein his Majesty desired that justice might be done to the party agriev'd, opposed him vigorously, though they made bold too with a point of conscience in the case, and went against the judgment of the best divines of all parties. It hath been observed, that whensoever his Majesty hath had the most urgent occasions for Supply, others of them have made it their business to trinkle with the members of Parliament for obstructing it, unless the king would buy it with a new law against the fanaticks. And hence it is that the wisdom of his Majesty and the Parliament must be exposed to after-ages for such a superfœtation of Acts in his reign about the same business. And no sooner can his Majesty upon his own best reasons try to obviate this inconvenience, but our Author, who had before outshot Sibthorp and Manwaring in their own bows, is now for retrenching his authority, and moreover calumniates the State with a likelyhood, and the reasons thereof, ' of the Return of Popery into this Nation.' And this hath been his first method by the 'fanaticks raising disturbance:' whereupon if I have raked farther into things than I would have done, the Author's indiscretion will I hope excuse me, and gather all the blame for reviving those things which were to be buried in oblivion. But, by what appears, I cannot see that there is any probability of disturbance in the State but by men of his spirit and principles.

The second way whereby the fanatick party, he saith, may at last work the ruin of the Church, is 'by combining with the Atheists; for their union is like the mixture of nitre and charcoal, it carries all before it without mercy or resistance.' So, it seems, when you have made gunpowder of the atheists and fanaticks, we are like to be blown up with Popery. And so will the larks too. But his zeal spends itself most against the atheists, because they use to 'jeer the parsons.' That they may do, and no atheists neither; for really, while clergymen will, having so serious an office, play the drols and the boon-companions, and make merry with the Scriptures, not only among themselves, but in gentlemen's company, 'tis impossible but that they should meet with at least an unlucky repartee sometimes, and grow by degrees to be a tayle and contempt to the people. Nay, even that which our Author always magnifies, the reputation, the interest, the secular grandeur of the Church, is indeed the very thing which renders them ridiculous to many, and looks as improper and buffoonish, as to have seen the porter lately in the good Doctor's cassock and girdle. For, so they tell me, that there are no where more atheists than at Rome, because men seeing that princely garb and pomp of the clergy, and observing the life and manners, think therefore the meaner of religion. For certainly the reputation and interest of the clergy was first gained by abstracting themselves from the world, attending their callings, humility, strictness of doctrine, and the same strictness in conversation: and things are best preserved by the same means they were at first attained. But if our Author had been as concerned against atheisme as he is against their disrespect of his function, he should have been content that the fanatick preachers might have spent some of their pulpit-sweat upon the atheists, and made a noise in their ears about 'faith, communion with God, attendance upon ordinances,' which he himself jeers at so pleasantly. Neither do I like upon the same reasons his manner of discourse with the atheists, where he complains that ours are not like those good atheists of former times, who never did thrust themselves into publick cares and concerns, 'minding nothing but love, wine, and poetry.' Nor, in another place, 'put the case the clergy were cheats and juglers, yet it must be allowed they are necessary instruments of State to awe the common people into fear and obedience, because nothing else can so effectually enslave them' ('tis this, it seems, our Author would be at) 'as the fear of invisible powers, and the dismall apprehensions of the world to come: and for this very reason, though there were no other, it is fit they should be allowed the same honour and respect as would be acknowledged their due, if they were sincere and honest men.' No atheist could have said better. How mendicant a cause has he here made of it! They will say, they see where the shoo wrings him, and that though this be some ingenuity in him, yet it is but little Policy. Nay, perhaps they will say, that they are no atheists neither, but only, I know not by what fate, every day one or other of the clergy does or saith some so ridiculous and foolish thing, or some so pretty accident befalls them, that in our Author's words, 'a man must be very splenetick that can refrain from laughter.' I would have quoted the page here, but that the Author has, I think for evasion sake, omitted to number them in this whole Preface. But whether there be any atheists or no, which I question more than witches, I do not, for all this, take our Author to be one, though some would conclude it out of his principles, others out of his expressions. Yet really, I think he hath done that sort of men so much service in his books by his ill-handling, and while he personates one party, making all religion ridiculous, that they will never be able to requite him but with the same manner. He hath opened them a whole treasure of words and sentences, universally applicable, where they may rifle or chuse things, which their pitiful wit, as he calls it, would never have been able to invent and flourish. But truly, as the simple Parliament 5° Eliz. never imagined what consequence that clause in the Wednesday Fast would have to Puritanism, neither did he what his periods would have to atheism; and yet, though he is so more excusable, I hope I may have the same leave on him, as he on that Parliament, to censure his impertinence. To close this: I know a lady that chid her master of the horse, for correcting the page that had sworn a great oath. 'For,' saith she, 'the boy did therein show only the generosity of his courage, and his acknowledgement of a Deity.' And indeed he hath approv'd his Religion, and justified himself from atheism, much after the same manner.

The third way and last (which I, being tired, am very glad of) by which the fanaticks may raise disturbances, and so introduce Popery, is by joyning crafty and sacrilegious statesmen into the confederacy. But really here he doth speak concerning king and counsellors at such a rate, and describe and characterize some men so, whomsoever he intends, that though I know there are no such, I dare not touch; it is too hazardous. 'Tis true he passes his complement ill-favouredly enough. 'The Church has at present an impregnable affiance in the wisdom &c. of so gracious a prince, that is not capable of such counsels, should they be suggested to him: though certainly no man that is worthy to be admitted to his Majestie's favour or privacy can be supposed so fool-hardy or presumptuous as to offer such weak and dishonourable advice to so wise and able a prince; yet princes are mortal, and if ever hereafter (and some time or other it must happen) the crown should chance to settle upon a young and unexperienced head, this is usually the first thing in which such princes are abused by their keepers and guardians, &c.' But this complement is no better, at best, than if, discoursing with a man of another, I should take him by the beard. Upon such occasions in company, we use to ask, 'Sir, whom do you mean?' I am sure our Author takes it alwayes for granted that his Answerer intends him upon more indefinite and less direct provocations. But our Author does even personate some men as speaking at present against the Church: 'They will intangle your affairs, indanger your safety, hazard your crown. All the reward you shall have to compensate your misfortunes by following Church counsels, shall be that a few churchmen, or such-like people, shall cry you up for a saint or a martyr.' Still '*your, your,*' as if it were a close discourse unto his Majesty himself. Though if this were the worst that they said, or that the Author fathers upon them, I wish the King might never have better counsellors about him. But if the Author be secure, for the present, in his Majestie's reign, fears not Popery, not forsaking the Church, not assuming the Church revenues, why is he so provident? why put things in men's heads they never thought of? why stir such an odious, seditious, impertinent, unseasonable discourse? why take this very minute of time, but that he hath mischief, to say no worse, in his heart? He had no such remote conceit (for all his talk) of an infant coming to the crown. He is not so weak but he knows too much, and is too well instructed, to speak to so little purpose. That would have been like a set of Elizabeth players, that in the country having worn-out and over-acted all the playes they brought with them from London, laid their wits together to make a new one of their own. No less man than Julius Cæsar was the argument; and one of the chief parts was Moses perswading Julius Cæsar not to make war against his own countrey, nor pass the Rubicon. If our Author did not speak of our present times (to do which nevertheless had been sufficiently false and absurd), but writ all this meerly out of his providence for after-ages, I shall no more call him Bayes, for he is just such a 'second Moses.' I ask pardon if I have said too much; but I shall deserve none, if I meddle any further with so improbable and dangerous a business.

To conclude, the Author gives us one ground more, and perhaps more seditiously insinuated than any of the former; that is, if 'it should so prove,' that is, if the 'fanaticks, by their wanton and unreasonable opposition to the ingenious and moderate discipline of the Church of England, shall give their governours too much reason to suspect that they are never to be kept in order by a milder and more gentle government than that of the Church of Rome, and force them at last to scourge them into better manners, with the briars and thorns of their discipline.' It seems, then, that the discipline contended about is worth such an alteration. It seems that he knows something more than I did believe of the design in the late times before the War. Whom doth he mean by our governours? the King? No, for he is a single person. The Parliament, or the Bishops.

I have now done; after I have (which is, I think, due) given the Reader and the Author a short account how I came to write this Book, and in this manner. First of all, I was offended at the presumption and arrogance of his stile; whereas there is nothing either of wit or eloquence in all his books worthy of a reader's, and more unfit for his own, taking notice of. Then, his infinite tautology was burdensome, which seemed like marching a company round a hall upon a pay-day so often, till, if the muster-master were not attentive, they might receive the pay of a regiment. All the variety of his treat is *pork* (he knows the story), but so little disguised by good cookery, that it discovers the miserableness, or rather the penury, of the host. When I observed how he inveighs against the '*trading part*' of the Nation, I thought he deserved to be within the '*five-mile Act*,' and not to come within that distance of any corporation. I could not patiently see how irreverently he treated kings and princes, as if they had been no better than King Phys and King Ush of Brantford. I thought his profanation of the Scripture intolerable; for though he alledges that 'tis only in order to shew how it was misapplyed by the fanaticks, he might have done that too, and yet preserved the dignity and reverence of those Sacred Writings; which he hath not done, but on the contrary, he hath, in what is properly his own, taken the most of all his ornaments and imbellishments thence, in a scurrilous and sacrilegious style; insomuch that, were it honest, I will undertake out of him to make a better, that is a more rediculous and profaner book, than all the 'Friendly Debates' bound up together. Methought I never saw a more bold and wicked attempt than that of reducing grace, and making it a meer FABLE, of which he gives us the MORAL. I was sorry to see that even prayer could not be admitted to be a virtue, having thought hitherto it had been a grace, and a peculiar gift of the Spirit; but I considered that that prayer ought to be discouraged, in order to prefer the Liturgy. He seem'd to speak so little like a divine in all those matters, that the poet might as well have pretended to be the Bishop Davenant, and that description of the poet's of prayer and praise was better than our Author's on the same subject. Canto the 6th, where he likens prayers to the Ocean:

> 'For prayer the Ocean is, where diversly
> Men steer their course each to a several coast;
> Where all our interests so discordant lye,
> That half beg winds, by which the rest are lost.'

And praise he compares to the union of fanaticks and atheists, &c., that is, gunpowder; 'praise is devotion fit for mighty minds, &c.'

> 'Its utmost force, like powder, is unknown.
> And though weak kings excess of praise may fear,
> Yet when 'tis here, like powder, dangerous grown,
> Heaven's vault receives what would the palace tear.'

Indeed all Astragen appeared to me the better 'scheme of religion.' But it is unnecessary here to recapitulate all, one by one, what I have in the former Discourse taken notice of. I shall only add what gave, if not the greatest, yet the last impulse to my writing. I had observed in his first Book, page 57, that he had said 'some pert and pragmatical divines had filled the world with a buzze and noise of the Divine Spirit;' which seemed to me so horribly irreverent, as if he had taken similitude from the hum and buz of the humble-bee in the Rehearsal.

In the same Book, I have before mentioned, that most unsafe passage of our 'Saviour being not only in an hot fit of zeal, but in a seeming fury and transport of passion.' And striving to unhook himself hence, page 152 of his second Book, swallows it deeper, saying, 'Our Blessed Saviour did in that action take upon Him the person and priviledge of a Jewish Zelot.' Take upon Him the person, that is, *personam induere*. And what part did He play? of a Jewish zealot.

The second Person of the Trinity (may I repeat

these things without offence?) to take upon Him the person of a Jewish zealot, that is, of a notorious rogue and cut-throat!

This seemed to proceed from too slight an apprehension and knowledge of the duty we owe to our Saviour. And last of all, in this Preface, as before quoted, he saith, the 'Nonconformist preachers do spend most of their pulpit-sweat in making a noise about communion with God.' So that there is not one Person of the Trinity that he hath not done despite to; and lest he should have distinct communion with the Father, the Son, and the Holy Ghost, for which he mocks his Answerer, he hath spoken evil distinctly of the Father, distinctly of the Son, and distinctly of the Holy Ghost. That only remained behind, wherein our Author might surpass the character given to Aretine, a famous man of his faculty.

> Qui giace il Aretino,
> Chi de tutti mal disse fuor d' Iddio:
> Ma di questo si scusa, perche no 'l conobbe.

> Here lies Aretine,
> Who spoke evil of all, except God only;
> But of this he beggs excuse, because he did not know Him.

And now I have done. And I shall think myself largely recompensed for this trouble, if any one that hath been formerly of another mind shall learn by this example, that it is not impossible to be merry and

228   THE REHEARSAL TRANSPROSED.

angry as long time as I have been writing, without profaning and violating those things which are and ought to be most sacred.

Finis.

END OF PART I.

NOTE.

For Notes and Illustrations elucidative of the 'Rehearsal Transprosed,' both Parts, see end of the present Volume. G.

THE REHEARSAL TRANSPROSED:

PART II.

1673.

REPROOF, p. 67.

If you have any thing to object against it, do your worst.
You know the Press is open.

Licensed the 1st of May
1673.

By the Author and Licenser of the
Ecclesiastical Polity.

THE

REHEARSALL

TRANSPROS'D:

The SECOND PART.

Occasioned by Two Letters: The first Printed, by a nameless Author, Intituled, A Reproof, &c.
The Second Letter left for me at a Friends House, Dated Nov. 3, 1 6 7 3. *Subscribed* J. G. *and concluding with these words;* If thou darest to Print or Publish any Lie or Libel against Doctor *Parker,* By the Eternal God I will cut thy Throat.

Answered by ANDREW MARVEL.

LONDON,
Printed for Nathaniel Ponder *at the* Peacock *in* Chancery Lane *near* Fleet-Street, 1673.

THE REHEARSAL TRANSPROS'D:

THE SECOND PART.

THE Author of the Ecclesiastical Polity (why not Doctor Sermon?) doubts, with some reason, whether he has not in that study 'lost his understanding.' [The last line of his Preface to the Rep(roof).] To convince himself, therefore, and others of the contrary, he attempts to shew here at the beginning, that he not only knows as yet what he does, but remembers still the very circumstances of his actions. He tells me: 'I had heard from him sooner, had he not, immediately after he undertook my correction, been prevented by a dull and lazy distemper; but being now recruited, &c.' [Reproof, page 1.] Sooner or later imports not, it comes much to the same account. No Naturalist has determin'd the certain time of a mountain's pregnancy, how long it goes before it be deliver'd; but one has told us what kind of child it always produces. And as for his 'dull and lazy distemper,' the courtesie was no less superfluous to inform me of what most men have been long since fully satisfyed upon undeniable testimony. What is the world concerned in the revolutions of his health, or the courses of physick that he runs through at Spring and Fall? Plutarch, indeed, gives us the minutes of Alexander the Great's sickness after his last debauch; and the Dutch historian Aytzema is so punctual in the late Prince of Orange's malady, as even to chronicle in folio what days he did *excernere dura*, when *fœtida*, and when *fæces laudabiles*. What then? must it therefore follow that this Orange Doctor, by having commenced in this prince's train, is grown so considerable, that the 'temper of his mind,' the 'juncture of his affairs,' and the 'state of his body,' should be transmitted to posterity? that after-ages must read in what moon his invention was fluent, and in what *epocha* costive? that as in his late Preface he enter'd his 'closer importance' upon record, so in this voluminous pamphlet his close-stool too should be register'd? But suppose he were of such moment, he is too hard put to it, and but ill-befriended that he must do himself that office. Was there not one true Englishman left to help him? Ungrateful world, that when he has 'lost his labour and understanding' [The last line of Preface to Reproof] in writing them an Ecclesiastical Polity, would not afford him some other pen for his own Ecclesiastical History! But he is so self-sufficient, and an *At-all* of so many capacities, that he would excommunicate any man who should have presumed to intermeddle so far within his province. Has he been an Author? He is too the Licenser. Has he been a father? He will stand too for god-father. Is he then to be marryed? he asks his own banes [=bans] in print. And now after he thinks himself cured, and in wedding and writing case, he cannot forbear nevertheless but he must be publishing his diseases. Had he acted Pyramus, he would have been Moon-shine too, and the Hole in the Wall. That first author of Ecclesiastical Polity, Nero, was of the same temper. He could not be contented with the Roman Empire unless he were too his own Præcentor; and he in the same manner, out of meer charity, when he apprehended death, lamented only the detriment that mankind must sustain in losing so considerable a fidler. When a man is once possess'd with this fanatick kind of spirit, he imagines, if a shoulder do but itch, that the world has gall'd it with leaning on't so long, and therefore he wisely shrugs to remove the globe to the other. If he chance but to sneeze, he salutes himself, and courteously prays that the 'foundations of the earth' be not shaken. And even so the Author of the Ecclesiastical Polity, ever since he crept up to be but the weather-cock of a steeple, he trembles and creaks at every puff of wind that blows him about, as if the Church of England 'were falling, and the State totter'd.' And then after men are once come to mistake themselves as so necessary, it is no wonder if they impute it for a great obligation as oft as they condescend to give the publick an account of their privacies. There is not any so undecent circumstance of their life but they think it worthy to be committed to paper, and, foul as it is, yet they forthwith send it away to the Printer. And now all Christendom doubtless has taken notice that the Author of the Ecclesiastical Polity has lain-in of a 'dull and lazy distemper,' and to be sure the ecclesiasticks of his faculty have deeply sympathized with his condition. The news will, after the rebound of some months, reach Constantinople and Agra; and as soon as they hear of his recovery, the Mufti and the Mulla will certainly send to congratulate him. But however, he has, methinks, not dealt so kindly herein with his native Country as their universal concernment for him might have deserved. For though indeed there must needs be a mighty profit upon the exportation of his Book, and those especially beyond the Line will think it a great advantage to buy the account of his health at any rate with so large a volume into the bargain; yet he might, out of gratitude to our curiosity, have advertis'd us at home the cheaper way, by the same Gazette in which he cries his Book to make it vendible. Whereas the inserting it thus in so thick an octavo is a most palpable project upon men's affections, and next to imposing his Book upon the Church-wardens of every parish, and the Chapters of all the cathedrals. As well as men love him, yet they desire not that his sickness should be as chargeable to the countrey as a Visitation. Nay, even the clergy scruple at the price, and take it ill, that as oft as their Archdeacon comes abroad again in print, they should be oblig'd in this manner to pay procurations and synodals. But of all men it falls most severely upon the Nonconformists, who, having been exhausted with so many other penalties formerly, cannot so well afford to buy their penance so dear, and take off his Books every year in commutation. 'Tis true, he has been kind to them, and to such a degree that he hath done more service to their cause by writing against it, than all their own authors that ever writ for them. But that therefore being so contrary to his intention, the accident diminishes the courtesie. And if yet for 'old acquaintance' sake they could be content to give somewhat for 'a book in some places erroneous, in some places scarce sense, and of ill consequence' [Gregory, p. 104; concerning the English Bible] they compute that if 'the Reproof to the Rehearsal Transpros'd, in a Discourse to its Author, by the Author of the Ecclesiastical Policy,' be of the same nature, and at the same price, it is, however, better of the two to buy an English Bible with all its faults. He is return'd to be a 'precious man' indeed, more precious than ever heretofore at the University; if, since he arose to be the Author of the Ecclesiastical Polity, a poor fanatick that has been of his intimacy cannot be inform'd how he does under the prodigal expence of five shillings.

He cannot sure take it unkindly if I enter into a further consultation of the nature of his indisposition, and the remedies, seeing he has so voluntarily interessed me therein, and his readers; for the officious always spring game to the curious. The disease being, as he relates, so dull and lazy, I should think at first that it might have been a lethargy; and whereas he imagines himself recruited, that he has only in order to a cure (as is usual in that case) been cast into a feaver. For he has forgot himself most extreamly, and his whole Discourse, as proceeding from a man in the confines of two so contrary distempers, partakes all thorow equally of stupidity and raving.

But when I reflect further upon the symptoms, and his description, it seems more probably to be the *Abelteria*, a Greek discomposure, and to which those of his constitution are generally subject. The malignity of this affects the mind rather than the body, and therefore lies further beyond the reach of physick. When once it takes a man, he is desperate, and there is no more possibility of his recovery: nor is that strange, it being the property of those that have it, by how much they grow worse, to conceive always that they are in a better condition.

Some indeed will have it, that under those terms of 'a dull and lazy distemper' he calumniates a more active and stirring disease (as the spleen and the scurvy do oftentimes bear the blame of another infirmity), and that it is no Grecian malady, but derives its name from a countrey much nearer. But that 'distemper is so unsuitable to the civility of his education and the gravity of his profession' [Reproof, p. 1], that I question much whether it could be so clownish and licentious (bold though it be) to accost a personage of his figure and character. Yet who knows after that new alliance in the year 1665 betwixt nature and divinity, that amorous season of his *Tentamina Physico-Theologica* (if he were the Author), whether his nature may not have given his divinity the slip, and running its own random, have met with some misadventure? For even then he had learnt how Aristotle worshipped his wench under show of sacrificing to a goddess. [Tent. Phys. p. 2.] He inform'd us so early how Stilpo disputing before the Areopagites that Minerva could not be a God, because she was a woman, and therefore a goddess, Theodorus somewhat smuttily ask'd him, whether he had seen her without her shift. [Idem, p. 14.] And this reparty [=repartee] of Theodorus he recommends there for so ingenious, that he ranks it among his colours why that philosopher, who called himself God, should not be counted an atheist; though I can scarce discern any more wit or theology in it then[1]

[1] =than. So is it throughout, with, I think, only four exceptions. I print accordingly 'then' and 'than' just as they occur; and this explanation must suffice for all. G.

in his own argument lately among a knot of eminent divines, the women being present—that the rest of the clergymen's wives were but dish-clouts, his own a goddess; and they had been perfectly quit, had but Stilpo now cap'd Theodorus, by telling him that they were all, however, no more than needed to scowre his mouth after so slovenly a comparison. In the same Book he demonstrates at large how impossible it was (though Epicurus his opinion) for mankind to be produced at first from certain vesicles or pimples of the earth. [Tent. Phys. from p. 68 to p. 77 and p. 112.] You would wonder to see how solidly and elaborately, with what dint of reason he confutes so dangerous an heresy, to the great instruction doubtless and advantage of Sir John Hinton and Dr. Chamberlain. [Idem, from p. 99 to p. 108.] Then he takes their office out of their hands, and proceeds immediately to read a public Lecture of the figure and use of the vessels of generation, and more especially those of the female. [Idem, p. 106.] Like a forward chick, he pecks through Dr. Harvye's egg-shell, and tells us that most famous physician was not so cunning as he should have been in the chief mystery of the seminal business. [Reproof, p. 227.] At last this blushing gentleman, this very picture of modesty, in open terms undertakes to explain the pleasure annex'd to the act of procreation [Tent. Phys. p. 108], and is so tickled with the imagination (presaging too, perhaps, that it might ere long be his fortune to dine with a God (so he stiles the Archbishop), and bed a Goddess (so he calls his mistress), that although he censures Lucretius for speaking so broad, yet he cannot refrain from using his own words: 'that 'twas so excessively sweet, as to be the solace not only of mankind but the Deities.' [*Divum hominumque voluptas.*] And all this stir is there made by the present Author of the Ecclesiastical Polity, in order, forsooth, to prove God's providence; as if that could not be or were not sufficiently evidenced without his gossiping collections of naked midwifery. Insomuch that one who understood not beyond his Latine might justly doubt, whether by the *Tentamina Physico-Theologica* he meant indeed the essays of his divinity, or the temptations of his nature. Neither can it in reason seem strange if the vigorous and frequent contemplation of such objects transported him further, and her too, as well as other creatures, might (to use his own phrase), 'out of that vehement and unbridled concupiscence, rush *in furias ignemque*' [Tent. Phys. page 105], thorow fire and water upon a dangerous experiment against the 'pimples of the earth and Paracelsus his limbeck.' [Tent. Phys. p. 73.] For he himself, in a succeeding Book (said to be his) [Cens. Plat. Phil. p. 211], the 'Censure of the Platonick Philosophy,' confesses 'that if in any respect virtue and religion intrench upon the liberty of our natures, 'tis in the instances of sensuality; and that when the man is divided from the beast, and his reason separated from the inferiour and brutish appetites, then arise irregular and unreasonable desires, &c.;' so that by his own acknowledgment, it is not impossible but the man in him may at some time have been obliged to carry the brute a pick-a-pack. Only there is this difference betwixt his beast and others, that his mind, it seems, is more subject to irregular and unreasonable desires when abstracted within itself; whereas the reason of other men suffers most in conjunction with the inferiour and brutish appetites. So that although in the same Book he magnifies those spruce gentlemen the Platonists, [Cens. Plat. Phil. p. 19] ' as being professedly the most generous contemners of women in the world;' and affirms, ' that their amours (for they were accused of sodomy) were not kindled by lust and petulancy, but were pure and cleanly enough to become angels and separated souls;' though in the usual pompous explication of his own perfections he glories [Idem, p. 15] ' that he hath tasted less of sensual delights than he thinks any one placed in the said circumstances and capacities ; for he hath hitherto scarce employed any of his senses but that of seeing;'—notwithstanding all those preventive insinuations, I see no reason to trust him further then I would the curate of Ikham, with his maid Mary Parker. But I rather suspect that where he stops short in the career of a sentence—[Idem, p. 123] ' that he thinks nothing concerns him so much as those designs that aspire to serve his dearest'—the rest was bawdy. For though he were on the road to Canterbury, let any female but cross his way, 'tis odds that his beast will stumble, and throw his Archdeaconship in the cart-rut, with his whole tridentine portmantle of polity and theology. Yet though I speak these things with some certainty, to evidence them to others would require a more difficult scrutiny. For whatsoever 'twas that befell him, he has been so concern'd of late to stop all avenues and every cranny of intelligence, that were he to pass through the discipline of sweating, there could not have been more strictness about the doors and the windows. And then his physicians, on the other side, are shut up as close by the obligation of their faculty, having all of them sworn secrecy to Hippocrates. Neither is it indeed at first sight probable that, if he were so obnoxious to them, one of so 'sweet a nature' should so openly declare himself against the Nonconformists. Had he been cured by a Jew, so great a prince as the Author of the Ecclesiastical Polity would surely, either out of his clemency or his wisdom, have been gracious to the whole tribe; and for his doctor's sake, have at least conniv'd at their Synagogue. He is not the first that Phys. has whisper'd out his kingdom: [Rehearsal Comedy, p. 17, 18]; and yet if he thought the matter once secured from discovery, I question much whether any other tie could hold him. For I know none so loose from all the restrictions of humanity as some within his girdle; and were there a Court of faculties for that purpose, he could not take out more ample dispensations from common ingenuity and gratitude. So that there could not have been more conformity betwixt the person and the disease, and an 'implacable divine' could never be better fitted, than with that distemper which his Italian author can tell him does sometimes make truce, but never admits a pacification [*fa tregua, ma non mai pace*]. But he is, I perceive, a very 'secret one,' in another sense then formerly, and perhaps did only publish his malady the better to disguise it; so that I will not, out of respect, press this point further. If he should by giving so partial an account fail of a cure, he is the more excusable; for it will have been the first time that his modesty did him prejudice. Yet this caution, for humanity's sake, I would leave with him; that he trust not too much to the asse's milk in his Hicringill's Dispensatory [Gregory (Greybeard), p. 119]; for every one knows, that if he have no better specifick, he will ever and anon be troubled with the reliques.

But whatever old mischief may possibly lurk in his body, I am told by one, who pretends to the best intelligence, that this was a new disease, which spred much through the nation about last autumn. I hear not that any dyed of it; and therefore its name is not yet read of in the bills of mortality. To be short; as I am certainly inform'd, he was sick of the Rehearsal Transpros'd. Then, indeed, the Rehearsal Transpros'd deserved a Reproof for exceeding its commission. I am sorry if that should occasion a distemper which I ordered as physick; the Rehearsal Transpros'd being, too, only a particular prescription in his case, and not to be applyed to others without special direction. But some curious persons would be licking at it; and most men finding it not distastful to the palate, it grew in a short time to be of common use in the shops. I perceive that it wrought a sensible alteration in all that took it; but varying in some for the better, in others for the worse, according to the difference of their complexions. Some were swoln up to the throat, some their heads turn'd round, and others it made their hearts ake; but all these were but a few in number; most men found only a little tingling in their ears, and after its greatest violence, it discharged itself in an innocent fit of uncessant laughter. But the greatest harm it did was to the Author of the Ecclesiastical Polity, for whose good it was principally intended: for before he had half taken it, his spirits began to fail him, and it put him past not only 'the common drudgeries' of preaching and reading prayers, but those other things too which he stiles 'the innocent comforts of humane life.' So that he laid it by for a considerable time, and was resolv'd to have taken no more of it, finding it so contrary to his nature. In that interval, his humours being stir'd, the predomineering choler in a short time diffus'd it self so through his body ecclesiastick, that it struck him into a deep jaundice; and his soul seem'd to have set up a gilt vehicle of the new lacker. The great little animal was on a sudden turn'd so yellow, and grown withall so unwieldly, that he might have past current for the elephant upon a guinny. For, as he had long since foretold, 'having been so inconsiderate as to write books, and faln so lately under the severe lash of one that knew him not' [Cens. Plat. Phil. p. 1], it was his concurring misfortune to be now 'exposed to the severer commands of those that knew him.' The cause was at present much altered from what in his Preface to Bishop Bramhall, and over and above the importunity of the Bookseller, he was now obliged to write in canonical obedience. But his yellow coife rendered him very unfit to appear in publick, and being troubled thus with the jaundice, and under a necessity of exercising at the same time all the remainders yet left him of reason, wit, or invention, 'tis probable that he found indeed cause to complain of a 'dull and lazy distemper,' and now too late repented 'that he had sold himself into so great a slavery.' [Idem, p. 1.] However, having driven himself into that condition, he must now needs go through with his task; and therefore the time too being limited, he hastened to bring himself in plight by such common remedies as were next to hand, writing too all the while by girds and snatches hand over head. His other self Hicringill (who seems very well informed of all his distempers, and of this particularly) had told him that a louse was good against the jaundice, and the Author of the Ecclesiastical Polity himself had for all events the 'Sacrament of Lousiness' by him of his own preparation [Reproof, p. 112] : so that this being much easier to be procured than the tribute of fleas was to be collected, there is no doubt to be made but that he tryed the vertue of this medicine. And as the Tartars cracking the same vermine with their teeth are used to wish solemnly that they had their enemies at the like advantage; so methinks I see how he snapp'd them e're they got down, and ever [and] anon prayed betwixt the teeth for the Nonconformists. But he had heard how his old accquaintance Doctor Rabelais, upon examination for his degree, answer'd that if his Gargantua were sick, he would prescribe him *pilulas evangelicas, ex centum libris aloes et myrrhæ*. He computed thence, that in his own case the dose must be proportionable betwixt the civil and the ecclesiastical giant. And if so, that though all prisons should be depopulated, though Beggars-bush pillaged, though the *phthiriases* of all former persecutors revived, yet the quantity would not be sufficient; but as once the incense of all Arabia was spent on one funeral, so the lice of all the world must be consumed upon his malady. But what he most consider'd was, that this must necessarily end in an utter dissolution of the government of the Phthirophagi, and that contrary to all good Ecclesiastical Polity, the 'Presidents of the sacred

Rites' (for the other orders of men 'twas less matter) should, in reference to his cure, be depriv'd of that 'lean and slender subsistence' which was yet left them. This would have been a sacrilege greater, because more universal, than to have rifled the louse out of St. Francis his bosom. So that upon this Algebra and prospect, he desisted at last from the lousy diet, partly out of his good nature, partly out of his conscience, and partly out of impossibility. And had he at the same time betaken himself in good earnest to the *Extractum Apostoli* of Faith, Hope, and Charity, as a succedaneum (for even his second Rabelais, Doctor Hicringill [Gregory, p. 93], renders them equivalent to a louse), he had been certainly cured both mind and body. But some doubt there is that his Shop Divines [Reproof, p. 21] have not the right composition of that medicine. However, he was not now in case or disposition to take it; and the Rehearsal Transpros'd, which after many a grimasse he had now at last gulp'd down, had so terribly disorder'd him, that he had quite forgot there was any such remedy in the ancient praxis of Christianity [Pref. to Eccl. Pol. p. 1]. But this gentleman of 'so tame,' if you will believe him, 'and softly an humour, of so cold a complexion, that he scarse thinks himself capable of hot and passionate impressions;' he that is only offended at them 'who will not suffer themselves to be embraced by those whose unbounded embraces would comprehend all' [Cens. Plat. Phil. p. 25], and '*quan-*

quam alias præmitis sit indolis' [Tent. Phys. p. 109], was altered beyond all imagination. I cannot determine whether I being but a new unlicensed practitioner, and the Rehearsal Transpros'd my first experiment, there might be some errour in the preparation, and it were too 'strong of the mineral,' or whether indeed it were the extraordinary foulness of his stomack. But it hath brought up such ulcerous stuff as never was seen; and whereas I intended it only for a diaphoretick, to cast him into a breathing sweat, it hath had upon him all the effects of a vomit. Turnip-tops, frogs, rotten eggs, brass-coppers, grasshoppers, pins, mushrooms, &c. wrapt up together in such balls of slime and choler, that they would have burst the Dragon, and in good earnest seem to have something supernatural. Insomuch that he seems not so fit at present for the Archdeacon's seat, as to take his place below in the Church among the *Energumeni*. But it is possible that after so notorious an evacuation he may do better for the future; and it is more than visible that either his disease or his nature cannot hold out much longer. Therefore I shall not grudge from time to time to lend him my best assistance, though I hope that this iteration will do his business, and carry off all the dregs of his distemper. And now from what I have said hitherto, and that I may begin so far an accommodation betwixt us, I shall, if he please, recant, and yield that the 'asswaging his concupiscence, and wreaking his malice, has been the highest pinnacle of his Ecclesiastical infelicity.'

Having treated him in as short a method as so chronical a malady would admit, I shall now be inforced to remove some dirt, that I may make my way cleaner to come at him, for otherwise there is no passing; but then I shall quickly have dispatch'd with him. He saith [Reproof, p. 1], 'I have cowardly and dishonourably accosted him in such a clownish and licentious a way of writing, as I knew to be unsuitable both to the civility of his education and the gravity of his profession.' I thought I had in the close of my former Book, and all thorow, sufficiently satisfy'd him of the reasons and way of my proceeding with him; but seeing he hath it seems so soon forgot them (as men willingly do what it is grievous to remember), I shall now at more leisure refresh his memory, and deduce the order of my thoughts upon that and this occasion.

Those that take upon themselves to be Writers are moved to it either by ambition or charity: imagining that they shall do therein something to make themselves famous, or that they can communicate something that may be delightful and profitable to mankind. But therefore it is either way an envious and dangerous imployment. For, how well soever it be intended, the world will have some pretence to suspect, that the Author hath both too good a conceit of his own sufficiency, and that by undertaking to teach them he implicitly accuses their ignorance: so that not to write at all is much the safer course of life. But if a man's fate or genius prompt him otherwise, 'tis necessary that he be copious in matter, solid in reason, methodical in the order of his work; and that the subject be well chosen, the season well fix'd, and, to be short, that his whole production be matur'd to see the light by a just course of time and judicious deliberation. Otherwise, though with some of these conditions he may perhaps attain commendation; yet without them all he cannot deserve pardon. For indeed, whosoever he be that comes in print, whereas he might have sate at home in quiet, does either make a treat, or send a chalenge to all readers; in which cases, the first, it concerns him to have no scarcity of provisions, and in the other, to be compleatly arm'd; for if anything be amiss on either part, men are subject to scorn the weakness of the attaque, or laugh at the meanness of the entertainment. In conclusion, the Author of the Ecclesiastical Polity hath in his own particular very fully stated and comprehended this whole matter; for he saith here in his Preface to the reader, that [Preface to Reply, p. *penult*] 'if his book have any effect' (I suppose he means any good effect), 'he hath a double reward' (that is, both the publick and his private satisfaction); 'but if it have none' (that is impossible), 'that then he hath his own reward' (that is sure to be accounted none of the wisest) : and indeed this reward too is double; for if he fails of his design, he saith [Idem, p. *ult.*] 'he must confess that he hath lost his labour and his understanding.' This is the common condition, to which every man that will write a Book must be content with patience to submit.

But among all the differences of writing, he that does publish an invective does it at his utmost peril; and 'tis but just that it should be so. For a man's credit is of so natural and high concernment to him, that the preserving of it better was perhaps none of the least inducements at first to enter into the bonds of society and civil government; as that government too must at one time or other be dissolved where men's reputation cannot be under security. 'Tis dearer than life itself; and (to use a thought something perhaps too delicate, yet not altogether unreasonable) if beside the laws of murther, men have thought fit, out of respect to humane nature, that whatsoever else moves to the death of man should be forfeit to pious uses, why should there not as well be deodands for reputation? And this I intend not only of those who publish ignominious falshoods, to whom no quarter ought to be granted, but even of such partly who, by a truth too officious, shall procure any man's infamy. For 'tis better that evil men should be left in an undisturbed possession of their repute, how unjustly soever they may have acquired it, then that the exchange and credit of mankind should be universally shaken, wherein the best too will suffer and be involved. It is one thing to do that which is justifiable, but another that which is commendable; and I suppose every prudent Writer aims at both: but how can the Author of an invective, though never so truely founded, expect approbation (unless from such as love to see mischief at other men's expence), who, in a world all furnished with subjects of praise, instruction, and learned inquiry, shall studiously chuse and set himself apart to comment upon the blemishes and imperfections of some particular person? Such men do seldom miss too of '*their own reward;*' for whereas those that treat of innocent and benign argument are represented by the Muses, they that make it their business to set out others ill-favouredly do pass for Satyres, and themselves are sure to be personated with prick-ears, wrinkled horns, and cloven feet.

Yet if for once to write in that stile may be lawful, discreet, or necessary, to do it a second time is lyable to greater censure. Not so much because the aftermeath seldom or never equals the first herbage (a caution not unfit, however, for all authors), as that bystanders will begin then to suspect that what they look'd on first as an accident with some divertisement, do's rather proceed from a natural malignity of temper. For few readers are so ill-natured but that they are quickly tired with personal and passionate discourses;

and when the contest comes to be continued and repeated, if they interest themselves at all, they usually incline to think that the justice lies on the weaker side. But whether the last appeal of writers lie to the readers or to a man's own ultimate recollection, this invective way cannot be truly satisfactory either to themselves or others. For it is a prædatory course of life, and indeed but a privateering upon reputation; wherein all that stock of credit, which an honest man perhaps hath all his age been toyling for, is in an hour or two's reading plunder'd from him by a free-booter. So that whatsoever be the success, he that chances in these contests to be superiour can at best (for that too is disputable) be accounted of the two the less unfortunate. And certainly (as it was usual of old for any man who had but casually acted in an unlucky rencounter) he that hath had his pen once in the reputation of another, ought to withdraw, and disappear for some time, till he has undergone and past through all the ceremonies of expiation.

But if the credit of all men whatsoever be, and ought to be, so well guarded both by nature, law, and discretion, the clergy certainly, of all others, ought to be kept and preserv'd sacred in their reputation. For they being men of the same spirit with others, and no less subject to humane passions, but confined within the regularity of their function, it is indeed unmanly, whatsoever scuffle others may make among themselves, to vilifie or treat them with those affronts, which nothing but the respect of decency or conscience could hinder them from resenting as well as others. But (which is more considerable) whoever too shall fix upon them an ill report, does thereby frustrate the very effect of their ministry in proportion. For though baptism is not to be vacated by the contrary intention of him that officiates, yet few men will or can be persuaded by his doctrine whose practice they conceive to be opposite. A conversation differing from doctrine is spiritual non-sence; neither will men believe by the ear, when their eye informs them otherwise. If an artificer indeed make his work fit for men's wearing, it is sufficient; or if he that sells have good of the kind, men inquire no further. No man's shooe wrings him the more because of the heterodoxy or the tipling of his shoemaker; and a billet burns as well though bought of whatsoever woodmonger; but the clergy being men dedicate by their vocation to teach what is truth, what falshood, to deter men from vice, and lead them unto all virtue, 'tis expected from them, and with good reason, that they should define their opinion by their manners. And therefore men ought to be chary of aspersing them on either account, but even reflect upon their failings with some reverence. A clergyman ought to have treble damages, both for his tithes and his credit; and it were to be wish'd that with the same ease that their maintenance comes in from the fruits of men's labour, they had too no less proportion out of the yearly increase of every man's reputation: the rest would thrive the better for it. Their virtues are to be celebrated with all incouragement; and if their vices be not notoriously palpable, let the eye, as it defends its organ, so conceal the object by connivence.

And yet nevertheless, and all that has been said before being granted, it may so chance that to write, and that satyrically, and that a second time and a third, and this too even against a clergyman, may be not only excusable, but necessary. That I may spare a tedious recapitulation, I shall prove all the rest upon the strongest instance, that is in the case of a clergyman. For it is not impossible that a man by evil arts may have crept into the Church thorow the belfry or at the windows. 'Tis not improbable that, having so got in, he should foul the pulpit, and afterwards the press, with opinions destructive to humane society and the Christian religion; that he should illustrate so corrupt doctrines with as ill a conversation, and adorn the lasciviousness of his life with an equal petulancy of stile and language. In such a concurrence of misdemeanors what is to be done? Why certainly, how pernicious soever this must be in the example and consequence, yet before any private man undertake to obviate it, he ought to expect the judgment of the Diocesan, and the method of the ecclesiastical discipline. There was in the ancient times of Christianity a wholsome usage, but now obsolete, which went very far in preventing all these occasions. For whosoever was to receive ordination, his name was first published to the congregation, in the same way as the banes [=bans] of those that enter into matrimony; and if any could object a sufficient cause against him that was proposed, he was not to be admitted to the ministry. He that would be a preacher was to be first himself commented upon by the people, and in the stile of those ages was said *prædicari*. But since that circumspection has been devolved into the single oversight of the later Bishops, it cannot be otherwise but some one or other may sometimes escape into the Church who were much fitter to be shut out of doors. Yet then if our great pastors should but exercise the wisdom of common shepheards, by parting with one to stop the infection of the whole flock, when his rottenness grew notorious; or if our clergy would but use the instinct of other creatures, and chase the blown deer out of their herd, such mischiefs might quickly be remedied. But, on the contrary, it happens not seldom that this necessary duty (which is so great a part of true Ecclesiastical Politie) is not only neglected, but that persons so dangerous are rather encouraged by their superiors, and he that upon their omission shall but single out one of them, yet shall be exposed to the general outcry of the faculty, and be pursued with bell, book, and candle, as a declared and publick enemy of the clergy. Whereas they ought to consider that by this way of proceeding, they themselves do render that universal which was but individual, and affix a personal crime upon their whole order; and, for want of separating from one obnoxious, do contribute to the causes of separation, justifying so far that schism which they condemn. In this case, and supposing such a failure of justice in those whose province it is to prevent or punish, I ask again, what is to be done? Why, certainly the next thing had been to admonish him in particular, as a friend does his friend, or one Christian another. But he that hath once printed an ill book has thereby condens'd his words on purpose, lest they should be carried away by the wind; he has diffused his poyson so publickly, in design that it might be beyond his own recollection, and put himself deliberately past the reach of any private admonition. In this case it is that I think a clergyman is laid open to the pen of any one that knows how to manage it; and that every person who has either wit, learning, or sobriety, is licensed, if debauch'd, to curb him; if erroneous, to catechize him; and if foul-mouth'd and biting, to muzzle him. For they do but abuse themselves who shall any longer consider or reverence such an one as a clergyman, who as oft as he undresses degrades himself, and would never have come into the

Church but to take sanctuary. Rather, wheresoever men shall find the footing of so wanton a satyr out of his own bounds, the neighbourhood ought, notwithstanding all his pretended capering divinity, to hunt him thorow the woods with hounds and horn, home to his harbour.

How far and whether at all the Author of the Ecclesiastical Politie is culpable on these accounts, I must refer to the reader's judgment upon perusal of my first and this my second Book, though I could much rather wish that men would be at leisure to take the length of him out of his own discourses. But had he not appear'd so to me, I should never have molested him, adventur'd myself, or interested the publick by writing in this manner. For I am too conscious of mine own imperfections to rake into and dilate upon the failings of other men; and though I carry always some ill nature about me, yet it is, I hope, no more than is in this world necessary for a preservative; but as for the clergy, the memory of mine own extraction, and much more my sense of the sanctity of their function, ingage me peculiarly to esteem and honour them. Insomuch that for their sakes I bear much respect even to their poor wives, of whom I may say (as Bishop Bramhall comparing the Readers with the Preachers, and who understood both), that 'if they come short of other women in point of efficacy, yet they have the advantage of other women in point of security.' [Bishop

Bramhall's Vindication, page 160, 161.] And though I am not so inamour'd of them as to worship 'em for Goddesses, yet I am so far from rejecting them as 'dish-clouts,' that what the Author of Ecclesiastical Politie [Preface to Bishop Bramhall, page 41] affirms of the clergy of the Church of England, 'I dare averre' concerning their wives, 'that, taking them under all their disadvantages, they are at this very time vastly the furthest off from being justly contemptible (to mention no other order or profession of women) of any clergymen's wives in the world. The preëminence is so evident, that it clears the comparison from all possible suspicion of being proud or odious.'

Being of this temper, there could be no great appearance of my being over forward to come out in print in such a stile against one of his cloth, unless upon some very extraordinary occasion. And such this occasion seemed to me, and so urgent and justifiable, that it might absolve me in any reader's opinion. For this sharpness of stile does indeed for the most part naturally flow from the humour of the Writer: and therefore 'tis observable that few are guilty of it but either those that write too young (when it resembles the acidity of juices strained from the fruits before they be matured), or else those that write too old (and then it is like the sowrness of liquors which being near corrupting turn eager), and both these are generally disrelish'd; or if men do admit them for sawce, yet he must be very thirsty that will take a draught of 'em; whereas the generousest wine drops from the grape naturally without pressing, and though piquant hath its sweetness. And though I cannot arrogate so much as even the similitude of those good qualities to my writing, yet I dare say that never was there a more pregnant ripeness in the causes. For having read one, two, three, and now four Books of the same Author, and of the same subject, which was no less then that weighty matter of Ecclesiastical Politie and all its dependances, I observed first that there was no name to them,—a thing of very ill example. For every one that will treat of so nice and tender argument ought to affix his name, thereby to make himself responsible to the public for any damage that may arise by his undertaking. Otherwise, though he has a license in his pocket, or be perhaps the Licenser, it is but a more authoriz'd way of libelling; and it looks too like a man that shall lay a train of gunpowder, and then retire to some obscure place, from whence, after he has applyed his match, he may solace himself with the mischief; or, though it be not so design'd, yet the effect is not more probably to stop a flame than to propagate it, and instead of preserving, to subvert and blow up the government; whereas if men were obliged to leave that anonymous and sculking method both of writing and licensing, they would certainly grow more careful what opinions they vented, what expressions they used, and we might have miss'd many books that have of late come out by the same authority contrary to all good manners, and even to the doctrine of our Church under which they take protection. Had there been no other cause but this, it might have sufficed; and when Ecclesiastical Politie [Preface to Ecclesiastical Politie, page 16: 'Let the author of the "Friendly Debate" be careful how he layes aside his vizor'] marched Incognito, and Theology went on mumming, it was no less allowable for any one to use the license of mascarade [masquerade] to show him and the rest of 'em the consequence of such practice.

But beside this, when I perused his Books, and others of the same patern, I saw that they plainly incroached upon other men's vocations, and that a sort of divines, among whom he always acted the highest parts, had clann'd together to set up above those of the King and Duke a new company of comedians.[1] Such was their dramatick and scenical way of scribling, and they did so teem with new Plays perpetually, that there was no post nor pillar so sacred that was exempt, no not even the walls of Paul's itself, much less the Temple-gate, from the pasting up of the titles. Insomuch that I have seen a lacquey that could not read, having been sent to take down the Play for the

[1] Pref[ace] to Ecc[lesiastical] Pol[itie], page 16, 'many things are only design'd to set off his reasonings with a comical humour and pleasantness.'

afternoon, has by mistake brought away the title of a new book of theology. Yet if they did it well, they might perhaps in time get some custom ; but, alas, those great men in the pulpit how ridiculous do they appear on a stage! and he that has all his life been cramp'd in a reading-pew, at what a loss must he be when he comes to tread in whatsoever theater ! They are so unfit to bear a part among any civil and judicious company, that whatsoever place they may hold in the Church, I am confident they must make all their friends to be but receiv'd into the nursery. And had not Mr. Killigrew foreseen that they must of course within a little time fall to dirt of themselves, he would ere this, to be sure, have trounced the Author of the Ecclesiastical Politie, for intrenching upon his patent. But he knew they were below his neglect, and the Pit would quickly do their business, and not only hiss but pelt them off the stage. And I, that had sate so long more quiet than all the rest of the spectators, could not at last restrain myself from using also the liberty of the House, and revenging the expense of my time and money, by representing the Author of the comedy call'd the Ecclesiastical Politie in that Farse of mine own, the Rehearsal Transpros'd.

Neither yet was this all that deserved reprehension in his Writings. He useth such a ruffian-like stile, and upon which, to my knowledge, he peculiarly values himself, that any one would suspect he had travell'd and convers'd all his life-time either among the nation of the Bravos and Filoux, or else been educated in the academy of the Venetian galleys, which he himself was in his second Book so apprehensive of, that he never rested until he had found in his third how to supply [Eccl. Pol. p. 223] them with slaves out of the Nonconformists. [Cens. Plat. Phil. p. 1.] But I perceive since, that men of his parts can arrive at those perfections sitting but in their closets and overhearing the watermen, which others, after their long voyages and observation, neither would nor could ever attain to. Then the arrogance which runs through all his Books is insupportable, boasting proudly of himself, vilifying and censuring others to such a degree, that, as I never heard any thing equal, so neither any thing like it, but the mountebanks abroad, who, after a deal of scaffold pageantry to draw audience, entertain them by decrying all others with a panegyrick of their own balsam. There is scarce any sort and rank of men ancient or modern, scarce any particular person, though of the most established and just reputation, but he does, if he meet them, not hale them into his way, to inveigh against them and trample upon them, nay, even such as have but a book, or two, or three before (perhaps a page, perhaps a line) been happy in his good opinion. And this he does for the most part in the most bitter manner that is possible: I know not whether I may properly call it satyrical, but let it go so for once; for what he wants in wit he supplies, however, in good will; and where the conceit is deficient, he makes it out always with railing. He scarce ever opens his mouth but that he may bite; nor bites, but that from the vesicles of his gums he may infuse a venom. Had he been but innocently dull, he might have been sure no man would have medled with him: but when there was no end of his buttering one Book upon another, and he still writ worse and worse, with less vigour alwayes, but more virulence, that perpetual grating did indeed set my teeth on edge, and I thought that even the most candid readers would out of their equity not take it amiss, if at last he did, by hearing ill himself, lose part of that pleasure which he had so frequently taken in traducing and speaking hitherto ill of others. For no man needs letters of mart against one that is an open pirate of other men's credit: and I remember within our time one Simons, who robbed alwayes upon the Bricolle, that is to say, never interrupted the passengers, but still set upon the thieves themselves, after, like Sir John Falstaff, they were gorged with a booty; and by this way, so ingenious that it was scarce criminal, he lived secure and unmolested all his dayes, with the reputation of a judge rather than a highwayman. But my greatest incentive was, as I told him in my former pamphlet, the perniciousness of the whole design of his Books; tending, in my opinion, to the disturbance of all government, the misrepresenting of the generous and prudent counsels of his Majesty, and raising a mis-intelligence betwixt him and his people; beside his calumniating the whole foraign Protestancy, his stirring up of persecution against those at home, and his mangling even of Religion itself and Christianity: and to this purpose he suited befitting principles, and to those a language as harmonious: seeming to have forgot not only all Scripture rules, but even all Scripture expressions; unless where he either distorts them to his own interpretation, or attempts to make them ridiculous to others; insomuch that, of all the Books that ever I read, I must needs say I never saw a Divine guilty of so much ribaldry and prophaneness. Which though it was a matter of such decency to his undertaking, that I account it to have been even necessary, yet in the whole I look'd upon it as so uncanonical and impious, that it would bear an higher and more deserved accusation than that of Onias, the son of Simeon the Just, for officiating in a woman's zone instead of the priestly girdle, and for the sacred pectoral wearing his mistress's stomacher. I must confess, that when all these things centred together upon my imagination, and I saw that none of his superiors offer'd to interpose against an evil so great in itself, and as to me appear'd so publick in the consequence and mischief, I could hold no longer, and I, though the most unfit of many, assumed upon him the priviledge (if any such priviledge there be) of an English Zelote.

Otherwise I indeed look'd upon him, whosoever he were, as a person in parts much my superior, until the cause, as he took and handled it, had depress'd and levell'd his understanding; neither could I ever discover before such an exuberance either in mine own abilities, which I am sensible how mean, or yet in my inclination, that should tempt me from that modest retiredness to which I had all my lifetime hitherto been addicted. And truly after I had written, I had so slender an opinion of mine own performance, that I can attribute the acceptance which it found only to his favour, who had so handled the matter, that nothing could have come out at that time against him but must be assured of welcom. And that among the other more weighty causes, by reason of his unspeakable arrogance before mention'd: a vice so generally odious, that to repress it is no less grateful; so that Lucretius might better have said that to be '*Divum hominumque voluptas;*' there being scarce any spectacle more pleasing to God and Man than to see the proud humbled. But could I have imagined that my Book could have had either so good or so ill a reception as it diversely met with, I have so much respect to those whom he calls the vulgar, and to whom he bids always universal contempt and defiance, as a rout of wolves and tigers, apes and baboons [Cons. Plat. Phil.

p. 34, 35], that I should however have bestow'd more pains upon it: I know not whether with better success. Yet the errours of that not being now revocable but by asking pardon of whosoever may have innocently mistaken my Book, and declaring, which I do, that if any thing therein do tend to the disparagement of the Church of England, I wish it unsaid, as it was unthought, and do hereby utterly disclaim it; I took it to be part of my gratitude to go no more to sea, having been sufficiently toss'd for one man upon the billows of applause and obloquy to put me in mind of a ship-wrack, which, when the waves go high, may either way happen. And as to the Author of the Ecclesiastical Polity himself, whose person I was so far ignorant of that I could only take aim at his errours, and much less could intend any other of that function, but those few who might assume to themselves his character; I found, nevertheless, after the writing of that Book, that natural relenting of mind which most men feel after they have done an harsh though necessary action. Insomuch that had it been in my power to have set him right again in men's opinions, as it was in his to set himself wrong, I should have certainly done it. But for that, he and every one else may please to believe as they shall see occasion. But this, however, must be evident which follows.

Whereas I had in that Book, as is in that stile usual, intermixed things apparently fabulous with others probably true, and that partly out of my uncertainty of the Author, and partly that if he pleas'd he might continue so; it seems, however, that I chanced to come so near his form that it started him, and he thought fit to discover himself. Hereupon, and having understood what he was about, I thought it my duty, if possible, to break off this ruder intercourse for the future, and reduce the matter unto a more manly way of argument. I therefore took care to advertise him that I heard from several hands, that if in the answer intended there were any unjust and personal reflections, it would tend much to the disreputation of himself and some persons whom he most esteemed, and that there was preparation made to that purpose. Upon this he sent me word, that if any Answer were intended, 'twas more than he was acquainted with, or would concern himself about; and assured me my private reputation, nor no man's else, should ever be injured in publick by his consent. I do not by quoting this answer of his pretend to sue his word, to which he is no more a slave than to the Venetian galleys (such men being at liberty to comment upon their own as well as other texts at their pleasure). Nevertheless before this, and at that present time, as well as ever since, I understood that he had sent out a general *siquis* thorow his own province and the other, to make inquisition concerning me. He voiced my Book all over as a most pernicious engine bent against the whole body of the clergy. And upon that pretence he summon'd in all that ow'd suit and service to his Court, or the Church of England. The whole *posse Archidiaconatus* was raised to repress me, and great riding there was, and sending post every way to pick out the ablest ecclesiastical drolls to prepare an Answer. Some came in daily as voluntiers, and others were more mercenary. For certainly there was never such an hubbub made about a sorry book; and, since the day of St. Bartholomew, there has not appear'd so great an expectation of an universal donative. Some one flatter'd himself with being at least a Surrogate; another was so modest as to set up with being but a Paritor; while the most generous hoped only to be graciously smiled upon and well treated at a good dinner. But the more hungry starvelings generally look'd upon it as an immediate call to a benefice; and he that could but write an Answer, whatsoever it were, took it for the most dexterous, cheap, and legal way of simony. So that, as is usual upon those occasions, there arose no small competition and mutiny among the pretenders; and it being impossible to satisfie them all, many an one departed with a sad heart and dejected countenance, when their Answers would not pass muster. For it was not every book that could now be admitted. 'Twas requir'd upon this occasion to gain a license, that there should be some wit more than ordinary, which most of them could not be at the expense of; some measure of impudence, which few of them would pretend to; and above all, such a proportion of falshood as might alone have supply'd the other defects, and made their books current; but scarce any of them would do it out of good conscience. For that indeed was now the principal business, and the only argument that, as he had handled it, remain'd to this cause; and therefore the Author of the Ecclesiastical Polity had altered his lodgings to a Calumny Office, and kept open-chamber for all comers, that he might be supplyed himself, or supply others, as there was occasion. But though he had been a little choice at first, the informations came in so slenderly, that he was glad to make use of any thing rather than sit out: and there was at last nothing so slight but it grew material; nothing so false, but he resolved it should go for truth; and what wanted in matter, he would make out with invention and artifice. So that he and his remaining camarades [=comrades] seem'd to have set up a glass-house, the model of which he had observed from the height of his window in the neighbourhood, and the art he had been initiated into ever since from the manufacture (he will criticize because not orifacture) of soape-bubbles he improv'd by degrees to the mysterie of making glass-drops, and thence in running leaps mounted by these virtues to be Fellow of the Royal Society, Doctor of Divinity, Parson, Prebend, and Archdeacon. The furnace was so hot of itself that there needed no coals, much less any one to blow them. One burnt the weed, another calcined the flint, a third melted down that mixture; but he himself fashion'd all with his breath, and polished with his stile; till out of a meer jelly of sand and ashes he had furnish'd a whole cupboard of things so brittle and incoherent, that the least touch would break them again in pieces, so transparent that every man might see thorow them.

In the mean time such care was used, that the license of my Book was recall'd, and the Rehearsal Transprosed was dubbed a theological book, only to bring it under the verge of that jurisdiction, on purpose that it might be prohibited. It hath indeed been usual to degrade a priest, or scrape a shaven crown, to deface his character before he were deliver'd over to secular justice; but this was a strange and contrary method to force a poor book into holy orders, that so it might be subjected to censure and execution by the Ordinary. This was an honour which, to my knowledge, the poor book neither affected nor deserved; though indeed it might have deserved it as well as the Preface to Bishop Bramhall, which occasion'd its writing; and that 'tis true came out in state, under the title of a theological book, in the printed catalogue of that year, as several others do of the same nature. When he had thus provided that my book should not speak for it self, and moreover used means, which having proved ineffectual I shall not particularize, to obstruct me from liberty of ever vindicating it for the future, it seem'd to him the most favourable season that ever was, or could have been invented, to keep his promise, and to publish his answers, to preserve 'my private reputation.' For one Answer would not suffice; but therefore, to fit his ware for the purse and fancies of all chapmen, and to ingratiate not only the booksellers, but the pedlers, he order'd the matter so, and digested it into several volumes, that a man might buy a groat, sixpence, a shilling, eighteen pence, half-a-crown, or five shillings'-worth of theological wit and verity, as he saw occasion. The rest issued promiscuously; only before that which was to bear his own character, and the other which was to be call'd Hicringill's, were divulged, he procured that I should be asked by good authority, whether the Rehearsal Transprosed were of my doing, which I under my hand avowed. By this means he had gained, however, three points, as he imagined. The first, that he should thereby have some months' time more to mature two such excellent pieces, which he intended as the Hercules' pillars and *ne-plus-ultras* of the reason, wit, sobriety, good-breeding, and orthodoxy of the clergy of the Church of England. The next, that he should now be able to take such certain aim at me, that he might, every shot he made, hit me in the eye, or at least (for I have to do with a very critical adversary) in its cavity, for I suppose his first arrow must have struck the eye out. And the last, doubtless, that having let me know 'that he would not concern himself,' and 'assur'd me that my private reputation, nor any man's else, should ever by him be injur'd in publick'—he might now be understood I was the professed Author —give by these books so ample testimonial of his own veracity. Though for some other reasons beside this last, I had rather conceive it might have been more expedient for him not to have been so inquisitive of the Author, or at least, after he had learnt it, not to have taken that notice of me. Not that I assume to myself any of those lineaments wherewith he describes me; but however, after I had own'd the Rehearsal Transpros'd, whatsoever in either of his books he reflects upon the Author he must acknowledge as said by himself of me, and directed to me. At last, when all other plots and clancular contrivance against me had failed him, these two books also, which he had kept in reserve, were in some haste printed off; his day of marriage too drawing fast on, which he intended to calendar by a victory, and would perhaps have been deferr'd longer by the friends, had he not first signaliz'd his prowess. So that now there were no less than half a dozen Answers out against me (not to mention several other pamphlets, wherein the authors or booksellers, by drawing-in but by head and shoulders one line perhaps concerning the Rehearsal Transpros'd, or by only naming it, hoped to procure vent or better their livelyhood). He had thus got a *sixiesme du valet* in his hand already, and if he can but show three more of the same honour to make a *quatorze*, I am repiqued inevitably and spoyled for a gamester by a dignitary much superior to him of Lincoln. There were no less than six Scaramuccios together upon the stage, all of them of the same gravity and behaviour, the same tone, the same habit, that it was impossible to discern which was the true Author of the Ecclesiastical Politie. I believe he imitated the wisdom of some other princes, who have sometimes been perswaded by their servants to disguise several others in the regal garb, that the enemy might not know in the battel whom to single. But for my part, though I know that several gentlemen, and some of them divines, are commonly named as the authors of those books, yet they are persons for the most part of more candour, learning, and good judgment, than that I should suspect the truth of it, or that they could possibly descend to so mean and contrary an undertaking. And even that 'Gregory Greybeard,' which alone of all the six pretends to a father, and to be writ by one that hath not only a surname, but a christen-name also, it sounds so strangely and unlike the name of any human creature, that rather than so, it seems to me a word of cipher, like the Smectymnus formerly of the Presbyterians; and so Hicringill, to denote the club of this whole party. But it is more probably by much the issue of the very same Author of the Ecclesiastical Politie. If it should be any other, 'tis a thing more remarkable than what is reported of the two learned brothers of St. Marthe, who being twins, and living to a great age, were so like one another, that they were not to be distinguish'd, but that one wore a plain-band and the other a ruff; nay, their minds had no less similitude, insomuch that having withdrawn all day to study at any time on the same subject, when they came to compare at night, they should find that they had lit for the most part upon the same conceptions. For he that shall read the Reproof to the Rehearsal Transpros'd, and then this Hicringill, will discern so little difference in their expressions, humour, and thoughts (such as no man else could have hit upon), as he must necessarily infer and conclude that they are the works of one and the same artificer; and so much I can prove, that if any one were not of his penning, yet all of them pass'd under his inspection, approbation, or license. So that upon perusal of all those books that have appear'd in so many several shapes against me—first 'Rosemary and Bayes,' then the 'Common Places,' next the 'Transproser Rehears'd,' fourthly 'S'too him, Bays,' afterwards the 'Reproof,' and in fine 'Gregory Graybeard'[1] —I find plainly that 'tis but the same ghost that hath

---

[1] See our ESSAY for notices of all these 'Replies' to Marvell. G.

haunted me in those differing dresses and vehicles. Insomuch that, upon consideration of so various an identity, methinks, after so many years, I begin to understand Doctor Donne's Progress of the Soul, which pass'd through no fewer revolutions, and had hitherto puzzled all its readers. For

> 'This great soul, which here amongst us now
> Does dwell, and to which Luther and Mahomet were
> Prisons of flesh—this soul, which oft did tear
> And mend the wracks of th' Empire and late Rome,
> And liv'd when every great change did come,' (st. 7)

did nevertheless fix itself at first in so mean a condition, as is scarce credible, in a chast and innocent apple (st. 9). But that being soon pluck'd, it betook itself into a mandrake, and

> 'To show that in Love's business he should still
> A dealer be, and be us'd well or ill,
> His apples kindle, his leaves force of conception kill.' (st. 15)

('Tis pity that his Curate of Ickham was not acquainted with its virtues.) From this it took its flight into a sparrow, and lived a chirping life, as is there described:

> 'Already this hot cock, in bush and tree,
> In field and tent, o'erflutters its next hen,' &c. (st. 20)

From thence it drop'd, I know not how, into a little fish (st. 23); after that into another little fish (st. 25), and there learnt the art of tipling, which it practis'd for some time in that moderate proportion. But next, in its third swimming leap, it pitch'd into a whale (st.

31), and grew up to be the great Leviathan—'Now drinks he up seas—' (st. 34)

> ... 'and ever as he went,
> He spouted rivers up.' (st. 32)

Immediately after this, the soul by some misadventure dwindled into a mouse, but a very busie mouse, and of great design, so that

> ... 'being late taught that great things might by less
> Be slain, to gallant mischief it doth itself address.' (st. 38)

and pick'd out no less opposite than an elephant to buckle with,

> 'Who, foe to none, suspects no enemies,' &c. (st. 39)

and having crept up thorow his trunk, was gnawing his brain-strings asunder; but suddenly was crush'd under the ruines of so great an adversary. In process of time it enter'd into a wolf, and infested Abel's flock (st. 41):

> 'Abel, as white and mild as his sheep were,
> Who, in that trade of church and kingdoms, there
> Was the first type;'

but being hindred by a vigilant bitch (st. 42), the wolf corrupted her to his purpose; yet at last was taken in a trap and kill'd. But straight it entered into the young Lycisca (st. 43), that was new-knotted, and the whelp growing up, was imploy'd by Abel in keeping the same flock; but the mungrel was not to be trusted, for partaking of both natures (st. 45),

'He, as his damme, from sheep drove wolves away,
And, as his sire, he made them his own prey.
Five years he liv'd, and cozened with his trade:'

and then coming at last to be discovered,

'From dogs a wolf, from wolves a dog hath fled,
And like a spy, to both sides false, he perishèd.'

The soul, being then at a loss, got admittance into an ape, which being very facetious and full of gambolls, grew into great favour with Madam Siphatecia; but for some ugly tricks, and making too bold with his mistresse's apron, he was with a great stone knock'd dead by Thelemite, her brother. After this soul had passed thorow so many brutes, and been hunted from post to pillar, its last receptacle was in the humane nature, and it housed itself in a female conception; which, after it came to years of consent, was married to Cain by the name of Themech. This was the sum of that witty fable of Doctor Donne's, which, if it do not perfectly suit with all the transmigrations of mine Answerer, the Author of the Ecclesiastical Politie, nor equal the Progress of so great a prince, yet whoever will be so curious as himself to read that poem, may follow the parallel much farther than I have done, lest I should be tedious to the reader by too long and exact a similitude. But if it do not quadrate here, the resemblance will perhaps be more visible upon the examination of what remains to be considered next to the '*gravity of his profession*,' that is, the '*civility of his education,*' which he charges me by my former book to have discomposed. For it is the interest of the publick, especially he appealing to it upon this particular, that it should remain upon record how syllogistical a life his hath been to the stile and principles that he has manag'd and prosecuted.

Whoever shall go back to trace his original, will quickly be at a stand, and find themselves so soon involved in the fabulous age, that they will run astray, and be benighted in his history before noon. They will find his Saturn to have reign'd much later than William the Conquerour; or if, like a true-born Arcadian, he derive himself from before the moon, it must be understood concerning the last change. I cannot yet learn, though he hath imployed me about it, who was his grandfather; but, as modern as he must have been, 'tis the certainer heraldry to extract him from a ' vesicle of the earth,' and let him go for the grandson of a pimple. For no prince, how great soever, begets his predecessors; and the noblest rivers are not navigable to the fountain. Even the parentage of the Nile is yet in obscurity, and 'tis a dispute among authors whether Snow be not the head of his pedigree. I read indeed, as long ago as in the reign of Edward the Fourth, concerning one Henry Parker, a Carmelite Friar, who having preach'd against the secular grandeur and pomp of the clergy in those times, was forced to make a publick recantation at Paul's-Cross. But this is too obsolete : and though otherwise the analogy might easily be propagated, yet I suppose the honest monk kept to his vow of continence; and besides, should the Author of the Ecclesiastical Politie descend from that line, it would make too great a solecism in his scutcheon. There was also in the latter end of Queen Elizabeth, and beginning of King James, one Robert Parker, the author of another kind of Ecclesiastical Politie, a learned but severe Nonconformist, who writ also the book *De Cruce*, for which he was forced to cross the seas. But neither can I find him to come within the proportion of time or scale of his genealogy. Therefore, to come nearer, I find in the reign of the late King Charles one Humfrey Parker, yeoman, who, together with Mr. Chancey, for opposing the rails about the Communion Table at Ware, was sentenced to make a solemn submission and acknowledgment of his fault, as he did accordingly. There are several arguments that might incline me to think the Author of the Ecclesiastical Politie is com'd of his succession, and one particularly, because in the record I read 'that this Humfrey took a journey upon this occasion into Northamptonshire, the seat of the Answerer's family. But that which seems to come nearest home to him and the chronology of his grandfather, is in the year 1640, in a petition from the city of London and several counties to the then Parliament; complaining, among other things, of Martin Parker's ballads, in disgrace of religion, to the increase of all vice, and withdrawing of people from reading, studying, and hearing the Word of God and other good books. 'Tis not at all unlikely that this, as an hereditary provocation, hath stuck upon him ever since, and that he swore at the altar, when he was but nine years old, to be aveng'd for this affront to his lineage. We see often that the signature of the grandfather revives upon the child, and, as some rivers diving for a while under ground, make a bridge of the parents to spring up again at that interval. Hence, doubtless, hath proceeded all his peek against the Nonconformists; hence that unquenchable Nemesis against the City; hence it is that he hath taken upon him to defend in gross at this time the whole mass of enormityes, right or wrong, then complained of in that petition: all this mischief for a ballad-maker's sake of the kindred. The Duke of Muscovy indeed declared war against Poland because he and his nation had been vilifyed by a Polish poet; but the author of the Ecclesiastical Politie would, it seems, disturb the peace of Christendom for the good old cause of a superannuated chanter of Saffron-Hill and Pye-Corner. But though indeed he doth not write his books in the Smithfield meetre, yet they are all blank ballad, and the subject and consequence 'to the disgrace of religion, the increase of all vice, and withdrawing people from reading, studying, and hearing the Word of God and other good books,' is exactly the same. So that he may when he will put in for letters of administration in the Prerogative Court, and enter his claim too with the Heralds; for every one will yield him to be the next-of-kin to that Author; or let him but produce his own writings, 'tis evidence sufficient. If it should prove otherwise, the fault is in his own obscurity, that hath left all the neighbourhood and me in the dark; and let him make what shift he will to procure himself a grandfather, for I have taken pains enough, I am sure, to help him to one.

But however, for that matter, let the worst come to the worst, he had a mother undeniably, and probably a father: otherwise he would be shrewdly disappointed, and in a worse case than Prince Prettyman lamenting,

' What oracle this secret can evince,
Sometimes a fisher's son, sometimes a prince:
It is a secret great, as is the world,
In which I, like the soul, am toss'd and hurl'd.'
(Rehearsal Comedy, p. 27.)

And he might with good reason exclaim more pathetically : ' Bring in my father ; why d'ye keep him from me ? Although a fisherman, he is my father.'

' Was ever son yet brought to this distress,
To be for being a son made fatherless ?
O you just heavens, rob me not of a father :
The being of a son take from me rather.' (Idem, p. 26.)

His mother is said to have been an honest yeoman's daughter, and to have been his father's servant, with whom she lived with good reputation, and so ever since her marriage; except what disgrace may have reflected from her issue, which being her grief and misfortune, ought not to be her scandal. But though he came of a good mother, he had a very ill sire. He was a man bred toward the Law, and betook himself, as his best practice, to be a sub-committee-man, or, as the stile ran, one of the Assistant Committee in Northamptonshire. In the rapine of that employment, and what he got by picking the teeth of his masters, he sustain'd himself till he had raked together some little estate. And then, being a man for the purpose, and that had begun his fortune out of the sequestration of the estates of the King's Party, he, to perfect it the more, proceeded to take away their lives; not in the hot and military way (which diminishes always the offence), but in the cooler blood and sedentary execution of an High Court of Justice. Accordingly he was preferr'd to be one of that number that gave sentence against the three Lords, Capel, Holland, and Hamilton, who were beheaded. By this learning in the Law he became worthy of the degree of a serjeant, and sometimes to go the Circuit, till for misdemeanor he was petition'd against. But for a taste of his abilities, and the more to reingratiate himself, he printed, in the year 1650, a very remarkable Book, called 'The Government of the People of England, precedent and present the same. *Ad subscribentes confirmandum, Dubitantes informandum, Oppo-*

nentes convincendum; and underneath, *Multa videntur quae non sunt, multa sunt quae non videntur.* Under that ingraven two hands joyn'd, with the motto, *Ut uniamur;* and beneath a sheaf of arrows, with this device, *Vis unita fortior;* and to conclude, *Concordia parvae res crescunt, discordia dilabuntur.*' A most hieroglyphical title, and sufficient to have supplied the mantlings and atchievements of the family! By these parents he was sent to Oxford, with intention to breed him up to the ministry. There in a short time he enter'd himself into the company of some young students who were used to fast and pray weekly together; but for their refection fed sometimes on broth, from whence they were commonly called Grewellers; only it was observed that he was wont still to put more graves than all the rest in his porridge. And after that he pick'd acquaintance not only with the brotherhood at Wadham Colledge, but with the sisterhood too, at another old Elsibeth's, one Elizabeth Hampton's, a plain devout woman, where he train'd himself up in hearing their sermons and prayers, receiving also the Sacrament in the house, till he had gain'd such proficience, that he too began to exercise in that Meeting, and was esteem'd one of the preciousest young men in the University. But when thus, after several years' approbation, he was even ready to have taken the charge, not of an 'admiring drove or heard,' as he now calls them, but of a flock upon him, by great misfortune the King came in by the miraculous providence of God, influencing the distractions of some, the good affections of others, and the weariness of all towards that happy Restauration, after so many sufferings, to his regal crown and dignity. Nevertheless he broke not off yet from his former habitudes; and though it were now too late to obviate this inconvenience, yet he persisted as far as in him was—that is, by praying, caballing, and discoursing—to obstruct the restoring of the episcopal government, revenues, and authority. Insomuch that, finding himself discountenanced on those accounts by the then Warden of Wadham, he shifted colledges to Trinity, and, when there, went away without his degree, scrupling, forsooth, the Subscription then required. From thence he came to London, where he spent a considerable time in creeping into all corners and companies, horoscoping up and down concerning the duration of the Government; not considering anything as best, but as most lasting and most profitable. And after having many times cast a figure, he at last satisfyed himself that the Episcopal Government would endure as long as this King lived; and from thence forward cast about how to be admitted into the Church of England, and find the high-way to her preferments. In order to this he daily enlarged, not only his conversation, but his conscience, and was made free of some of the town-vices; imagining, like Muleasses King of Tunis (for I take witness that on all occasions I treat him rather above his quality than otherwise), that by hiding himself among the onions, he should escape being traced by his perfumes. Ignorant and mistaken man, that thought it necessary to part with any virtue to get a living; or that the Church of England did not require and incourage more sobriety than he could ever be guilty of; whereas it hath alwayes been fruitful of men who, together with obedience to that discipline, have lived to the envy of the Nonconformists in their conversation, and without such could never either have been preserved so long, or after so long a dissipation have ever recover'd. But neither was this yet, in his opinion, sufficient; and therefore he resolv'd to try a shorter path, which some few men have trod not unsuccessfully; that is, to print a Book; if that would not do, a second; if not that, a third of an higher extraction, and so forward, to give experiment against their former party of a keen stile and a ductile judgement. His first proof-piece was in the year 1665, the *Tentamina Physico-Theologica:* a tedious transcript of his common-place book, wherein there is very little of his own, but the arrogance and the unparalleled censoriousness that he exercises over all other Writers, besides his undutiful inveying even then against the 'vesicles of the earth' for meer bubbles, as he did shortly after against his father's memory, and in his mother's presence, before several witnesses, for a couple of 'whining phanaticks.' However, he accounted it a safe Book on all sides, it being of so trite and confessed an argument, that few judicious men would read it to examine the errours; and in so rough and scabbed a Latine, that a man must have long nails, and those sharper than ordinary, to distinguish betwixt the skin and the disease, the faults and the grammar: to omit his usual volume and circumference of periods, which, though he takes alwayes to be his chiefest strength, yet indeed, like too great a line, weakens the defence, and requires too many men to make it good. But the cause being against Atheism, he was secure that none would attaque him. For whether there be any Atheists is some controversie; and he is compurgator for most of 'em; or if there be such, yet they know the bastions are all undermined, and they should be blown up as soon as enter'd. But let him show me any Atheist that he hath reduced by his Book, unless he may pretend to have converted some (as in the old Florentine Wars) by meer tiring them out and perfect weariness. In this treatise, however, it was difficult for him to have hedged in the Nonconformists; only here and there he sprinkles a glittering ore, to give hopes of a vein underneath of such metal as might by a skilful hand be founded into any figure; and having shown, as he thought, sufficiently, that he believ'd there was a God, he imagin'd that thenceforward, write what and against whom he would, it might pass as indisputably; that all would be current which past his touch-stone; that as his predecessor, Midas, turn'd into gold whatsoever he touched, so every thing by his handling should be transmuted to orthodoxy. When he had cook'd-up these musty collections, he makes his first invitation to his 'old acquaintance' my lord Archbishop of Canterbury, who had never seen before nor heard of him. But I must confess he furbishes-up his Grace in so glorious an Epistle, that had not my Lord been long since proof against the most spiritual flattery, the Dedication only, without ever reading the Book, might have serv'd to have fix'd him from that instant as his favourite. Yet all this I perceive did not his work, but his Grace was so unmindful, or rather so prudent, that the gentleman thought it necessary to spur-up again the next year with another new Book, to show more plainly what he would be at. This he dedicates to Doctor Bathurst; and to evidence from the very Epistle that he was ready to renounce that very education, the civility of which he is so tender of as to blame me for disordering it, he picks occasion to tell him: 'to your prevailing advice, Sir, do I owe my first rescue from the chains and fetters of an unhappy education.' But in the Book, which he calls 'A free and impartial Censure of the Platonick Philosophy' (censure 'tis sure to be, whatsoever he writes), he speaks out, and demonstrates himself ready and equipp'd to surrender not only the Cause, but betray his Party without making any conditions for them, and to appear forthwith himself in the head of the contrary interest. Which, supposing the dispute to be just, yet in him was so mercenary, that none would have descended to act his part but a divine of fortune. And even lawyers take themselves excused from being of counsel for the King himself, in a cause where they have been entertain'd and instructed by their client. But so flippant he was and forward in this book, that in despight of all chronology, he could introduce Plato to inveigh against Calvin, and from the Platoniques he could miraculously hook-in a Discourse against the Nonconformists. [Cens. Plat. Phil. p. 26, 27, 28, &c.] After this feat of activity he was ready to leap over the moon: no scruple of conscience could stand in his way, and no preferment seemed too high for him; for about this time, I find that having taken a turn at Cambridge to qualifie himself, he was received within doors to be my Lord Archbishop's other chaplain, and into some degree of favour; which, considering the difference of their humours and ages, was somewhat surprizing. But whether indeed, in times of heat and faction, the most temperate spirits may sometimes chance to take delight in one that is spightful, and make some use of him; or whether it be that even the most grave and serious persons do for relaxation divert themselves willingly by whiles with a creature that is unlucky, mimical, and gamesome,—so it was. And thenceforward the nimble gentleman danced upon bell-ropes, vaulted from steeple to steeple, and cut capers out of one dignity to another. Having thus dexterously stuck his groat in Lambeth wainscot, it may easily be conceived he would be unwilling to lose it; and therefore he concern'd himself highly, and even to jealousie, in upholding now that palace, which, if falling, he would out of instinct be the first should leave it. His Majesty about that time labouring to effect his constant promises of Indulgence to his people, the Author therefore walking with his own shadow in the evening, took a great fright lest all were agoe. And in this conceit being resolv'd to make good his figure, and that one government should not last any longer than the other, he set himself to write those dangerous Books which I have now to do with; wherein he first makes all that he will to be Law, and then whatsoever is Law to be Divinity. And I shall appeal to all readers, and I hope make it good, that never in any age, by any man (that I may not say any Churchman), have there been published discourses either so erroneously founded, or so foully managed, or of so pernicious consequence. In conclusion, this is that man who insists so much, and stirrops himself upon the 'gravity of his profession' and the 'civility of his education;' which if he had in the least observed in respect either to himself or others, I should, I could never have made so bold with him. And nevertheless, it being so necessary to represent him in his own likeness, that it may appear what he is to others and to himself, if possibly he might at last correct his indecencies, I have not committed any fault of stile, nor even this tediousness, but in his imitation. I have not used any harsh expressions but what were suitable to that 'civility of education' which he practises, and that 'gravity of profession' which he hath set up of; and even therein I have taken care, beside what my nature hath taken care for, to shoot below the mark, and not to retaliate to the same degree; being willing, as I must yield him the preference for many good qualities, so in his worst, however, to give him the precedence. And yet withall that it hath been thus far the odiousest task that ever I undertook, and has look'd to me all the while like the cruelty of a living dissection, which, however it may tend to publick instruction, and though I have pick'd out the most noxious creature to be anatomatiz'd, yet doth scarce excuse or recompence the offensiveness of the scent and fouling of my fingers. Therefore I will here break off abruptly, leaving many a vein not laid open, and many a passage not search'd into; nor read any further upon this 'Soul of the World,' or prosecute afresh its allegory from the apple, the mandrake, the sparrow, the fishes, the mouse, the mungrel, the ape, unto the day of marriage, but leave the moral to the judicious. And I could here take advantage, perhaps plausibly enough, to put a final conclusion to this whole Book; for if a man hath taken off his railing, he hath therein answered his argument.

But if I have undergone the drudgery of the more loathsome part already, I will not defraud my self of what is more truly pleasant, and remains behind the lighter burthen—the conflict with, if it may be so call'd, his reason. For his whole Book is, according to his usual address, a letter to me, and it concerns my civility to return an answer to every part of it. He hath ask'd me many questions, and I take my self obliged to resolve them. And he hath promis'd me the press shall be open; neither would I therefore be behindhand with him in courtesie. So that I have now only three things of which he hath made it necessary that I caution the Reader. The first is, not to be misled by a pestilent way that he has of youing me, and so making me an epidemical person, affixing thereby what hath ever, he pretends to have been said or done by any in the cause of Nonconformity at any time, to my account, although it hath never enter'd into my Book or imagination; and he had been more kind, if, as sometimes, he does out of civility, he had thou'd me to the end of the chapter. The second is, not on the other part to impute any errors or weakness of mine to the Nonconformists, nor mistake me for one of them (not that I fly it as a reproach, but rather honour the most scrupulous); for I write only what I think befits all men in humanity, Christianity, and prudence towards Dissenters. The last is, not to think that I am any such old acquaintance as he claims, to insinuate me of dis-ingenuity, for of our acquaintance I shall give account hereafter.

That which gave me the first occasion of writing was, as I have said formerly, his third crambe, of the same purulent matter and virulent stile, the Preface to Bishop Bramhall; and against that and its incomparable extravagancies was my whole discourse bent and levell'd. Only about the middle of mine I touch'd in passing upon some points of his other treatises, that is, the 'Power of the Magistrate, Conscience, Morality, Debauchery, Persecution,' &c. But he, whether by mistake or on purpose, turns my method quite backward, and, avoiding that which was direct for what is but collateral, begins in his second page, in his usual military metaphors of 'Attack, Front and Rear,' &c., with the ninety-seventh of my Book. This, however, is an accident that hath befallen other great commanders as well as himself. For his ancient friend, William the Conqueror, at the battel of Hastings, had in the same manner the back of his cuirasses placed before, by the error of him that put them on. The thing is ominous, I doubt, to the Author of the Ecclesiastical Politie, and assuredly (as the Duke then said), 'This day his fortune will turn, and he will be a King or nothing before night.' Yet I will not decline the pursuit, but plod on after him in his own way thorow thick and thin, hill or dale, over hedge and ditch, wherever he leads; till I have laid hand on him, and delivered him bound either to Reason or Laughter, to Justice or Pity. If at any turn he gives me the least opportunity to be serious, I shall gladly take it; but where he prevaricates or is scurrilous (and where is he not?), I shall treat him betwixt jest and earnest. That which is solid and sharp, being imp'd by something more light and airy, may carry further and pierce deeper, and therefore I shall look to it as well as I can, that mine arrows be well pointed, and of mine own whetting; but for the feathers, I must borrow them out of his wing. Neither yet would I have this similitude improv'd to his disparagement; for he is a bird of prey and an high-flyer, and though he hath lessen'd himself by the height of his place, he cannot certainly be other than an eagle, and perhaps the same fate may attend him.

First, therefore, as to the power of the magistrate, he saith in gross, that 'the supream government of every Commonwealth must of necessity be universal, uncontroulable, indispensable, unlimited, and absolute in all affairs whatsoever that concern the interests of mankind and the ends of government; as well in matters of religion as in all other civil concerns.' [Eccl. Pol. p. 27, 28, 35, &c.] This is, I confess, pretty strongly worded, and drawn up, doubtless, by the advice of his counsel learned. But if these be terms yet unknown in our Law, we must refer it to the supream government 'to define their signification.' [Idem, p. 109.] However, if it be not law, 'tis pity but it were so. 'Tis the very *elixir potestatis* and *magisterium Domini:* so fine a thing, that no man living but would be inamour'd with it; for, wot ye well, it is 'a power,' he saith, 'established' of yore, at or before the beginning of the world, ere there was any such thing known or thought of as periwigs or glass-coaches, 'by the unalterable dictates of natural reason and universal practice and consent of nations.' Only in 'the Jewish commonwealth, for some peculiar reasons of State,' [Eccl. Pol. p. 32] (which he knows, but will not tell us), 'twas for some time otherwise. But this power was 'antecedent to Christ' Himself [Idem, p. 35], and it was so well founded, that there was none, or very little need of the authority of the Scripture in the case, and therefore 'the Scripture rather supposes than asserts this jurisdiction.' Yet in our Saviour's time, and for some while after, there was such 'a posture of affairs' [Idem, p. 37, 38] and 'such an happy juncture of affairs' [Idem, p. 40] (how mechanically he expresses it!), that while the Heathen princes enjoy'd this power by the antecedent right of soveraignty, and accordingly exercised it over Christians, 'twas also necessary to supply it among them 'by miracles of severity.' But 'when once Christianity became the imperial religion, this power began to resettle where nature had placed it' [Idem, p. 48]; and so the world jogged on, and 'its affairs were competently well governed (though better or worse, according to the wisdom and vigilance of the several Emperors') [Idem, p. 54], till the Bishop of Rome, seeing this Power to be so rich and beautiful a creature, began to cast a sweet eye on her, and, by the address of his constant sollicitation and courtship, carried her sheer away from all the princes of Christendom. So this jewel of the crown was for several hundred of years imbezel'd, till Henry the Eighth and other princes found it again by chance in the ruines of an old monastery at the Reformation. But though the 'wisdom of the elder ages had always practised this power' [Eccl. Pol. p. 32], yet 'since that governors have not been thorowly instructed in its nature and extent.' [Idem, p. 58; idem, p. 229.] 'Government hath not been rightly understood nor duly managed; the Reformation hath not been able to resettle princes in their full and natural rights.' [Idem, p. 58.] What will not the man deserve that can show them better, and teach governors a receipt against so chronical negligence and ignorance? 'So little have princes understood their own interests; so fatal has been their miscarriage.' [Idem, p. 19.] Send for a physician ere they be all out of hope, and while there is yet some life in 'm. But he will do well to make sure of his fee beforehand; as those that sold the icterus, a bird good against the jaundice, hid it till they were payed, lest the buyer at first sight [might] be cured. The great secret, after all, is, 'that the prince may and hath power to transfer the exercise of the priesthood upon another, and that he may if he please reserve it to himself.' [Idem, p. 32.] Is this all? The notion is something new indeed; but he hath deduced it very well, and 'tis pretty probable: though I have known the time, and many others may remember it, when it would not have been granted. I make account the Author of the Ecclesiastical Politie is sufficiently impowred by the whole clergy, at least of England; and doubtless therefore his Majesty, among other princes, will, if he find it good, and for his service, accept the donation, not much inferiour to that of Constantine. 'Tis a great piece of gratitude now in them, and 'twould have done well and more seasonably, had his late Majesty before the War been informed by them in this particular and the dependances. But I have some reason to be jealous that the Author of the Ecclesiastical Politie is not thus liberal without some design; that he hath some job or other to be done; and how unlimited and absolute soever he hath made and declared the magistrate, there is some condition annex'd, upon failure of which this fiefe shall reincamerate. For he was of another opinion in his Preface to Bishop Bramhall, when he said, 'all government does and must owe its quiet and continuance to the Churche's patronage.' [Eccl. Pol. p. 30.] Yes: there is another croisade [=crusade] to be undertaken; and he hath a project in his head to ingage all princes in a war against Nonconformity, a second *bellum Archidiaconale*. [Pref. to Eccl. Pol. p. 46.] For though he was resolved to run his head against a wall, and very ingenuously professes there too, that 'if he had spoke reason, he had, without any more adoe, carry'd the cause; if he had not, he was content to lose his labour,' he intended not it should go so easily. But in that very first Book, while he was in the sweetest temper, in his natural serenity and most benign inclinations, not heated or provok'd by any adversary, and before he had expected one minute what so strong a reason, what so perswasive eloquence might have effected with the Nonconformists, joyn'd with that interest which he had so many years been creating amongst them, even then at the same time he sounds another trumpet than that in Sheere-Lane, to horse and hem-in his auditory. He proclaims them, for meer dissenting upon tenderness of conscience, ' Villains, Hypocrites, Rebels, Schismaticks, and the greatest and most notorious hereticks.' [Pref. Eccl. Pol. p. 241, 273, 319.] He summons therefore the magistrate to do his office, that is, to impose ceremonies which he owns to be indifferent upon those that hold the contrary, with the severest penalties and the strictest execution. What is this but to put governors upon the tenters, to invent how possibly they may run their subjects into disobedience, and then to invent and apply the tortures for their disobeying? As for the poor subjects, there is no help for them; but he gives them very excellent and ghostly counsel to 'abide their sad fate' with patience and resignation; but in stead of them he layes his imposition now upon the magistrate, and leaves him not so much as the power to will nor chuse, but he must govern by the laws of the Author of the Ecclesiastical Politie. [Eccl. Pol. 321.] He 'must scourge them into order. He must chastise them out of their peevishness, and lash them into obedience.' [Eccl. Pol. p. 325.] 'There is no remedy but the rod and correction.' [Idem, 272.] 'He must restrain them with more rigour than unsanctifyed villains. He must expose them to the correction of the publick rods and axes.' [Idem, 219.] Is this at last all the business why he hath been building up all this while that necessary, universal, uncontroulable, indispensable, unlimited, absolute power of governors; only to gratifie the humour and arrogance of an unnecessary, universal, uncontroulable, [in]dispensable, unlimited, and absolute archdeacon? Still ' *must, must, must.*' But what if the supream magistrate won't? Why, '*must*' again, [Idem, 271] eight times at least in little more than one page, and thorow his whole Book proportionably. This is (and let him make a quibble on't if he please) like Doctor Rabelais his setting Julius Cæsar to beat mustard; and just as worshipful an imployment, if he should prefer his Majesty from his kingdom and Whitehall to the government of his ancient palace of Bridewell. But laws and impositions, he saith, signifie nothing without penalties, nor these without acting up roundly by rigorous executions. Therefore, that he might be true to his own principles, if the supream magistrate be disobedient, he hath provided against him too, pretty severely. He hath denounced that in that case men deserve to perish like Sardanapalus; that such a prince 'deserves to be king of the night;' and, to conclude, he affirms that 'princes unless they will be resolute,' that is, to do what he would have them, 'they must not govern.' [Eccl. Pol. p. 271.] 'Tis come to *noli igitur regnare:* they had need to take heed of him, it seems, and how they behave themselves. But they may very well take all this kindly of him and as an honour, for it is no less authority than he exercises over God Almighty; for he will have it that God too 'must of necessity have vested princes in at least as much power as was absolutely necessary to the nature and ends of government.' [Idem, p. 40.] And what the Author's ends are, we have and shall take occasion more particularly to examine hereafter.

What needs there further for evidence in this matter? or if men would out of love to justice be more exactly inform'd, let them but read, if their patience will not last longer, the contents at least of the several chapters of his Ecclesiastical Politie, in this and the other matters. It is sufficient punishment for some offenders to be placed in publick with their Book or its title affix'd before them. But because he will not be satisfy'd with that, I shall presume so far on my readers as to trace him thorow the maze of what in the

Reproof he would answer. He insults first, because he saith [Reproof, p. 3] I expose an innocent and undeniable proposition of his, that the magistrate hath such a power as is before described to govern and conduct the consciences of his subjects in affairs of religion; and yet I say not a word in its confutation: but he forgets, that where I quote that, I in the very next line subjoyn thus, and page 22 he explains himself more fully: 'That unless princes have power to bind their subjects to that religion that they apprehend most advantageous to publick peace and tranquillity, and restrain those religious mistakes that tend to its subversion, they are no better than statues and images of authority. [Rehearsal Transpros'd, p. 97.] And this I several times inculcated into him; but of this he takes not the least notice, I warrant you: 'tis all hush'd. Is not this, now, a candid Reprover? But because I know he will hereupon be wriggling, I will shew him that these words cannot be interpreted otherwise by him than according to their first appearance and full latitude. He cannot mean it in matters of ceremony, which indeed he ought to have kept to, but that the subject, it seems, turn'd into an argument, and led him further to confess and speak out what was in the bottom. For concerning ceremonies he saith indeed, 'That 'tis absolutely necessary that governors injoyn matters of no great moment and consequence in themselves, thereby to avoid the evil that would naturally attend upon their being not injoyn'd; so that when they are determin'd, though perhaps they are of no great use to the Common-wealth in themselves, yet they have at least this considerable usefulness, as to prevent many great mischiefs that would probably follow if they were not determined. [Eccl. Pol. p. 322.] A most memorable passage, and that deserves to be recorded as the full sum and state of the controversie. Yet he most ingenuously professes that 'all that concerns religious worship is no part of religion itself, but only an instrument, &c.; and therefore, though the Christian laws command us by some exterior signs to express our interior piety, yet they have no where set down any particular expressions of worship and adoration.' [Idem, p. 99.] So also 'all rituals and ceremonies and postures and manners of performing the outward expressions of devotion are not in their own nature capable of being parts of religion.' [Idem, p. 206.] And thus in many other places: so that he hath gained nothing by the first objection which he hath raised, but a proposition not so undeniable, nor very innocent, that the prince hath power to bind his subjects to that religion which he apprehends most advantageous, &c. [Reproof, p. 6.] His next exception against me is very material: that I have quoted so many passages out of his Book. It has, I believe, indeed anger'd him, as it has been no small trouble to me: but how can I help it? I wish he would be pleas'd to teach me an art (for if any man in the world, he hath it) to answer a Book without 'turning over the leaves' (for that in a former Answer offended him), or without citing the passages. In the mean time, if to transcribe so much out of him must render a man, as he therefore stiles me, 'a *scandalous plagiary*,' I must plead guilty; but by the same law, whoever shall either be witness or prosecutor, in behalf of the king, for treasonable words, may be indicted for an highwayman. After this he asks me roundly whether I do seriously believe that his Majesty has no power in matters of religion. Let him first make good his own assertions, which I have charged him with, and then I will tell him more of my mind. Yet because he questions me of my belief (which I believe he never yet did to any man in his own parsonages, or either at Ickham or Chartham), I do, however, count myself obliged to give him some answer, as much as he can challenge of me; that is, I most certainly do believe that the supream magistrate hath some power, but not all power, in matters of religion. And particularly to advance so much further to our Author of the Ecclesiastical Politie, I do not believe that princes have power to bind their subjects to that religion that they apprehend most advantageous. And I will give him a reason too of this my belief. He himself saith (and it is worthy to be taken good notice of), 'that the Fanaticks of late have so embroiled Christendom, that

Christian princes begin to be of a perswasion, that Christianity is an enemy to government.' [Eccl. Pol. p. 179.] Now it is therefore to be presumed, that he is very conversant and intimate with all the princes of Christendom. But I suppose that they reveal'd this secret of State to him only in confidence, for I never before heard of it in publick: and it is not so ingenuously or prudently done of him to proclaim in print the subject of a familiar discourse and private conference with them. This sure will make princes more cautelous [=cautious] for the future whom they chuse for their ministers, and to believe that even he, unless he be better at keeping a secret, is not so fit to be of their Privy-counsel; no not in affairs ecclesiastical. But if it be so (as who dare controvert it after so authentical authority as the Author's of the Ecclesiastical Politie?) that princes are indeed perswaded that Christianity is an enemy to government, it is not so safe to acknowledge that they have power to bind to what religion they apprehend most advantageous. Especially if it should chance that so pliable a gentleman should be at their elbow, who, out of excess of Conformity, indulges the greatest Nonconformity imaginable. 'We condemn,' saith he, 'neither Turks nor Papists for their forms and postures of adoration (unless they fall under one or both of the obliquities aforesaid). Let them but address the same worship to its proper object, and we will never stand stiffly with them about their outward rites and ceremonies of its expression, but will freely allow them to conform to the significant customs of their countrey, as we do to those of ours.' [Defence Eccl. Pol. p. 286.] 'Tis most graciously done that his we-ship will allow them it. Will he not sound a trumpet too when he has done, to give them leave to go to dinner? In due time sure there will be an hat for him, to make him in requital the cardinal-deacon. But why will he not carry the good humour thorow, and be as merciful to his neighbours? all abroad, and nothing at home? There have been and are several rights and customs too in the countries of England, which do neither countenance vice nor disgrace the Deity; and these dissenting people do address the same worship to its due and proper object. But (not to prevent [=anticipate] myself) should he now, that is so clear as to matter of ceremonies, be back'd at the same time with another fellow-prebend of his, no less frank in religion, who should tell the princes that he abhors being a papist as much as being a presbyterian [Dr. Pierce against Baxter, p. 167], and will as soon be a Turk as he will be either, what might become of us, if the princes were satisfy'd of their own power, and of these men's discretion? It might breed no small alteration in the affairs of Christendom. For whatsoever the papists be, there are many things to be said why the Turks' is a very advantageous religion.

Then he quotes his Majestie's Declaration to make good his 'making use of that supream power in ecclesiastical matters, which is not only inherent in the crown, but has been declared and recognized to be so by several statutes and Acts of Parliament.' [Reproof, p. 3.] I honour the quotation, and am come not long since from swearing religiously to own that supremacy. And it is surely the more valid for having received from the Author of the Ecclesiastical Politie this confirmation. Only it might have been wish'd that all his books had not been writ directly counter to it, and, under pretence of gratifying him with titles, he had not cut him out of the exercise and liberty of his jurisdiction. But having in his Ecclesiastical Politie created himself Perpetual Dictator, *nequid res-clerica detrimenti capiat*, and marching every where with four-and-twenty rods and axes before him, he deputes the consul to be indeed both his *Magister Equitum* and his *Pontifex Maximus:* but all along speaks in the '*us*' and the '*we*' of himself, and treats the good civil uncontroulable magistrate with the '*must, must,*' to evidence his own rigorous superiority. And in that only place where he seems to give the magistrate some little license, he doth it with so ill a grace, and stigmatizes both the magistrate and the people with such a mark and character, that 'twould put a generous prince upon some deliberation whether he were best to make use of an authority so ignominiously granted.

For all that is to be obtained is this, and in these terms [Eccl. Pol. pp. 63, 64]: 'Should any prince through unhappy miscarriages in the State be brought into such straits and exigences of affairs as that he cannot restrain the headlong inclinations of his subjects without the hazard of raising such commotions and disturbances as perhaps he can never be able to allay, and so should be forced in spight of himself to indulge them their liberty in their fancies and persuasions about Religion; yet, unless he will divest himself of a more material and more necessary part of his authority than if he should grant away his power of the militia, or his prerogative of ratifying civil laws,—unless, I say, he will thus hazard his crown, and make himself too weak for government by renouncing the best part of his supremacy, he MUST lay an obligation upon all persons to whom he grants this religious freedom, to profess that it is matter of meer favour and indulgence, and that he has as much power to govern all the publick affairs of Religion as any other matters that are either conducive or prejudicial to the publick peace and quiet of the Commonwealth. And if they be brought to this declaration, they will but confess themselves (to say no worse) turbulent and seditious persons, by acknowledging that they refuse their obedience to those laws which the supream authority has just power to impose.' I know not whether all these solemnities were duely observed in the late Declaration, or whether the failing in some of these rituals may have rendered it less sacred. But our Author's concession here looks something like the Cardinal Antonio's suffrage, when he could not have his man chosen: *Sia dunque Pamfilio papa al nome del diavolo.* However, this, such as it is, joyned with the former quotation, does amount to some kind of sanction, and the parties concern'd may do well to consider of it.

He inquires next 'whether I have never read or heard of any publick disturbances, under pretence of religion.' [Reproof, p. 7.] Yes, I have, and whosoever shall do so deserves to be severely punish'd. 'Whether I have not heard of the merry pranks of John of Leyden and the Anabaptists of Germany.' [Idem, p. 8.] Yes, and they were handled as they deserved. Nay, moreover, I have heard of the Anabaptists too of New-England, in a book printed in the year 1673, intituled 'Mr. Baxter baptiz'd in blood,' which came out under the license of the Author of the Ecclesiastical Politie; being therefore, as is to be supposed, a book of theological nature. It was indeed a piece of Ecclesiastical History, which he thought, it seems, very fit 'to reconcile to the present juncture of affairs, and recommend to the genius of the age: faithfully relating the cruel, barbarous, and bloody murther of Mr. Baxter, an orthodox minister, who was kill'd by the Anabaptists, and his skin most cruelly flea'd off from his body.' And yet from beginning to end there never was a compleater falshood invented. But after the Author of the Ecclesiastical Politie had in so many books of his own indeavour'd to harangue up the Nation into fury against tender consciences, there could not have been contrived by the wit of man any thing more hopeful to have blooded them upon the Nonconformists than such a spectacle, and at the end of his orations to flourish the skin of an orthodox minister in this manner flea'd off by the Anabaptists. So that *se non era vero, fu ben trovato.* And in good earnest I dare not swear but it was the Author of the Ecclesiastical Politie's own handy-work. Several words I observe that he frequently and peculiarly makes use of in his other books, 'concerns, villains, villanies, booby, &c.' But as for his 'brisk and laboured periods,' they may be traced every where. What say you to this, for example? 'As the profession of the gospel is a most sacred thing, the doctrine of the gospel a most holy rule, the Author of our religion an exemplar and pattern of meekness,—so when Christians renounce this sacred profession, lay aside this Holy Gospel, and abrenunciate Christ the pattern of meekness, they soon become the most desperate villains in the world.' [Baxter's Baptism, p. 1.] (Ay, very truly said, were it but rightly applyed.) Never in my life did I read any thing that more lively expresses and nicks the energy of our Author's sense, or the rotundity and cadence of his numbers: and so in many places more, too long to be instanced. And indeed what reason could there be, what likelyhood that any other man should go so far out of the way with such a book to him who was the most improper Licenser of things of that nature? unless he may have therefore been thought the most proper Licenser, because he had given so many testimonies as books of his good inclination to such matters; and that (not only in history, but even in doctrine too) he did not so nearly consider the truth as the interest. And therefore, if perhaps he were not the Author, yet I dare undertake that when he came to the licensing of that pamphlet, he felt such an expansion of heart, such an adlubescence of mind, and such an exaltation of spirit, that betwixt joy and love he could scarcely refrain from kissing it. And this no man living can deny, that either if he thought there were any fault in it, he took care to correct and fit it for the press with that advantage that it came out; or else he found it so satisfactory, that it past his approbation without any amendment, and so transporting, that he forgot to keep a copy for his own justification. And truly, had it not chanced that there was present and immediate proof upon the place to convict the forgery as soon as published, it might probably have had the effect for which it was designed. However, no thanks to the Licenser, who either was also the Author, or the more criminal of the two; by how much the Licenser is alwayes presumed to have the stricter inspection, the better judgment, and more honesty, and is therefore intrusted by my Lord Archbishop to give the stamp of publick authority. So that whereas this Author saith that [Eccl. Pol. p. 76] 'had we but an Act of Parliament to abridge preachers the use of fulsome and luscious metaphors, it might perhaps be an effectual cure of all our distempers' (what of the 'dull and lazy' one too?), 'let not the reader smile at the odness of the proposal.' (Neither, is not that lawful before it come to be enacted, as certainly it will upon his recommendation?) I must rather say, that had we but an Act of Parliament to abridge Licensers from publishing falsehoods, how sweet soever and luscious, and to command and inable them to authorize truth, there would be a sensible amendment in our modern History, Polity, and Theology. I know he will take it unkindly that this should be revived after, he will say, he hath given so ample satisfaction since for it in his testimonial to the contrary. But he may please to consider that this was since the late Act of General Pardon; that it all happen'd since the writing of the Reproof; that he hath only given a masterly certificate as it were from a Justice of Peace, instead of making an humble recantation as an Offender; that it is but the same law which he every where would exact of the Nonconformists, and the same right which he does Mr. B. in the Preface to Bishop Bramhall. Had he but, as they say indeed he complimented the Anabaptists on this occasion, so printed it too, 'that he esteem'd them to be the nearest to truth of all the Dissenters from the Church of England,' it had been some sign of penitence and integrity, and amounted to some degree of restitution.

From this of the Anabaptists he falls as severely upon the word '*unhoopable*,' which I, it seems, used in representing his '*unlimited*,' &c. But whereas I only threw it out like an empty cask to amuze him, knowing that I had a whale to deal with, and lest he should overset me, he runs away with it as a very serious business, and so moyles himself with tumbling and tossing it, that he is in danger of melting his spermaceti. A cork, I see, will serve without an hook; and instead of an harping-iron, this grave and ponderous creature may, like eeles, be taken and pull'd up only with bobbing. What adoe he makes with tubs, kilderkins, hogsheads, and their dimensions, that you might suspect him first to have served as gager of the Lambeth brewing! I wonder that he should descend to so low imployment; but even that prudent Emperor Claudius publish'd an edict *De bene picandis doliis*. And I perceive that a person of considerable ecclesiastical tunnage did very lately 'resemble the Church of England, with its ceremonies, to a vessel, which *must* of *necessity* be composed of staves, hoops, withs and pins; but if the pins were pulled out, then of consequence the withs slacken, the hoops ungird, and the staves fall all asunder into confusion;' so that you see the trope of an 'hoop' is not so apocryphal. And I should have thought that, if not out of respect to the Church of England, yet had it been only out of reverence to Cornelius his tub, among the rest, it might have becomed the Author of the Ecclesiastical Politie upon this occasion to have been something more serious.

And no less does he intangle himself in another line of mine, weak enough, I confess, yet though of but a single hair, strong enough to land him. 'Tis where I chanc'd to say, that 'he hath given here the magistrate so infinite a power, that it is extended to impotency, as a streight line continued grows a circle.' Here indeed I am hard put to it; and I begin too late to be sensible of my rashness in provoking so terrible an adversary. But in good earnest I thought it enough when I wrote it, that in any small segment of a great circle the curvature is not perceptible, but rectifies more by how much the figure is extended. And at the same time I reflected, that if mine Author should carp at it (for I foresaw very well all the way where he would take hold, and where he would as soon eat his fingers), I would refer him, as being an ecclesiastical mathematician, to Cardinal Cusanus his treatise *De Docta Ignorantia*, p. 10, c. xiv., where he might see in the diagram *quod infinita linea sit trian-*

gulus, and p. 11, c. xv. *quod ille triangulus sit circulus.* But if this will not satisfie him, let him try conclusions with his own girdle, which circumscribes something that is infinite.

And no less considerable is that which he undertakes 'to maintain, that all figures are hoopable:' and I, on the contrary, will defend, that if he can make that good, he hath found out the circle of the quadrature.

From hence he runs out into Plays, designing, as he told us his friend did of the 'Friendly Debate, [Pref. to Eccl. Pol. p. 16] to set off his reasonings with a comical humour and pleasantness.' I must here acknowledge the defect of my reading. For Du-Foy I have not heard of, and it might better have become him to have quoted, instead of the Conquest, the Archbishop of Granada. But for what he recites out of the Rehearsal and the Kings of Branford [Brentford], I understand it better; and seeing he is pleas'd to alter the scene, I shall joyn with him, and try whether the humour of Bayes be so worn out that it may not give the auditory a second daye's diversion. For indeed 'tis too ceremonious and tiresome to repeat so often upon all occasions the Author of the Ecclesiastical Politie, and though I bear him great respect, yet I had rather of the two offend him than my readers. He does indeed complain of it something pathetically that I should have fix'd that name upon him; and in good earnest, could I have yet in all this while invented any name more consonant and agreeable to his character, I would have chang'd for it. Neither did I at first make use of the Rehearsal so much in order to make merry with him, as for a more publick and serious advantage. For having observed that he and others of his coat did, for want either of reading, wit, or piety, as oft as they would be facetious, make bold with the Scripture; thinking too, perhaps, that being so long acquainted, they might be more familiar with it; I had a mind to show them by this example, that there was not so much need of prophaneness to be ridiculous, or to take the Sacred Writings in vain; but that if they did but take up at adventure any book that was commonly read, known, or approved of, they had the same and better opportunity than out of the Bible, to gather thence variety, allusion, and matter sufficient to make the people merry: and I hope I have attain'd my end in some measure. But beside this, I have now one reason more, and his own authority, to treat him under this title, he having been since so far in love with the name, as even to send to Co'chester to procure him as much Bayes as would serve for a facing. [Reproof, p. 20.] One thing, indeed, he objects with some fading colour, that there is an errour in chronology, the play of the Rehearsal not having been made publick till after his first book came out; which yet is something excusable, seeing it was publish'd before his second or third, and to be sure, however, before mine. But you know, Mr. Bayes, that you wanted not the opportunity to see it long before it was printed; and that comedy, as all judicious and lasting things ought, was long considered of ere it was thought fit to come abroad. Had you follow'd the same example, and not divulged and promulgated your Preface to Bishop Bramhall, as you confess, 'before your thoughts were cool enough, or could possibly be so, to review or correct the indecencies either of its stile or contrivance;' had you 'but had either leisure or patience to examine it,' all this labour might have been spared betwixt you and me; and I, for mine own part, should never have 'tired either yourself or the reader.' [Preface to Bp. Bramhall, p. 2 and p. last.] But that I may be quit with you for so weighty an *emendatio temporum*, have you not observed that your Hicringill, or Gregory, though not published till after your Reproof, foretells of it nevertheless, threatning what a vengeance-book was impending over me? 'That I must shortly be disciplined by another hand; advising me to say my prayers, and tremble at the rod that was coming upon me, except I thought it the wisest way to save the *hangman* a labour.' [Gregory, p. 196.] It is a title so honourable, that I should scarce have adventur'd to give it him; but seeing he thinks fit to assume it, you may shift and divide it as you can betwixt you. This was, I confess, the most authentick way of prophecy imaginable, it being fulfill'd beforehand; but the worst piece of chronology that ever I heard of. Indeed, Mr. Bayes, it appears to me very evident that, as I told you before, this Hicringill was your own book, and it was licens'd too by yourself, as certainly as 'Baxter baptiz'd in blood.' The strains and recherches are all along exactly the same with those of the Reproof. Read but, for example, in the very same page [Gregory, p. 196], in answer to what I say of the King of Poland's being obliged to wear that countrey habit: 'For which unsufferable affront to his Majestie's our gracious soveraign his crown and dignity, hereditary and not elective, and at the good-will either of people or Parliament, I leave him to be chastiz'd for this bold intrenchment and invasion of our King's prerogative and title to his crown.' [Idem, p. 224.] Then read your Reproof: 'This is an impudent intrenchment upon his Majestie's crown and prerogative; for the Polish kingdom being hereditary and not elective, the Parliament deals with their Kings as &c.' [Reproof, p. 498.] Was there ever such a double pick-lock of the Law, to find out such a dangerous inuendo? But thus those twin-books sympathize all thorow, although the Reproof was brought forth a considerable time before the other. Only, Mr. Bayes, as when in the Rehearsal you once resolv'd that for your 'first Prologue you would come out in a long black veil, with an huge hangman behind you, with a furr'd cap and his sword drawn [Rehearsal Comedy, page 7];' you could not for a long time determine whether the Reproof or Hicringill should be 'the Prologue for the Epilogue, or the Epilogue for the Prologue;' [Ibid. page 7] whether your first or your second self should come foremost. But having several things in your two Books, some fit, as you thought, to be said in another's person, and others in your own, you stood a great while thumming the busk of your 'comfortable importance,' whether to divine 'which of these two should first be hatched, and which leg should go first.' [Ibid. page 30.] And from this irresolution and controversie arose this most gross and yet most subtil errour in your chronology, which would require another Scaliger to reform it. The case is parallel; and you were even so puzzled betwixt those two books, as you were at Canterbury betwixt your two capacities, how you should take place not only of others, but even of yourself; whether as you were archdeacon, or as you were youngest prebend; and, though an alternative had been more advisable, you determined that in all interviews with yourself (which are not so frequent except in your looking-glass), and in all publick solemnities among others, the arch-deacon should both in place and time have the precedence.

Having I hope thus far done you right in matter of Chronology, I shall indeavour no less to satisfie you in point of Comedy, and your politick argument concerning the danger of a distinct jurisdiction in civil affairs and those of conscience, which you very weightily fetch from the two kings of Branford. And therefore be pleased to accept as serious a reply from the same author: 'To conclude, Sir, the place you fill has more than amply exacted the talents of a wary pilot, and all these threatning storms, which, like impregnant clouds, do hover o'r our heads (when they once are grasp'd but by the eye of reason), melt into fruitful showres of blessings on the people.' [Rehearsal Comedy, p. 12.] Or, if you have something to object against this, take your answer from the kings themselves at their restauration. 'Now mortals that hear how we tilt and career, with wonder will fear the event of such things as shall never appear.' [Idem, p. 44.] For no less causeless are the apprehensions which you raise up, Mr. Bayes, concerning consciencious people under an equal government.

I cannot now but take some notice of another argument: your threatning me here and in several other places with the loss of my ears [Reproof, p. 25, 31, 75], which, however, are yet in good plight, and apprehend no other danger, Mr. Bayes, but to be of your auditory. But it is no less than you have projected against all the Nonconformists, to the great prejudice of the Nation, in wasting so unseasonably so much good timber to make whipping-posts for them and pillories. This hath been a considerable part indeed of the Ecclesiastical Politie, and doubtless a most effectual means of conversion, and bringing men over to the Church of England. I cannot tell where you have learnt it, unless from the wisdom and piety of the Tartars, in the year 1240. [Del Rio, page 144.] Though they left upon every man's head one ear standing, yet [they] fill'd no less than nine huge sacks with the ears that they cut off of the Christians. But there is no peril, as far as I perceive, to either of us; for my ears, Mr. Bayes, do not so much as glow for all your talking of them, and I will secure yours at least upon one account; for you are so far from running away, like Evagrius [Socrates. l. iv. c. 18] for fear of a bishoprick, that much less will you, like Ammonius, cut off one of your own ears to render yourself uncapable of that office.

There follows one thing more which I know is personally intended to me, but you have couch'd it so darkly, that at first I could myself scarce understand it. You tell of an antique medal,

'On the reverse whereof was gravèd
Th' alliance betwixt Christ and David;'
[Reproof, p. 27]

and desire me to tell you in what emperor's time it was coyned. Why, it was, as I remember, in the year 1650, and of 'the government of the people of England precedent and present the same.' But if you would hereby insinuate any thing either concerning myself or my father, I shall once for all unriddle in two or three lines the mysterie of this your quotation, because otherwise such nodding reflexions impress the Reader more effectually than your more 'brisk and laboured calumnies,' which at other times you word more plainly and vent more openly against us. This therefore is a greater errour in chronology than your former; for as to myself, I never had any, not the remotest relation to publick matters, nor correspondence with the persons then predominant, until the year 1657, when indeed I enter'd into an imployment, for which I was not altogether improper, and which I consider'd to be the most innocent and inoffensive toward his Majestie's affairs of any in that usurped and irregular government, to which all men were then exposed. And this I accordingly discharg'd without disobliging any one person, there having been opportunity and endeavours, since his Majestie's happy return, to have discover'd had it been otherwise. But as to my father, he dyed before ever the War broke out, having lived with some measure of reputation, both for piety and learning; and he was moreover a Conformist to the established rites of the Church of England, though I confess none of the most over-running or eager in them. I desire you, Mr. Bayes, to make my excuse to the readers for having troubled them so far with my private affairs, by your occasion. But whether they will so easily admit my excuse for you, I know not, you having by the servility of your performances since manifested, that, had you then been of age sufficient, you would not have declined a more homely imployment, which, as you may read in Philip de Comines, another Oliver, a barber, discharged under Lewis the Eleventh. For the rest, as to the distich you have here quoted, whosoever was its author, it might better have become your divinity to have supprest so profane an allusion; but that, as I have told you before, and shall often have occasion, you have a singular snickering after Scripture drollery. It may seem to some by the manner of your expression as if you had a mind to ascribe it to me; but I resign all my interest in it to you, and most men that are conversant about town know very well who was the Author, who dyed some years since; and it may concern you, for some reasons not out of respect to be named, to take heed that you come not to resemble him in two of his capacities.

There remain still behind some figures of brass which you bestow upon me, as ' *Colossus of Brass*,' in requital to which I can onely return you *colosseros*. ' Brass upon brass is false heraldry ;' but salt upon salt is not. ' *Brazen brow*, *Out-brazen*, *Bruss-copper*,' and I know not how many more of the same metal and statuary. I cannot possibly learn or imagine where you have improved your talent to such proficience, unless perhaps you have practised with a modern divine who is said to have appear'd not many years ago, and preached in the copper-mines of Sweden. And indeed, such is your performance here all along, and much more hereafter when you treat concerning the most sacred arguments, that I suspect it is not all your own; but (though I shall not therefore call you a '*scandalous plagiary*') that you have attracted by force of phantasy some extraordinary spirit to your assistance. As Cicero said on another occasion,

> ... Multa quidem ipse,
> Multa sed et Daemon tibi suggerit.

So that I hope the readers will in so unequal a contest assist me also, at le[a]st with their good wishes, and should I be worsted in such discourse, or rather absolutely decline it, that yet they will not think the worse of me. Had he but wrote like a man only, I might possibly have answer'd him; but where there appears something more than humane in the business, I may well be excused.

But though in his railing he is more than man, he hath as moderate and reasonable a reasoning as other mortals; and that being therefore more proportionable to my weakness, I shall deal with as soon as I can find it; for it hath that advantage, that it is for the most part invisible. But in the mean time I shall, to show him how justly I might have declined all this trouble, quote him two authors, the one civil, the other ecclesiastical, so nearly related to himself and this controversie, that till he has answer'd them, I account my self under no obligation. The first his fellow-chaplain Doctor Tomkins, who in the last act at Oxford, the question being, *An summae potestates civiles gaudeant potestate clavium?* held it in the negative, and being urged with all the testimonies and arguments to the contrary out of the Ecclesiastical Politie, the professor was fain to help him out at a dead lift, disavowing his authority in the face of the whole country and university in plain terms: *Non stamus hujus authoritati.* Now where two persons so eminent and equal in learning—the two say-masters of orthodoxy, and of whom all theology must ask license—are of so contrary opinion in the very fundamentals of Ecclesiastical government, is it not time to have a general vacation, and that all private process should be respited till so dangerous a division betwixt the two 'pins of the Church of England' be again cemented? The other is the supposed father of the Author of the Ecclesiastical Politie (for as long as his book is nameless, I can always speak of him only at random) in that tract before mentioned, 'The Government of the people of England precedent and present the same.' It was writ to spirit men to subscribe to the ingagement 'to be true and faithful to the Commonwealth as then established, without a king or the house of lords:' and there he asserts that '*populus suo magistratu prior est tempore, natura et dignitate: quia populus magistratum constituit, et quia populus sine magistratu esse potest, sed magistratus sine populo non potest esse.*' Also out of another classical author, '*Vindiciae contra tyrannos,*' he affirms: '*Reges sunt a populo, et sunt constituti causa populi.*' More, he undertakes to prove that the kings of England had no negative voice rightfully and by law, but that it was contrary to the law and their oath at coronation. And then *a fortiori*, that the lords neither can have any negative upon the people. That Acts of Parliament may pass and be valid without consent of the lords spiritual: and many other passages of an higher nature, if higher could be, which I cite not, lest the very reading of them should prejudice the publick, that book being the very quintessence of a subcommittee-man turn'd serjeant-at-law, and of the high court of justice. It befitted our Author to have wash'd off the blood from his own threshold before he had accused others: and no man is ingaged to answer his ' necessary, universal, uncontroulable, unappealable, indispensable, unlimited, absolute magistrate,' as long as his own father stands upon record against him, and he 'spends not so much as one quibble in his confutation.' Nevertheless I will supererogate and use all the means possible to find some more cleanly spot in him: though indeed he does all over so wallow and coat himself in dirt, that he is almost impenetrable, and unless his skin were flea'd off like Baxter's, there is no touching him without pollution.

He expostulates with me for 'perverting the whole

design of his book.' [Reproof, pp. 17, 30.] What, do I know the designs that are managed betwixt him and his book when they are together in private? But when any discourse is made publick, it must abide the common interpretation; and *sit liber reus, testis et judex*. You know very well that, though no man ever spoke more perspicuously and fully then Calvin concerning the obedience due to magistrates, yet for one particular passage, '*de privatis hominibus semper loquor, nam si qui nunc sint populares magistratus*,' &c. he is upon all occasions dressed up by yourself and others of your make as the bugbear of princes. [Idem, p. 381.] Therefore, Mr. Bayes, you should have done well to admonish your book, if it would needs be treating of government, yet by his example to have learnt discretion, and to weigh every word; for you cannot imagine what hurt a silly well-meaning book may do in the world, far from its intention; but if it have, on the contrary, a felonious intention, and not having the fear of God before its eyes, as I doubt yours has not, you know then that it may do more mischief than you can ever make amends for. And this is all the matter depending betwixt your book and me, for ought I can perceive by you. The contest is rather of the truth of fact than the truth of opinion, and a dispute rather of the eye than the understanding. Your book hath said so and so concerning the magistrate, as you have seen in my former quotations.

And now you come, and would bear me down with more than ordinary confidence that your Book said no such thing, or else you understand its sense better than itself. Therefore, pray let us see, Mr. Bayes, what you have to alledge : but in the mean time what have my readers and I to do but to pity one another? I must quote all over again, and they read it all, and you will affirm and deny, deny and affirm, without any regard to truth or honesty; and yet all this and more we must indure out of love to justice. But I hope at least, Mr. Bayes, that if I do convince you that the quotations are right on my part, you will be so ingenuous as to put me upon no further trouble, but confess your book misunderstood you, and was in an errour. For if there be no fault in the matter, why should you deny it?

You say [Reproof, p. 25] that what you affirm'd of the magistrate's authority to take upon him the exercise of the priesthood, was only 'as things stood in the bare state of nature' [Idem, p. 27]; and though you said the magistrate's power was antecedent to Christ, 'yet its continuance depends meerly upon his confirmation, in that' (very politically said) 'whatever prince does not reverse a former grant, confirms it.' [Eccl. Pol. pp. 31-32.] Let us see how it is possible that these should be either your words or meaning. 'The priestly and the royal office in the first ages of the world, and for well nigh 2500 years, descended together and upon the same person.' Then 'this' same 'power, because it must be seated somewhere, can only properly belong to him in whom the supream power resides.' Then, 'for he alone having authority to assign to every subject his proper function, and among others this of the priesthood, as he may transfer the exercise thereof to another, so may he, if he please, reserve it to himself.' And therefore 'this the wisdom of the elder ages always practised.' Can there be any thing more plain under heaven, than that you distinguish the elder times against these, and having done so, then assert that what was constant in those former times remains still the same, and that of necessity? But go on: 'this' same 'power was firmly establish'd in the world by the unalterable dictates of *natural* reason and universal practice and consent of nations.' And then, 'though in the Jewish commonwealth, for peculiar reasons of State, the two offices of king and priest were separated, yet the power of the priest remained subject to the other.' [Eccl. Pol. p. 32.] But this was only a present interruption; for then, 'our Saviour at His birth came not to diminish the *natural* rights of princes,' so that all of them (for the Jewish commonwealth was already dissolved by the Romane power, and by His coming) were reinstated certainly in the royal and priestly office as before, 'for He came not to set up any new models of polity.' [Idem, p. 33.] But however, 'when Christianity had prevail'd long after to be the imperial religion, then its government began to resettle where *nature* had placed it' [Eccl. Pol. p. 48]: nay, so far it went, that 'therefore the Divine Providence did begin to withdraw the miraculous power of the Church' [Idem, p. 49], (and you can tell us why too here, though the Jewish reasons of State, for some peculiar reason, you thought fit should be private;) 'for the necessity ceased, the power of miracles being now as well supplyed by the *natural* and ordinary power of the prince.' [Idem, p. 54.] And then came the Pope, as you told us before; and then came the Reformation, which was almost as bad, it seems. For 'though it wrought wonderful alterations in the Christian world, yet it has not been able' (but you, it seems, have been able) 'to resettle princes in their full and *natural* rights in reference to the concerns of religion.' [Idem, p. 56.] Now, Mr. Bayes, what is become of your excuse, that you 'affirmed this power in the bare state of nature, but not under the guidance of revelation, nor indifferently to all ages and periods of the church, under whatsoever positive laws and different institutions'? [Reproof, p. 21]; whereas your whole business has been to prove that princes and mankind are herein still under the bare state of nature, though your Book perhaps did not intend it. But pray therefore reprove your Book; 'reprove even your Reproof; and if that will not serve, take it under correction;' but if it prove incorrigible, I know not what course I should advise you to take with such a rascal. For it hath said beside, 'to what purpose should Christ grant princes a new commission, when this power was already so firmly established in the world by the unalterable dictate of natural reason, &c.?' And this perhaps, out of your natural indulgence to your own book, you took no notice of. But by this means what becomes of that confirmation of Christ's which you speak of? [Reproof, p. 28.] For, as your Book argues very strongly, it must have been either an usurpation or impertinent. And whereas you say, 'that though the magistrates were vested with an ancient and antecedent right, yet its continuance, ever since our Saviour commenced His empire, depends meerly upon His confirmation, in that whatsoever prince does not reverse a former grant, confirms it:' howsoever the truth prove to be in fact, yet it is not much obliged to your argument. For that 'who does not reverse a former grant, confirms it,' supposes that the power of nature was equal, if not superior, to that of our Saviour. For where a new and superior power is introduced, all former grants are null, unless they be expressly confirmed. And so, if the power of Christ were superior to that of nature, and He hath not positively confirmed that authority of the civil magistrate, it is absolutely extinguished, and the magistrate hath no power at all left him, but runs into a *praemunire* by exercising it. Beside, you call the original of the magistrate's authority the 'unalterable dictate of natural reason:' so Christ's confirmation could have signifyed nothing. For what is unalterable is unconfirmable; and yet this too was in the state of depraved nature. Nevertheless such is your inconsistence, that you own our Saviour's authority to be superior. [Eccl. Pol. p. 34.] And it befitted you so to do; for, if you will believe Him, 'all power was given Him in heaven and earth.' [Matt. xxviii. 18.] And He did not confirm it, and therefore He did confirm it. For 'the Scripture,' you say, 'rather supposes than asserts it,' and 'every prince not reversing a former grant, confirms it.' This is your argument. Nay, but further, if you read p. 40, there is a solemn renunciation, as full as could be drawn up by counsel, of any power of Christ in the whole matter. 'We derive not therefore the magistrate's ecclesiastical jurisdiction from any grant of our Saviour's; but from an antecedent right wherewith all sovereign power was indued before ever He was born into the world.' [Eccl. Pol. p. 40.] Here is an ingagement with a witness, beyond that of 1650. Father's 'nown son. And 'will you be true and faithful to the government establish'd, without Christ, &c.?' And is the Reproof, then, writ to prove 'that the government of England precedent to Christ and present is the same'? and '*ad subscribentes confirmandum, dubitantes informandum, opponentes convincendum*'? For in this I suppose 'twas not your Book's fault only, but you and it were both of the same opinion; which is the reason that you say, 'We derive it not:' that is sure you and your book. For if you meant it otherwise, you should have done well to shew your plenipotence from all those that authorized you. However, methinks, betwixt you and your book, you might have had more wit than to have excluded any grant of our Saviour's whatsoever, unless (as indeed you treat Him like other princes and '*crown'd heads*,' only allowing Him a power something less than to others, and more moderate) you confine His everlasting kingdom to the day of His birth, and date His dominion that is infinite from *anno Domini et anno regni nostri primo*. And now, after all this, I leave it to the most candid or severest reader to judge, whether for one in your case to affirm 'that you spoke of the magistrate's exercising the priesthood in his own person, only in the bare state of nature;' and 'that you did not make the magistrate's power independent herein from Christ;' be not a flat contradiction to yourself, and so outfacing to all ingenuity, that had you not first wash'd your face in Stygian water, it were impossible for you to persist without blushing. And what detriment the Church of England might suffer upon this occasion, I leave it to themselves to consider. But I perceive some are wiser than some; and, though you were so forward as to undertake this side of the argument, yet it was so order'd betwixt you, or somewhere else, that Dr. Tomkins should defend the contrary. For the Church of England is so intelligent as not to trust all in one Doctor's bottom : but knows that it is good having two strings to the ecclesiastical bow, that if one break, the other may hold.

Neither, considering what you have thrown out upon this occasion, was it at all improperly said by me, that if the King might exercise the priesthood in his own person, it was all the reason of the world that he should too assume the revenue. [Reproof, p. 22.] This, though it were the only passage in my whole Book that could possibly be perverted to an ill sense in this matter, is by you and the rest of your Scaramuccios invidiously applyed, and aggravated both here and in many other places at large, as if it had been seriously intended by me for his Majestie's assuming the Church revenue. Whereas it appears to have been meant quite contrary, and only to represent your malice in defaming the government, or those persons eminently instrumental under his Majesty both in Church and State, as if there were some such counsel or design on foot; and to show you how ridiculous your fear was (if it were not counterfeit) of any such matter, and to fright you something the more with your own argument. For, indeed, though you accuse me as if I put his Majesty in mind to violate his coronation oath [Reproof, p. 24] for preserving the rights of the Church, it was all that I said only to put you in mind, that, if the magistrate may exercise the priesthood in his own person, any such coronation-oath was in itself invalid, as being contrary to 'the unalterable dictates of natural reason;' and that, if he did exercise the priesthood himself, he was by that oath perjured, unless he himself also assumed the revenue. For though you are pleasant, and say that by the same reason he may as well, because he is the supream civil magistrate, assume the revenues of the laity; the argument holds not; for as much as the ecclesiastical maintenance is annex'd to the function, and this being extinguished, that devolves naturally upon the king; or, the king exercising the function himself, the revenue is so much the more due to him and such other lay persons as he shall depute under him instead of the clergy. But this being a thing so dissonant to mine own and other men's ordinary conceptions (though I shall show you in a fitter place here-after why you ought still to continue in the same opinion), I left you to be responsible for your own consequences: for that you may understand, Mr. Bayes, that I am none of those that, were I in capacity, could give any so pernicious advice, I tell you and desire you henceforward to take notice of it—that I am so far from thinking enviously of the revenue of the Church of England, that (though I will not, as you do, call that sacriledge which makes up the estates of so many of the nobility and gentry of England, and of which the Church too hath its part, if it be sacriledge) that I think in my conscience it is all but too little, and wish with all my heart that there could be some way found out to augment it. But in the mean time, to tell you my heart (for what needs dissembling among friends?), I am inclinable to think, as the revenue now stands, there is sometimes an errour in the distribution. And for example, I think it is a shame that such an one as you should, for writing of political, flattering, persecuting, scandalous Books, be recompens'd with more preferment than would comfortably maintain ten godly orthodox and conformable ministers, who take care of the people's souls committed to their charge, and reside among them. Whereas you, as being too great for your sacred employment, must be exercising it by your spiritual deputy or deputies, and one of them so notorious, that, though married, it was his usual practice, under pretence of studying late at night for his sermons, to lye with his maid, Mary Parker before mentioned, and instead of instructing your parish in the ' fruits of the spirit,' he gave them an example of the 'works of the flesh,' which are these: 'adultery, fornication, uncleanness, lasciviousness, &c.' [Gal. v. 19]; so far indeed excusable, if, as 'tis said, after he had finished the work, he attempted to administer something to undoe it again, and make the fruit abortive. You in the mean time, as if you were an exempt of the clergy, and as parson can transmit over the cure of souls to your curate, saunter about city and countrey whither your gilt coach and extravagance will carry you, starving your people and pampering your horses, so that a poor man cannot approach their heels without dying for't. I speak not of stale achronisms, but of things that really happen'd all since the writing of your Reproof, and which deserve one better. For what reason can you alledge why you should gluttonize and devour as much as would honestly suffice so many of your brethren that take pains in the Word, like the great eater of Kent, when you are either so unable or so 'dull and lazy' that you do not one man's labour? This is the great bane and scandal of the Church, that such livings as more immediately belong to it should be the worst supplyed, and that you and some few ingrossers like you should represent yourselves by so ignorant and vicious curates, men not fit to be mentioned in the same Collect, and upon whom indeed the Spirit of grace cannot descend but by miracle; and while things are no better order'd, it is not strange at all if Nonconformity take root and spread further among consciencious persons, nor that the revenue of the Church, though in itself too slender, should nevertheless appear too great and envious by the manner of distribution. This is more then I should have said, had not you by your unseasonable discourses drawn it out of me, but however is intended principally to yourself; though as long as the Church shall not think fit to repress such Writers, it is unavoidable but that some faults already too visible should be mention'd.

But to proceed: you say, 'that I have upbraided you, with ascribing an infinite jurisdiction to princes without any regard to the divine laws' [Reproof, p. 20], and that you 'give an ecclesiastical authority to the civil magistrate absolutely paramount to any other jurisdiction; whereas you meant it, you say, only in defiance to the claim of any other humane power. [Idem, p. 15, 16.] What shall I answer in this case? Will you not remember that you say your 'power of the prince is antecedent to Christ; that it was established such by the unalterable dictates of natural reason; that God of necessity must have given them such power'? If it be antecedent to Christ, how is it accountable to Him? If established by natural reason, does it not result only from man as a loose and free agent, however produced, and though from the 'vesicles of the earth,' yet acting by nature? and if God of necessity must give the magistrate this power, do you not make God accountable rather to him? and may not the magistrate bring his action against the Deity *de potestate imminuta*, or accuse him *læsæ majestatis?* So that hereby the sum of your doctrine appears to be (if without offence I may name it) that your priestly and uncontroulable power of the civil magistrate is antecedent to Christ, contemporary to the world, nay at least co-eternal, if not pre-eternal, to God himself. And this is the more strongly confirmed by your asserting, which I told you of, that the 'magistrate hath power to bind his subjects to that religion that he apprehends most advantageous to publick peace and tranquillity:' so that he may, if he chuse his religion, chuse his God too, unto whose jurisdiction he will be accountable; and if he begin to think, as you say he does, 'that Christianity is an enemy to government,' he may make use of paganism. But still you clamour 'that when you asserted the soveraign power to be absolute and uncontroulable, 'twas not to be understood so in regard to God.' (Why then, pray, do not brave it and justifie yourself at this rate, but make your submission humbly, and acknowledge your offence as an honest man should do.) And that 'when you said it was absolute and unlimited, no man, unless he would give his mind to misunderstanding, could understand it in any other sense than that it was not confined to matters purely civil, but extended its jurisdiction to matters of Ecclesiastical importance' (that is the word, it seems, in all senses, 'comfortable,' 'close,' 'ecclesiastical'), 'upon which account alone you determin'd it to be absolute, universal, and uncontroulable.' Why, I perceive you did not, or would not, observe what I had all the while been driving at, and of what I was all along jealous; that the thing would not end there, but that, as you had given to certain uses, and for certain valuable considerations, an 'universal and absolute' power to the prince in ecclesiasticals, so you would, if it were but out of revenge, bestow the same upon him in civils.

But you say: 'there was never a man of such immodesty in the world to charge you with these things; whereas you know no Writer, ancient or modern, that hath so vehemently and industriously asserted the contrary, spending two whole chapters in your first book to prove, that the opinion of the unlimited humane authority was no less than rank atheism and blasphemy, and subverts the power of all government, and safety of all societies.' [Reproof, p. 21.] Ay, a very good man are you: hold you there. But I hinted to you once before, Mr. Bayes, that this writing forsooth against Atheism from the first hath stood you in very good stead, and under pretence of confuting Mr. Hobbs (who, I believe, could explain himself as innocently as you have done), you have usher'd in whatsoever principles men lay to his charge, only disguised under another notion to make them more venerable. Nay, in good earnest, I do not see but your '*Behemoth*' exceeds his '*Leviathan*' some foot long, in whatsoever he saith of the power of the magistrate in matters of religion and civils; save that you have levyed the 'invisible powers' to your assistance, the better to fright men out of their wits, their consciences, and their proprieties [=properties]. I have told you in my former Book that I do really believe you are no atheist, and, however, I know you have so much wit as to keep it to your self, though not perhaps to avoid some opinions which, if followed home, might in due time lead to it. But to what purpose is it, atheism or not atheism, and what difference in the matter, if under pretext of divinity an 'uncontroulable principle' be insinuated and obtruded to the invasion of all the rights of mankind and priviledges of reason; if an 'unlimited and absolute power' be challenged in things of ecclesiastical as well as civil, and of civil as well as those of ecclesiastical consideration? and I think under one or other of these all are comprehended.

I have something a troublesome and unnecessary task herein, if I were to deal with a person of ordinary ingenuity; for his Book is in print, and I have also in print charged this upon him, and nevertheless by this last Book he puts me again upon this double drudgery —to prove first that he said it, and afterwards to prove that he meant what he said. But, though I know this is only a piece of his art, hoping to tire out the auditory, not out of any belief of his own innocence, yet a guilty person ought not to be debarred from making the best of his own case, and I hope the Readers will, by his tedious evasions and tergiversations in a thing so evident, be the rather provoked to do him justice. Having therefore sufficiently witnessed his words, I shall now proceed to manifest his intention. And to that purpose I shall alledge one or two material passages; the first in his first Book, the Ecclesiastical Politie. [Eccl. Pol. p. 215.]

He saith, ' 'Tis better to submit to the unreasonable impositions of Nero and Caligula, than to hazard the dissolution of the State.' What he means here by 'dissolution of the State,' he might have done well to have expressed: but what the 'unreasonable impositions' are, cannot be understood otherwise than either in matters of religion or of propriety; and how both those emperors acquitted themselves on those two accounts, appears in their History. For as to Nero, beside his personal vices, which can scarce be imitated or paralleled but by Caligula, I will but succinctly mention how he behav'd himself to the publick in the course of his government. If men bequeath'd nothing to him by their last wills and testaments in token of gratitude to the prince, he confiscated the whole estate, and fined all lawyers whatsoever by whose advice such wills had been drawn. He decreed that, though there were never but one informer, it should suffice to convict men of treason, either for words or actions. Whensoever he bestowed an office, he did it with these instructions: 'You understand what I have need of, and therefore let us make it our business, that no man may have anything which he can call his own.' Beside so many particular instances of savage cruelty, he design'd to cut off the heads of all the governors of provinces; to poyson the whole senate at a dinner; to burn the city, and at the same time to turn out wild beasts among the people, to terrifie them from quenching the fire. A blazing star appearing, he resolv'd to divert the omen from his own head, by the massacre of all the nobility and the most considerable persons in Rome. He did cause the city of Rome to be set on fire, and so carelessly, that divers of his officers being taken with fire and flax in their hands, and in the very act, yet were let go for fear of offending him, and some houses not being so easily burnt, he took care to have them beaten down with engines. And though it was manifest how it was designed and acted, he derived the crime of all this upon the innocent Christians. He sacrilegiously took the donatives from the temples, and melted down the images of the very tutelar gods of Rome to make money. He contemned all religions, and particularly is reckon'd to have been the first persecutor of Christianity. He affirmed publickly, that 'none of his predecessors had known their own power:' the very same words in a manner, and spoke in the same sense, as those of our Author, that 'governors have not been throughly instructed in the nature and extent of their power' [Eccl. Pol. p. 58]; and the other: 'that no nation hath rightly understood and duely managed government, because they have not chain'd their Nonconformists to the oare, and condemned them to the galleys.' [Idem, p. 223.] The con-

clusion of this tragedy is common : how Nero was by
the Senate proclaim'd an enemy to the State, and sentenced to be punish'd after the ancient manner; that
is, to be stripp'd naked, and his head held up with a
fork, till he were whipp'd unto death; but this by another death he prevented. This is I suppose one, Mr.
Bayes, of your 'uncontroulable magistrates,' these his
'unreasonable impositions,' and this your 'dissolution
of the government;' and you think it was better that
this Nero had still reign'd, than that Galba should have
succeeded. I would all of you that are of that mind
had such governors. And thus much concerning Nero.

But now as to Caligula and his impositions. What
disposition he was of, he manifested by his 'wishing
that all the people of Rome had but one neck:' beside
that, he was used to 'lament the unhappiness of his
time, because it was not signalized by any publick
calamity' (as if there needed any other calamity but
his government, and he himself had not abundantly
supply'd the defect of any other misfortune); 'whereas,'
said he, 'the reign of Augustus was felicitated by the
defeat of Varus and his legions, as Tiberius his was
memorable for the fall of the amphitheatre at Fidenæ'
(in the ruines of which twenty thousand men perish'd);
'but my unfortunate prosperity will leave me in danger
of being inglorious after death and forgotten.' But he
took good and effectual care to the contrary. He was
often heard to say that he 'would certainly reduce

things into such a condition, that the lawyers should not have any thing to say or do but what he thought just and equitable :' and he was as good as his word. The things may be seen in particular in his history, his whole reign having been a pandect of rapine and tyranny, and his rule by which he proceeded, ' that he might do what he pleas'd with whom he pleas'd.' As to the ' sacred rites and their presidents,' take one instance. The priest being ready to offer a sacrifice at the altar, he took upon himself, ' according to the unalterable dictates of natural reason, to exercise the priesthood in person,' and having vested himself as in the power so too in the sacerdotal habit, he took up the mallet, and feigning to knock the beast down, in stead thereof struck down the officer who stood by with the knife. Which should methinks be a sufficient caution unto churchmen hereafter, how they trust the civil magistrate with exercising the tooles of the priesthood. But this is nothing in respect of what follows. He commanded that the statue of Jupiter Olympius, among many other, should be brought over from Greece, and their heads taken off to place his in the room of 'm. He seated himself often in the middle betwixt Castor and Pollux to be adored by the people. He built a temple to himself, and appointed priests to his own divinity: and even then there wanted not ambitious men, who by favour aspired to that office, or purchased it by simony, upon any ecclesiastical vacancy. The sacrifices appointed for his own worship were peacocks, pheasants, and all other the delicatest fowl and of greatest rarity. He took upon him the ensigns of all the gods: the lion from Hercules, the caps from the Castors, the ivy and thyrsis from Liber, the caduceus from Mercury, the sword, helmet, and buckler from Mars, the crown, bow, arrows, and Graces from Apollo. He made love to the Moon, and pretended to her imbraces. But more then this, he commanded that his image should be set up in the temple at Jerusalem, and that the temple should be dedicated only to him, and he there to be worship'd under the name of the New Jupiter. He caused his statues moreover to be placed in the Jews' synagogues, to be there adored; insomuch that the great Grotius does most accurately deduce and expound the 2 Thessalonians, chap. ii. 3d and 4th verses concerning him (though differing therein from other interpreters), and that St. Paul adventur'd to call him the ' son of perdition, that is worthy to die in the most miserable manner,' as he did afterwards, 'and the adversary, that is, the enemy of God;' and that ' his sitting as God in the temple of God was to be meant of his command to erect his image there, though it were not effected, yet however seeing he did his best to have it done.' And this, Mr. Bayes, is your other magistrate, who 'understood, it seems, the nature and extent of his power' [Eccl. Pol. p. 21]; and, as you would have princes do, 'made inflexible laws under the severest penalties, and acted up roundly to them.' [Idem, p. 271.] But when all people were weary of him, one Cassius Chærea, a tribune of one of the prætorian cohorts, for many affronts receiv'd from him, and among others that of giving Priapus and Venus for the word, undertook his death; and so happen'd the 'dissolution' of his 'government.' Nevertheless I shall not decide here what submission was to be made either to Nero's or his impositions; but only remember what your Doctor Heylin said concerning King Edward the Sixth. 'It shall be left to the reader's judgment whether the king was either better studyed in his own concernments, or seem'd to be worse principled in matters which concern'd the church.' [Heylin, Ref. p. 132.] And in another place, 'King Edward's death I cannot reckon for an infelicity to the Church of England, he being ill principled in himself, and easily inclined to embrace such counsells.' [Idem, Pref. Ref. p. 4.] Neither will you, I hope, affirm that the loss of these two emperors was any grievous judgment upon the Roman Commonwealth, or a very sad affliction to the State of Christianity. This same Caligula was he that took so great affection to Incitatus, a fleet and metalled courser, that beside a stable of marble, a manger of ivory, housing-cloaths of purple, and a poictrell of precious stones, he furnish'd him an house very nobly, and appointed him a family to entertain those who rendered visits to his '*equinity*' and his '*hinnibility*' (words of yours on another occasion), and to treat such guests as were invited with the more magnificence. Nay, so far did he carry on this humour, that 'tis said, had he not been prevented, he design'd to have made this race-horse consul; as fit, however, for that office as his master to be emperor. What pity it is, Mr. Bayes, that you did not live in that fortunate age, when desert was so well rewarded and understood, when preferments were so current! Certainly one of your heels and mettle would quickly have arrived to be something more than an archdeacon. If an horse had so great a Court, and so rich furniture, and stood so fair for election, what might not such a one as you have expected! Give me leave, Mr. Bayes, having been so long in your debt, to requite and cap you with an ancient distich: but if I 'thou' you this once, it is not out of disrespect, but only to repeat it the more faithfully. Had you then lived,

> 'Thou shouldst have had a silver stye,
> And she herself have pigg'd thee by.'

So that there would have been no occasion for you to have coveted, as you do, your neighbour Prebend's house, but you should have begun at last, as Nero said, to dwell like yourself, and have been installed in a palace suitable to your dignity. But though those happy dayes are past and gone, you need not grumble; unless nothing will suffice you, and you are so ambitious of a fortune, that you cannot be content with the spirituals of Simon Magus, and the temporals of Caligula.

' *Hactenus*,' saith Grotius upon the place, '*impium principem descripsit, nunc venit ad impium doctorem;*' so that the field lies open (were it not against good huntmanship to course two hares at once) to run your doctoral similitude here through your *Prote Ennoia*, showing herself at so many windows; your doctrines and deceits tending '*ut homines ad flagitia impelleres aut in flagitiis detineres;*' your attempting to fly with the assistance of two other spirits. But I will let all these things rest till another occasion shall offer; nor am I at present in humour to be too severe upon you. Only pray let me show you, Mr. Bayes, with how much reason you have recommended to the publick the civil magistrate Caligula, seeing you do so particularly resemble him. Who that shall but cast his eye upon you in your Writings can take any other representation of you then that you have not only usurped the winged bonnet from Mercury, the thyrses and ivy from Bacchus, the bow and arrows and the Graces from Apollo, the lion from Hercules, the sword, buckler, and head-piece from Mars; but that you have even stolen the Cerberus from Pluto, and the snakes and torches from the Furies? And though I will not strain it so high as that ' you exalt yourself above all that is called God in the temple,' yet it is notorious that you pretend to more worship than belongs you in the cathedrall. Nor does it look otherwise when men see you crowd yourself in between the Dean and the senior Prebend, then like Caligula's taking the middle between Castor and Pollux. 'Tis the same imperial spirit that makes you justle so for place, that out of your seeking for pre-eminence you have almost made a schism in the church of Canterbury; and it concerns Christian princes to take care how you rise higher, lest the ancient ecclesiastical controversies be revived, to the 'disturbance of the publick tranquillity, and the ends of government.' Then, as Caligula had his images in the synagogues, so have you your curates at Ickham and Chartham; for they 'having no power,' you know, 'are no better than statues and images of authority.' [Eccl. Pol. p. 120.] But Mr. Lee of Ickham, in particular, is so like you, that if both your heads were cut off and '*transpros'd*' on each other's shoulders, no man living but would take you one for the other. But to omit these, I shall, as in the case of Don Sebastian, show by some more private marks of your body and mind, that though you might have imposed upon the Parthians for a Pseudo-Nero, it is impossible you should be a Perkin-Caligula, but the very original. First, he had a singular quality for which he admired himself, and gave it a peculiar name of *adiatrepsia*, which was his unmoved constancy in assisting at and looking upon the most horrid executions: and no less is your unrelenting and undaunted resolution in first condemning the Nonconformists to 'the galleys, the pillories, the whipping-posts, the publick rods and axes,' and afterwards beholding the execution with an ordinary sedateness and judicial temper of spirit. He had beside this a peculiar antipathy, which was the reason that it was made an hainous and capital offence in his reign to name but a goat upon whatsoever occasion. And the same aversion have you, if not to a greater height; insomuch that, I having but mentioned a goat in my former Book, and under the disguised names too of *crabe* and *cabre*, you do as good as accuse me of animating therefore the subjects to rebellion. [Reproof, p. 210.] He was moreover, as I told you, ingaged in a great intrigue of courtship with the Moon, like that of your camarade Bayes: 'Where shall I thy true love know, thou pretty pretty Moon? To-morrow soon, ere it be noon, on Mount Vesuvio.' [Rehearsal Comedy, p. 51.] And you in like manner boast yourself to be married to a goddess; but which of them 'tis I know not, for Selene was adored under the figure of Minerva: but 'tis most probably Luna, for you courted her in the language of Bayes his Eclipse, but something more smutty, as I could rehearse to you from a good hand, were it not too broad for any man's mouth but yours; and that I would not have you blame me again for 'betraying publickly the mirth and freedom of private conversation.' [Reproof, p. 244.] The last token of your

Caligulism shall be the sacrifices which he appointed of pheasants and peacocks to his deity: and accordingly your friend the Author of the 'Friendly Debate' hath sacrificed a pheasant, and I have sacrificed a peacock to your divinity: and I hope it will be therefore henceforth and for ever to me propitious and favourable. Now that I have thus far represented in the persons of Caligula and Nero what it was that you meant in your former argument, and what those impositions are which you instruct princes to practise, and their people to submit to, I shall dismiss this testimony, after I have mentioned one imposition more of Caligula's, and indeed very laudable, which, if you also will submit to, I would recommend to your graver consideration. He condemned those authors, whose writings gave no satisfaction to the publick, either to blur them over with a spunge, or lick them out with their tongues; unless they rather chose to be disciplin'd with ferulaes, in commutation of penance, or to be duck'd over head and ears in the next river: a punishment which, were it but for your incorrigible faculty of railing and scolding, you could scarce, under so gentle a government, have avoided.

But to pass over, Mr. Bayes, from your 'Roman Empire,' and come nearer home; the second testimony that I shall produce out of your own Book of the same nature shall be what you reply upon me concerning the Vicar of Brackley in Northamptonshire, your countryman Doctor Sibthorpe, and who commenced Doctor much after the same manner that you did. His sermon is extant in the History, and some heads and points of it I gave you in my first book as a pinne-paper of your modern orthodoxy, and the very flour of your brann (not of the Church of England, as you would suggest) in the doctrine of some men in the late times concerning impositions, and I shall here sift it after your grinding. Here in the Reproof [Reproof, from p. 366 to p. 376] you undertake to tell the story of that Doctor's sermon; which you needed not, for the sermon is yet extant, beside what is legible in Archbishop Abbot's Narrative: but you also adventure to justifie it, and Manwaring's case also, which you allow to be the same with Sibthorpe's. [Idem, p. 371.] But whereas you limit the matter to the indiscretion only of a country Vicar or so, I gave you those particular relations for an example of what was then the doctrine *à la mode* at that time in most of your pulpits, and which you here attempt to bring again in fashion. You defend that Loan, and the carrying of it on in that manner; and if there were any illegal design of absolute government promoted, you ascribe it to 'the impudence of the members of Parliament;' to the 'assaults they then made upon the royal power by their bold and unreasonable demands;' to their 'bringing things to that pass, that nothing must be done unless the King would either grant away all his power to them or keep it all to himself;' to the 'rudeness and insolence of their demands; so that the King must sometimes govern without them, or not at all.' And as to those persons and members that were imprisoned for refusing the Loan, you say 'they had forgot the respect they ought [=owed] to their prince, and the duty they ought [=owed] to God;' that the 'King was forced on those courses by the stubbornness of Presbyterian Parliaments' (No, Sir, it was by the flattery of Archidiaconal preachers); that as things then stood betwixt him and his Parliaments, 'punctilios of law were superseded; their demands were disloyal and unreasonable:' all 'good and ingenuous subjects ought not to have stood then so curiously upon precedents and nicetyes of old custom.' And in conclusion you determine *ex tripode* [Reproof, p. 376], that 'whatever that Parliament or the refusers of the Loan were by the laws of the Land, they were even then most notorious rebels by all the laws of the Gospel.' It is worth taking notice more particularly that the Parliament which you have thus qualifyed was the Parliament 3° *Caroli*, which I have heard by unprejudiced men to have been an assembly of the most loyal, prudent, and upright English spirits that any age could have produced. Their actions are upon record, and by them, not by your perishing and false glosses and relations, will posterity judge concerning them. And if we had no other effects and laws from them but the 'Petition of Right,' it were sufficient to eternize their memory among all men that wear an English heart in their bosome. But it is too much for you to make their process however, and to arraign a Parliament as traytors by an Ecclesiastical bill of attainder. 'You dare,' you say, 'determine them so.' It is indeed like your fellow Bayes his draw-can-Sir—

> 'You huff, you strut, look big and stare,
> And all this you can do because you dare.'

But I assure you, notwithstanding your complaint 'of ecclesiastical laws being in a manner cancelled by the opposition of civil constitutions' [Eccl. Pol. p. 20], it will never be well in England as long as that doctrine holds, that men though loyal by the laws of the Land, yet are most notorious rebells by all the laws of the Gospel. Here is divinity indeed, not on God's name I am sure, nor the King's; whose, then, you may consider. You say indeed, 'if Doctor Sibthorpe intermedled with the King's absolute power of imposing taxes without consent in Parliament, he went beyond his own commission.' [Reproof, p. 370.] But why might he not, Sir, as well as you? Where is your commission, unless what he might not preach you have license to print, and that alters the case? 'Tis, it seems, no matter; for Manwaring, you say, for 'his zeal in the cause of loyalty was punished with preferments to defie the pragmaticalness of that Parliament' [Idem, p. 374]; and so was Sibthorpe; and so you doubtless expect to be, if you be not already sufficiently punished with preferments for the same merit. You will do well to register your name in some office of address, or rather with the clerks of both Houses; that if any new occasion of preferment should start, they may not escape you, nor you, according to your deserts, be forgotten. In conclusion, these kind of Sermons were not the least inducement of that petition wherein I told you Martin Parker's ballads were complained of; the very next article but one being against 'such as preached that subjects have no propriety [=property] in their estates, but that the king may take from them what he pleaseth, and that all is the king's, and he is bound by no law.' In this Petition, though I find sundry things intermix'd which had better been omitted, yet it is no wonder if, having this just cause of complaint, their pen being in their hand, they dashed out farther than was fitting against the clergy.

And now I hope I have pretty well evidenced that your Book hath said what it did say, and that you meant what you said, and it was but the self-same design which both of you managed together. And yet, Mr. Bayes, you think this is hard dealing, when you betwixt ranting and whining affirm this your grand thesis of the unlimited and absolute magistrate [Reproof, p. 9] 'to be so granted and undoubted a truth, that it is plainly ratifyed by the unanimous consent of all mankind. Nay' (inhumane!), 'when a man has demonstrated its certainty from that unavoidable influence that religion alwayes has upon the peace of kingdomes.' [Ibid.] But when beside you have drawn up 'a brief and plain account of the parts, the coherence, and the design' [Idem, p. 17]; when you have provided with equal care and caution too 'against the inconveniences of both extreams, unlimited power on the one hand, and unbounded license on the other;' when the bounds you have proposed are 'so easie to be observed, and so unnecessary to be transgressed, by all parties concern'd; that governors only take care not to impose things certainly and apparently evil' [Idem, p. 18], and that subjects be not allowed to plead conscience for disobedience in any other case;' and when you have so carefully avoided 'all kind of severity more than is absolutely necessary.' Alas, good sir, have you so, and nevertheless do they misuse you? Where is your witness? But pray what are indeed these bounds that you have set? Let us consider; though when you have made the magistrate once unlimited, I know not whether he gave you leave again to set bounds to him. But indeed they are, as you say, very easie. Only that he take care not to impose things certainly and apparently evil. But what things are so, you take not so much care to inform him. Oh, I have it: 'He may command any thing in the worship of God that does not tend to debauch men's practices, or their conceptions of the Deity.' [Eccl. Pol. p. 66.] But I was of opinion that the magistrate would think fit not only to refrain from imposing things certainly and apparently evil, but that he would even have shun'd 'the appearance of evil;' I am sure, if he won't, his subjects for their part ought both as men, and more as Christians, to follow that maxime. But therefore in such weighty cases who shall be the Expositor, who the Judge betwixt people and magistrate? One would have thought the Scripture should for good reason have decided a case of conscience. No, it may as to matter of obedience to the magistrate; but as to the magistrate's ecclesiastical power of commanding, it has rather supposed it, and Christ Himself, being as you make Him but Nature's successor, thought not fit to meddle with it. Why, then, we must have something else, 'a guardian of humane nature' (you know whence the word comes), to decide the business. In conclusion (though it be unusual, yet some precedents there are in the Roman Empire), you declare your self the magistrate and judge of all controversies, without expecting the suffrages of the prince or people. We are like to be well govern'd, then, Mr. Bayes; are we not, think you, all well taught and edifyed? Pray tell me first whether you be a lawful prince. But that is not so much matter neither; for some Usurpers, because of the tenderness of their title, have thought fit to carry with the greatest clemency and equality to the people, and to make very good and wholsome laws for the publick. What yours are, I must intreat the Readers to see at least in the contents of the seventh and eighth chapters of your Ecclesiastical Politie; where you tell them strange stories, and argue at a wild rate, and, knowing they were such dunces as that they would not comprehend your reasoning, you fall out upon your poor distressed subjects, and rogue and rascal them in the most significant terms of rebells, traytors, villains, schismaticks, and the most notorious hereticks, and, which you avow from the beginning of the Book to have been your design, you muster up all Christian princes to 'Neronize' and 'Caligulize' them, unless they themselves, the princes, will chuse for their omission to be 'Uilenspiegled' and 'Sardanapalized' by you. But the bounds which you boast yourself to have so wisely and equally determined betwixt the magistrate and the people are so inconsiderable and low, that any man may without weights leap plum over them. If any subject do take that which is commanded to be apparently evil, he needs but, as I quoted you in my former Book, consider that 'if there be any sin in the command, he that imposes it shall answer for it, not the man whose duty it is to obey; for the commands of authority' (mark but here the gradation of his capering divinity) 'will warrant my obedience, my obedience will hallow or at least excuse my action, and so secure me from sin, if not from errour.' And in another place, which I have since taken more notice of: 'Publick peace and tranquillity is a thing in itself so good and necessary, that there are very few actions that it will not render virtuous, whatever they are in themselves, wherever they happen to be useful and instrumental to its attainment.' [Eccl. Pol. p. 317.] Was there ever any man that writ of things of so high consequence, as to concern men's reason, honesty, and salvation, at so profligate and loose a rate? I will not be tedious, but those whole chapters are such stuff. You should have told us which actions were excused, and which were hallow'd, that we might have known how to shew them respect according to their several qualities. You should have caused the magistrate to enter into good and sufficient security, and be bound in a round sum to save the subject harmless. And the penalty of the bonds should have differ'd, what in case he run the subject only into errour, and what in case of sin, and the day too should have been expressed, although it had been but the Day of Judgment. And in the other place, if there be so few actions that the 'publick peace' will not render virtuous whatever they are in themselves, it had been kindly done of you, Mr. Bayes, to enumerate them, and to have gratifyed our curiosity with shewing us the whole process and manner of the transmutation. And no less arbitrary and conjectural is that expression concerning the magistrate's power: 'The same Providence that intrusted princes with the government of humane affairs must of necessity have vested them with at least as much power as was absolutely necessary to the nature and ends of government.' [Eccl. Pol. p. 40.] You should have done well to have given us the date when Providence intrusted the several princes, and by what means it was brought about. You should have prescribed just how much power was intrusted; for if it were a *depositum*, it is fit that there should be a great exactness in order to account for it. But suppose Providence should have intrusted them with a little more power than were absolutely necessary, whether or no would it have been absolutely destructive? A small errour in the quantity leads on to great absurdities. Neither will the same proportion agree with all politick bodies. The Turk, the Pope, the Emperour, the King of France, the King of Poland, and so on, are not all intrusted with the same power; but some of 'm have more and some perhaps less than is absolutely necessary. 'Tis pity that you were not at the Admensuration, and that you, like Apollo, did not order the balance of government, or fill the cartridges and distribute them to each magistrate according to his calibre. Then whereas you say that 'Providence must of necessity have intrusted the magistrate with at least as much power as was absolutely necessary,' you ought to have consider'd whether, according to your usual exactness, necessity upon necessity 'be not false heraldry:' and when you add to the nature and ends of government, you should have exprest what those were; for Authors are very much divided about it. You say, 'publick peace and tranquillity.' Why but some, for the attainment of that, hold it to be necessary that subjects should have no arms, others that they should have no wealth, no propriety [=property], and a third that they should have no understanding, no learning, nor letters. You have indeed exprest your self in another place of the same Book that 'there is no creature so ungovernable as a wealthy Fanatick.' Now you that say, 'princes must have at least as much power as is necessary to the ends of government,' should also have weigh'd how much wealth at least, and how much religion at least, was necessary to make a man 'a wealthy Fanatick,' that princes might have calculated better how to govern them. Whether a dram of wealth mixed with a pound of conscience, or whether a scruple of conscience infused in a thousand pounds a year, do compound 'a wealthy Fanatick.' For otherwise there may be a great errour in the dose of government; and you may, even during your 'dull and lazy distemper,' have had experience how necessary it is to be exact in the preparation and quantity, though it were but of *Callimelanos.* The word Fanatick is of a large acceptation. The Papists are Fanaticks; the Presbyterians, the Independents, the Anabaptists of New England, and I know not how many more, are Fanaticks. The Parliament 3° *Caroli*, that drew up the Petition of Right, and others that you mention, excluding that of Forty, were Presbyterian, Fanatical, Puritanical, and rebellious Parliaments. Who knows at this rate where Fanaticism will end, and whether, according to your notion, every man who has an estate, or who asserts propriety [=property], may not in a short time be deemed a Fanatick; nay, whether you yourself, that were formerly a Fanatick in point of religion, may not, now you are grown so wealthy, upon that account at least turn Presbyterian? Moreover, in your '*Censure*' too '*of Platonick Philosophy*,' when you first made courtship to Ecclesiastical Politie (but the intrigue was not so avowed and publick), you have said, 'governours must keep their subjects from sinking into too much ignorance or rising to too much knowledge in matters of—' (I wonder what this — should mean : it is not sure of those designs that aspire to serve your dearest——) 'for the former renders them salvage [=savage], which is apparently destructive to government; the latter makes them proud, conceited, and zealous, that breeds contempt of governours, and sets them upon headless plots and designs of reformation, that usually proceed to rebellion, &c.' I see now that it is to be supplyed, 'or rising to too much knowledge in matters of'—— Religion. You that do, as if it were in Rogation Week, perambulate the bounds of government, and leave them 'so easie to be understood, and so unnecessary to be transgressed,' why would you here have conceal'd them; or was it that in this manner you drew a line betwixt the prince and the subject, to serve ever after for their boundary? Will you believe me? seeing you had blamed me for saying that 'you have extended the prince's power to impotency, as a streight line continued grows a circle;' when I saw this streight line of yours, I took my compasses, and divaricating them for experiment, I drew the circular line all along thorow it, that you could not see what was become of it, and without the least offence to the figure upon either account. But here again, Mr. Bayes, or — to use a Chaucer's word for change — Mr. Limitour, you are much out and too indefinite. You should, if you would have said any thing to the purpose, have read a lecture here to princes upon the centers of knowledge and ignorance, and how and when they gravitate and levitate. But as you failed in the matter of wealth and fanaticisme, and you did not instruct them how to know when their subjects were fat or lean enough, when they were honest or dishonest enough; so you have here disappointed governours extremely, who would have been glad to have behaved themselves well, and to have ruled with good reputation, that they are at an absolute loss to know how to diet their subjects, and to distinguish when their people are fools enough, and when wise enough, or how much ignorance would suffice a reasonable man. But however, upon this survey, if the rule hold good, that an indefinite is equipollent to an universal, I collect from these two passages of yours last quoted, that you are pretty well satisfyed that 'Providence having of necessity intrusted princes with at least as much power as is absolutely necessary to the nature and ends of government,' they ought for peace and tranquillitie's sake (for 'tis '*must*' too in this, out of your '*Platonic Philosophy*') to keep their subjects from arms, from letters, and from propriety [=property]. For, as you said formerly, 'there are few actions' (whether of the governour or of the people) 'which that nobler end of publick tranquillity will not render virtuous, whatsoever the actions be in their own nature.' How others will judge of it, I know not, or how far princes will think that expedient which you affirm necessary: but certainly if this course were once effectually taken, the whole year would consist of halcyon holidayes, and the whole world, free from storms and tempests, would be lull'd and dandled into a brumal quiet.

Neither are you more distinct in the matter of necessity, wherein, it being the original from which you first derive all this absolute and unlimited government, it behoved you, if ever, to have '*shown your heraldry.*' For though necessity be a very honourable name of good extraction and alliance, yet there are several families of the Necessities, as in yours of Dayes;

and though some of 'm are patrician, yet others are plebeian. There is, first of all, a necessity that some have talk'd of, and which I mention'd to you in my former Book, that was pre-eternal to all things, and exercised dominion not only over all humane things, but over Jupiter himself and the rest of the Deities, and drove the great iron nail thorough the axletree of Nature. I have some suspicion that you would have men understand it of yourself, and that you are that necessity. For what can you be less or other, who have given an absolute and unlimited power to princes, who have made Nature pre-existent to our Saviour and pre-eminent, and have therefore forced Him to subscribe to its dictates, and confirm its grants, though to His own derogation and prejudice; who have obliged Providence to dispense power to the magistrate according to your good pleasure, and herein have claim'd to yourself that universal dictatorship of necessity over God. and man, though it were but *clavi figendi causa*, and to strike thorow all government, humane and divine, with the great hammer? There is another, which may be named the necessity of the neck, or Caligula's necessity, before spoke of; that is, that the whole body of the people should have but one neck. Do you mean this? for it is very useful and virtuous toward the attainment of 'publick tranquillity and the ends of government.' A third is the necessity of the calf, which in this case would be very considerable to the magistrate. For the calves of the legs being placed behind, where they are altogether unuseful, it were necessary in some men's opinions to place the calf rather before for defense, lest men should break their shins by making more haste than good speed. You may then reckon necessity of State, to which in former times it was usual to oppose impossibility : and of kin to these is necessity that has no law, and that necessity where the King loses his right, that is, when nothing is to be had. And lastly, there is one sort of men, for whose sake there is a common maxime establish'd, that there is an absolute necessity they should have good memories. I have thus far gratified your indefiniteness by this enumeration, that you may henceforward pick and chuse a necessity as you shall see occasion. And in the mean time, that I may furnish you with a christen-name as well as a sir-name, and set you up for an Author, you may please henceforward to write yourself Mr. Necessity Bayes. But though the necessity you speak of does more or less partake of all or most of those I have mention'd, it seems to me rather reducible to that of the calf. That is to say, you do hereby seem to imagine, that Providence should have contrived all things according to the utmost perfection, or that which you conceive would have been most to your purpose. Whereas in the shape of man's body, and in the frame of the world, there are many things indeed lyable to objection, and which might have been better, if we should give ear to proud and curious spirits. But we must nevertheless be content with such bodies, and to inhabit such an earth as it has pleased God to allot us. And so also in the government of the world, it were desirable that men might live in perpetual peace, in a state of good nature, without law or magistrate, because by the universal equity and rectitude of manners they would be superfluous. And had God intended it so, it would so have succeeded, and He would have sway'd and temper'd the mind and affections of mankind, so that their innocence should have expressed that of the Angels, and the tranquillity of His dominion here below should have resembled that in Heaven. But, alas, that state of perfection was dissolv'd in the first instance, and was shorter-liv'd than anarchy, scarce of one day's continuance. And ever since the first brother sacrificed the other to revenge, because his offering was better accepted [Genesis iv. 4-5], slaughter and war has made up half the business in the world, and oftentimes upon the same quarrel, and with like success. So that, as God has hitherto, instead of an eternal Spring, a standing serenity, and perpetual sunshine, subjected mankind to the dismal influence of comets from above, to thunder, and lightning, and tempests from the middle region, and from the lower surface to the raging of the seas and the tottering of earthquakes, beside all other the innumerable calamities to which humane life is exposed, He has in like manner distinguish'd the government of the world by the intermitting seasons of discord, war, and publick disturbance. Neither has He so order'd it only (as men endeavour to express it) by meer permission, but sometimes out of complacency. For though it may happen that both the parties may be guilty of War, as both of Schisme, yet there are many cases in which War is just, and few, however, where there is not more justice on one side than the other. To repell an invasion from abroad, or extinguish an usurpation at home, would not require a long consultation with conscience. The Jews themselves learnt at last that 'twas lawful to fight a battel on the Sabbath-day, rather then submit their throats to the enemy: and had all sectaries been of the opinion of some Anabaptists and others, that all war is unlawful, they would have afforded matter rather of derision than disturbance. Nevertheless it is most certain, that tranquillity in government is by all just means to be sought after; and it might easily be attain'd and preserved, did those that most pretend to it, sincerely labour it. But men have oftentimes, as I have partly show'd you in your own doctrine, other ends of government, and that to compass them require other means than will consist with so specious a title. How should such persons arrive at their design'd port but by disturbance? For if there were a dead calm always, and the wind blew from no corner, there would be no navigation. You will object perhaps, and I stand corrected, that though there should not be a breath of air, it might be performed by galleys: and 'tis indeed the very thing proposed in your Ecclesiastical Politie, that you might be row'd in state over the ocean of publick tranquillity by the publick slavery. But because you are subject to misconstrue even true English, I will explain my self as distinctly as I can, and as close as possible, what is mine own opinion in this matter of the magistrate and government; that, seeing I have blamed you where I thought you blameworthy, you may have as fair hold of me too, if you can find where to fix your accusation.

The power of the magistrate does most certainly issue from the divine authority. The obedience due to that power is by divine command; and subjects are bound, both as men and as Christians, to obey the magistrate actively in all things where their duty to God intercedes not, and however passively, that is, either by leaving their countrey, or if they cannot do that (the magistrate, or the reason of their own occasions hindring them), then by suffering patiently at home, without giving the least publick disturbance. But the dispute concerning the magistrate's power ought to be superfluous; for that it is certainly founded upon his commission from God, and for the most part sufficiently fortified with all humane advantages. There are few soveraign princes so abridged, but that, if they be not contented, they may envy their own fortune. But the modester question (if men will needs be medling with matters above them) would be, how far it is advisable for a prince to exert and push the rigour of that power which no man can deny him; for princes, as they derive the right of succession from their ancestors, so they inherit from that ancient and illustrious extraction a generosity that runs in the blood above the allay of the rest of mankind. And being moreover at so much ease of honour and fortune, that they are free from the gripes of avarice and twinges of ambition, they are the more disposed to an universal benignity toward their subjects. What prince that sees so many millions of men, either labouring industriously toward his revenue, or adventuring their lives in his service, and all of them performing his commands with a religious obedience, but conceives at the same time a relenting tenderness over them, whereof others out of the narrowness of their minds cannot be capable? But if this gracious temper be inconsistent with the 'nature and ends of government,' it behoves them to be aware, and by the rougher methods to provide for their own and the people's security. For though princes are not, as in some barbarous parts of the world, sworn as 'twere upon the almanack, and violate their coronation-oath unless the seasons of the year be very punctual, yet (abating only for an extraordinary accident from heaven) they are responsible to Him that gave them their commission for the happiness or infelicity of their subjects during the term of their government. It is within their power, depends upon their counsels, and they cannot fail of a prosperous reign, but by a mistaken choice betwixt rigour or moderation. But whoever shall cast his eye thorow the history of all ages, will find that nothing has alwayes succeeded better with princes then the clemency of government; and that those, on the contrary, who have taken the sanguinary course, have been unfortunate to themselves and the people, the consequences not being separable. For whether that royal and magnanimous gentleness spring from a propensity of their nature, or be acquired and confirmed by good and prudent consideration, it draws along with it all the effects of Policy. The wealth of a shepherd depends upon the multitude of his flock, the goodness of their pasture, and the quietness of their feeding; and princes, whose dominion over mankind resembles in some measure that of man over other creatures, cannot expect any considerable increase to themselves, if by continual terrour they amaze, shatter, and hare their people, driving them into woods, and running them upon precipices. Nay, even if this similitude were pursued to the uttermost, and the 'absolute and unlimited' power over rational beings were so desirable as some, for their own sinister ends, will alwayes be suggesting to governors, there is not any so proper and certain way of attaining it as by this softness of handling. If men do but compute how charming an efficacy one word, and more, one good action, has from a superior upon those under him, it can scarce be reckon'd how powerful a magick there is in a prince who shall, by a constant tenour of humanity in government, go on daily gaining upon the affections of his people. There is not any priviledge so dear, but it may be extorted from subjects by good usage, and by keeping them alwayes up in their good humour. I will not say what one prince may compass within his own time, or what a second, though surely much may be done; but it is enough if a great and durable design be accomplish'd in the third life; and supposing an hereditary succession of any three taking up still where the other left, and dealing still in that fair and tender way of management, it is impossible but that, even without reach or intention upon the prince's part, all should fall into his hand, and in so short a time the very memory or thoughts of any such thing as publick liberty would, as it were by consent, expire and be for ever extinguish'd. So that whatever the power of the magistrate be in the institution, it is much safer for them not to do that with the left hand which they may do with the right, nor by an extraordinary, what they may effect by the ordinary, way of government. A prince that goes to the top of his power is like him that shall go to the bottom of his treasure. And therefore it is very unadvisable, however, to put a great stress upon little things, and where the obedience will not countervail the experiment. It is like a man that knits all his force to throw an inconsiderable weight; he both strains his arm with it, falls short, and makes no impression; whereas he that chuses a just weight, does neither find himself the weaker after he has deliver'd it, and reaches the length he aim'd at. And this I doubt has been the case in laying on so much load upon account of things at best only indifferent and ceremonious. But as it is the wisdom and virtue of a prince to rule in this manner, so he hath that advantage that his safety herein is fortified by his duty, and as being a Christian magistrate, he has the stronger obligation upon him to govern his subjects in this Christian manner. Even during the Law under the Mosaical dispensation, in that regal chapter of the 17th of Deuteronomy, it is solemnly commanded that when the king sits upon the throne of his kingdome, he shall write him a copy of the Law in a Book out of that which is before the priests the Levites, and it shall be with him, and he shall read therein all the dayes of his life, that he may learn to fear the Lord his God, to keep all the words of the Law, and these statutes to do them: that his heart be not lifted up over his brethren, and that he turn not aside from the commandment to the right hand or to the left, to the end he may prolong his dayes in the kingdom, he and his children. And though our Saviour came to abrogate the ceremonial part of the Law, yet this was so essential to the magistrate's duty, that he confirmed and established it stronger by His doctrine. He declares indeed, that those Christians are blessed who are 'persecuted for righteousness sake' [Matt. v. 10], and when 'men shall revile, persecute, and say all manner of evil' [Ibid. v. 11] against them; but it does not therefore follow that the magistrate by fulfilling that prediction does gain any of the beatitudes. Rather he is invited to the contrary course, for as much as 'the merciful are blessed' [Ibid. v. 7], for they shall 'obtain mercy,' and 'blessed are the meek, for they shall inherit the earth.' And so, in the xiii[th] to the Romans, where the duty of the subject is so fully and excellently described, 'tis nevertheless as to the magistrate said that he is not, which is to say he ought not, to be a 'terrour to good works, but to the evil.' Neither is it fair for any man to speak as though our Saviour had in a manner balked the whole business of the magistrate's duty intermixed with His jurisdiction. For whatsoever Christ did generally dictate, unless where He speaks to men under the express capacity and notion of subjects, is equally bound upon the magistrate as well as the people. And where He denounces 'woe' to them that shall 'offend one of His little ones that believe in Him' [Ibid. xviii. 6], and whoso doth it, that 'it were better for him that a milstone were hanged about his neck, and that he were drowned in the sea,' it is said without reservation either to prince or subject. Neither where the Apostle Paul speaks of the 'tribulation' [Romans ii. 9] which God recompences to the troublers of Christianity, is there any exempt jurisdiction to be pleaded. The power of princes is not improperly resembled and derived down by paternal authority, and that which a master hath in his family; and in the 6th to the Ephesians, where the rules are given of domestick obedience, yet both parents are forbid too from 'provoking their children to wrath,' and masters that they do not 'threaten their servants.' [Eph. vi. 4, 5, and 9.] Indeed, although Christ did not assume an earthly and visible kingdome, yet He by the gospel gave law to princes and subjects, obliging all mankind to such a peaceable and gentle frame of spirit as would be the greatest and most lasting security to government, rendering the people tractable to superiors, and the magistrate not grievous in the exercise of his dominion. And He knew very well that without dethroning the princes of the world at present, yet by the constant preaching of that benevolous and amiable doctrine, by the assimilating and charitable love of the first Christians, and by their signal patience under all their sufferings and torments, all opposition would be worn out, and all princes should make place for a Christian Empire. Neither, therefore, did He or the Apostles, or the primitive Christians that trode on in their steps, notwithstanding their obedience to the magistrate, intermit the declaring and propagating the whole Christian doctrine; in the doing of which, if I can express it so with decency, they did an act of the most direct and highest contumacy and disobedience to those that then governed. And so it did and always will happen, that whereas Christianity is indeed most certainly the greatest friend to government, and takes the greatest care, makes the best provision of any doctrine whatsoever for the preserving of its authority; yet where the magistrate does clash with the rules and ends of Christianity, he does of consequence subvert his own power, and undermine his own foundation; not by any malignity that there is in the Religion, but by a distinct efficacy that it has in maintaining itself thorow all opposition. But when once Christianity had in this regular and direct way obtained the soveraignty, ecclesiastical persons in whose keeping the counterparts of Christian doctrine, and example, are most properly deposited, began exceedingly to degenerate. For the former sincerity and devotion of the teachers, joyned with their abstinence from riches or secular honours and imployments, had, as it will do always, render'd them in the opinion of others worthy of that which they most contemned and avoided, and by how much they fled they were the more follow'd by a devout liberality: and good reason it was, that as the people did partake of their spirituals, so should they too of the people's temporals: neither could any plenty then seem envious, when the donors saw them to be so good stewards of what they gave them, converting little to their own profit, but dispensing the most part to pious and charitable uses. But in those dayes *venenum*, as it was said, *infusum est Ecclesiæ*, and Religion having brought forth Riches, the daughter devoured the mother. Not that I think any reward can be too great for one that is faithful in the discharge of so sacred an office; but those that can go upright under the load of wealth make up the lesser number of mankind, and for the most part they that seek it more earnestly do the worse deserve it. Too many of that order did then begin to sleight their own function, although of all others the most eligible and worthy: consisting in the sweetness of a contemplative life, the inestimable care of men's souls, a freedom from the common occasions of vice, and from the mechanical drudgery of raking together a fortune. That which was an office before was now turn'd into a benefice, and one would not suffice the appetite, but they introduced the polygamy of Pluralities. Non-residence was so legal, that it was almost grown to a science, and a man might have compil'd a systeme of its several terms of art and distinctions. They follow'd the Courts of princes, and intangled themselves in secular affairs, beyond what is lawful or convenient to the sanctity of their vocation : and from that unnatural copulation of ecclesiastical and temporal together have those monsters of practice and opinion been begotten, with which the world has been ever since infested; they incumbred Christianity (that is the most short and plain Religion) with an innumerable rabble of rites and ceremonies; neglecting the sincere and solid for a Mosaical rubbish that tends nothing to edification, and which our Saviour had swept out of His temple. They affected pre-eminence, and ruled their flock by constraint, lording it over God's inheritance. [1 Peter v. 2-3.] They rent the universal Church in pieces, sometimes about the observation of a festival, otherwhiles about their scuffles for precedence. By degrees they bearded princes themselves, and challenged so exempt a jurisdiction, that it was resolved even the concubines of priests were not within the cognizance of the civil magistrate. In conclusion, they let the reins loose to their own covetousness, ambition, pride, ignorance, formality, and contentions : and could never take up again. Insomuch that well-nigh ever since it has been more than half the business of princes to regulate the brabbles and quarrels that have been unnecessarily sow'd by some of the clergy; and they have brought the world to that pass, that indeed it cannot longer subsist then kings shall have and exercise an ecclesiastical supremacy as far as it can be stretched. And when the best function was by these means the worst corrupted, so far have they been from returning to the good and ancient wayes of Christianity, that all their endeavours have bent to the 'establishing of their iniquity by laws' [Hab. ii. 12], and propagating it by the most indirect methods of humane policy. They have strove constantly to make all Reformation not only ridiculous but impossible, and to draw princes into their confederacy. Unto which end, although they had accumulated the wealth of most kingdoms into their own coffers, and grasped at all jurisdiction, as oft as there was any fear of a Reformation they have been very liberal again of power and treasure to dispose and inable the magistrate to war and violence. There have never been wanting among them such as would set the magistrate upon the 'pinnacle of the temple,' and showing him all the power, wealth, and glory of the kingdoms of the earth, have proffered the prince all, so he would be tempted to 'fall down and worship them.' [Matt. iv. 8-9.] So that the ecclesiastical wisdom has resembled that after the Deluge, which having once wash'd the world clean from that filth of luxury and impiety that it had in so long a time been contracting, men thought it wonderful politick, instead of trusting to God's promise, and following righteousness, the only security against God's judgments, to erect an impregnable Babel of power, that should reach to heaven. But all such vain attempts are still by the Divine Providence turn'd into confusion. In the mean time nations, it is true, have by this means been run up into schismes, heresies, and rebellions, which are indeed crimes of the highest nature and of the most pernicious consequence; but do not in the least diminish, yea rather aggravate, the guilt of those men who have alwayes design'd to secure their own misdemeanors by publick oppression. For all governments and societies of men, and so the ecclesiastical, do in process of long time gather an irregularity, and wear away much of their primitive institution. And therefore the true wisdom of all ages hath been to review at fit periods those errours, defects, or excesses, that have insensibly crept on into the publick administration; to brush the dust of the wheels, and oyl them again, or, if it be found advisable, to chuse a set of new ones. And this Reformation is most easily and with least disturbance to be effected by the Society itself, no single men being forbidden by any magistrate to amend their own manners, and much more all Societies having the liberty to bring themselves within compass. But if men themselves shall omit their duty in this matter, the only just and lawful way remains by the magistrate, who, having the greatest trust and interest in preserving the publick welfare, had need take care to redress in good season whatsoever corruptions that may indanger and infect the government. Otherwise, if the Society itself shall be so far from correcting its own exorbitancies, as to defend them even to the offence and invasion of the universality; and if princes shall not take the advantage of their errours to reduce them to reason; this work, being on both sides neglected, falls to the people's share, from which God defend every good government! For though all commotions be unlawful, yet by this means they prove unavoidable. In all things that are insensible there is nevertheless a natural force alwayes operating to expel and reject whatsoever is contrary to their subsistence. And the sensible but brutish creatures herd together as if it were in counsel against their common inconveniencies, and imbolden'd by their multitude, rebel even against man, their lord and master. And the 'common people' in all places partake so much of sense and nature, that, could they be imagined and contrived to be irrational, yet they would ferment and tumultuate at last for their own preservation. Yet neither do they want the use of reason, and perhaps their aggregated judgment discerns most truly the errours of government, forasmuch as they are the first, to be sure, that smart under them. In this only they come to be short-sighted, that though they know the diseases, they understand not the remedies; and though good patients, they are ill physicians. The magistrate only is authorized, qualified, and capable to make a just and effectual Reformation, and especially among the Ecclesiasticks. For in all experience, as far as I can remember, they have never been forward to save the prince that labour. If they had, there would have been no Wickliffe, no Husse, no Luther in history. Or at least, upon so notable an emergency as the last, the Church of Rome would then in the Council of Trent have thought of rectifying itself in good earnest, that it might have recover'd its ancient character; whereas it left the same divisions much wider, and the Christian people of the world to suffer, Protestants under Popish governors, Popish under Protestants, rather then let go any point of interested ambition. The instances made by the emperour, and by the king of France, with their proposals for Reformation, the indeavours of sundry great and religious prelates, and among the rest the archbishop of Granada, whom I named on a former occasion, all came to nothing; and I wish our later times did not furnish us with parallels of the same nature. What I have said thus far concerning the Ecclesiasticks, I have said with great regret; and it would be yet greater, did not the imputation upon such particular persons as are culpable on these accounts set off the multitude of those that are commendable for the contrary with a fuller lustre. But as to our Church, as I wish that none therein could come within this reflexion, yet truly there are not so many notorious defects in its government, that any can suspect me to have directed this discourse to those reverend persons that are the guides of it; and who, if they would but add a little more moderation to their great prudence, might quickly mend what is to be mended, to the great quiet of themselves, and edification of the people. In this one matter only of the ceremonial controversie in our Church, I must confess my want of capacity, which I have reason in all other things to acknowledge; and though indeed our ecclesiastical governours have the law herein upon their side, it befitted them, however, to have seen that the dispute should have been managed even on their part with more humanity; which having been otherwise, has drawn me, as it might any man else, beyond mine own diffidence, to say what I thought expedient. Even the Church of Rome, which cannot be thought the most negligent of things that concern her interest, does not, that I know of, lay any great stress upon rituals and ceremonials, so men agree in doctrine: nor do I remember that they have persecuted any upon that account, but left the several churches in the priviledge of their own fashion. Insomuch that in the very ritual of the Mass, the most religious part of their worship, the Mosarabe ceremonies are allowed where formerly practised, in which horses and fencings are introduced after the manner of the Moores, which Antonius of Valtellina affirmed to have a great mysterie and signification in them, but that thereby that Mass so differ'd from the Roman, that no Italian would think it were a Mass, should he see it celebrated. I have as much as possible disingaged my mind from all bias and partiality, to think how or what prudence men of so great piety and learning as the guides of our Church could find out all along, it being now near an hundred and fifty years, to press on and continue still impositions in these matters. On the Nonconformists' part it is plain that they have persisted in this dispute, because they have, or think they have, the direct authority of Scripture on their side, and to keep themselves as remote as might be from the return of that Religion from which they had Reformed: whereas on the other side, in the former times rigour was heighten'd with rigour, and innovation multiplyed by innovation, that no man can conjecture where it would have ended. But whatever design the ecclesiastical instruments managed, it is yet to me the greatest mysterie in the world how the civil magistrate could be perswaded to interest himself with all the severity of his power in a matter so unnecessary, so trivial, and so pernicious to the publick quiet. For had things been left in their own state of indifferency, it is well known that the English nation is generally neither so void of understanding, civility, obedience, or devotion, but that they would long ago have voluntarily closed and faln naturally into those reverent manners of worship which would sufficiently have exprest and suited with their Religion. And when things were carried on to an extraordinary height by the rulers of the Church, they suffered long, and even to extremity; which is as much as could by any magistrate be expected, unless that too were made a crime, and they must suffer for suffering. It is true, at last men proceeded beyond the bounds of Christian moderation and patience; and there fell out those dismal effects, which, if they cannot be forgotten, ought to be alwayes deplored, always avoided. To conclude this matter thus far, there is no command in Scripture that injoyns the Christian magistrate to lay any such impositions: and that promise, 'that Kings shall be nursing-fathers to the Church' [Isaiah xlix. 23], is so far from warranting any such thing, that it rather implyes the contrary; neither that they should so pamper the clergy and humour their weaknesses, as to forget that in our Church the national multitude is more properly included, and that as nursing-fathers they ought to be careful lest they overlay any of their children. Those therefore that ascribe an absolute and unlimited power to the magistrate, will not, I hope, deny them peremptorily to proceed within the bounds of their own discretion. And if our Saviour has reserved some cases to His own jurisdiction, as I shall treat hereafter, no prince, I hope, will think it a diminution, but that rather he is thereby discharged and eased of that part of government wherein there would have been the most trouble, and can be the least advantage.

And that can be only in CASE OF CONSCIENCE, which is the second thing that in your pleasant and droling manner you have chose to insist upon. I have in some measure shown you, Mr. Necessity Bayes, how many absurdities you have incurred in managing the 'absolute and unlimited' ecclesiastical power of the magistrate as well as civil. That you may the more exalt that, you continue as in your former Books to revile and debase conscience, so that you may put it out of countenance, and out of all good conceit with itself. 'Most men's minds or consciences,' you have said, 'are weak, silly, and ignorant things, acted by fond [=foolish] and absurd principles.' [Eccl. Pol. p. 7.] You say, men talk of it as of 'some distinct puppet within them, or as if it were a Pope in their bellies' [Reproof, p. 10]; whereas 'conscience,' you say, is 'an indeterminate thing, and has no more certain a signification than the clinking of a bell, that is, as every man fancies.' [Idem, p. 86.] I understand, sir, what you mean; 'as the fool thinks, so the conscience tinks.' Commend me to you, Mr. Bayes, for a good conscience-maker. Who that were in his wits would trouble himself with a thing so inconsiderable? And yet the mischief is, that this is that by which every man must be excused or accused. But the good again of that mischief is, that this will have no effect till the Day of judgment. In the mean time, I take it, I assure you, to be as serious a thing as you would make it ridiculous; and what I fancy by it, is humane reason guided by the Scripture in order to salvation. What you determine it to be, is to be seen more particularly in the third chapter of your Ecclesiastical Politie [Eccl. Pol. p. 87], and summarily in the contents: and you reproach me for representing it as if you there 'confined the whole duty of conscience to the inward thoughts of the mind and its perswasions;' and this (to avoid tediousness, and that I may not return your immodest answer) I shall refer to the Reader. If, as there you say, 'the inward actions of the mind and matters of meer conscience' be made terms convertible; if 'mankind have a liberty of conscience as far as concerns their judgments, but not their practices;' if 'the nature of Christian liberty relate to our thoughts and not to our actions;' if 'Christian liberty consist in the restauration of the mind of man to its natural liberty from the yoke of the ceremonial law;' I durst almost trust your self, though I have no great inducement to confide in you, with the arbitration betwixt us. For if the inward actions of the mind only be the matters of meer conscience, do you not confine the whole duty of conscience to the inward thought and perswasions of the mind? Or, if a man would help you over the stile, and allow something to be conscience that is not meer conscience, do not you evacuate it again in saying, that men have a liberty of conscience as far as concerns their judgments, but not their practices? So that here is a second commitment, and you have confined conscience back again to the inward thoughts only and perswasions of the mind.

Nay even, if Christian liberty consist in the restauration of the mind of man to its natural liberty from the Mosaical Law, does not that too, according to your doctrine here, dispense only with our judgments, but our practice is still, or may be, bound up to the observance of all the Mosaical institutions? So that if you please you may keep the lye to your self, of which you are so liberal, or let it remain in the middle, till it be decided whom it of right belongs to, and let him take it and make his best on't. But in this of the Jewish Law you are indeed very distinct, and as dogmatical as a man would wish. For you say, that 'if the Proconsul of Judæa should publish an edict that all Christians shall submit to circumcision out of regard to the eternal obligation to the Law of Moses, that were a manifest violence to the freedom of the Gospel: but whatever else he may command, so he pretend not to any warrant of divine authority, whatever abuse it may be of his own power, it is no abuse of Christian liberty.' [Defence, p. 413.] So that you do not determine that it would be so much as an abuse of his own power, but you do determine, that if he do command not only circumcision, but whatsoever else (how strangely comprehensive are those words!), it is no abuse of Christian liberty. But you are so far in love with this notion, that you say the 'Mosaical dispensation being cancell'd by the Gospel, those indifferent things that had been made necessary by a divine positive command return'd to their own nature, to be used or omitted only as occasion should direct.' [Eccl. Pol. p. 96.] So that here you plainly assert what you left disputable in the former passage, that the magistrate may, if he please, lawfully introduce and set up the Jewish Religion again among Christians. 'Tis a sad case in the mean time, and truly if our Saviour's cancelling the Mosaical Law do but render the same indifferent, I am afraid that His confirming of the magistrate's ecclesiastical power, that you told us of, is not much better, and had no greater validity. But I do not now wonder that you said it was in the power of the magistrate to establish what Religion he took to be most advantageous; for I see you are an honest man of your word, and meant it in good earnest. He may command whatsoever he pleases. He may set up the whole Jewish Religion as occasion shall direct. Whether, in God's name, will these ceremonies of ours lead us at last? what shall we come to? I see there is nothing divine or humane so unalterable or so sacred, no liberty that belongs to men or to Christians, that you are not ready to violate and prostitute to your own end; and you will turn any thing Jew or Heathen, and preach up others to it, rather than lose a speculation, or be foyl'd in an argument. Whereas no man hath devested himself of any natural liberty, as he is a man, by professing himself a Christian, but one liberty operates within the other more effectually, and strengthen themselves better by that double title. Especially if your rule hold in this case, 'that our Saviour hath confirmed what He hath not reversed.' For as to this particular of the Mosaical Law, Christ has abrogated it for ever in perpetuity; and it must sure be a very pretty doctrine this of yours, that so the antecedent necessity be taken away, the magistrate may erect it again by a subsequent. So, in conclusion, our Saviour has done just nothing; neither indeed could He by your argument: and the Christian subject being only at liberty in his judgement, is notwithstanding obliged in obedience to conform to the whole Jewish ceremonial, as oft as the magistrate may think it expedient. But I say, you ought to know and acknowledge that our Saviour has establish'd Christianity to indure till His second coming; and hath in the institution of that Religion condescended, though He might have exacted both, to be Himself treated without ceremony, so that were supplyed by reality. For Christianity has obliged men to very hard duty, and ransacks their very thoughts, not being contented with an unblameableness as to the Law, nor with an external righteousness: it aims all at that which is sincere and solid, and having laid that weight upon the conscience which will be found sufficient for any honest man to walk under, it hath not pressed and loaded men further with the burthen of ritual and ceremonial traditions and impositions. For whether indeed they be so heavy as they appear to the scrupulous, yet they are not so light, to be sure, as you would perswade men: and most creatures know when they have their just load, nor can you make them go if you add more. In conclusion, it is most certain that as our Saviour has exacted those duties which are necessary with more declarative strictness from Christians then was under any other religion, and thereby bound the conscience to a severer scrutiny within itself over all our performances; so hath He gratified them on the other part with larger exemptions and priviledges from things indifferent and unnecessary. And it is a gross abuse, whosoever strives to limit Christian liberty only from the Jewish ceremonial Law, which you too will hardly grant us. But whatsoever general rules, laws, and precepts are given in Scripture, and more particularly in the New Testament, to direct the magistrate in the moderation of his power in things of this nature, do make up the great charter of Christian liberty, and they may justly plead it. 'Tis true that the decision and punishment of those that shall transgress therein if they be supreme magistrates is reserved to God's tribunal, and the appeal thither, which you almost laugh at, is the most proper: but the Law by which those that offend their weak brother will then be proceeded upon is very legible, both having been dictated by our Saviour Himself and by His apostles. Yet though the supreme magistrate cannot be questioned, I am not at all doubtful but that he may punish any such transgression in his subalternals and substitutes : and if it would please God to inspire the hearts of princes to curb that sanguinary and unchristian spirit of those that for their own corrupt ends make government so uneasie to princes, so that we might once come to the experiment how happy a prince and people might be under a plain and true Christian administration, I believe all men, and especially princes, would be so satisfy'd, and in love with it, that they would make it treason to give them any contrary counsel.

But the occasion of all this medly and hoch-poch that you make in matters of meer conscience, and of mixt conscience, in the liberty of Christians as to their judgment, but not to their practice, of the magistrate's power to impose things by a subsequent, so he do it not by an antecedent necessity, is from your ignorance of divine and humane things, which makes you jumble them so together that you cannot distinguish of their several obligations. Or else, it is your voluntary and affected perverting of your own knowlege, in the same manner as in Turky they turn themselves so long giddy, till they can neither think nor see what is before them, and fall down in an extasie fit for inspiration. Or, it is that you may thus contribute to your own maxime, and seeing 'governors must keep their people from sinking into too much ignorance, or rising to too much knowledge in matters of——' to do your part in muffling them up to play before you at the blind-man-buff of conscience. [Defence, p. 413.] For whereas you quote out of the first of Peter, c. ii. v. 13 and 15, 'Submit to every ordinance of man for the Lord's sake, for so is the will of God, that with well-doing you may put to silence the ignorance of foolish men,' it appears as if you had on purpose omitted what comes between in the latter end of the 13th and the whole 14th verse, 'Whether it be to the king as supreme, or unto governors, as unto them that are sent by him for the punishment of evil-doers, and for the praise of them that do well:' and you neglect in the 16th verse, 'As free, and not using your liberty as a cloak of maliciousness,' the conclusion 'but as the servants of God:' and 'as *free*' you print in the common character, that men may not, unless they look in the Bible, discern that it is part of the text. These are pretty little contrivances. But if this be consider'd in the whole, it seems to me that 'by every ordinance of man' is not meant every law of man, but the governors themselves, whether supreme or substitute. And that submission not to be intended singly concerning an active obedience: for few men will offer to say that if ordinances should be interpreted by laws, men ought so to obey '*every*' law; for their duty is described 'as free,' and 'as the servants of God;' so that whensoever those come to be contradistinguished, not man but God is to be obey'd. And therefore this Apostle, and so all the rest, did actively disobey by preaching the gospel, and in particular Saint Paul perceiv'd another kind of '*necessity*' than yours; 'necessity was laid upon him to preach the gospel.' [1 Cor. ix. 16.] And you may find in the ixth to the Hebrews that those ordinances which you contend still to be lawful, are absolutely voided. For 'the first covenant also had ordinances of divine service, and a worldly sanctuary.' [Heb. ix. 1.] And v. 10, it 'stood only in meats and drinks and divers washings and carnal ordinances imposed on them until the time of Reformation.' And you cannot unless you shut your eyes but discern Col. ii. 14, that our 'Saviour has blotted out the hand-writing of ordinances, and taken it out of the way, nailing it to His cross.' Neither in the xiiith to the Romans does it appear to me otherwise than that therefore men ought not to contemn, contradict, resist the magistrate, who indeed is the ordinance of God according to that text and others; but in the same place it is evident that, as to active obedience to governours in particular cases, the matter must be decided betwixt God and every man's conscience. And I must still desire you to remember that by conscience I understand humane reason acting by the rule of Scripture, in order to obedience to God and a man's own salvation. But you, not content to have said that the 'magistrate hath power to make that a particular of the Divine Law which God hath not made so' [Eccl. Pol. p. 80], do avowedly and plainly make all humane laws that do not countenance vice, or disgrace the Deity, to be particulars of the Divine Law, and that to break any other law then such is a sin, and that 'all laws civil as well as ecclesiastical equally oblige the conscience,' and upon pain of damnation. So that hereby whatsoever is enacted on earth is at the same time enacted in heaven. Every law carries along with it the pain of excommunication. Whatsoever the magistrate binds on earth is bound in heaven: and he delivers every man who transgresses in cart-wheels, and the number of horses in his team, or that buries not in flannel, over to Satan. There is no Christian magistrate, but, if he thought the matter went so high, he would be very tender how he made laws, and rather then multiply them to the damnation of his good subjects, he would bear with many a public inconvenience. But this desperate maxime (though what I am going to say is unavoidable, yet I do it with reverence) does impose upon God's conscience, that He must make that a sin which was not so before the magistrate commanded the duty; it makes God to be the magistrate's minister; and whereas the lawgiver contents himself with the penalty that the law exacts in case of failure, nevertheless at the same time he obliges God to execute damnation upon the offender. I am almost confident that the Divine Justice would never have been thus far at the magistrate's beck, but that you have told God that 'He must of necessity grant him at least thus much power;' and therefore I must confess there is no help for it. Will you never be ashamed of this damning and damned doctrine? It were better that all Uniformity had never been invented, then that it should be upheld by such Theology. But I will not fall into a further transport, seeing some allowance is to be given you, by reason of your ancient acquaintance, and your present friendship with the Nonconformists; which obliges you to do them all good offices, and therefore, like that Italian, you would not do them an half-courtesie, but contrive to kill their bodies and damn their souls with one labour. Are there not many customs that have gained the force of laws? Are there not many persons that are ignorant of several laws that are made? Are there not many laws that by disuse are grown obsolete and stand yet unrepealed? What would you in this case advise God to do with poor sinners? Will nothing serve but Hellfire? or will you agree that there may be some gentler Limbo prepared for them, where they may sweat out their guiltiness? It is impossible in such gross absurdities, but that a man should speak to the quick, though never so desirous to treat of sacred things with due reverence. But moreover, whatsoever obligations may be put upon mankind, they are to be expounded by that great and fundamental law of mercy. And therefore it was that our Saviour, even in the case of a divine positive law, declared accordingly and interpreted the meaning of 'I will have mercy and not sacrifice' [Hosea vi. 6], as a general dispensation in all things that come within that respect and consideration. But to proceed further: I say, with submission still to better judgments, and especially to superiors, that I conceive the magistrate, as in Scripture described, is the ordinance of God constituting him, and the ordinance of man assenting to his dominion. For there is not now any express revelation, no inspiration of a prophet, nor unction of that nature as to the declaring of that particular person that is to govern. Only God hath in general commanded and disposed men to be governed. And the particular person reigns according to that right, more or less respectively, which under God's providence he or his predecessors have lawfully acquired over the subject. Therefore I take the magistrate's power to be from God, only in a providential constitution; and the nature of which is very well and reverently expressed by princes themselves, 'By the grace of God King of &c.;' but I do not understand that God has thereby imparted and devolved to the magistrate His Divine jurisdiction. God, that sees into the thoughts of men's hearts, and to whom both prince and subjects are accountable, 'sees not as man sees' [1 Sam. xvi. 7], nor judges as he judges; but is His own measure and the first rectitude. But for the magistrate, it is surely sufficient that God has fortify'd him with a divine law, that he may not be resisted:

but his administration is humane; neither is it possible either for him to exact or men to pay him more then a civil obedience in those laws which he constituteth. Otherwise it were in his power not only, as some and Caligula for example, to decree that he is God, but even to be so. God surely, although it does for the most part or ought to fall out that the same action is a sin against God, and a disobedience to the humane law, punishes the fact so far as He sees and knows in Himself that it is sinful and contrary to the eternal rule of justice: but an humane law can create only an humane obligation; and unless the breach chance likewise to be against some express Divine Law, I cannot see but that the offendor is guilty not to God, but onely to the magistrate, and hath expiated his offence by undergoing the penalty.

I should be very sorry to disseminate, in a matter so weighty, any errour, nay even an unseasonable or dangerous truth; none being more desirous or more sensible of the necessity of publick obedience. And therefore as I have consulted none to make them conscious or culpable of what mistake I may run into, so if any shall convince me of one herein, I shall ingenuously retract it. But if this appear to be sufficient in reason for the preserving of government, 'tis probable that it will prove to be so likewise in fact, and that there is no further provision made for the magistrate. I do suppose therefore that the true stress and force of laws lyes in their aptitude and convenience for the general good of the people; and no magistrate is so wanton as to make laws meerly out of the pleasure of legislation, but out of the prospect of some utility to the publick. Few subjects are so capable as to imagine any further obligation: neither does that opinion lean towards atheism, but proceeds rather from an honourable apprehension concerning God, that He could not institute government to the prejudice of mankind, or exact obedience to laws that are destructive to society. Therefore, as long as the magistrate shall provide laws that appear useful in the experiment [=experience], the whole people will stand by him to exact obedience from the refractary, and pursue them like a common enemy. But if it fall out otherwise, that the laws are inconvenient in the practice, men are so sensible of that, and so dull in divinity, that, should the legislator persist never so much, he would [be in] danger to be left in the field very single; and should you, Mr. Necessity Bayes, inculcate your heart out, the auditory would scarce be converted. Indeed, how is it possible to imagine, and to what purpose, that ever any magistrate should make laws but for a general advantage? and who again but would be glad to abrogate them when he finds them pernicious to his government? and therefore it is very usual to make at first probationary laws, and for some term of years only; that both the law-giver and the subject may see at leisure how proper they are and suitable to the effect for which they were intended. And indeed all laws however are but probationers of Time; and though meant for perpetuity, yet, when unprofitable, do as they were made by common consent, so expire by universal neglect, and without repeal grow obsolete. There is again, beside the convenience of a law, another security in the penalty. For because few laws are so perfect or convenient, but that some man will out of a vicious temper or interest transgress them, the penalties too of pecuniary mulcts, or of life, or limme, or liberty and whatsoever else, are necessary, and doubtless the magistrate does therein hold the balance of Justice, and weigh the punishment as near as may be, that it should be proportionable to the offence. And out of that care it is, that governors make the same fault sometimes capital, otherwhiles pecuniary, other, imprisonment, &c.; but that, whatsoever it is, being once undergone, all men reckon that the magistrate and justice are satisfied. For indeed how can humane laws bind beyond the declared intention of the magistrate in them? They who obey them find therein their convenience and reward, they who break them the punishment: and upon those two wheels all government hath turned. But to make all obedience matter of salvation, is a note that I believe no tyrant ever thought of: and it would be some trouble to calculate, when a law is alter'd here upon

Earth, and the same offence shall one year be capital, and the next year perhaps thought fit to be finable, how far the judicature of Heaven takes the same measures, as it is a sin, in the damnation. Or suppose the crime be pardon'd here, why should not the malefactor plead it too in Heaven? or how came it that 'the parliament 3° *Caroli*, whatsoever they were by the laws of the land, were notorious rebels by all the laws of the Gospel'? [Reproof, p. 376.] You say they are no laws unless they oblige the conscience. It is no great matter, however: for if they be not laws, they are at least halters; and the obligation of that without conscience will be sufficiently effectual. It was, you know, an order in one government that he that proposed a new law should appear with an halter about his neck in the assembly; it being thought reasonable that he should know his own neck would be concerned as well as others' in the inconvenience. But for such an ecclesiastical law-giver as you, I know not what *memento* were competent; who bring in a law that whosoever shall disobey any statute, nay any by-law, though he deserves not to be hang'd, nor to be fined ten pounds, yet shall in a trice and the very same moment be damned. You should, before you thus confounded all humane and divine things together, have at least reflected upon affairs nearer your understanding: to what purpose, then, have all those former contests been managed, whether episcopacy were *jure divino* or *jure humano?* whether residence in a man's living were by divine or by canon law? in which last controversie the archbishop, whom I minded you of at your *siege of Granada*, determined it to be of divine obligation. But the Pope said, that to declare that the non-resident should incur the deprivation of the benefice, would be a readier way and much more effectual. And that is indeed too experienced a truth, that humane penalties do more powerfully affect men's obedience than divine obligations. But therefore, as it is unlawful to palliate with God, and enervate His laws into an humane only and politick consideration; so is it, on the other side, unlawful and unnecessary to give to common and civil constitutions a divine sanction; and it is so far from an owning of God's jurisdiction, that it is an invasion upon it. Now, that I may more manifestly and further evidence that, how horrid soever this opinion be which I object to you, yet I have not in the least aggravated your sense or words, it may be necessary, knowing what manner of man I have to deal with, to press you and instance a little closer in that one particular of the *jejunium Cecilianum*, or the Wednesday Fast, in the 5° *Elizabethæ*, to which purpose it is material that the original clause be cited. 'Tis thus: ' And because no manner of person shall misjudge of the intent of this statute containing orders to eat fish, and forbear eating of flesh, but that the same is properly intended and meant politickly for the increase of fishermen and mariners, and repairing of port-towns and navigation, and not for superstition to be maintained in, in choice of meats; be it enacted, that whosoever shall by teaching, writing, or open speech notifie that any eating of fish or forbidding of flesh, mentioned in this Act, is of any necessity for the saving of the soul of man, or that it is the service of God, otherwise then as other politick laws are and be, then that such persons shall be punish'd as spreaders of false news. This Act to last for ten years, &c.' [Rastall, 5 Eliz. c. v. p. 378.] Now upon consideration of what you maintain and quote out of a late learned Prelate, whom you leave nameless, that you might have the honour of it, 'then the law is no law at all, and if it be not tyed upon the conscience, it is no sin to break it, and to keep it is no duty' [Eccl. Pol. p. 59]; and adding hereunto what you say in the Reproof, upon this occasion, 'I will challenge you and all your party of mankind to maintain that whatever enacts a law with this proviso, that it shall not bind in conscience, enacts no law; whether therefore the clause were added by Cecil or by the Parliament, I am not concerned; and though you should throw in the Queen and Convocation, and all, I care not, I will declare that they were all miserably out in their divinity' [Reproof, p. 33, 34]: I say, considering this, I am very jealous that neither your late learned Prelate nor you ever read the clause, but took it up at adventure. For there is not a word of conscience in the whole clause; and if you would mount what is said to mean conscience, the clause does not however exclude it, for it runs, you see, thus: 'or that it is the service of God otherwise then as all other politick laws are and be.' Indeed at this rate you may say and make what you please. But it is plain that this clause which is a part of the Act, and you call impertinent, was inserted with most exemplary and christian prudence, to avoid not only apparent manifest evil, but the 'very appearance of evil' [1 Thess. v. 22], and to show the perswasion of those times, though it prove so contrary to yours, that the ordinances of meats and drinks were so abolish'd by our Saviour, that this Act could not concern men in their salvation: and therefore too they made it but a probationer, that the subject also might have time to try the convenience or inconvenience. Therefore, Sir, I would advise you to go to your statute-book, and see whether the Act be continued or repealed; least at any time you have incurr'd not only the penalty of 'false news,' 'by teaching, writing, and open speech,' but lest you have unwittingly run yourself into damnation, according to your own doctrine, by disobeying the Act. But as to your 'throwing in the Queen and Convocation too, and that they were all wretchedly out in divinity,' you might have considered whether Archbishop Parker were not there among them, who methinks, how light soever all the rest were, might have weighed something in your balance. This, however, is according to your wonted bravery, Mr. Bayes, and, as your camarade [=comrade] said of the criticks, so Queen, Parliament, Convocation, when they are not of your mind, 'have no more wit in them than so many hobby-horses' [Rehearsal Comedy, p. 8]: and, as Mr. Johnson replyed thereupon, 'you have said enough of them in conscience.' You are, it seems, yourself the man you mention in your Platonick Philosophy : '*Celsa qui mentis ab arce Despicis errantes, humana Senacula ridens.*' [Cens. Plat. Phil. p. 18.] And you look down upon these '*odde*' passages of humane laws, at the same time you make them divine, as very despicable. [Idem, p. 18.] Since you are come to be the Cardinal-Deacon, you look, as you say the Cardinals of Rome express it, upon all secular affairs as the '*undershrievalties of that life*,' with great *sossiego* and calmness. From what I have alledg'd of yours in this clause, I hope it is evident. that you do maintain not only that statute, but all others to bind under pain of damnation. What need I trouble myself in proving it out on you ? 'Tis what you contend avowedly to make us believe. 'God has annexed,' you say, 'the same penalties to disobedience to man's laws as His own.' [Eccl. Pol. p. 260.] Henceforth, I pray, do not criticize so severely upon Calvine, nor upbraid him with his *horrendum decretum* of divine predestination ; for at this rate you will make every humane law as horrible and terrible. Take heed of hooking things up to heaven in this manner; for, though you look for some advantage from it, you may chance to raise them above your reach, and if you do not fasten and rivet them very well when you have them there, they will come down again with such a swinge, that if you stand not out of the way, they may bear you down further than you thought of. I assure you I am sore afraid, and very sory for it, that not only you, but all your clergy of England, are in a way to be damned. For there is a law that hath all the force and validity that any ecclesiastical or civil constitution can carry among us, and something more to boot; which was perhaps the reason that you said the Anabaptists were so much in the right; that is, in the order of publick Baptism in the Common Prayer Book. For the words are these: 'The priest, if they shall certifie him that the child may well indure it, shall dip it in the water discreetly and warily; but if they do certifie that the child is weak, it shall suffice to pour water upon it.' This is in a matter of no less moment than the Sacrament of initiation into Christianity: and you know very well what is nevertheless the practice, and you have in your doctrine informed us of the consequence. Therefore, in my humble opinion, it were better for you, Mr. Bayes, to speak civilly of princes, whensoever, like nursing-fathers or nursing-mothers, they speak tenderly of things relating to the conscience and salvation of their subjects: though, indeed, either it seems they must themselves learn a new divinity, or teach you better manners. And you would do well and wisely not to stretch, gold-beat, and wier-draw humane laws thus to heaven; lest they grow thereby too slender to hold, and lose in strength what they gain by extension and rarefaction. Reverend Mr. Hooker ought to have serv'd you for a better example, who, though he was willing to drive this nail as far as it would go, yet, having spent his whole eighth book in sifting the obligation of humane laws, concludes his whole Ecclesiastical Politie with these words : 'Disobedience therefore unto laws which are made by the magistrate is not a thing of so small account as some would make it. However, too rigorous it were, that the breach of every humane law should be held a deadly sin. A mean there is between those extremities, if so be we can find it out.' You might have done wisely to have imitated his modesty. And no less pernicious is all that you say further in this matter which I named '*publick conscience.*' Forasmuch as you said, that 'in cases of publick concern men's wills and judgments are to be directed and determined by the commands and determinations of the *publick conscience.*' She is a Lady doubtless of great quality and virtue; I should be glad to know her lodging, and be better acquainted with her: though often it happens that there is little difference betwixt publick and prostitute. But, she being very generous, 'if there be any sin in her commands, will her self answer for it,' and discharge you of all danger; 'she will warrant your obedience, and hallow, or at least excuse, your action.' Do what you will with her, 'she will secure you from sin, if not from errour.' She 'will render your actions virtuous, whatever they are in themselves.' 'Tis the best woman that ever was born. And further, 'a doubting conscience must alwayes at least as much fright us from disobeying as from obeying any humane law.' Ay, *private conscience* is a meer trollop to her, an old beldam superannuate, and a bulbegger fit to fright children. These '*at-leasts*' are the very spirit and flame of casual theology. Frighted at least as much on this side, and frighted at least as much on that side. What will become at this rate of the poor simple doubter? He will be in as bad a case as you, when you were distracted betwixt your bookseller and your '*comfortable importance;*' or, like a horse, he may stand and starve between two equal hay-cocks; or hang in an '*at-least*' betwixt heaven and hell till the day of judgment. Nay, but to avoid that inconvenience, 'if we would speak properly, the commands of authority perfectly determine and evacuate all doubtfulness and irresolution of conscience' [Eccl. Pol. p. 287]; so that now, instead of what the Apostle said, 'he that doubts is damned if he eat' [Romans xiv. 23], the business is sheer altered, and if he doubts, he is therefore damned. And all your seventh and eighth chapters of Ecclesiastical Politie swarm with such affirmative and imperative divinity. So that you need not have astonish'd your self, when you find it out, after long consideration, 'that my Book was rather a censure than a confutation' (yet that too others will judge of): neither ought you to have taken it so ill, though I had only 'squirted,' as you call it, at your thesis and corollaries, unless you knew that syringing had been, 'if we would speak properly,' more suitable to your distemper. But to conclude this matter. Whatsoever 'villainy,' you say, 'there is in those men's religion who distinguish betwixt grace and morality,' and how modern soever that orthodoxy, I am sure these opinions of yours are of an higher tincture: but because it is a theology of your own begetting, 'tis reason to let you too have the naming of it. But 'tis likely to prove a very wicked wretch; and should it grow up, as in probability, at this rate under your instruction and education, its malice would soon supply its age, and 'twill take very desperate courses: and what end it will come to, you may easily imagine. I hope, nevertheless, that this doctrine is yet an alien in our Church, and therefore, if for some notorious offence it come to its twelve godfathers, let it have, however, its priviledge, and be tryed *per medietatem conscientiae*. There is one thing more in your discussion of Christian liberty concerning the Gnosticks, [with] whom you very frequently parallel the Nonconformists; which, would

I seek for new matter of mirth, or stir up fresh controversies, does administer me abundant occasion. But I shall defer that till your Diagnosticks be better. For I am afraid you take that, as you do many things else, upon trust; and should you, upon further consultation with your Chronologers, discern that their heresie began not till after the death of the Apostles, you would be shrewdly disappointed to find yourself guilty of the *Pseudonymos Gnosis*, in that particular. That which in my former Book I call'd your third play, of Moral Grace, you here act over again, but with so trivial levity, that indeed I perceive I did you injury in calling it so; for I see it is but an old farse new vamp'd. And truly here especially, but thorow your whole Reproof, it seems that you do not trouble your self so much about the weight of the matter, as disquiet your mind with an emulation of wit, of which you ought to be a good husband, for you come by it very hardly. Whether I have any at all, I know not; neither, further then it is not fit for me to reject any good quality wherewith God may have indued me, do I much care; but would be glad to part with it very easily for any thing intellectual, that is solid and useful. Neither therefore do I at all complain or trouble myself, though I see you borrow or steal it before my face, and that you 'turn' (with what felicity let others judge) 'three parts of my own book,' as you say you could, 'upon me.' Much good do you with it; I will never question you for't. But, therefore, when you should have been treating here with due gravity concerning the most serious subject perhaps in all Christianity, you fall a-mousing about the definition of a quibble. You need not upbraid me with that which is the best of your science; and I foresee within a few pages that I shall discover you to be much better at it than I am, and that you are (if it be a quibble, it befits you) a meer word-pecker. You have, contrary to all architecture and good œconomy, made a snow-house in your upper roome, which indeed was philosophically done of you, seeing you bear your head so high as if it were in or above the middle region, and so you thought it secure from melting. But you did not at the same time consider that your brain is so hot, that the wit is dissolv'd by it, and is always dripping away at the icicles of your nose. But it freezes again, I confess, as soon as it falls down; and hence it proceeds that there is no passage in my Book, deep or shallow, but with a chill and key-cold conceit you can ice it in a moment, and slide shere over it without scatches. But having done that, you show your self mightily offended that I have upon this subject of grace told you, that ' if it be resolved into morality, I think a man may almost as well make God too to be only a notional and moral existence.' I have told you that I foresaw every where at what you would be carping; so I did here, and nevertheless thought fit to express it so upon good deliberation:

and could you now have held your tongue, you had heard no more of it; whereas, now I am obliged frankly to satisfie you of my severall reasons. And 'tis first upon occasion of your *Tentamina Physico-Theologica* before mentioned, which you dedicated to my Lord Archbishop; it being your first address to Ecclesiastical Fortune, and an essay, by writing against Atheisme, to gain authority to whatsoever doctrine you should afterwards disseminate. I should not say what follows, did I think I could thereby offend my Lord Archbishop, who, having the oversight of this whole church upon him, does of course, and conscientiously doubtless, transmit such applicatory discourses to his chaplains. So I suppose you bespoke Doctor Grigg to make a favourable report in your behalf, and give you, as he did, a cast of his office in the license. I must deduce the thing to make it clear to you. As soon as I open'd the Book at the title, and saw the author's name, if you be the same person, I met with '*typis* A. M.;' but we two not being then acquainted, surely you could not prophesie that I should be the man that should print you in so legible a character in a first, and now this second edition. Next after that ' *venales,*' which I could not reconcile either in gender or number, but concerning you and your book; that henceforwards you were both alike venal; you indeed, as in an auction, to be sold by inch of candle. Where? '*apud* Jo. Sherley.' Ay, there it was where you and your book both lodged at one another's expense. For whatever others are, you were then a meer '*shop divine*' [Reproof, p. 21], and did so nibble all his library, and dirty them with your thumbs, that the poor man had not one new book left, but was fain to sell them all at second hand. But where was his shop? '*Ad insigne pelicani.*' A very emblematical sign, where you digged and pick'd your very heart-blood and brains out to nourish your young '*tentamina.*' Where was this? '*In parva Britannia.*' You should have done well to have printed us the map of it; for I find it not in your Heylin, who misled you 'on the South-side of the Lake Leman.' But wherever you live, you will take a course to make it '*little Britaine.*' This is not all: '*et apud* Sam. Thompson,' to direct men further; and you were to be had at as many places as Buckworth's lozenges. '*In coemeterio Divi Pauli:*' bury him out of the way, 'tis no matter; but '*ad insigne capitis episcopi,*' at the sign of the Bishop's-head, there you are sure to be heard of. And, to convince men that this was not all pure chance, but there was something of design and wit in't, turne but over the leaf, and you meet full bob, '*Reverendissimo in Christo patri et domino, domino Gilberto, providentia divina, archiepiscopo Cantuariensi, totius Angliae primati et metropolitana; et augustissimo principi, Carolo secundo, Magnae Britanniae, Franciae et Hiberniae regi, a secretioribus consiliis.*' So here you *apud* Jo. Sherley *in parva Britannia*, and my Lord Archbishop, *totius Angliae primas*, and *Carolus secundus Magnae Britanniae rex*, are brought to an enterview, and to set up a triumvirate together. But I was at first surprized by your marshalling and commaes, not being able readily to distinguish whether it were not dedicated also to the king, and which of the two was the other's privy counsellor. Well, to proceed: '*Nullus dubito quin mireris pedibus tuis provolvi recentem quendam ignotae frontis clientulum ;*' and well he might, for he knew not yet the height and breadth of your forehead : had he, to remark it the better, it being so unknown, set a brand upon it, it had been some courtesie to the publick. '*Et forsan obstupescis.*' 'Tis an uncivil supposition, did you not since lessen it by affirming in your Hicringill : ' *Clerus Britannicus stupor mundi.*' 'Suppose, Mr. Bayes,—you may suppose, it seems, what you please ; I have nothing to do with your suppose,—suppose, quoth a !' [Rehearsal Com. p. 7]—but you intend to make him amends : *hominis fiduciam*. This salves it indeed a little : for truly, if any thing in the world could rebate the vigour of so acute and solid a judgment, it must have 'stounded him to reflect upon your confidence, then in that address, but much more in your latter writings. But ' *Qui faelicius litaturus sperarem studiorum primitias quam si in summi pontificis dextram libandas submitterem ?*' Pretty well. ' *Tum quod animae germinantis impetum repressorint quorum potius intererat tenella conaminum germina radiis maturantibus inspirasse.*' The inspiring with beams is a new invention. But, sweet germinating soul, what was it did betide thee? was it changed in the cradle? Alas for't! You were whimp'ring, I doubt, already, as you did afterwards to Doctor Bathurst, about 'the chains and fetters of an unhappy' (yet civil) 'education.' '*Si vero jubare vestro afflentur:*' do you mean sun-burning or blasting? '*fiet forte*' (suppose again, though it were '*quod non est supponendum*') '*ut indies maturescant, dum tandem studia nostra ad meliorem frugem pervenerint.*' You found Ecclesiastical Polities, Defences, Prefaces, Reproofs, even now stirring within you, '*ut plerumque solent adolescentium partus minus vigoris et maturitatis adipisci.*' Do you mean it literally? You do, to be sure, where you speak in the next line of enjoying '*felici genio et sorte,*' which was all you cared for, and which you promised yourself '*tanti syderis aspectu:*' take heed you become not '*syderatus,*' for that is worse than a fanatick. '*Sibi postulat immensa Numinis majestas sacratissimos et prorsus augustos Mecaenates.*' Nay, then I see you did indeed dedicate the book both to my lord archbishop and the king, and in that precedence; or otherwise you have given my lord a title which he would not have thank'd you for: but the whole expression, had any one but you, Mr. Bayes, used it, is very pedantical; for, though you were scraping about for a Mecænas, God, to be sure, stands not in need of one, or, however, not of your chusing. But now your theology thickens upon us: '*cum pro aris dimicaverim, cujus potius auxilia implorarem quam vestra, venerande antistes, qui iis tanquam numen tutelare praesideas?*' Here, however, you make my lord indeed but a '*tanquam*' Deity; but expect a little. '*Non video cujus tantundem intersit ut victor evadam, quantum summi pontificis: nempe si optimo Numini imperium abrogetur, quid sequitur, nisi protinus maximo pontifici abrogandum esse?*' Really, Mr. Bayes, very closely argued, and from an efficacious topick. But here you have made my lord '*summus pontifex*' and '*pontifex maximus*,' to the great disparagement of the other old gentleman you speak of; but, which is more, the pegging-out of the prince, who might otherwise by your latter law have pretended a title to the place, and exercised it in person. Beside that you have curtal'd '*optimus maximus*' from the Deity, and made him glad to go half with the Bishop, lest he should leave him nothing. But at last it comes in plain terms: '*adeo res eadem sit de Numine bene mereri atque de vestra Clementia;*' which I can English no otherwise but thus, 'insomuch that it is the very same thing to deserve well of God as of your Grace.' That afterwards is prity concerning yourself: '*hosce gigantum fraterculos non sat duxi expugnare nisi ut fabulantur superos,*' &c., making that what had been but fabled of the Gods, you had atchiev'd in good earnest. Had my lord seen't, or had but Sir Francis Vere, he would for certain have spit in your mouth; but your last collect is something strange, praying for him, '*ut sero tandem in triumphantis ecclesiae gloriam et dignitatem*' (that '*dignitatem*' comes off at last very poorly) '*cooptetur.*' 'Tis true, better late than never; but to pray that it may be very late before a man get to heaven, hath, I confess, been done in the case of a secular prince once by a heathen poet; but was not so decent a piece of chaplainship towards my Lord Archbishop. I see you writ, Mr. Bayes, here after the copy of Mr. Croxton, and others in the former times, '*sanctissime pater*' and '*sanctitas vestra, Spiritus Sancti effusissime plenus; optimus maximusque in terris; quo rectior non stat regula et quo prior est corrigenda religio.*' These were fine compliments to be bandyed among ecclesiasticks. But what was in your mind, Mr. Bayes, to write this letter, when, a year after, you appeal to Doctor Bathurst, 'that it was, he knew, one of your greatest designs in this world to be one of the most unconcerned men in't'? [Cens. Plat. Phil. p. 1.] You did it out of the meere abstracted generosity of your heart, and writ only your letters-testimonial in this manner on my Lord Archbishop's behalf. For what I perceive, you had by this breath only cool'd your own porridge, and things were not as they should be, till upon further solicitation you began to foresee and tell your friends 'that you were exceedingly straitned in time' [Idem, p. 184, 242]; and then, a little after, were all cock-a-hoop ' upon the very point of your departure to' London. ' My dearest Coz. ('where you before us in the sun-beams buz')' [Rehearsal Com. p. 36]. From Trin. Col. Oxon. May 2.' Though you are so fertil, that when a man hath once begun, he can scarcely give over laughing, I have not forgotten that my occasion of quoting this your Epistle was, to shew you might take it well I express'd your notion of God so modestly; when in the very treatise where you confound atheism from Pelion to Ossa, from top to bottom, yet you would at the same time for your own ends deify a person you had never seen, and worship an unknown God. But you were so hungry at that time, that you would have adored an onion, so it had cryed 'Come, eat me.'

Another reason why I said to you, that to resolve grace into morality was almost the same as to make God a notional and moral existence, was from a passage I met with in your *Platonick Philosophy*. 'From all which premises we see that God's benignity, goodness, and beneficence consist in a gracious propensity to let forth the communication of its fulness to His creatures, which being lodged in the Divine will, does not only suppose its freedom, but is also subject to its determinations; so that though it may incline, yet it cannot either command or destroy its liberty; because if it should, it would not only interfere —' [Cens. Plat. Phil. p. 164.] Here is indeed material intellectual puff-past[e]; Pinners-hall has nothing like it. This is to show how excellent you are at quoiting a pea to stick upon the point of a needle. But what would, I know not what, not only interfere with? Why, 'not only with God's moral accomplishments, but it would withall be inconsistent with itself.' God's moral accomplishments! If it were an oath, I should not think it binds me: but in the mean time methinks it has something in it bordering upon blasphemy: but we laymen do not distinguish well when the clergy blaspheme and when they speak reverently. You perhaps, Mr. Bayes, intended it very well and honourably, but you had talked yourself round, and wanted a better word only; for I must confess 'twere proper enough to speak of the '*moral accomplishments*' of some young gentleman at the Inns of Court that were upon his preferment; but I do not remember to have heard it used at any time upon this occasion. I hope you see by this time that a man might at your rate of talking have made God as well only a 'notional and moral existence.' And to make the preaching of any other doctrine ridiculous, you fall into such a desperate fit of blasphemy as I never heard any man but your self; you indeed have it often. 'The Nonconformist Preachers,' you say, 'make a grievous noise of the Lord Christ, talk loud of getting an interest in the Lord Christ, tell fine romances of the secret amours between the believing soul and the Lord Christ, and prodigious stories of the miraculous feats of faith in the Lord Christ.' [Reproof, p. 56.] Did ever divine rattle out such profane balderdash! I cannot refrain, Sir, to tell you that you are not fit to have Christ in your mouth. You talk like a mountebanke, and seem to know so little of our Saviour as if you had never convers'd but with Salvator Winter. Is this our great champion against Atheisme? is this he that tells young gentlemen ' they are not acquainted with any histories, unless that perhaps of the follies and amours of the French Court? Alas, young gentlemen, you are too rash and forward; your confidence swells above your understandings. 'Tis not for you to pretend to Atheisme. 'Tis too great a priviledge for boys and novices. 'Tis sawciness for you to be profane and to censure religion, impudence and ill manners.' [Pref. Eccl. Pol. from p. 22 to p. 45.] It were so indeed in the presence of so great an artist. They ought to expect till you have instructed them better in't, and set up an Academy and a publick-lecture to that purpose. What distinction do you make betwixt 'the amours of the French Court' and the secret amours betwixt the believing soul and the Lord Christ? What betwixt the 'feats of faith' in the 11th to the Hebrews, and the chivalry of Don Belianis or Don Quixote? What between the romances of the Lord Christ, and those of the grand Cyrus or Cleopatra? None at all. Tell me truly, as you are wont to conjure me, ' and by the tyes of ancient friendship,' was it not here that, as you told Doctor Bathurst, 'the recreation you took to frame your thoughts and conceptions into words did almost equal the ravishing delight you derive from their first births and discoveries'? [Cens. Plat. Phil. p. 3.] It is an uncomely thing to pass immediately from such foul expressions into any discourse of so serious a subject without some more cleanly transition; and a man had need wash himself first before he handles any place of Scripture, after you have so bemired the argument. 'Tis the fifth to the Galatians, where you had before expounded the fruits of the Spirit to be meer moral virtues, and the '*joy*' [Eccl. Pol. p. 72], '*peace*,' and '*faith*' [Defense, p. 327], there spoken of, to be only '*peaceableness, chearfulness,* and *faithfulness*' [Reproof, p. 320]; as if they had been no more than the three homiletical conversable virtues, *veritas, comitas,* and *urbanitas;* and truly you do so face me out in justifying this your interpretation, that I was almost ready to have yielded it up and confess my self in the wrong. Neither did I think it any thing extraordinary if you had chanced once in your life to have understood a thing rightly, or for myself to have been more than once mistaken; but you do so insult and vociferate upon it, like one of your bulky princes who had the trumpet ready to sound whensoever he hit the ball at Tennis, that I have a mind to try a little further whether you were not in the errour. In that of '*faith*,' you say 'that whensoever other acceptations it has in Scripture, 'tis to be expounded here of faithfulness in opposition to the perfidiousness of the Gnosticks; *peace*, of peaceableness in opposition to the contentiousness of the Gnosticks.' 'Tis pity that you could not invent too how '*joy*' should mean ' *chearfulness*,' in opposition to the ' *melancholy*' of the Gnosticks. And you say that ' faith here is reckoned up as one of the fruits of the Christian faith, and therefore must be something distinct from it, and therefore can be nothing but the virtue of fidelity.' [Reproof, p. 121.] Whereas it is plainly enumerated as a fruit of the Spirit of God here in the 22d verse; and 'tis strange you should be so sleepy as not have seen in the 5th verse, ' For we through the Spirit wait for the hope of righteousness by faith :' but you had indeed a particular reason to wink at that in this controversy. And in the 6th verse, ' in Jesus Christ faith only availeth which worketh by love.' So that you have mis-interpreted the place only out of love to your notion, and by this pretence to enervate the grace and work of God's Spirit. For even Grotius too, who is of great reputation with all men, and ought with you to have more authority than ordinary, does in his Annotation on this text expound faith to be here *aperta professio verae fidei*, an open profession of the true faith, *et opponitur haeresibus*. So that, if I might advise you as a friend, 'twere convenient for you to quit your comment, though being your own, it must needs be dear to you; and observe rather the Apostle's rule in the last verse of the same chapter, 'let us not be desirous of vain-glory, provoking one another, envying one another.' But of all that you say in this business, nothing is more pleasant then where, arguing this matter, you say to me, 'if you have credit enough to borrow a Bible in the neighbourhood, you will quickly find (if you can find the Epistle) that St. Paul is there describing the opposite effects between the flesh and the spirit; and therefore as all the fruits of the flesh there reckoned up are immoral vices, so must all the fruits of the spirit there opposed to them be moral virtues.' [Eccl. Pol. p. 118.] It follows not. For those that speak distinguishingly of grace understand thereby an extraordinary work of God's Spirit, subduing their wills, and heightning men's performances beyond the possibility of our endeavours. But no fanatick, nor unfanatick, ever doubted but that men have pravity enough to be wicked, without any extraordinary assistance of some other spirit. So that you argue, men have sufficient power of their own to do that which is evil; therefore they have sufficient power also of themselves by an ordinary influence to do that which is good and adequate to salvation. I deny not nevertheless that some sins are so desperate and of so high malice and contrivance, that no man could invent them out of his own ingenuity, or practice them in his own confidence, but must be strengthned thereto by supernatural auxiliaries; and then indeed the opposition you speak of betwixt immoral vices and moral virtues, or, as others, betwixt sin and grace, is more full and runs parallel. And seeing you are talking of Gnosticks (but I have lately given you a caution about them, and I cannot find in history how the Gnosticks had already made an inrode upon the Galatians), Simon Magus, that goes for one of them with you, is one that mounted above the humane pitch in his performances, and men 'tell us prodigious stories of the miraculous feats' that he did, but it was by the extraordinary assistance of two devils, one, it seems, not having been sufficient. But, as to the main controversie of the Nonconformists distinguishing betwixt Grace and Morality, you only shew therein the malice of your wit. Whereas there is none of them but acknowledges morality to be absolutely necessary, and that without it Christianity is nothing; but, however, that to render men capable of salvation, there is a more extraordinary influence of God's Spirit required and promised. You in the mean time make merry with it, and as in your Reproof (to shew your skill in anatomy) you will have conscience to be seated in the *glandula pinealis* ('twas civily done, however, that you placed it not in some other *glandule*). So, in your Defence, you say, ' It were an easie task for a man that understands the anatomy of the brain, the structure of the spleen and hypochondria,' the divarications ' of the nerves, their twistings about the veins and arteries, and the sympathy of the parts, to give as certain and mechanical an account of all its fanatick freaks and phrensies, as of any vital or animal function in the body. The philosophy of a Fanatick being as intelligible by the laws of mechanisme, as the motion of the heart and circulation of the blood, and there are some treatises that give a more exact and consistent hypothesis of enthusiasme than any Des Cartes has given of the natural results of matter and motion.' [Defense, p. 342.] 'Tis very well said, and what was to be expected from one as you, of whose philosophy and religion the mechanisme is so visible in the '*tentamina*,' concerning that sophisme of nature [Tent. p. 105], and the '*vehemens et effraenata venerei coitus cupiditas et exquisitissima voluptas*,' though there is a maxime on the other side, '*omne animal triste est post coitum, praeter gallum gallinaceum et sacellanum gratis fornicantem.*' But this hypothesis of yours, confounding the extraordinary influx of God's Spirit for the power of nature, seems to arise from your being ill-principled, and not well-read in the doctrine of the Church of England concerning original sin, which you make 'not to be a crime, but an infelicity inflicted by God Himself upon mankind, as a punishment of Adam's sin, and what is an act of His' (that was God's) 'will can be no fault of ours.' [Defense, p. 198.] We should be all engaged to you, would you carry this point thorow and make it good.

And another reason of your opinion is, your too high conceit of men's good works; as if, contrary to the stream of the Scripture, we could be thereby justified. For though you would make all the party of English Nonconformists answer for one passage in Flaccus Illyricus, '*bona opera sunt perniciosa ad salutem*' [Reproof, p. 74], 'tis falsely imposed upon them by you; and 'twere well that you understood Flaccus himself rightly; for whosoever shall, to the prejudice of our Saviour's merit, and debasing the operation of the Holy Ghost, attribute too much to his own natural vigour and performances, will be in some danger of finding his '*bona opera perniciosa ad salutem.*' For mine own part, I have, I confess, some reason, perhaps particular to my self, to be diffident of mine own '*moral accomplishments,*' and therefore may be the more inclinable to think I have a necessity of some extraordinary assistance to sway the weakness of my belief, and to strengthen me in good duties. If you be stronger, I am glad of it; and let every man, after he has read and consider'd what we have of it in the Scripture, and what even in our Common Prayer Book, take what course and opinion he thinks the safest. But this controversie is of so high a nature, that it overthrows your maxime, that 'all things disputable are little:' and the matter is so serious, that it is not fit for you and me to treat of it in such a mixed and perfunctory stile. You have already been answer'd upon this subject by one who at least rivals you in the knowledge and practice either of grace or morality. And as to your 'chalenge' to all the world 'to produce any ancient writer that has understood this matter otherwise then you have done' [Reproof, p. 53]; if you will but have a little patience, I am told that it will be accepted and complyed with. Therefore I shall not at present oblige my self further to this dispute: and indeed, though what I could say might perhaps add not much weight or moment to the better understanding of it, yet neither, on the other side, do I think you a fit man to be discoursed with of such matters. For to what purpose should I make a secret of that which you make it your business to divulge and propagate among all, but especially female, companies? Are not you the same person that say, 'of all things in the world you would not make your son a preacher'? 'Twas seasonably and timely considered. 'For 'tis better being drunk twice than making one sermon.' Do not you 'invey against the drudgery of that sacred office,' to which nevertheless you have so many titles? But yet you say, 'you can indure it pretty well, and it goes pleasantly off, when you have a company of handsome young women for your auditory? but the old jades do quite disgust you, and they are mobled up like so many judges.' Are not you he that think it below your dignity to step down to the private prayers in the family; and that an honest gentleman of your old acquaintance lodging with you in your chamber, you left him to his devotions, and told him you had in the mean while spent your time to as good purpose in reading of Plutarch? Do not you jeer the women when they are serious, and tell them, 'you are troubled with sin, I warrant you: 'tis nothing but some fond scruple the minister has put into your head; let them learn of you, for you your self have not sinned this quarter of a year'? Is it not you that entertain them with a leading narrative, of 'a certain lady that stray'd up into your chamber, where you drank her up to such an height till you had drunk her down, and lay'd her upon your bed till you had recover'd her'? You told a lady of better quality, that 'in case Popery were introduced, you would be one of the first to comply with it.' What must others then do, think you, after your so illustrious example? Is not this, think you, 'very edifying doctrine for the white aprons'? Yet, I assure you, I would not have told you of it, but that I have very good authority for't. In the mean time, therefore, if you will take my advice, do not you intermeddle further in this dispute; but make friends as soon as you can both with Grace and Virtue: for, how inconsiderable soever you may imagine them at present, you may at some time or other stand in need of both their assistance. You draw into this brangle, too, reverend Mr. Hooker, though he is unconcern'd in it, and you use his name continually as a piece of inchantment only, that you understand not. For I have commission to tell you that you said in good company, 'Hang Mr. Hooker's Ecclesiastical Politie; it was a long-winded book, and you never had the patience to read it; but it was no matter, you would alwayes upbraid the Nonconformists with him, for you knew the rogues had not read it neither.' And truly this is your usual practice and ingenuity as to other authors.

The fourth thing which I transiently objected to you was, your asserting that it was necessary TO PUNISH MEN MORE SEVERELY FOR THEIR ERROURS IN RELIGIOUS PERSWASIONS THEN FOR THEIR IMMORALITIES AND DEBAUCHERIES: and upon this therefore you greedily fix, pretending to some advantage. You say, 'that I have exhibited so foul a charge against you, without referring so much as to one passage of yours to make it good, and that therefore I prove nothing at all, but that I have a bold face and a foul mouth. For we all know' [Reproof, p. 66], you say (what 'we' are you? I doubt you stand single, and no man else will vouch for you), 'that you are not unskilful in improving the smallest and most inconsiderable advantages; that had you been furnish'd with any shadow of proof, you would have smother'd it,' &c. Really I began upon this your confidence to misdoubt my self, being very willing to believe that you had some reliques of honesty, especially in a matter that would be manifest and evident to all men that would have recourse to my former Book. Hereupon I went to it my self. There I found : 'Having thus inabled the prince, dispensed with conscience, and fitted up a moral religion for that conscience, to show how much those moral virtues are to be valued, p. 53 of his Preface to the Ecclesiastical Politie, he affirms that it is absolutely necessary to the peace and happiness of kingdoms that there be set up a more severe government over men's consciences and religious perswasions than over their vices and immoralities : and p. 55 of the same, that princes may with less hazard give liberty to men's vices and debaucheries than their consciences.' [Rehearsal Transpros'd, p. 100, 101.] Then, again, I find that I have quoted you, speaking of honest and well-meaning men, to have said, ' So easie is it for men to deserve to be punished for their consciences, that there is no nation in the world in which, were government rightly understood and duly managed, mistakes and abuses of religion would not supply the galleys with vastly greater numbers than villany.' [Rehearsal Transprosed, p. 301.] For that I cited your p. 223; and I immediately add, ' p. 44 of the Ecclesiastical Politie he saith of all villains the well-meaning zelote is the most dangerous.' [Idem, p. 314.] Do I not by all this so much as refer to one passage of yours ? And again, under the title of *Debauchery Tolerated* (forasmuch as you advise in that p. 55 rather to tolerate that than conscience), I refer in my p. 119, which is no great distance, to the very same passages. And it had been needless to cite any more, your Book being full and crawling all over with such expressions. And further (for, having been desirous you should take notice of it, I have reminded you in several places), I find I have objected the same to you, 'and that you are contented the Nonconformists should be exposed to the pillories, whipping-posts, galleys, rods, and axes, and, moreover and above, to all other punishments whatsoever, provided they be of a severer nature than those that are inflicted on men for their immoralities, &c. So that although a man should be guilty of all those heinous enormities not to be named among Christians, beside all lesser peccadillos expressly against the Ten Commandments, or such other part of the divine law as shall be of the magistrate's making, he shall be in a better condition and more gently handled than a well-meaning zelot.' [Rehearsal Transprosed, p. 318, 319.] Is here, again, no reference so much as to one passage? no shadow of proof? Gentle Reader, what shall we do with this man, that puts us continually upon such tedious task in things so notorious? And you, Mr. Bayes, in what a miserable case are you, so distracted that you know neither what to do, nor what you do! Whereas I told you there was a maxime establish'd for one sort of men, that 'tis necessary they should have good memories; yet such is my fate to have to do with such a man all along and thorow; insomuch that, though I am no forward undertaker, I think I can manifest to you when you are at leisure, that in the Reproof (a Book but of 528 pages) you are guilty of at least a thousand falshoods: therefore I hope men will not be too forward to be imposed upon by you. But for my self, I am therefore so little moved with all the aspersions and ill language wherewith you have fraught your discourse, that I can only say your tongue is not made of bone [Cens. Plat. Phil. p. 1] : or that, whatever other slave you be, which yourself owned, you are not (that I may suit you with a Cardinal's phrase) a slave of your word. Whereas, next after this *tentamen* of your veracity, you tax me for saying, ' 'Tis demonstrable that for one war upon a fanatick or religious account, there have been an hundred occasioned by the thirst and glory of empire; and more have sprung from the contentiousness and ambition of some of the clergy' [Reproof, p. 70],—to give no less essay of your candor, you fall on turning and wresting that, quite forgetting what follows and was direct to the matter in hand: ' but the most of all from the corruption of manners, and alwayes fatal debauchery.' [Rehearsal Transprosed, p. 316.] But, however, you say, ' if this were true, 'tis lamentable impertinent; for all the wars that do concern our present debate are rebellions, and not invasions.' Who told you that? But 'tis probable rebellions as well as invasions have sprung from the same turbulence. I, for my part, left it applicable either way, and therefore, if it will do you any service, you may, if you please, add rebellions too into the scale, and I will submit it to be weigh'd by the reader. And whereas you would confound my terms, as if it were all one, a war upon a fanatick or religious account [Reproof, p. 70], and a war from the contentiousness and ambition of the clergy; I suppose few that read it, beside your self, but will perceive that the religious or fanaticks are directly opposed there and distinguish'd from the predominant clergy. But as to your business of Algebra, and your computation of an hundred wars, or an hundred and one, it is, I confess, very ingenious : 'tis worth my quoting : ' If an hundred have been occasioned by thirst and glory of empire, then if more, by the ambition and contentiousness of the clergy, there have been at least an hundred and one of the last.' [Eccl. Pol. p. 216.] As to this, be pleased to read that passage in your Ecclesiastical Politie, where you say, ' 'tis easie for one Commonwealth that has gained by rebellion to produce an hundred that it has hazarded, if not utterly ruined :' if you will first name me an hundred Commonwealths, I will join issue with you; and I will drop clergy against commonwealth, till one of us come at the end of our reckoning. You then cite me for having said on occasion of your greater rigour against Nonconformity than Debauchery, ' that comparisons of vice are dangerous;' which 'jumps,' you say, ' with as wise a paradox of the Stoicks, that all crimes are equal.' [Reproof, p. 71.] This of yours is a very strong consequence, and if it will hold, I ask your pardon; for I assure you I did not intend it so. But however you can wring this against my known meaning, that of the Stoicks suits much better with a passage of your own formerly quoted, 'that all laws, civil as well as ecclesiastical, equally oblige the conscience.' [Reproof, p. 34.] If they equally oblige the conscience, a common understanding would think that all crimes are equal. But as to the hinge of the controversie—that is the danger to the publick, you affirming that ' debauchery or immorality rarely proves so dangerous as either serious or affected pretenses of religion' [Idem, p. 68] (pity it were that serious pretenses should prove so)—take but out at adventure any one kingdom for instance, and work your question upon it, I suppose you will find the contrary: but I know upon what ground and reason principally you maintain this maxime. It is from your hatred and fear of Reformation; wherein you tread in the very footsteps of Doctor Heylin and some others, who have deliberately applyed themselves to vilifie and make odious the foreign, and even the English Reformation, than which they could not have invented anything more obliging to the Romish Church, and meritorious. For the foreign Reformation was indeed wrought out of the fire, and increased in those other countries, either by the wars and persecutions stirred up against it, or else did itself draw the sword in defence of the just civil liberties (for it seldome can happen but that tyranny in religion introduces it self by an invasion of propriety [=property]). And therefore it was that our severall princes, and particularly King James (who was conscientious and knowing as any man in that point), have ingaged both their swords and pens, both reason of State and of Religion, not only their publick but their private conscience, in that quarrel: and if there must always be wars, I know no cause more justifiable, nor any design which were in prudence more fitting to be still prosecuted and continued. Divers also of our Bishops and eminentest men in our Church have appear'd in the justifying of the foreign Reformation. For otherwise, though ours was indeed brought about something more peaceably, the Church of Rome, if we should single out ourselves from other Protestants, would have found us more weak, if not more pliable, and might urge the same, if not stronger and more efficacious arguments against us. But you may at this rate of 'the danger of serious pretenses of religion,' say in your usual confidence that, whosoever our princes were, and throw-in King James too, and King Charles, and Parliaments, Bishops, and Convocations and all, you 'must and will declare that they were miserably out in their divinity.' And upon the same reason and apprehension it is that you would be thus severe at home, and do raise this outcry against Nonconformity in balance to Debauchery; that you may thereby quench the good inclination of my Lords the Bishops, either as to a revisal of themselves, or moderation towards others; incense his Majesty against so estimable a part of his people; infuriate and inviperate the nation against peaceable Dissenters; and all to amuse men from observing, or to perswade them into the protecting of your own irregularities. Hence it is that you say, 'tender consciences, instead of being complyed with, *must* be restrained with more peremptory and unyielding rigour than naked and unsanctified villainy.' [Eccl. Pol. p. 272.] Hence, ' if governours would consider seriously into what exorbitances peevish and untoward principles about religion naturally improve themselves, they could not but perceive it to be as much their concernment to punish them with the severest inflictions as any whatsoever principles of rebellion in the state.' [Idem, p. 18.] Nay, once you appeal to governours themselves (which is an extraordinary piece of civility in you), 'to judge whether it does not concern them with as much vigilance and severity either to prevent their rise, or suppress their growth, as to punish any the foulest crimes of immorality.' [Idem, p. 18.] 'Tis something like the story of Gondomar this, who from the example of a mother that whip'd her girle beforehand, least she should break the pitcher, argued that Sir Walter Rawleigh's head should be cut off before he went to Guiana. Indeed it is the very wisdom of Herod, who, lest there should a king be born among them, massacred all the children at Bethlehem. [Matt. ii. 16.] So they must be prevented, or so suppressed. As (and more then) any of the foulest immorality, as (and more then) any principles of rebellion. So here is a law, that not to kneel at the Lord's Supper shall be more penall than murther; not to wear a surplice, more criminall than adultery; and to omit the cross in baptisme, less pardonable than perjury. If this were once, as you would have it, enacted, and that the whole conventicle should forfeit their lives and estates, as in other cases of treason, do you think that 'God has annexed the same penalties' too here 'to disobedience to man's laws as His own'? You have already thrown-in 'Queen and Convocation and all;' but if you will maintain this maxime, you must too throw-in our Saviour and Apostles and all, and 'declare that they are no less miserably out in their divinity.' But you imagine, doubtless, and do not a little applaud yourself for the invention, that by the doctrine of punishing Nonconformity more severely than the foulest immorality, you have made yourself the head of a party, and a world of people will clutter henceforward to shelter themselves under the wing of your patronage. I confess it is a great and brave undertaking, and which, I believe, none ever managed before, nor will be so hardy as to take it up again for the future. Let it be ingraven on your tomb. But perhaps, nevertheless, you may fail in your account; and though you reckon your function to be a drudgery, and do in your printed Books debase, as much as you dare, the value of the Bible under the scornful name of '*the English Bible;*' and not only satyrize the Nonconformists' sermons, but traduce all preaching, and make it seem unnecessary, that so the Liturgy might be sufficient for salvation,—I believe you will find very few that will come up to you. For whether it be the laity, there are not many of them such Libertines but they would be glad to learn better, and once a week to be told of their faults by an exemplary teacher. And though you brave it like a landlord, and that the ' clergy are possess'd by as good right of their revenues as any seculars' (only it were to be wish'd that benefices were hereditary), they have a rustick kind of opinion that you ought to do something for't, and that whereas you have the tythe of their labour, they should have the whole of yours. This perhaps you think unreasonable : but they think too, worse, that you may well abide to give them good example; forasmuch as you are paid for living soberly and honestly among them, whereas they must be good at their own expence. And this is, and hath been alwayes, their clownish humour, that they may see something for their money: neither are any almost so debauch'd that they will grudge their dues to a grave, learned, and pious minister; but most think for such an one nothing is too much, and for the contrary nothing too little. This you think hard dealing here in your Reproof [Reproof,

p. 339]; and yet I assure you, there it pinches. And moreover, though you would pretend never so much to be the landlord of your living, if you do not behave your self there as you should do, I think there is a very legal way to divest you of your propriety [=property], and there is a trust reposed in some persons to look to your manners. Neither, on the other side, are the clergy so generally depraved that they need fly to you for sanctuary: and I know many of them that conne you little thank for so scandalous a doctrine. For those of them, indeed, that are among them debauch'd and immoral, there could not any thing more inveagling or more seasonable have been calculated. You have gained your self immortal renown, and how they chuckle and hug themselves and you for the invention! 'It is a crime in a clergyman to be happy, nay, to be a man. And if he will but be unkind and uncivil to himself, they will love him for that, if for nothing else.' [Reproof, p. 335.] There spoke an Archdeacon. But you should not serve your self in such occasions of so equivocal and applicable expressions, lest ill use should be made of them beyond your intention. Who can tell whether the good Doctor at York last Shrove-Tuesday were unkind and uncivil to himself? Your Curate of Ickham, when he had laid with his maid, whether was not he kind to himself? And even you, when you dissolved that precious lady in good sack at your chamber, were not you kind to your self? And when you first got your '*dull and lazy distemper*,' were not you unkind to yourself? Men are too prone to expound such passages to their own inclinations, and some wag may chance to write an history of the clergies' kindnesses to themselves, and their unkindnesses: therefore let me request you, Mr. Bayes, the next time to define how that word '*unkind to himself*,' or '*uncivil to himself*,' is to be understood properly for the future. But in good earnest, were it not for some that are unkind to themselves, you and your fellows would soon forfeit all the clergies' reputation. But of all your freaks upon this subject of punishing Nonconformity beyond the foulest immorality, there is none so capricious as the Declaration which you have without any occasion administred on my part, and, with a boldness beyond all precedent, drawn up in his Majestie's name. Yet seeing you are here so obligingly courteous to me, as to promise me your license and the liberty of the press in these words, p. 67 of your Reproof, thus: 'If you, or he, or any body else, have ought to object against it, you know the press is open,' do your worst. I accept the favour, and seeing your Declaration, I doubt, hath not so well been taken notice of for want of the character in which such publick matters ought to be promulged, I have, in return of your civility, prevailed with my Printer to do you a cast of his office.

By the Archdeacon:

A DECLARATION *for the tolerating of* DEBAUCHERY,

BAYES R.

WHEREAS ever since our happy Restauration we have, out of our special zeal and care for the interest and security of the Church of England, executed with all severity all penal laws against whatsoever sort of Nonconformists and Recusants; but yet finding, by the sad experience of 12 years, how ineffectual all forcible courses are either to reduce or restrain Dissenters, We think ourself obliged to make use of that 'unhoopable power' that is naturally inherent in us; not granted by Christ, but belonging to us and our predecessors under the broad seal of nature next and immediately before Him. By vertue whereof we have and claim an absolute dominion not only over the consciences of all our subjects, but over all the laws of God and man, so as to repeal or dispense with their obligation, as shall from time to time seem good to our royal will and pleasure. And therefore, that we may obviate and prevent those mischiefs that are likely to befal our kingdom from the sobriety and demureness of the Nonconformists, our Will and Pleasure is to give a free and uncontroulable licence to all manner of vice and debauchery; and of our princely grace and favour we release to all our loving subjects the obligation of the Ten Commandments, and all laws of God, and statutes of this realm whatsoever, contrary to the contents of this our Declaration: and we require of all judges, justices, and other officers whatsoever, that the execution of all manner of penalties annexed to the laws aforesaid, whether by pillories, whipping-posts, gallies, rods, or axes, &c. be immediately suspended, and they are hereby suspended. From whence we hope, by the blessing of God, to give some check and allay to the insolence of fanatick spirits, and by debauching our good people out of all tenderness of conscience, to free our kingdoms from those great and grievous annoyances, wherewith they perpetually disturb our government, and at last bring back all the advantages of peace and good fellowship, both to our self and all our loving subjects, &c.

Given at our Archidiaconal Court, the 1st day of May 1673. GOD SAVE THE KING: And ———— the Inventor.

LONDON:
Printed for *James Collins*, at the King's-Arms, in *Ludgate-Street*, 1673.

The thing, **Mr.** Bayes, is very judiciously drawn up by you: only I am surprized thus to see it conclude with an *&c.* For it is true that I have heard in the former time of the '*et-caetera* oath,' and there was another dignitary, who like you penn'd declarations; yet I never saw before an '*et-caetera*' Declaration. But I cannot comprehend by what license from his Majesty, or upon what occasion from me, you have publish'd so daringly this paper. For if you have any conceal'd criticism upon those words, '*debauchery tolerated*,' I explain'd what I meant by what I quoted out of you, and accused you no further then what those words signified and imported. And the fact stood thus: His Majesty before his happy return transmitted hither a gracious Declaration concerning Liberty to tender consciences, and hath ever since pursued it. You, on the contrary, declare, p. 55 before quoted, and in many passages the same, 'that princes may with less hazard give liberty to men's vices and debaucheries then to their consciences.' But a toleration or indulgence to conscience has been thought advisable. Do not you then maintain that 'a liberty to vice and debauchery was the more advisable of the two? And was not this enough to charge you in the terms of '*debauchery tolerated*'? But as for his Majesty, he had sufficiently manifested his judgment both of the one and the other by a Declaration of indulgence to tender consciences, and by a Proclamation against Debauchery: so that you had little reason to raise so malapert an allusion, and profane his name in a mock declaration, which indeed is your own and no man's else, and is not unsuitable to your principles and practice. Yet whatsoever mischief you intended by it (for some you intend always), I am perswaded you were partly transported by the ornament that you thought it would be to your Book. Nay, I do not think but you took it for a great piece of wit; so great, that for its sake and two or three speeches that you make for the Parliament men, you writ the whole book; or else I had scaped both Reproof and Correction. But because I have observed how careful you are to find out, before you attempt a great jump of wit, some convenient rise, and you would not doubtless have penn'd so notable a declaration without some precedent, I cast about where to meet with it, and after a little searching, I found this in the *Caesares Juliani*, where that emperour having undertaken to marshal his predecessors under the patronage of some proper Deity, when he comes to Constantine does thus satyrically represent him : 'But Constantine not being able among all the Gods to find a pattern of his own life, casting his eye about saw the Goddess of Luxury near him, and straight ran to her. She hereupon receiving him delicately and embracing him, tricked him up in woman's cloaths, and conducted him to the Goddess of Intemperance, finding his son returned, and making to all men this public proclamation :

'Let all men take notice, of whatsoever condition and quality, whether they be adulterers, or murtherers, or guilty of any other immorality, vice, or debauchery, that hereby they are warranted and invited to continue boldly and confidently in the same; and I declare that, upon dipping themselves only in this water, they are, and shall be so reputed, pure and blameless to all intents and purposes. And moreover, as oft as they shall renew and frequent such other vices, immoralities, or debaucheries, I do hereby give and grant to them and every one of them respectively, that by thumping his breast, or giving but himself a pat on the forehead, he shall thereupon be immediately discharged and absolved of all guilt and penalty therefore incurred, any law or statute to the contrary notwithstanding.'

This is in the 99th page of that book printed at Paris 1583, to prevent any such accident for the future as that of the epistle to Marcellinus; for I am sensible of the great trouble I thereby gave you, though you have it recompensed by the great reputation you have acquired by your learned criticismes upon it. But, good Mr. Bayes, surely you were hard set, that you had no body here to go to but Julian the Apostate for an invention. Or however, if you had contracted some acquaintance or similitude with him, you could not have pick'd out a more unhappy instance for your imitation than this present. For as he in this Proclamation ingratefully derides Constantine, so do you traduce his Majesty by your Declaration, which deserves to perish with your Book: whereas he by his Proclamation against debauchery hath sufficiently testifyed his judgement, and as he hath resembled Constantine in his patience and industry toward composing (howsoever obstructed) the Ecclesiastical differences among us, so in his largess and munificence to the Church hath far exceeded him.

And this leads me directly to your fifth play, Mr. Bayes, of PERSECUTION RECOMMENDED; though I might perhaps more properly have call'd it a *spectacle*, and exceeding whatsoever was exhibited at any time among the Romans for cruelty [Reproof, p. 73]. I had hereupon said, that 'Julian himself, who was first a reader and held forth in the Christian churches before he turn'd apostate, and then persecutor, could not have outdone you either in irony or cruelty' [Rehearsal

Transprosed, p. 318]: and for the truth of that I refer to your whole Ecclesiastical Politie. You return me in answer to this passage (for in my whole Book I have but this once mentioned him) : ' you bring the emperour Julian upon the stage, as a more cruel and execrable monster of persecution than Antichrist or the Dragon himself, and you throw your slaver upon him with so much scorn and rudeness, that the people take him for as very a rake-shame as Bishop Bonner or Pope Hildebrand.' [Reproof, p. 73.] You are very gentle, Mr. Bayes, and good-natured to extremity; which makes me the more wonder at this transport, for in your whole Book there are not above one or two like instances, and you have imbraced no man's quarrel with more concernment and vehemency. There must be something extraordinary in it. Had I then known that he was so old an acquaintance of yours as I since find in your *Platonick Philosophy*, or had I imagined that he was so near of kin to you, and one of your '*dearest cuzzes*,' I should perhaps, according to the rules of conversation, have spoke of him with more respect; but however I am cautioned sufficiently for the future. Especially seeing he has so ample testimonial from you, ' that he was a very civil person, a great virtuoso, and though somewhat heathenishly inclined, yet he had nothing of a persecuting spirit in him against Christians, as may be seen at large in Ammianus Marcel. l. 22.' And you add immediately:

'unless you will suppose, as he did, that there is no such effectual way of persecuting an established Church as by suspending all Ecclesiastical proceedings against Schismaticks and Hereticks, and granting an unlimited universal toleration.' I do not suppose it, but you do; and it is one of the greatest arguments in your Ecclesiastical Politie against toleration or indulgence. Therefore let us see what your Ammianus saith : ' But when Julian observed that he was now free to do what he would, he revealed his secret design, and by plain and absolute edicts commanded that the temples should be open'd, sacrifices offer'd, and the worship of the Gods restored : and to strengthen the effect of what he had proposed to himself, he therefore called the Christian Bishops that were at odds with one another, and their divided people, together into his palace, admonishing them that laying aside their intestine quarrels, every one should boldly exercise without all disturbance his own religion; which he therefore did, that this liberty increasing their dissentions, he might be secured thenceforward against the unanimating of the Christian people, for he had found by experience that no beasts were so cruel against man as Christians for the most part are inveterate against one another.' [Ammianus, l. 22, p. 225.] So it was then, and so you would still have it. But what have you yet gain'd by this author? Under his toleration they grew to a better understanding and union ; under his persecution they cemented still closer; and so it will always probably succeed: whereas in the former flourishing times, the Church was so miserably rent by the factions and contests of the then Bishops: and so was Julian's experiment, and so I hope will all others of that kind be frustrated. But further, does not your Ammianus tell you of 'a most inhumane edict, and in respect to Julian's memory fit to be buried in perpetual silence,—that no grammarian or rhetorician should presume to teach any Christian'? [Ammianus, l. 25, p. 316; l. 22, p. 239.] This he twice mentions with the same remark. Does he not tell you that Apollo's Temple at Antiochia 'being burnt down,' whether by chance and Asclepiades the Heathen Philosopher's candle, or otherwise, 'he upon meer suspicion caused the Christians to be question'd and tormented more severely then usual, and commanded their great church at Antioch to be shut up thenceforward.' [Idem, l. 23, p. 257.] He saith too 'that Julian left behind him there a turbulent and cruel governour on purpose, affirming that he was not worthy of the place, but the people deserved to be so handled:' so that this Author makes as much herein against your '*great virtuoso*' as could be expected from one that was no Christian, and in Julian's service. Let this therefore serve as a return to you for my 5° *ad Marcellinum*, on which you spend so many pages: for this is your Fifth Play, you know, and this is your *Marcellinus:* only you have made him but Marcel; and have, out of a certain instinct, nibbled off the end of him, least he should at any time fly in your face. But if upon occasion of this Marcellinus you had here too remember'd St. Austin 18 *de Civitate Dei*, you might have been better informed concerning your Julian. Or if you will not admit him, would you but have given as much credit to Gregory Nazianzen, or to Chrysostome, and Nectarius, and all the Ecclesiastical writers, of that time, as to Ammianus Marcellinus an heathen soldier, you could not sure have had so good an opinion of him. I have, upon this occasion from you, made a collection whereby to manifest that during his short raign there was by his means and under his authority as great, if not greater, ravage and cruelty exercised then in any of the former persecutions: but I will not so far gratifie your ignorance or your falshood. You perhaps, because his is not reckoned among the ten persecutions, thought there had been no more, neither in his time, nor Pope Hildebrand's, nor Bishop Bonner's, nor since. But I have truly a better esteem of your reading, and that all this comes from that good inclination you have to such matters; so that you either sneer them off at the end of your nose as old impertinent stories, to jeer out our credulity, or do openly aver a known falshood in defence of Julian, for whom you have so great a friendship, and whose actions you approve of. But no man will think the better of your cause for your justifying it by panegyricks of Julian the Apostate and Cardinal Granvell. The ripping-up of bellies, and tearing of men's bowels, the whipping of virgins, digging out their eyes, pulling forth their teeth, cutting off hands and tongues, breaking of legs, boyling of men in caldrons, grilling them on gridirons, roasting them on spits, fricassing them in frying-pans, were but a small part of the felicities of Julian's Empire, 'that *virtuoso*, and who had nothing of a persecuting spirit against Christians.' He was, I see, an excellent cook for your palate: and what ragousts had here been for you to have furnish'd the Mazarines on your table! you that can relish nothing less then 'pillories, whipping-posts, galleys, rods and axes'! 'Tis true, nevertheless, that I find not any edict of his against Christians: for his malice solaced it self in a more subtle way, by interpreting an old statute about the violating of temples; and under colour of that he proceeded against them, and caus'd them either to abjure their faith or quit their estates; and if they chose the last, he subjected them notwithstanding to death and the most exquisite torments. Truly, Mr. Bayes, you have a very notable face, and many men I meet very like you. Caligula before, how great a resemblance was there betwixt you! And now Julian, one would almost swear you were spit out of his mouth. He set up a nickname for the Christians, to mark them out to be knock'd o' th' head: so do you give the Nonconformists the name of Fanaticks, as he them of Galileans; but the great Galilean was too hard for him. Pray, Sir, who are these Fanaticks? Most of 'm, I assure you, better men then yourself, of truer principles then you are, and more conformable to the doctrine of the Church of England: only you, by the advantage of some knick-knacks, have got the ascendant over them, and left them in the lurch, so that now you have the priviledge to miscall, abuse, and triumph over them at your pleasure. And above all, the pestilence of Julian's wit and yours is incomparable but betwixt you. There is not any more visible token of a mean spirit, than to taunt and scoff at those in affliction, and for a man by virulent jeers to exasperate and impoyson the wounds of his own giving. Such words are like chaw'd bullets; and, as if it were not sufficient to shoot thorow, you invenom them with your spittle. Neither is any torment to an ingenuous mind so sensible as to be so insulted over, and for him that undertakes to be their judge to pelt them with such expressions of malice, as the condemned themselves, *in curiae egressu*, would not have used though it were their priviledge. There is a certain civility due to such as suffer, and to ' bruise a broken reed' is inhumane. Nevertheless, such was Julian's practice, and when he seized the estates of the Christians, it was, he said, but to discharge them of this worldly pelf; that being quit of such baggage, they might march on to heaven with better expedition.

When he tormented them he was not only a reader, but a preacher, and instructed them that it was their part only to be 'patient under affliction' [Romans xii. 12], for so Christ their king had commanded them. And you in like manner point out the wealthy Fanaticks to the magistrate as ungovernable creatures; mark forth an hundred '*systematical-rat-pushpin-shop-divines*' for the publick vengeance; laugh at the calamities of the City when in ashes; interdict and embargue all traffick till the ceremonies be complyed with; and smile at 'some that would be thought wonderfully grave and solemn statesmen, who labour with mighty projects of trade and manufacture, while those things which you your self allow to be perhaps of no great use to the commonwealth are not submitted to.' You tell a man, that if he 'has not a good conscience, yet he has a brazen wall;' that 'there is little difference betwixt a soft head and a tender conscience;' that ' weakness of conscience alwayes proceeds in some measure from want of wit;' therefore that men should actively obey at all adventures, because 'they have the publick wisdom to warrant them, and their own folly to excuse them;' you call the scrupulous Dissenters so many '*old boyes*,' and would 'have them lashed out of their peevishness.' But why do I reproach you with these things, which I am perswaded, nay certain, that you take for an honour? I oblige you by the very repetition, and you clap and crow at the wit and malice of your expressions. So some men find a second entertainment in the savoryness of their own belches. Therefore I will not further gratifie you herein, or nauseate the reader: your whole book of Ecclesiastical Politie having been writ not with a pen but a stilletto, and with an intention so un-theological, that the writer might not unjustly be tryed upon the statute for stabbing. Methinks I discern now what secret impulse directed you in your learned exercitations concerning *tintinnabulum* and *clangor;* though you knew it not, but your bell, like that in Spain which forbodes no good, tinkled of its own accord, and rung itself backward. You are indeed a meer *tintinnabulum* yourself, and if with your leave I may transfer the expression, though ' you spoke with the tongues of men and angels, not having charity you are become as sounding brass, or a tinkling cymbal.' [1 Cor. xiii. 1.] But whereas you are of a dimension small enough to hang in the ear of an hobby-horse, yet you raise a noise and *clangor* like the *Stentoro-phonick;* sounding the trumpet of War, and ringing the *tocsain* of Persecution. Insomuch that, not content to have press'd and muster'd up all the princes of Christendon in your service, you raise too the Ecclesiastical Militia and the Train-bands of the Church in your quarrel. 'When men's consciences,' you say, 'are so squeamish or so humoursome as that they will rise against the customs and injunctions of the Church they live in, she *must* scourge them into order, and chastise them, not so much for their fond [=foolish] perswasion as for their troublesome peevishness.' You will teach her to be a very shrew, if she will take your counsel. Was it not enough that 'he *must*' and 'they *must*,' but 'she *must*' too? Suppose she has not a mind, and that she will not suffer you to wear the britches. You could have said no more to her had she been your '*comfortable importance*.' Really, if you be so masterful in the Church, I doubt you will learn to play reaks at home. But if she find herself not well or not well used, I would advise her to appeal to Julian: for he made a law that women married should have liberty to divorce themselves from their husbands.

I have thus far instanced that though you are not so great a conjurer as Julian, yet it is not your fault if you have not been as severe a persecutor. I come now to your sixth and last play of PUSH-PIN DIVINITY. For as in all other things, so in this too, you tread on Mr. Bayes his heels; 'who, whereas every one makes five acts to one Play, what does me he but make five Playes to one plot; by which means the auditors have every day a new thing, and then upon Saturday, to make a close of all (for he ever begins upon a Monday), he makes you up a sixth Play that sums up the whole matter to them, and all that for fear they should have forgot it.' [Rehearsal Comedy, p. 33.] So do you here recapitulate all your former profaneness, with some additions, pretending to represent the Nonconformists' divinity. The expressions are your own, 'whether conversion be performed in an instant, or whether it be divided into several acts and scenes. As first, the work of vocation is the prologue. Secondly, this vocation infuseth faith only, say some; but faith and repentance, say others. And then, thirdly, this faith must be acted, so that it seems believers may have faith before they act it, *i.e.* they may believe before they believe. Fourthly, by this act we apprehend Christ's person, and by this apprehension we are united to Him. Fifthly, from this union proceed the benefits first of justification, then of sanctification, &c.' These are, I perceive, what you call 'the scholastick nothings of faith and justification.' You understand nothing but the union of benefices: these other things you laugh at, as so many ten real differences in the same thing. And yet, if one would call over the muster-role of your self, he should find near as many differences; and you would have been sory that any of them should be omitted: Fellow of the Royal Society; Doctor of Divinity, Chaplain to my Lord-Archbishop, Parson of Ickham, Parson of Chartham, Prebend of Canterbury, Archdeacon of Canterbury, &c. Yet, methinks, if you be so delicate and scrupulous in a tautology of religion as you pretend this to be, you ought to be eased in this tautology of livings and dignities. Had you been well catechized in Bishop Usher's body of divinity, or, because you will slight him as a 'systematical' Bishop, would you but once read Mr. Hooker's life, p. 17, or his sermon of justification, p. 520, you might for his sake, if not for the Apostle's, speak at least, if not think, more reverently concerning these doctrines or speculation. Then you go on, 'whether the word and sacrament have only a moral operation in the conversion of a sinner, as a man draws an horse to him by the sight of provender, or a hog after him by the ratling of beans,' and so on till you come to, 'Blessed Apostle, shouldst thou but make a visit to the Christian world, how wouldst thou stand aghast to see such a vast body of modern orthodox faith framed out of thy writings, &c.! How would it recover to thy memory all that gibberish in which thou wert so idely busie while thou satest at the feet of Rabbi Gamaliel!' How came Saint Paul and you so well acquainted? I doubt you are not in a fit pickle to speak with him; and if he saw what you write, it would recover to his memory his fighting with beasts at Ephesus. What do you tell him of Gamaliel? 'tis a wonder you tell him not too, that 'much learning has made him mad.' [Acts xxvi. 24.] Blessed Mr. Bayes, that were brought up at the feet of Elizabeth Hampton, should she but make a visit to Holywell, and read those scandalous volumes that you have written and published, she would go near, although she were bed-rid, to kick you; did she but see that so 'precious' a young man of her own education should in this manner stir up persecution, trample under foot the graces of God's Spirit, cry down the observation of the Lord's day [Hierome, p. 95 to p. 103], vilifie and mock the English Bible, 'as not in every particular the word of God, nor in any one thing the words of the prophets, nor of Christ, nor the Apostles; as a book in some places erroneous, in some scarce sense, and of dangerous consequences, &c.' [Idem, p. 104 and 105 to p. 128]; that you should lead men off from searching the Scriptures, dispute against the work of preaching, and sum up the whole duty of man (which an excellent though unknown writer [Idem, p. 262 to p. 272] of our Church has done at another kind of rate) in six burlesque lines of rhime doggrel:

'By the liturgy daily pray,
So pray and praise God every day;
The Apostles' Creed believe also;
Do as you would be done unto;
Receive the Sacrament as well as you can;
This is the whole duty of man;'

and maintain that this catch 'is to be preferr'd before all the sermons that have been preached for this six-and-thirty years by the Nonconformists' [Reproof, p. 98];—did she but see these very passages here, and how, under colour of some particular Author that does not please you, you run down and baffle that serious business of regeneration, justification, sanctification, election, vocation, adoption, which the Apostle Paul hath, beside others, with so much labour illustrated and distinguish'd; and did she but perceive that you have done all this and worse, only '*as a horse*' to gain '*provender*,' or '*like a hog*' to procure yourself '*beans*,' I dare say the good old woman (although she was not strait-handed to her ability) would grudge all the oatmeal that you spent her in grewel, and wish the skillet had boyled over.

But for ' your desiring for the present, though you could be very large upon this subject, that those who would be further satisfied in the mysterie would repair to Pinne-makers Hall every Tuesday about ten a-clock in the forenoon,' it is not the first conventicle in your lifetime that you have invited men to, though I suppose this now was only meant as a better direction to informers; but in return to the wit of it, this being one of your most happy rencounters, you should have considered that the best part of your own '*push-pin divinity*' was fetched as far as from Aberford, a town in Yorkshire which subsists wholly on that trade, and from whence you have furnish'd yourself with pins in abundance to set up with.

Thus at last, as you mock at men for ' passing through so many stages of regeneration,' I have clamber'd as well as I could over these six stages of your Theology. And I cannot but, upon reflexion, wonder that so good a cause as that of Conformity could not be managed by better doctrine and argument. But certainly if any thing more material could have faln within the circuit of humane reason, or could that have been fitted up with a better stile or more polish'd language, we could not have failed of it. For you are, it seems, the last resort of theological understanding, and a man deservedly chosen out of the whole body of the clergy for this glorious enterprize. A man that, while I am writing these lines, is proclaim'd, even under Doctor Tomkins his *imprimatur*, by another mascarade divine, to be ' *the wonder of this age*' [Free and impartial Enquiry, &c. p. 33]; and so you will be of the future. Give me leave therefore, Mr. Bayes, to sit in the pit and clap my hands among the herd of your humble admirers.

I have thus far made good my former charge against you, and submitted partly to make my self the Defendant out of my service to the Readers, and candor towards you; but henceforward I shall take my liberty. And now, when I look over the rest of your Book, it makes me very good sport to see you play more tricks then a dancing-bear for the recreation of the spectators. But you were afraid you should want company, and therefore, instead of delivering bills about, or being usher'd through the streets by the bearward and his musick with the usual ceremony, you have printed a Preface to the reader even before my Reproof: 'You have no other civility to request of the Reader then only to desire him, that if he shall think what you have written worth his perusal, to read it over with an unprejudiced mind, and an ordinary attention.' Ay, pray come in, pray come in, gentlemen. You shall have the rarest sport that ever was seen. Every man for his five shillings, and welcom. Whether or no a man can think it worth his perusal before he has read it over, it had been more seasonable to advise men to an ordinary frugality and an unprejudiced pocket. The remainder of my business here with you is only to pick up and down your flowers of the bear-garden. But how to begin with you, or where to end, is unsearchable: for indeed there was never such a Book written, except those of your other Bayes, of which 'tis excellently said :

'If it be true that monstrous births presage
The following mischiefs that afflict the age,
And sad disasters to the State proclaim,
Playes without head or tail may do the same.'
[Rehearsal Comedy, Epilogue.]

The empire of atoms is more in order, and Chance itself has a better method. Therefore I shall be obliged to write too at adventure, and sit by you, scumming off whatsoever comes uppermost, as it rises.

You had deliberately discours'd from p. 47 to p. 54 of your Ecclesiastical Politie, to which I refer, against all trade and traffick in opposition to Nonconformity; and that, while it was not rectified, 'to erect and incourage trading combinations was only to build so many nests of faction and sedition :' and you had reckon'd that the Nonconformists swarmed ' most in great cities and corporations ;' you had instructed men how Christ ' whipped the tradesmen out of the temple.' Your whole Book was an halloo to princes and all mankind to fall upon tender consciences with the severest rigour; and hereupon I said, ' 'twas some sign of the Nonconformists' peaceable temper, that you were not deified' [Reproof, p. 82 and p. 110]; and well I might say so. But you hereupon are in a terrible pelt that I have animated the rabble against you; but ' from me you fear no other weapon but a Spanish fig, or some more secret Italian dispatch.' No, no, set your heart at rest, Mr. Bayes; the very rabble are too judicious to meddle with you; and you need not apprehend or be jealous of any, unless it be the Cæcilian figs, or those others which were used at the first institution of the ceremony of *il fico*, which your obsequiousness would have digested, from what place soever you had suck'd 'm.

There was another fear upon you, lest, having been so liberal to the prince in ecclesiastical matters [Idem, from p. 164 to p. 180], the Church should sue you for dilapidations of its power; wherein you have done just nothing, unless you had retracted the very words and things which I have justified upon you, and by one word of confession you might have saved yourself and the reader all this labour. But your proud heart would not come down. But ' the priestly and the imperial power,' you now say, 'are both supream in their several kinds.' [Reproof, p. 178.] The priestly 'is in its kind supream, universal, and uncontroulable.' [Idem, p. 176.] Our Saviour 'deputed the apostolical order or succession of Apostles' (in which you have some interest) 'to superintend the affaires of the holy catholick Church.' [Idem, p. 167.] These 'may require obedience to their constitutions, under pain of the divine displeasure and the lash of the apostolical rod.' [Idem, p. 168.] I question it; if you will say Christ's constitutions, you say right; but yours are '*et-caetera*' constitutions. 'When the exterminating sentence is passed upon the offenders, it smites like the sword of an angel, &c. It cuts a man off from all the advantages of the communion of saints and of our Saviour's incarnation: and that is a capital execution.' Is it so? But at the rates that our excommunications are managed, and upon consideration for what matters they are inflicted, and by what sort of persons they are issued, I doubt that there will be every day fewer men of your opinion. And many will think, if it be but an affair of '*the day of judgment*,' that the Nonconformists may abide the tryal. But these discourses of yours, Mr. Bayes, have been the occasion that I have read several Books over, which otherwise I should never have thought of. And wondring with my self how it was possible that such a man as you should ever come to be intrusted with the keys, I met, in studying the point only as to your own particular, with some shrewd passages out of Archbishop Cranmer, subscribed by his own hand. ' In the admission of Bishops, Parsons, Vicars, and other Priests, there are divers comely ceremonies and solemnities used, which be not of necessity, but only for good order and seemly fashion : for if they were committed without such ceremonies, they were nevertheless truly committed. There is no more promise of God, that grace is given in committing the ecclesiastical office then it is in committing the civil. In the Apostles' time there was no appointing of ministers, but only the uniform consent of Christian multitudes among themselves to follow the advice of such as God had most induced with the spirit of wisdom and counsel. And when any were appointed or sent by the Apostles or others, the people did accept them, not for any supremacy, impery, or dominion that the Apostles had over them, but as good people ready to obey the advice of good counsellours. The bishops and priests were at one time, and were not two things, but one and the same office in the beginning of Christ's religion. Princes and governours may make a priest by the Scriptures, and that by the authority of God committed to them, and so may the people also by their election. In the New Testament he that is appointed to be a bishop or a priest needeth no consecration by Scripture ; for election or appointing thereto is sufficient. It is not against God's Law, but contrary, they ought indeed so to do :

and there be histories that witnesseth [*sic*] that some Christian princes and other laymen unconsecrate have done the same. They that be no priests may excommunicate also, if the Law allow thereunto.' This from so excellent a person, a most worthy prelate and most glorious martyr, with other things of the like nature, from authorities to you undeniable, have brought some odde thoughts into my head how you came to be a clergyman, or what kind of mungrel creature you are: which was the reason I told you, that you for your part ought to have stood fast to your maxime, that the magistrate may exercise the priesthood in his own person; though you have thought fit again in this book to disown it. [Reproof, p. 13 and 22; and from p. 164 to p. 180.] And then, withall, reflecting as to your particular, who do so studiously oblige the clergy by qualifying them for political and secular imployments, although there be many constitutions (and I thought them priviledges) against it; I begin to be of your mind, and that you are very capable of them, great or small: and I acknowledge your humility, who, being of so eminent parts, have not disdain'd, nevertheless, at first to exercise the office of the scavenger; in good time you may make a further progress.

You are offended at me [Idem, p. 106] for using you with so much familiarity, for you perceive that we are so 'intimately acquainted, as if we had either robbed orchards or lampooned the Court together.' You best know what you are good at; but I have had so little society with you, except in your books, that my ignorance may be excusable. But I suppose you spoke figuratively, and by 'robbing of orchards' you understood *Baldwin's-Garden;* and by 'lampooning the Court,' you meant *Three-Crane-Court;* and you might have inlarged with *Bond's-Stables* and the *Pall-Mall;* for I perceive you have had some conversation there which you would count it uncivil to commemorate, but neither do I remember that I was ever there in your company.

In the same page you accuse me ' with comparing his Majesty to a mad horse, kicking and flinging most terribly.' 'Tis unkindly done of you, to say no worse: and to leave the reader better possess'd against me, you quote not the place. The thing is below any answer, but to refer to the 110th page of my former book, being Horace's of Augustus.

I cannot omit, lest some should take it for an expression of mine, what follows, for you seem to have couch'd it so on purpose: 'This is too like the stubbornness of your shrew, that when she was duck'd over head and ears, stretched up the symbols, or, as your pin-divines would have it, the sacraments of lowsiness and cucoldry.' [Reproof, p. 112.] I have heard of some that have impoysoned with the Sacrament; of another Emperour that had his sirname from the font, Constantinus Capronymus, having marr'd it at his baptisme, as did also Wenceslaus; of witches that have imployed the *hostia* in their sorceries; and of hereticks who have administred the Sacrament in the impurest elements: but I never read before of a divine that had to such height-improved the invention. But for the sacrament of lowsiness I have formerly reckoned with you; for the sacrament of cuckoldry, cast up your own accounts. I cannot imagine where you took the rise, too, of this jump of wit, unless either from a secular, Andronicus Comnenus, who furnished an horn-gallery with a several stag's head for every man's wife he had to doo with: or from an ecclesiastick, who was in former times like you, a penner of Declarations, and fill'd a whole trunk with the single shooes of women (such was his humour) with whom he had the same occasion; this man having chosen the measure of the wive's foot, the other of the husband's head, to remain as the trophies of their lasciviousness. This is, I know, only a Julianisme, and you think, and are glad of the occasion, that as oft as you have to do with the Nonconformists, you have a liberty to speak prophanely, like those that will on purpose curse and swear the rather in civil company. For, I suppose, you make thus bold with the Sacraments because I mentioned an argument not very weak on their part, that to institute and impose ceremonies was to make so many new Sacraments; forasmuch as our Church declares, ' that they serve not only for decent order and godly discipline, but they are apt to stir up the dull mind of man to the remembrance of his duty to God, by some special and notable significancy whereby they may be edified.' And further, our Church defines a Sacrament 'an outward visible sign of an inward spiritual grace.' And I added, 'our Author besides makes them by his principle, when commanded, a new part of the divine law.' But to this I do not find that in a very large and noisome discourse you give any tolerable answer, but this jeer of ' sacraments of lowsiness and cuckoldry' [Reproof, from p. 180 to p. 204], as in your other book, that they cry '*sacraments, sacraments*,' as if you had been swearing a Dutch oath; save that you insist upon the old answer still, that 'divine institution is the only thing necessary to the nature and office of a Sacrament.' [Idem, p. 186.] Whereas I think, with submission, that by the same argument there can be no idolatry in the world. For idolatry is either worshipping a false God, or else the worshipping of a true God after a false manner. Now, may you not as well say, that because there is but one true God, therefore men cannot adore a false one; because there is but one true worship, men cannot practise superstition; as because there are but two true Sacraments, men cannot devise new ones? And though the Church allows them not for Sacraments, you may remember the case of Julian's soldiers at the burning of incense. It seems to me much the same as if, because 'God made man upright,' it were not possible for him to 'seek out many inventions.' [Eccles. vii. 29.] But enough of this; only I will furnish them with one argument more, though none of the weightiest, out of the Rationale of the Common Prayer [Rationale, p. 68], which you ought not to have been ignorant of, the Bishop instructing us that the Collects are by some of the ancients called *sacramenta*, 'either because their chief use was at the communion, or because they were uttered *per sacerdotem*.' At this rate there would indeed be '*sacraments, sacraments*.' I might pretend to be a shred of a sacrament; the whole Liturgy would be so many sacraments; nay, your Reproof might bustle to be a sacrament, as being uttered too *per sacerdotem*.

In many places of your Book, and sure you think it a lucky hit, you would fix upon me the old *Martin Marprelate* (in one page you do it four times): let me only desire you as often to remember Martin Parker [Reproof, p. 813], and your relation to him; for to my knowledge, if you do not make 'ballads to the disgrace of religion,' you are a singer of such ballads; and if you be curious, I will at a more convenient time rehearse them to you.

You had said our Saviour, in chasing the sellers out of the temple (tradesmen you call them), had 'put on, out of an hot fit of zeal, a seeming fury and transport of passion, and that he took upon him in that action the person and priviledge of a Jewish zelote.' [Preface to Eccl. Pol. p. 7, and Defence, p. 152.] This I found fault with in my former book [Reh. Tr. p. 324], and with good reason, if you would but consider that you say 'a well-meaning zelote is the worst of all villains.' You still defend it here by the examples of Phinees and Elias; and to have been 'a power, or at least a license, for private persons to execute by publick authority notorious malefactors upon the place, without form and process of Law.' [Reproof, p. 134.] This priviledge is very far-fetch'd, and long discontinued, if from the time of Phinees and Elias until our Saviour there were no new claim enter'd. But really it seems to me, by this and some other passages, that you do not attribute much belief to the miracles of our Saviour, among which, perhaps, this was one of the most remarkable. For, to omit other authors, Grotius, who ought to be of as much value with you as all the rest put together, interprets the text thus: '*Regni sui in hominum animos specimen aliquod Christus dederat asinorum accitu. Majus nunc et maxime admirabile edit in purganda aede paterna, nulla ut externa sola divina virtute venerabilis.*' Our Saviour, saith he, 'had given an experiment of His kingdom over the minds of men by His sending for the asses. He gives now a greater and most admirable proof thereof by this cleansing of His Father's house, which He did by the Majesty of his Divine power, not of any external violence.'

I had quoted upon occasion Mr. Hales his book of Schism, and Doctor Stillingfleet (who, though yet living, deserves the honour to be already cited for good authority) [Iren. p. 120] does the same, as I find since, stiling him 'as learned and judicious a divine as most our nation hath bred, in his excellent though little tract of Schisme' [Reproof, p. 143]; and transcribes the same passages. You hereupon laugh at me, for having said in his commendation that he was a man 'who had cleared himself from froath and groons.' Had I been the Author of that expression, it was not at all ridiculous, but is very proper and significant, and founded upon a Latine classical saying. But the best sport is, it is Mr. Hales his own words in that same book; and though Mr. Hooker were 'so long-winded an author' that you never could read him, methinks you might have had the patience upon this occasion to have perused Mr. Hales his book of eight pages. But to amend the matter, you say, 'the loftiest thing that can be said of so great a man as Mr. Hales is, that he was neither a mad man nor a fanatick.' I yield, Mr. Bayes, and instead of admiring 'that majesty and beauty which sits upon the forehead of masculine truth and generous honesty,' I will henceforward admire only the maidenly modesty and rosial blushes that bloom on your cheeks and inhabit your forehead. But this will not suffice: Mr. Hales you say, too, was a Socinian. I see you did not serve your fanatick prenticeship in vain. No man can tell you truth but he must presently be a Socinian. You have spent much paper in your Defence to decipher the fanatick deportment toward all adversaries: but, whether it be theirs or no, I am sure you have learnt it to the height. 'He has drop'd,' you say, 'some loose passages in that treatise, for which himself was then censured, and the book is still, though the Author be pardoned, because as he did not first publish it, so he afterward recanted it.' Most judicially said, and in the language of the tribunal. But who told you this fine story? Doctor Heylin, I warrant you; for as for yourself, it appears you never read him. But if Mr. Hales of Schisme be too loose for you, will you be pleased to admit my Lord Archbishop of Canterburie's authority, that the Schisme is alwayes the crime of those who give the occasion? But if neither Mr. Hales nor the late Lord Archbishop may be trusted in the matter, pray, Sir, inquire in the shops for *Copernicus of Schisme*, if there be any such treatise, for that author would have been the most proper to have solved the *phaenomena* either way.

You take occasion here, and in very many other places of your book, to tax me partly upon Bishop Bramhall's account [Reproof, p. 140] (and more of my Lord Archbishop Laud, Hugo Grotius, and others), as if I had traduced him under a seeming commendation. To this once for all. Had it not been for your Preface to Bishop Bramhall (which I will never pardon, because it drew me out into publick to be a Writer), I had never medled with him. But no man will fare the better or gain reputation by keeping you company: whereas you intrude yourself upon men of the best authority, by their names to render your self considerable. In that Preface you stuffed out the bishop with such bombast, you rung such an incessant peal of *in Laudem Thomae bum, bum, bum, sine fine*, that it would have made an horse break his halter. But now that I have wrought so good an effect, as to rescue him in some sort from you, and that you have since (which looks prettily) printed your *Preface* without his Book, I will not (though I have so fresh a temptation by your censure of Mr. Hales) further molest his memory, but let his life and death be buried together. And if I have in some historical passages writ too distinctly, I cannot ascribe whatsoever errour of that kind I may have committed to any other cause then the reading of ill books, which have perhaps vitiated my stile as well as others'. For ever since you were to be sold at 'Jo. Shirley's, Sam. Thompson's, Rich. Davis's, J. Martin's, James Collins's, Henry Hall's,' you have so perpetually pester'd the press with your own Books and obstructed better authors, that men have scarce had any thing else to read, and so your virulence has corrupted the age you live in. For, as I instanced to you in my former Book, your malignant remark even upon Bishop Bramhall, that, 'as far as the prejudice of the age would permit him, he was an acute philosopher;' I think it now pertinent to shew in some few examples more how civil you are to your friends, and of consequence how generous to your adversaries. First for friend Galen. 'I confess that Galen gave a kind of specimen in his book *de usu partium*, which though it is indeed a famous work, yet it is not so divine as to be writ by enthusiasme; but alwayes seem'd to me such a thing as might either be very much amended or much improved: which I do not say that I may extenuate Galen's commendation.' [Tent. p. 77.] No, I know you don't, just as 'you did not publish your Preface to impair Mr. B.'s esteem in the least, but to correct his scribbling humour, and for a warning to the rat-divines, and to show how the bishop baffled him without condescending to his "systematical and push-pin divinity".' [Idem, p. 106.] Then friend Harvy. 'In whatsoever manner therefore generation is performed, whether the man do only, &c. (which excellent Doctor Harvy guesses at, but not so ingeniously as he is wont).' And yet you were not acquainted with your 'comfortable importance.' Who next? 'I wonder how *Mercurius Trismegistus* could cousen those great counsellors of criticisme [Idem, p. 189], Lipsius, the Scaligers, &c., and I cannot but admire that Lipsius, Scaliger, Vossius, nay, and Grotius too, so many clearsighted men, should understand the thing wrong, as if they did it on set purpose.' [Tent. p. 188.] See more: 'our countrymen Sanford or Parker, in a most learned book of Christ's descending into hell, which, begun by Sanford, Parker finished, first attempted to accommodate, wrong and rashly, the theo-

logical history of the Gentiles to the sacred history:
but whoever was the first author, the venerable names
of Scaliger, Selden, Bochart, Vossius, ay, and Grotius
again, brought it in reputation; so that every man that
affects to be accounted a prime philologer sets up forthwith to accommodate of any fashion the Greek matters
to the Hebrew; the scabbado of which affectation does
so break out every day, &c.' [Idem, p. 265]; but they
got the itch it seems first of Grotius, and those other
scoundrels. 'Tis to be considered, Mr. Bayes, that you
are 'the wonder of this age;' so they must all subscribe
to you, and carry your Books after you. On: 'I do
not question but that great and honourable person Picus
Mirandula was a person of stupendious parts and learning: yet I am sure that those notions wherewith he
made the greatest noise in the world were but grand
and pompous futilities.' [Cens. Plat. Phil. p. 100.] For
the School doctors, you abuse them at every turn [Idem,
p. 68 and p. 93, and Reproof, p. 201]; and I could
away with it better but for one reason, which is, that
you say in the fifth leaf of your Preface, 'it was never
any part of the Church of England's design to exchange
the old School doctors for Calvinian systemes and syntagmes;' so that it is not so handsomely said of them
therefore that 'they are full of such stuff as makes fools
stare, and wise men laugh.' [Reproof, p. 200, 201.] But
whereas I had hereupon said, p. 213, that you had owned
the Schoolmen for authors of the Church of England's

divinity, you formally deny it, insulting with all your natural and acquired rudeness. It is not worth the Reader's trouble to interess him in such a foolish brabble; but if any one please to take the pains to inspect your Book again, as I have done, and quoted the leaf on this occasion, the most he can say will be that you have cheated me; but if you have done it so cunningly that it cannot be made out evidently, I am content to go by the loss. Yet for a collateral proof, how far to rely either upon your good faith or good memory in what you yourself write, let him take one instance where you quote me in my page 120. 'Thus when you cite for your own convenience that passage, that "rebellion is as the sin of witchcraft" [1 Sam. xv. 23], you are pleased to add too, that this text will scarce admit my interpretation; and yet you know no more what my interpretation would be than you do what witchcraft and rebellion are.' [Idem, p. 124.] You might have done me the favour, instead of saying 'I cite it for mine own convenience,' to have begun with my own words, 'I will allow him that rebellion is as the sin of witchcraft.' But that candor is not to be expected. Yet to show you that I know better what you write, and what your interpretation would be, then you do yourself, pray read in your Preface to Bishop Bramhall, 32 leaf; where you say, 'the clergy of England are as strongly principled against the hateful sin of rebellion as against witchcraft or idolatry.' Then see the text, 1 Sam. xv.

25, 'For rebellion is as the sin of witchcraft, and stubbornness is as iniquity and idolatry.' Now, Mr. Bayes, whether did I not at least guess shrowdly at your interpretation? But you are excusable, forasmuch as you confessed in that Preface, both at beginning and end, ' that you knew not what it would prove, nor had leisure nor patience to examine whether it were idle or not idle.' [Cens. Plat. Phil. p. 93.] Proceed : ' I might have added to them the late grand dogmatical master of modern orthodoxy, whose rude dogmatizing has occasioned as many controversies in the Christian Church as ever Manes and Valentinus did.' Had you told his name, it had been fairer; but by the project of that whole book it seems to be Calvine. So, Mr. Bayes, he is sped : you have done his work that he shall never lift up his head again. Yet 'Lucian is every where so abusive and bitter in his satyres against all sòrts of philosophers, that, if his mouth be any slander, they must have been a pack of the vilest villains that ever breathed.' [Idem, p. 6.] Nevertheless you say, 'some have slandered Plato himself, together with Socrates, as guilty of that unnatural sin of the lustful Sodomites; which calumny had never gained any credit with us, had it not been reported by some of the ancient Fathers; and yet it is too notorious to dissemble, that those Fathers were not only very careless in their relations concerning them, being apparently guilty of innumerable faults of memory, but also in many instances highly disingenuous;

insomuch that I find no prose-writer agree so much with their reports as Lucian, whose main design it was to abuse every thing that was grave and sober.' [Cens. Plat. Phil. p. 19, 20.] Well spoke for your clients, Mr. Bayes; ay, and for yourself too. For 'while you,' forsooth, 'take only that most delightful prospect to behold others scrambling and aspiring to those things which you contemn and trample upon, and while your palate is not surfeited and cloyed with the same repeated relishes' [Idém, p. 18] (for you were but newly come from your grewel), 'nor your eye quite weary of beholding the same repeated objects, yet you could have been highly contented (upon the account of a philosophic curiosity) to leave this present theater, that you might enter upon the next for the delight of being entertained with a new scene of things' [Idem, p. 16]; yet you handled it so, that by p. 242 you were 'upon the very point of your departure to London.' Go on and prosper. But 'had the pristine learning of Egypt been the same it was in later ages, it had been as great a disparagement to Moses as 'tis now justly reputed a commendation, that he was accomplished in all the Egyptian learning, and had amounted only to this, that he was a vain, trifling, superstitious fellow.' [Cens. Plat. Phil. p. 242; Idem, p. 101.] Why so? You put it, Mr. Bayes, too hard upon Moses. For neither did you intend it as a disparagement to Bishop Bramhall, that, 'as far as the prejudice of the age would permit him, he was an acute philosopher.' [Idem, p. 102.] Still, it 'is not my design, by representing those primitive sages as fools and dunces, to rob them of that esteem and veneration with which they have been deservedly honoured in all succeeding ages.' That is more gentle where you say, 'you might give account too of the mean abilities of Orpheus and Pythagoras, but that you delight not to speak too hardly of any virtuoso's ashes.' [Idem, p. 25.] But to conclude: whether do you handle our Saviour himself more softly? 'And then if we look into our Saviour's life, the unparalleled civility and obligingness of His deportment seems to be almost as high an evidence of the truth and divinity of His doctrine as His unparalleled miracles were. For it is altogether unimaginable that so sweet-natured a person should be so base and profligate an impostor, as He must have been if He had been one.' And yet yourself must, and do, avow that He was not so sweet-natured to the Scribes and Pharisees, Matt. xxiii. 15, 'Woe unto you Scribes and Pharisees, hypocrites, for ye compass sea and land to make one proselyte, and when he is made, you make him twofold more the child of hell than yourselves,' &c.; and so in many other places. You know too that He was once in a very 'hot fit of zeal, and a seeming fury and transport of passion.' You say too that, 'whereas the gentle and sweet-natured St. John was His darling disciple, you often find Him checking Peter's rude and unmannerly zeal.'

But, by the way, where is it that you find it so often? I cannot find it more then once, which was when He rebuked him for cutting off Malchus his ear (John xviii. 10): neither is He there so severe upon him as you are, to tax him with 'rudeness and unmannerliness.' But once is not often. You, I doubt, trusted herein too much to your memory, and thought He had checked his zeal four times, because the same thing is related by all the four Evangelists. I find, indeed, that our Saviour (John i. 22) check'd Peter for inquiring what should be of John; and ask'd him, 'What is that to thee?' But here He reproved not his zeal but his curiosity. And at another time (Matt. xiv. 31), when Peter walking on the water began to sink, He blamed his want of faith. And (Matt. xvi. 23) our Saviour said to him, 'Get thee behind Me, Satan, thou art an offence unto Me, for thou savourest not the things that be of God, but the things that be of men.' But this was not neither because of Peter's zeal, but the unseasonable care he had of our Saviour's preservation. And I do not at present remember that he was check'd oftener upon whatsoever occasion. This mistake arises from reading of Plutarch, when you should be at your Bible and devotions: and 'the ravishing delight you take in labouring your periods, and framing your own thoughts and conceptions into words,' makes you forget the text of Scripture. You were sure, and had some idea remaining, that somebody was check'd; and so it were for zeal (which was to your present purpose), it was not so much matter with you on whom it lighted. Whereas, indeed, I doubt it was that very John whom you oppose to Peter. For (Luke ix. 54) he, because a village of the Samaritans would not entertain our Saviour, would presently have 'commanded fire from heaven to consume them, as did Elias' (whom too you quoted for one of your zelotes). And him, indeed, our Saviour severely rebuked for that zeal, telling him 'he knew not what manner of spirit he was of.' And to this I might add Matt. x. 35 and Luke xx. 20, where the mother of Zebedee's children, and the sons, James and this John, would first have covenanted with our Saviour that He should grant them whatsoever they desired, and then made it the request of their family 'that they two might sit, one at His right hand, and the other at His left, in His kingdom;' for which He rebuked them, saying further, 'Whosoever will be great among you shall be your servant; and whoever will be the chief of you shall be the servant of all.' So that, indeed, I doubt you have robbed John to pay Peter with his 'rudeness and unmannerliness,' and in making it 'often,' you have mistook thus the number of the persons for the frequency of the time. But you may perhaps object, that this last of John was not a fault of zeal, but of ambition; nevertheless, because some men's zeal is only for pre-eminence, and thereupon they are often rude and unmannerly to their betters, I thought it not unseasonable to put you in mind of it on this occasion, that you might apply it to your self, and learn that, being an Archdeacon, you ought, instead of contending for superiority over others, 'to be their minister.' But I pray you reflect seriously upon this your mistake, and hereafter either read the English Bible more carefully, and 'the words' (but you will not allow them to be so) 'of our Saviour and the Apostles' [Hierome, p. 104], or else, like a *traditor*, lay it by for good and all, as 'a book in some places erroneous, in some places scarce sense, and of dangerous consequences, when every pert, bold, and conceited fellow takes upon himself to raise doctrines and opinions thence, contrary to the meaning of God in His Holy Word, and contrary to the mind and meaning of the Holy Ghost, &c.' [Idem, p. 105.]

But, to let these things be as they will, it is, however, too bold to say (but you durst not adventure further), that 'the civility of our Saviour's deportment was almost as high an evidence of the divinity of His doctrine as His unparalleled miracles, otherwise He had been a base and profligate impostor.' [Cens. Plat. Phil. p. 25.] You ought not to put such things as these upon cross and pile so, for ill use may be made of it, though it should be against your intention. And really, had you writ as much of Mahomet as you have here done of Christ and Moses, you [would] have put fair to be, as you have been the second author of Ecclesiastical Politie, so now of the *tre grandi impostori*. So that you see, I hope, by this time, if my stile hath differently deciphered the same person in different circumstances, where I learnt it, but have not yet attained the height of your faculty.

You condemn me for having, in my p. 309 [Reproof, p. 138], mentioned the reverend Bishop Andrews his form of consecration of a church or chappel, which I might have done at large, and inserted something of history that depends upon it: but I did not. Neither shall I now say any thing further, but only refer you to Archbishop Parker, p. 85, of his *Antiquitates Ecclesiae Britannicae*, where you may find what his judgment was in this case of things of the very same nature.

I had said, p. 166 of my Book, that I could quote my Lord Verulam to your confusion: hereupon you tell me the 'quotation of my Lord Verulam would have been more to the purpose, or the story of pork, which you say I know, but I say I do not know; or however, if I did, you might have had the manners to have told it for his Majestie's sake, because he knows how to make use of it.' [Reproof, p. 155.] You think you put me hard to it. I am sorry that I must trouble the Reader with such stuff, and these mean contests *de lana porcina*. But this is all the fleece a man can hope for in shearing you. I had told you, Sir (there was not a word of his Majesty), in my p. 300, alluding to your tautologies, 'that all the variety of your treat is pork (you know the story), but so little disguised by good cookery, that it discovers the miserableness, or rather the penury, of the host.' Now here have you brought my p. 166 into conjunction with my p. 300, that (which every man will discern) because my Lord Verulam was mentioned, you might make a quibble betwixt *pork* and *bacon*. Nor did I ever see a quibble fetched at greater distance, or more cunningly carried. But in whatsoever you undertake you are extraordinary, as (because I promised you before some instances in your Ecclesiastical Politie) where you are informing the world concerning some 'sects of men made up of sanctified fury, &c.' [Eccl. Pol. p. 150.] *Tois gar Presbuteroisin*, &c., which was to make a Greek quibble, forsooth, upon the Presbyterians, and of so many ages ago. Whereas the good old poet never dreamed of any such thing, or such a nation; and the chronology and geography of it varies as much as in the play of Moses and Julius Cæsar. A third instance shall be in an anagram you give us of Calvin, that is *Culina:* though it be in two languages that understand not one another, and the man spent very little in his kitchen, nor made provision for it, but all went to his study, and yet his whole inventory at his death mounted not to above seventy pounds sterling. This may serve for a specimen or scantling of your wit, and to shew how well you spent your time at both universities: 'which I do not say by any means to diminish your just commendation,' for certainly none ever quibbled with greater enthusiasme.

I shall upon this occasion take leave to digress a little further concerning Calvin and Geneva, to which you are every where a declared enemy. The town you might have spared, if not for his, yet for Sales his sake, the Bishop of Geneva, whose Book was thought fit to be licensed by your predecessor Doctor Heywood: though afterwards it was called in and burnt by proclamation, but the Doctor was 'punished with preferment.' But as to Calvin himself, it had been well that you had rather imitated the incomparable modesty and candor of Reverend Mr. Hooker in all his writings, and especially in this particular; but how should you imitate him whom, notwithstanding your challenging and defying the Nonconformists with his Ecclesiastical Politie, it seems you had never read? 'I think,' saith he, 'that Calvin was incomparably the wisest man that ever the French Church did enjoy, since it enjoyed him. Divine knowledge he gathered not by hearing or reading, so much as by teaching others. For though thousands were debtors to him as touching knowledge in that kind, yet he to none, but only to God the Author of that most blessed fountain, the book of life; and of the admirable dexterity of wit, together with the helps of other learning, which were his guides.' And I find the Reverend Bishop of Durham, Doctor Morton, in his little tract *de Pace Ecclesiastica*, had no less opinion of him. In that tract the Bishop, as also Bishop Davenant, Bishop Hall, and others, do with singular wisdom and piety treat concerning reconciliation of Protestants among themselves: a design much more probable and better timed then that which was set up by others for the accommodating of our Church with the Roman. There he saith, '*consulant illi, si placet, Lutherum, Melanchthonem, Jac. Andream Brentium. Nos Calvinum nostrum, Petrum Martyrum et Zanchium proferemus*' (we will produce, saith he, our Calvin), '*qui singuli in Ecclesia Christi veluti primae magnitudinis lumina fulserunt.*' And he adds upon occasion in the next page, '*Haec Calvinus tam pacate, tam placide, tamque indulgenter, ut jam non homo sed ipsa humanitas loqui videatur.*' It were endless to cite testimonies of all sorts of men, not only of the Protestant, but of the Romish perswasion, concerning that excellent person: but, indeed, he needs no more certain commendation then that he is traduced and accused by you. And whereas you tax him as pragmatical and intermedling with other men's matters; what could he do otherwise, all the learned men of Europe soliciting his approved judgment in the most weighty occasions? Nor therefore could he avoid that general correspondence by letters, of another stile, I am sure, than your letters are, who are therefore offended at him. Though you might have remember'd that there were some letters too writ to him by Archbishop Parker. But the design of you and those of your cast has been, and still it seems to continue, against all the foraign Churches: and you are but Heylin resuscitated, whose business it was by his scandalous Histories to blacken the whole Reformation, attributing (as Reverend Doctor Moulin well expresses it) and 'imputing the excesses that happened by the ordinary course of humane business unto Religion.' And he did it to so good purpose, that I believe his books have occasioned among us the defection of more Protestants unto the Romish Religion then any thing that themselves have writ in the points of controversie. And this distance from all other of the Reformed Churches hath been and is held up by you and your party so studiously, that beside what has been writ against them with all bitterness, they have even in cases of extremity and necessity refused to communicate with them. Hence it is that you say in your Preface: 'Therefore, Reader, I beg thy hearty prayers and endeavours for the peace and prosperity of the Church of England' (he had need when you do so dangerously interrupt it); 'for when that is gone, it will be very hard to find out another with which, if thou art either honest or wise, thou wilt be over-forward to joyn communion.' And why so? Truly I know not, unless it be for some more,

peculiar and ceremonial perfection that our Church
may have attained to above others. And this indeed
hath been alwayes magnifyed and esteemed to that
height by those of your bran and leaven, that even
our own kings and bishops have all along been cha-
racteriz'd by them well or ill, according as they promoted those matters or remitted them. As for Henry
the Eighth, he is a gone man, and his sacrilege will
never be pardon'd even in his successors. For Edward the Sixth, that miracle of princes, 'yet his death
was none of the infelicities of the Church of England.'
But might he not have lived to be wiser and better?
But in the blessed reign of Queen Mary (as in the
Preface of the Oxford statutes compiled in the time
of Archbishop Laud), '*potiunte rerum Maria, inter
incerta vacillans statuta viguit Academia, celebrantur
studia, enituit disciplina, et optanda temporum felici-
tate*' (if it could be had again for wishing) '*tabularum
defectus resarcivit innatus candor, et quicquid legibus
deerat moribus suppletum est.*' But then upon her
death there came in an iron age: '*Terras Astraea re-
liquit.*' For '*decurrente temporum serie*' (that is, in
Queen Elizabeth and King James his times) '*et vitiis et
legibus pariter laboratum est:*' all was quite spoyled;
yet sometimes she was Elizabeth and sometimes Old
Elisibeth with you thereafter, as she behaved herself
in the matter of Conformity. There in her *quinto*
Eliz. 'she was miserably out in her divinity.' And

then in *decimo tertio* she did no better when she was contented the Puritans should only subscribe the Articles of doctrine. But at other times she was pretty tolerable. King James was more busie then belong'd him, when he writ a letter to her in behalf of the Nonconformists: but after he succeeded her in England he made amends. But he had a great fault nevertheless, that he was so uncivil to the Arminians, even to such a degree as to stile 'Arminius the enemy of God, Arminianisme heresie, the Arminians hereticks and atheistical sectaries.' For though in England he advanced the Episcopal government, yet he had adhered to the doctrine of Calvin, which you and your tribe do so detest, that though a king please you never so well in matter of Conformity, yet unless he humour you too in Arminianisme or such devices, he cannot be assured of your good graces. And so it is too even as to the bishops. Archbishop Cranmer is subject to many exceptions. But Archbishop 'Parker was a prelate of great worth, and no less eminent in the Churche's cause.' But Archbishop 'Grindall was a man of another spirit; he having convers'd with Calvin and Beza abroad could not shake off their acquaintance, or was as willing to continue it as they: when Bishop of London, he condescended to have a French Church set up in the city,: when of York he entertained correspondence with Zanchy [=Zanchius], a divine of Heidelberg.' An hainous crime! 'Nay, but when he was Archbishop of Canterbury, he not only conniv'd at the Lectures which were newly set up by the Puritans, but even incouraged them.' A sad man was he! But then came Archbishop Whitgift, who repair'd all that had run to ruine 'by the negligence and remissness of some great bishops,' and by the zeal of the Grendalizing [=Grindal] lecturers. And yet this truly venerable Bishop could not escape censure too among you; for, though he were right in ceremonies, yet he was wrong in substance, and gave authority to the Articles of Lambeth, which run point-blank against the Arminian tenets. Therefore, notwithstanding all his merits, he can scarce be forgiven. But Archbishop Bancroft was a man, I trow, without exception. But then, as misfortune would have it, Archbishop Abbot succeeds him, and 'he was too facil and yielding in the exercise of that great office, and by his extraordinary remissness in exacting strict conformity to the prescribed orders of the Church in point of ceremony, he seemed to resolve those legal determinations to their first indifferency. And he brought in such an habit of Nonconformity, that the future reduction of those tender-conscienced men to a long-discontinued obedience was at the last interpreted an innovation.' This is out of your Doctor Heylin, who goes down with you for gospel, and is to you like meat, drink, and cloathing. All this adoe must be made for things that profit nothing (save that to you indeed they are very profitable), and according as great princes or eminent prelates are more or less ceremonious, so must they be ranked in your Calendar. By how much a man is more a Christian you account him the worse Bishop : and it is now grown, instead of the requisites in Scripture to that sacred office, a sufficient commendation to have been 'an admirable Ritualist.'

'Tis now time to return to our pork and bacon ; but because you cry 'pork, pork,' as often as any raven, I will first, to stay your stomach, give you the story of the pork, and the rather to satisfie another friend of mine, who did me the favour to interpret it of his Highness the Duke of York, when he contented himself the former year with the homely fare of the mariners at the Dogger-bank. It was at an audience of the embassadors of the Ætolians and Antiochus, in the Council of Achæa; Quintius, the Roman general, being present. Antiochus his embassadors boasted there very much of the potent armies of their King ; thundring out the hard names of Elymæans, Cadusians, Medians, &c. of which they consisted : whereupon Quintius, to take off the wonderment and terrour, replyed (and I will give you honest Philemon Holland for an interpreter) : 'Now, in faith, this is mine host of Chalcis up and down, a friendly man I assure you, and a good fellow in his house, and one that knoweth how to entertain his guests, and make them very welcom. We went upon a time to make merry with him, and I remember it was at Midsummer, when the dayes are longest and the sun at the hottest. And as we wondered how, at such a season of the year, he met with that plenty of venison, and such variety withall, the man, nothing so vain-glorious as these fellows are, smiled pleasantly upon us, and said we were welcom to a feast of good swine and no better: but well fare a good cook, my masters, who by his cunning hand, what with seasoning it, and what with serving it up with divers sawces, has made all this fair shew of wild flesh, and the same of sundry sorts.' Thus, Mr. Bayes, have I reveal'd to you this great mysterie of pork, of which you were so curious, and which tended only, as I told you, to show how jejune you were, who in all your matters, and even in that of railing, whereof you are most copious and the best furnished, yet are forced to serve up to the Reader continually the cold hashes of plain repetitions, to stuff out your Books and fill your table. I hope I have with this stay'd your stomach; and if you will but expect a little, I will too in convenient time bring in your Bacon.

You had, to make the ceremonies go down better with the Nonconformists, said, 'that 'twas no more for the magistrate to impose them, then to determine a new signification of words.' For it is your great art to make the ceremonies at once stupendiously necessary, and at the same time despicably little—both a fly and a whale:

> 'In whose vast bulk though store of oyle doth lye,
> We find more shape, more beauty in a fly.'
> Rehearsal Comedy, p. 40.

This I made merry with, as of good reason. For it would raise a very great disorder in the world to bouleverse so, and overturn the signification of all words: for even in the name of your function, if a man should but chance to lispe, it would make a dangerous alteration; but however, to impose' such contrary significations with the same penalties too would make wild work, and pester the nation with a whole swarm of informers. But in that debate I instanced in Augustus Cæsar, who was so shy of unusual words: and this you will needs have to be a notable mistake, because Julius Cæsar compiled a book *de Analogia*, forgetting that Suetonius [*In vita Aug.* 86 and 88] describes at large Augustus his hereditary exquisiteness in that particular. 'Those which delighted in new words, and those which affected old' (apply it to ceremonies), 'he equally dispised, both being alike contemptible:' insomuch that it was reported he displaced a Consular Lieutenant for a fault of orthography: and if orthography in worship were now as strictly observed, perhaps your spiritual lieutenancy might run the same risk.

I had chanced in my Book to speak of Hudibras

with that esteem which an excellent piece of wit upon whatsoever subject will alwayes merit. But you hereupon fall into such a fit and rupture of railing at me, that you have exceeded not only all the oyster-women and butter-whores, but even your self, pretending that I have done him some dishonour. Should I study a suitable return to you, I could not raise myself into more choler then to call you a 'jewel,' a 'glass-drop,' a '*tintinnabulum*,'—words that you, with some sympathy, delight in, and whose heraldry is to be pendant. As for you, I cannot restrain you of this liberty, who have wisely taken safeguard in the ecclesiastical function, and, foreseeing betimes what occasion you might have, thought fit to post yourself up in print that 'you are not valiant.' [Cens. Plat. Phil. p. 15.] Only I could have, for your own sake, wished you had not call'd me Judas, lest so eminent a divine as you are should appear more concerned for Hudibras than for your Saviour. For the rest, you may please to know, that whatever you have here said to me cannot either diminish or increase my esteem for that Author.

You foam again as in the falling-sickness [Reproof, p. 326] because I had said, that I thought God never intended the clergy for political and secular imployments, and you make it to be no less then blasphemy. If they be so enamour'd of those drudgeries, and have deputed you to maintain it, much good may it do them and you! But why should you upon no more occasion tell me, '*Fatuos et hujus terrae filios quod attinet*' (saith a Jewish Zelote) '*non magis nostro judicio prophetare possunt quam asinus et ranae.*' 'Asses and tadpoles may as soon expect the impressions of the Divine Spirit as such dunces and sots as you:' but these words of yours I suppose you pretend to be dictated by that Spirit. And further you say, 'the *Ruac Hakodesh* dwell in such a distemper'd and polluted mind as yours! it may as soon unite itself to a swine.' *Ruac Hakodesh*, Mr. Bayes! this is, as your other Bayes has it, 'A crust, a lasting crust, for your rogue critiques: I would fain see the proudest of them all but dare to nibble at this. If they do, this shall rub their gums for 'm, I promise you.' [Rehearsal Comedy, p. 14.] I doubt your *Ruac Hakodesh* is but at best a *Bath col*. But is not this of yours fine language, think you, for an *A. Sac. Dom.? O seytang aurang olanda bacalay samatay*. To show you, Mr. Bayes, that I too have been sometimes conversant with the Jewish Zelotes, I will tell you hereupon a story out of one of them, that shall, as yours, be nameless. There was among the Jews a certain kind of people that were called proselytes, which you may in English interpret turn-coats, concerning whom was that expression that I quoted you before of our Saviour's, Matt. xxiii. 15. 'Wo unto you, Scribes and Pharisees, hypocrites! for you compass sea and land to make a proselyte; and when he is made, you make him twofold more the child of hell than you yourselves.' Now what I shall tell you of these men, I would not have you to misapply unto such conscientious persons as have re-united themselves unto the discipline of our Church; for I wish that all the Nonconformists rather could find reason to do in like manner: but it relates particularly to your self, who, abandoning all modesty and Christianity toward your former party, have defiled and dishonour'd the Church that has receiv'd you into protection. But concerning these proselytes and turncoats it was that the Jews had that maxime, '*Proselyti et paederastae impediunt adventum Messiae?*' and again, '*Proselyti sunt sicut scabies Israeli;*' that they were like a scab or leprosie to Israel. Therefore, when a proselyte was circumcised, they first catechized him about the sincerity of his conversion; whether he did not do it, *ob adipiscendas divitias*, to make his fortune; *ob timorem*, for fear of some inconvenience; or lastly, *ob amorem erga aliquam Israeliticam*, whether there were not some woman in the bottom of the business. For they had a shrowd suspicion of them, '*quod non periti essent mandatorum, quodve inducerent vindictas, atque insuper quod forte eorum opera imitarentur Israelitae?*' and therefore it was '*quod proselyti opus habebant triumviratu;*' and they would not trust them until three men had examined and taken care that all were right. And if it chanced that both the man and the wife came together to be proselytes, they were used to separate and keep them apart for ninety dayes, '*ut dijudicari possit inter prolem in sanctitate genitam.*' Nay, moreover, there was a baptisme peculiarly solemn before they could be admitted, and a great ceremonial rationale by which it was to be administred. The whole body was to be dipped '*mersione una. Si, excepto apice minimi digiti, manebat adhuc in immunditia. Si quis capillosus admodum, omnem crinem capitis abluere necesse erat.*' And there were many other scrupulous niceties in this washing. As for the water, '*homo Gonorrhaeus non mundatur nisi in fonte: sed menstruosa et Proselytus in collectione aquarum.*' But put the case the same man were *Proselytus* and *Gonorrhaeus* too, though the Rabbies were very exact, I find not this decided; but it is easie to collect that he must have passed thorow both waters. They were so curious as to regulate what proportion too of water was sufficient, and the least quantity that could be allowed was *quatuor seae aquarum*, and the dimension *cubitus quadratus*, &c. Now, Mr. Bayes, I would gladly be satisfyed whether you have been rightly and duly proselyted according to these ceremonies (for you know that the Jewish ceremonies are not so abrogated but that the Proconsul may re-establish them), but particularly have you been drawn cross the river to Lambeth? Has not so much as the top of your little finger escaped ducking? Is there not one hair of your head but has been over head and ears in the river? All this ought to have been exactly observed (especially considering how much filth you brought about you), else you are not a true turncoat, but remain still in your uncleanness. And you might have had the advantage, in traversing thus the water, to have catched some of the prophecying 'tadpoles' you speak of. But really, there is your self, and some few more such proselytes to our Church, that are so impure creatures, that before you had been admitted into it, 'it had been absolutely necessary' for you to have passed thorow this cold-water ordeal.

You do three times at least in your Reproof [Reproof, p. 125], and in your Transproser Rehears'd well nigh half the book thorow, run upon an author J. M. which does not a little offend me. For why should any other man's reputation suffer in a contest betwixt you and me? But it is because you resolved to suspect that he had an hand in my former Book, wherein whether you deceive yourself or no, you deceive others extreamly. For by chance I had not seen him of two years before; but after I undertook writing, I did more carefully avoid either visiting or sending to him, least I should any way involve him in my consequences. And you might have understood, or I am sure your friend the author of the '*Common Places*' could have told you (he too had a slash at J. M. upon my account), that had he took you in hand, you would have had cause to repent the occasion, and not escap'd so easily as you did under my Transprosal. But I take it moreover very ill that you should have so mean an opinion of me, as not to think me competent to write such a simple Book as that without any assistance. It is a sign (however you upbraid me often as your old- acquaintance) that you did not know me well, and that we had not much conversation together. But because in your 115 p. you are so particular, 'you know a friend of ours, &c.' intending that J. M. and his answer to Salmasius, I think it here seasonable to acquit my promise to you in giving the reader a short trouble concerning my first acquaintance with you. J. M. was, and is, a man of great learning and sharpness of wit as any man. It was his misfortune, living in a tumultuous time, to be toss'd on the wrong side, and he writ *flagrante bello* certain dangerous treatises. His books of *Divorce* I know not whether you may have use of; but those upon which you take him at advantage were of no other nature then that which I mentioned to you, writ by your own father; only with this difference, that your father's, which I have by me, was written with the same design, but with much less wit or judgment, for which there was no remedy: unless you will supply his judgment with his High Court of Justice. At his Majestie's happy return, J. M. did partake, even as you your self did for all your huffing, of his regal clemency, and has ever since expiated himself in a retired silence. It was after that, I well remember it, that being one day at his house, I there first met you, and accidentally. Since that I have been scarce four or five times in your company, but, whether it were my foresight or my good fortune, I never contracted any friendship or confidence with you. But then it was, when you, as I told you, wander'd up and down Moor-fields astrologizing upon the duration of his Majestie's government, that you frequented J. M. incessantly, and haunted his house day by day. What discourses you there used, he is too generous to remember. But he never having in the least provoked you, for you to insult thus over his old age, to traduce him by your *Scaramuccios*, and in your own person, as a school master, who was born and hath lived much more ingenuously and liberally then your self; to have done all this, and lay at last my simple Book to his charge, without ever taking care to inform yourself better, which you had so easie opportunity to do; nay, when you your self too have said, to my knowledge, that you saw no such great matter in it but that I might be the Author: it is inhumanely and inhospitably done, and will I hope be a warning to all others, as it is to me, to avoid (I will not say such a Judas, but) a man that creeps into all companies, to jeer, trepan, and betray them.

But after this fresh example of romantick generosity and your John-like good-nature, you plunge over head and ears into History. That of Sibthorpe and Manwaring I had occasion before to speak of in better method. I shall therefore only renew your own request in your epistle to the reader, 'that they would peruse it with an unprejudiced mind and an ordinary attention,' and I shall leave the rest to their judgments. For I do not know but that you may have some peculiar dispensation to determine those in 3° *Caroli* to have been 'most notorious rebels,' notwithstanding that, in the year 1667, this present Parliament resolved in the most solemn and judicial manner, by a concurrence of the Lords with the Commons, 'that the judgment against them in 5 *Caroli* was illegal.' As to Manwaring's particular, whose cause you take up with a remarkable concernment, I cannot but attribute it to some extraordinary correspondence of genius betwixt you. His very name hath more influence and power upon you then Dr. Bathurst's talismans [Preface to Cens. Plat. Phil.]; and that very week that you uttered this history of Doctor Manwaring, comes out in the Gazette of the first of May (I know not by what sympathy) 'The History and Mystery of the Venereal Lues, being a more new and ample discovery of that disease, then yet hath been extant, with the medicines and methods of cure practised in Italy, Spain, Germany, Holland, France and England, &c., by J. Manwaring, Doctor of Physick.'

You launch out into a relation of the Conference

too at Worcester House betwixt the Episcopal and the Nonconformist Divines, by his Majestie's commission. What is most to be taken notice of is, that you say here and in several other places, that the Nonconformists had 'nothing of sin to object against those things from which they dissented.' I have heard to the contrary, that they did in eight, if not ten several instances; but it is not my business to enumerate either for them or you. Only I admire, I confess, that upon such an occasion they could not in any one thing be gratifyed, not so much as in forbearing the lessons of the Apocrypha. Insomuch that, as many remember very well, after a long tug at the Convocation-house about that matter, a good Doctor came out at last with great exultation, that 'they had carried it for Bel and the Dragon.'

I cannot omit what it seems you thought necessary to be said in defence of your cause, that 'none are better qualifyed for State affairs then church men, and none have acquitted themselves with greater art and success, and that things have rarely miscarried but when their counsels have not been effectually follow'd (as you shall shew also in the cases of Cardinal Granvile and Archbishop Laud).' Alas! what needed you to have gone so far about, when your own case all along, and even this your Reproof and this parallel, are so pregnant a demonstration of their abilities? And you acquit your promise, where you say that the wise and resolute ministry of Granvile was render'd not only successless but odious to the people. For as he was a man of extraordinary wisdom, courage, and fidelity, that sincerely pursued his Master's interest, faithfully executed his commands, and kept up the height of his authority; so, being an implacable divine, he saw to the bottom of the projects that were carryed on by the discontented Lords, and foresaw the tendency of factions in religion to disorders and seditions in the State.' I shall not suppose any one who reads this Book to have so little convers'd with the Modern History, as not to gather hence how ready you are to make good your word to the lady whom I mentioned, as to your Religion. But I have not yet heard of any Protestant, beside yourself and the Recorder of London, who hath of late years so publickly avowed the Inquisition, of which that Cardinal Granvile was the chief patron and instrument. And instead of that honourable character you give him, I shall refer you to Grotius, whom I chuse always to ply you with above all other authors. 'The government of the Netherlands was in appearance in Margaret, but in effect, and as to the power, was only in Granvile, in whom industry, vigilance, ambition, luxury, and avarice, and all manner indeed of good and evil, were remarkably visible, &c.' And therefore it is not the greatest instance of your prudence (whatsoever you thought in your 'meer conscience') to take this publick liberty of dogmatizing.

and to pick out that Cardinal (whom I never thought of) to be the precedent and parallel of Archbishop Laud's administration.

I should after this do you injury, did I not take notice that whereas in your Preface to Bishop Bramhall, in the fifth leaf before you conclude, I told you that you spoke scandalously and with leering reflexion upon the government and ministers of State, you try with the best of your skill to return it upon me. But so unfortunately, that, as alwayes, you sink deeper and quag yourself in your Roman Empire. 'Were it possible,' say you (and I abhor to hear you), 'that his Majesty should degenerate from the goodness of his nature, as much as they say Nero did;' and again, 'These are the Sejanus's that you described.' [Reproof, p. 288.] It will not serve your turn, this evasion. 'Tis like mine host in France, that when he swore *je renie Dieu*, interpreted it of the *Dieu Bacchus*. You spoke not a word there of Nero or Sejanus, or that could be applyed to either; unless you can give us Nero's coronation-oath, or Sejanus his cases of conscience, or at last instance in that emperour's 'being canonized for a Saint and Martyr:' so that for the wit and chronology of the business this too is calculated for the play of Moses and Julius Cæsar. But for the discretion and loyalty of it, you might have long since answered, as for other passages, did either the rabble or the statesmen think you considerable; whereas indeed they reckon you, it seems, among that sort of men, who have a privilege to say any thing with impunity. But for the Long Parliament you have indeed an ecclesiastical *non obstante* to say what you will. [Reproof, p. 400.] I shall only take up at one passage: 'To deal plainly with you, I have read most of the Long-Parliament speeches over, and, though I know you will chide me for calling a whole Parliament coxcombes, yet it is better to call them so then worse. Yet this censure I dare pass upon them, without any suspition of arrogance within my self, that they were for the most part no better then school-boys' declamations, &c.; all their discourses were much like yours, and accommodated to people that took confidence for reason, nonsense for mysteries, and rudeness for wit.' Ay, Mr. Bayes, 'they wanted some certain helps, helps for wit, which you, man of Art, have thought fit to make use of.' Ay, Sir, that's your position; and you do here aver, that no man yet the sun ever shone upon has parts sufficient to furnish out a stage, except it be with the help of your rules.' But I was misinform'd, I perceive, who thought you might have called them all the names in the rainbow but coxcombes, and never heard them arraign'd of 'want of wit' but by your abundance. But that you may not think altogether so meanly of them (though indeed who is the man either in the former or this age that is able to stand or appear before your profound eloquence and piercing judgment?), let me refer you, although many others might be cited, to two speeches of the Lord Falkland's: the first concerning Episcopacy, which begins, 'He is a great stranger to Israel, who knows not that this kingdom hath long laboured under many and great oppressions, &c.' The second speech was to the Lords, at the delivery of the Articles against the Lord Keeper, and begins, 'These Articles against my Lord Keeper being read, I may be bold to apply, &c.' And if you think these worthy of perusal, I shall expect your second opinion concerning the capacity and skill of those gentlemen both in history and oratory. But as for you, when Dr. Heylin's divinity shall go for orthodox, or his prevarications pass for History, you may then, and not before, be reputed a classical author. And all the 'Canterbury Tales' you have told in the Reproof will be Chronicle. There was just such another Italian acquaintance of yours, one Polydore Virgil, who, coming into England, was dignifyed and distinguish'd like you, being made both a prebend and an archdeacon; only you are not yet, as he was, come to be collector of the Peter-pence; but all in good time. This gentleman did too, even as you, oblige this Nation with a piece of history, which after he had writ he used a notable invention, which if you would but imitate, and burn all the Records of the times you write of, it were the only way imaginable to make you authentick.

As you are officious in your own stories, so you are very inquisitive and critical upon some that I have told you [Reproof, p. 401]; and for a great space of your book you run into such froth and growns and taplash of wit, that it deserves compassion. Insomuch that though men may perhaps believe that, as you yourself affirmed, 'you are not valiant' [Cens. Plat. Phil. p. 15], yet there is some reason to doubt the truth of what you say in the same place, 'that you are not miserable.' But you are more particularly concern'd to know who that Queen was, and of what country, that gave so ridiculous a town-seal. [Reproof, p. 503.] For wheresoever you can suspect any thing smutty underneath, you are wonderful curious to be thorowly informed. But I have already gratified you in pork, and am not bound to nauseate the reader to comply with your ignorance. I will tell you who that tyrant was that demanded so many bushels of fleas [Ibid.]: it was John Basiliwich, the great Duke of Muscovy, and it was of the citizens of Muskow that he required it, fining them for non-payment. But as for this Queen, it shall for certain reasons of State be a secret. Only, not to leave you wholly in the dark, if you please to speak with your fellow-chaplain of the copper-mines, he will inform you, for it is in that kingdom. And if he do not satisfie you, if you please to resort to me, I will shew you the medal of the city, with that device upon the reverse of it.

'Tis more then time that I left scumming you, for I perceive 'tis all the same stuff; and should I continue, I should leave you nothing in the bottom: therefore I shall only take notice of two things more very remarkable. The one is concerning the quotation out of St. Austin, which I speak of from p. 209 to 214 of my former Book: '*Signa quum* [*quae*] *ad res divinas pertinent Sacramenta appellantur.*' You had said, you would lay odds there was no such saying in St. Austin; and now, because your Answerer had said '*sunt Sacramenta*' instead of '*Sacramenta appellantur*' (which therefore you note in him as 'a boldness with the text for his own convenience and an improvement beyond modesty'), you think you are safe. But, good Mr. Bayes, whether or no doth an Archdeacon *pertinere* [*pertinet*] *ad res divinas?* And pray tell me what is the difference betwixt saying that you are an Archdeacon, or you are called an Archdeacon? But because I wonder'd you could not find it, when I myself had met with it *Ep. 5ta ad Marcellinum,* you say, 'you will not laugh at me; no, for I rather deserve to be scourged for so gross and impudent a falshood: whereas (as fortune would have it) the fourth is the last Epistle to Marcellinus that St. Austin ever writ, and if you had search'd after a fifth Epistle to him, you might have pored till the day of judgment.' Let all ingenuous men judge this matter. I quoted it only in the order of the Epistles, where the first to Marcellinus is the fifth Epistle. You say it should have been thus

set down by me, '*ad Marcellinmu, Epistola quinta ;*'
and that I quote it '*Ep. quinta ad Marcellinum.*' I do
not; but thus, '*Ep. 5ta ad Marcellinum.*' Mind first
how falsely you have transcribed my quotation to fit it
to your own turn; and then observe too upon what a
frivolous and mistaken ground, and about how slight a
matter, you molest the Reader: for, besides what is
here, there runs a repetition of this matter of Marcellinus, and others of less consequence, through the whole
Reproof. But, Mr. Bayes, this business is not yet ended
thus: I will save your 'poring till the day of judgment,' and help you to a fifth Epistle of St. Austin too
to Marcellinus. Take the edition *Lugduni, Anno* 1561.
And whereas you say that ' (as fortune would have it)
St. Austin never writ but four Epistles to Marcellinus,'
this is but your usual misfortune, to hamper yourself
worse, when you would dis-intangle your own errours.
For his 5th, 7th, 158th, and 159th, are his four Epistles
to Marcellinus. But you will find there, p. 1080, a 222d
Epistle, which is a fifth to the same person. It is noted
so all along in the head of the pages, and the contents
of it express before it begins: '*Longa et docta est haec
Epistola, tractans de Baptismo parvulorum contra Pela
gium*' (because it was against Pelagius, could you not,
or might you not see it?), '*quem tamen clementer in hac
Epistola tractat. Haec per exemplaris vetustatem diffi-
culter legi potuit, propter quod in aliquibus obscura est*'
(but not so obscure but you might have discerned it).

You say, you find none of the 'Nonconformists' dirty thumb-nails in your patron's library.' [Reproof, p. 195.] But have not you nor your poor 'leaf-turners' liberty to peruse the volumes? Or is there a peculiar reverence due to the books in that place, that no man does or may touch them? Or have you lost all your credit too 'apud Jo. Shirley in parva Britannia,' and is the Pelican grown hard-hearted? Could you but have reckon'd your five fingers, you had not mistaken. But this proceeds from your bragging of books (so usual with you) which you have not the patience to read over, no more then your own; or having cast your eye on the index, you imagine you have read the Author; for indeed here the index points but at four Epistles, but the *pollex* would have made them five.

The other passage of yours [Idem, from p. 422 to p. 426], and last which I purpose to recommend to the Reader, is indeed accompanyed with many extraordinary circumstances. It is not that wherein you accuse your Answerer to have given their degrees to Oliver and Ireton at Oxford, though it is notoriously known that it was a Bishop yet living who performed that ceremony. That is an untruth too slender to be taken notice of in a Book so pregnant as the Reproof. But it is the whole hinge, it seems, whereupon your design of writing has turned. For upon occasion of a certain 'Declaration published,' as you inform [us], 'after the Cheshire insurrection,' which you affirm to have been subscribed by your Answerer, and which you have kept in deck until this season, you pretend that you have dealt 'so roundly,' as you call it, with him and the party, and me too. Happy had it been for me that you had once understood how to speak truth. For had you not writ 'so roundly,' I had never intermeddled in these matters, and so the Reproof too had been spared. However, I have gain'd hereby so much learning as to know what is the figure of falshood. It seems 'tis circular, and in your phrase, to speak 'roundly;' and you have stretched it so till it is 'unhoopable.' But I therefore shall answer you square. It is known, and ready to be proved by thousands, that the Declaration mention'd was not writ by your Answerer nor any of his Party, but by the Fifth-monarchy men; and its effect vented itself in that wild insurrection of Vennor. You yourself, although you were not of so high a dispensation, yet were at that time of age sufficient, and stirring enough in your little sphere, to have understood it rightly. But it is a grievous thing to forego a falshood that is serviceable to the great design; and the 'ends of your publick government will at last excuse, if not hallow,' the most orbicular untruth. Hence it was that you were so forward to publish that Book of 'Baxter baptized in Blood.' And hence now it is that, as your last reserve of slander and malice, as you had essayed in the Preface to Bishop Bramhall, you throw this upon the body of the Nonconformists, upon me too, and your Answerer. Yet neither is this Declaration so mad as that which you have penn'd, pp. 64, 65, 66 of your Reproof, in the stile and name of his Majesty, with a boldness of which I think no age can bring a parallel. But, seeing neither that of Baxter, nor this attempt upon your Answerer and the Party, has had that bad effect which probably you had proposed, I shall not aggravate it further; but appeal to all men, whether the world be well used, when such railing Books, grounded upon voluntary and suborn'd suggestion and forgery, shall by publick License invade men's quiet and disturb their modesty, and stir up a tumult of writing; and yet, if any man shall but open his mouth to the contrary, and in defence of common ingenuity, the same person that invented or licensed the falshood shall have the priviledge likewise to prohibit the Truth and the Discovery. Only, Mr. Bayes, forasmuch as you do here avow that it was upon this occasion that you called for 'signal marks, acknowledgments, recantations,' &c., and seeing this occasion chances to be no occasion, pray learn henceforward to be something more deliberate in your railing against the Nonconformists. Perhaps, if you would use your incomparable *Suada*, and move them to repentance in a theological and Christian language, they might be prevailed with. For truly it do's befit all that have been accessory to the late mischiefs and crimes, to walk with great innocence and modesty, though, after the State has set them right, the Church cannot of right, as you would have it, demand another allegiance. But to think that railing will do the work, or for men to hear themselves called 'traytors, villains, schismaticks, hereticks,' and to have all mankind preach'd and harangu'd up to extirpate them, for meer Nonconformity; and this by such a person as you (which makes their suffering more infamous and odious to them), and for you to perswade them that all is wholsome for them and the good of their souls, and that therefore they should recant in your hands, it is just as if Rabshakeh should pretend, when he threat'ned the men of Jerusalem they should drink their own piss [2 Kings xviii. 27], that he prescribed them a remedy for the scurvy. Pray do but try a little, Mr. Bayes, for experiment, how you your self could away with this recanting; if you were to disgorge all you had swallowed, and swallow all you had disgorged, it would make you, I trow, look very simply, and cast you into a fit worse than of the *miserere* or the iliack passion. Were you to recant all your false doctrines, all your profanations of Scripture, all your Bear-garden and Billingsgate railing and scolding; nay, were you to recant (and in good conscience you ought to refund) for your estate got by plunder and sequestration, and High-Court of Justice; were you to recant for all the circles, semi-circles, complements, and segments in the Reproof; were you but to refund to your bookseller for all those books that you were fain to give away to disperse them, and for that mutual ' gratification' which you were not asham'd, notwithstanding all your dignities, to pillage him of before he could pay his printer: I doubt the least of these would come off with an ill grace, and 'twould go very hard and aukwardly with you. But, because this may be too severe, you have here solemnly ' protested that if your Answerer can convict you of any one forgery, it shall not suffice to ask him forgiveness upon your knees, but you will make him a publick recantation.' This thing of the Declarations, that it was subscribed by your Answerer, is a notorious and convict forgery. Therefore do but now go to him, and kneel down on your knees, and ask his blessing, and make but a private recantation, and I will say you are so far an honest man.

And now, being so near a period, I cannot but gratulate my good fortune rather then my wisdom, that I have travelled such an Author through with no more extravagancy. 'Tis some kind of deliverance to have found my way so well when I was to follow an *ignis fatuus.* Had he thought fit to make use of my admonition, there had been no occasion for this intercourse. But seeing he has chosen it, I hope there are few persons of candor who need strain their invention to supply my excuse; it being more easie to justifie to others, then to delight myself with this kind of writing. And among the most eminent, I hope my Lord Archbishop will not (if this be the man I take him for) misinterpret me; but that as he was once pleased to 'thank me, and acknowledge that I had done good service to the Church' in detecting to him another Doctor so effectually, that he voluntarily subscribed never to come more within any pulpit, although he is since 'punished' with a living of three hundred pounds a year: so now his Grace will not take it ill that I have also discovered this man to him, the tenure of whose divinity is *per saltum, sufflum, et pettum;* and whose purse and conscience, being link'd with the same ties, do make together the perfect character of an, &c.

What remains, Mr. Bayes, is to serve-in your *Bacon;* but because I would do it to the best advantage, I shall add something else for your better and more easie digestion. The first shall be your Ammianus Marcel, whom if you had, as I advised you, bit off at both ends, he could not probably have molested you. But in the 27th book, having described the contention of Damascus and Ursicinus for ecclesiastical pre-eminence, he adds, 'These kind of men ought indeed to be most sharply reprehended, who, having obtained what they covet, are secure to be inriched with the offerings of the ladies, and rowle about in coaches, curiously drest up, and eat more delicately then princes; whereas they might be truly happy, if, neglecting the grandeur and ostentation of the city, which they make an excuse for their vices, they would imitate, in their manner of living, such country prelates, who eating and drinking moderately, cloathing themselves homely, and looking humbly, recommend themselves thereby to the everlasting Deity, and those that truly worship Him, as modest and pure persons.' Again, in his 21st book, giving the character of Constantius, among other things he saith that 'He did confound the Christian Religion, which is a perfect and plain thing, *rem absolutam et simplicem*, with a grannamish and doating superstition, and instead of composing with gravity the perplexed questions which he excited, he promoted them further with a strife of words; so that the prelates trooping it up and down on the publick post-horses, and canterburing from synod, as they call it, to synod, whilest they indeavour to draw all rites within their jurisdiction, there were scarce any horses left to supply travellers.' If this be for your service, pray make use of it.

But lest you should say hereupon that your Ammianus was a Socinian, will you admit King James his judgment, who, after nineteen years' experience, tells the Parliament 'That the external government appear'd well; learned judges, settled peace, great plenty, so that it was to be thought every man might have sat in safety under his own vine and fig-tree; yet he was ashamed, and it made his hair to stand upright, to consider how his people have in this time been vexed and poll'd by the vile execution of projects, patents, bills of Conformity, and such like; which, beside the trouble of his people, have more exhausted their purses then subsidies would have done ?' You see that a Bill of Conformity (though it made not, in the phrase of your Preface, ' an archangel stare,' yet it) made a king's hair stand an end.

But lest you should say King James was an Arminian, I shall now bring in my Lord Verulam, whom you cannot refuse, having so often call'd for him. And I the rather quote him because a wise man is as it were eternal upon earth; and he speaks so judiciously and impartially, that it seems as if these very times which we now live in had been in his present prospect. There are two short treatises of these matters; one begins p. 129, the other p. 180, of his *Resuscitatio*. Pray, Mr. Bayes, let us both listen; for I assure you, before he has done, he will tell us many a wiser thing then is to be met with either in Ecclesiastical Politie or Rehearsal. ' The controversies themselves (saith he) I will not enter into, as judging that the disease requires rather rest then any other cure. Neither are they concerning the great parts of the worship of God, of which it is true, *non servata unitas in credendo nisi eadem sit in colendo*. Not as betwixt the East and West Church, about images, or between us and the Church of Rome about the adoration of the sacrament, &c., but we contend about ceremonies, and things indifferent, about the extern policy and government of the Church. And as to these we ought to remember that the ancient and true bounds of unity are, one faith, one baptism, and not one ceremony or policy. *Differentiae rituum commendant unitatem doctrinae*, the diversities of ceremonies do set forth the unity of doctrine; and *habet religio quae sunt aeternitatis, habet quae sunt temporis;* Religion hath parts which belong to eternity, and parts which pertain to time. If we did but know the virtue of silence and slowness to speak, commended by St. James [James i. 19], and would leave the overweaning and turbulent humours of these times, and revive the blessed proceedings of the Apostles and Primitive Fathers, which was in the like cases, not to enter into assertions and positions, but to deliver counsells and advices, we should need no other remedy at all. "Brother, there is reverence due to your counsel, but faith is not due to your affirmation." St. Paul was content to say, "I, and not the Lord"; but now men lightly say, "*not* I, but the Lord," nay and bind it with an heavy denunciation of His judgments to terrifie the simple; whereas saith that wise man, "the causeless curse shall not come." The remedies are, first, that there were an end made of this immodest and deformed manner of writing lately entertained, whereby matter of Religion is handled in the stile of the stage. But to leave all reverence and religious compassion toward evils, or indignation toward faults, and to turn religion into a comedy or satyre, to search and rip-up wounds with a laughing countenance, to intermix Scripture and scurrility sometimes in one sentence, is a thing far from the devout reverence of a Christian, and scant beseeming the honest regard of a sober man. Two principal causes have I ever known of Atheism: curious controversie, and profane scoffing. Now that these two are joyned in one, no doubt that sect will make no small progression. Job, speaking of the majesty and gravity of a judge, saith, "If I did smile, they believed it not" [Job xxix. 24]; that is, if I glanced upon conceit of mirth, yet men's minds were so possessed with the reverence of the action in hand, as they could not receive it. Much more ought not this to be among bishops and divines disputing about holy things. Truly, as I marvel that some of those preachers which call for Reformation (whom I am far from wronging so far as to joyn them with these scoffers) do not publish some Declaration in dislike that their cause should be thus solicited; so I hope assuredly that my Lords of the clergy have no intelligence with this interlibelling, but do altogether disallow that their cause should be thus defended. For though I observe in one of them many glosses, whereby the man would insinuate himself into their favours, yet I find it to be ordinary that many pressing and fawning persons do misconjecture of the humour of men in authority, and many times seek to gratifie them with that which they most dislike. Nevertheless, I note that there is not an indifferent hand carried to these pamphlets as they deserve: for the one sort fly in the dark, and the other is uttered openly. Next I find certain indiscreet and dangerous amplifications, as if the civil government, &c.' For it is impossible to omit any thing in those excellent discourses, without apparent injury to their Author and to the reader. And that which makes them more pertinent is, that he does not spare neither the Nonconformists, but gives them too their just charge; for neither then certainly, nor now, are they to be excused: though the unequal dealing used towards them doth justifie them the more, and hath not allowed place or leisure in this Book for me to particularize their failings.

But least you should except against my Lord Bacon, as a layman, 'not competent to judge of these ecclesiastical matters in comparison with the clergy, and who was but, as far as the prejudice of the age he lived in would permit him, an acute philosopher;' what say you to Doctor Stillingfleet in the Preface to his *Irenicon* from beginning to end? And in the Book itself from p. 117 to 123? I have made scruple to disguise the discourses of him and others, as some practise, to make them pass for mine own: and to quote them at length were unnecessary, being so easily found in the Author. But here in few pages you may find all that you have said with so many years' labour totally ruined.

But least you should reject Dr. Stillingfleet, as a Papist, may Bishop Usher, Dr. Hammond, Bishop Taylor, Chillingworth be allowed of? I have them all ready at hand for you. But they are all I doubt *suspectae fidei*, and you will believe none but your self.

This is that which hath seduced you, and, because you preach'd over your notes of Ecclesiastical Politie in a private congregation, without being interrupted, you imagined the whole world had been of that mind, and 'twould pass for œcumenical doctrine; whereas I despair not of seeing yet, by God's goodness, and the influence of his Majesty upon the prudence and moderation of my Lords the bishops, that if you still persist in your mischievous undertaking, you shall be but Simon Magus his sickle, to mow the whole field without any hand to manage it. It was in the latter end of Queen Elizabeth, after the long experiment of her reign, that my Lord Verulam writ his first discourse I quoted, and his second at the coming in of King James, as Dr. Stillingfleet's at the Restauration of his Majesty now reigning. But still is at the beginning of the reigns of our princes the proper seasons of redressing these ecclesiastical matters, and of taking firm measures for their future government; some rub has been interposed unhappily that has thrown all off the bias, and so lost the cast. Who is there that ever reads the Scriptures, unless he put on ecclesiastical spectacles (and those too have a fly ingraven upon them), but sees plainly what tenderness is due unto the scruples of Christians; that our Saviour hath taken conscience into His immediate protection, and how conformable the Apostles were to His rule therein, both as to doctrine and practice? What Englishman, reflecting seriously, but must think it hard that a man may be a Christian in Turky upon better conditions? That the French, Dutch, and the Walloons, even at Canterbury, may serve God here more freely then our own natives? That it shall be a priviledge among us to be an alien, while an home-born subject must pay the double-duty (nay forfeit his whole estate) for the Protestant Religion? What Christian can conceive how a man should lose his right to the sacraments for dissenting from the ceremonies? I think I objected that to you once; but you have never deigned, as far as I can observe, once to answer it. But who especially, that, as a wise man, weighs what it is to impose things unnecessary upon people obedient to all other laws, can advise the continuance of such counsels? For a prince to adventure all upon it, is like Duke Charles of Burgundy, that fought three battels for an imposition upon sheep-skins. For a clergyman to offer at persecution upon this ceremonial account, is (as is related of one of the Popes) to justifie his indignation for his peacock, by the example of God's anger for eating the forbidden fruit. But in you, Mr. Bayes, who are I know not well what, I look upon it as an effect of your madness, and only the 'staring of an arch-deacon.'

You say, 'that most' wise men ' were of opinion you should not answer me, only desire the world to compare it with your discourses: yet others' [Reproof, p. 527] ('tis uncivilly said both as to your self and them) overpowr'd 'you to this reply, against the bent of your own inclinations.' What 'others' was it? Was the devil in you? Or were there 'certain tyes upon you,' as Bayes saith, 'that you could not be disingaged from? and you writ for the sake of some ingenious persons and choice female spirits, that have a value for you? otherwise you would see them all hanged before you would ever more set pen to paper.' [Rehearsal Comedy, p. 8.] If I might advise you, Mr. Bayes, do so no more: for 'I verily believe you have writ a whole cart-load of things every whit as good as this, and yet the insolent rascalls turn them all back upon your hands again.' [Id. p. 15.] But do as you please, I have not paid you the tythe of what I owe you, but it lyes ready for you, when you please to send for it. You are a blatant Writer and a latrant; and for lesser crimes, though of the same nature, was Gnevoski, the Polander, sentenc'd to lye barking underneath the table. You put me in mind of the Hollanders in Batavia, who, having spent their other ammunition, charged with excrements; the purity of the savage Javaes could not abide it, but thereupon yielded them the victory: neither does it become me to contend for it.

I will conclude in a short story, and more seasonable, because, as your Reproof, it happen'd once at a wedding. Wenceslaus, the emperour, married the duke of Bavaria's daughter [Del. Rio. Mag. p. 317]; the duke, knowing the emperour's delights, brought along with him a cart full of jugling conjurers, who playing their tricks, Zytho, that was Wenceslaus his magician, '*accedens propius artificem Bavarum cum omni apparatu protinus devorat (ore ad aures dehiscente), calceos duntaxat, qui luto obsiti videbantur, expuens: secessumque inde petens, ventrem insolita esca gravem in solium aqua plenum exonerat, praestigiatoremque adhuc madidum spectatoribus restituit, passim deridendum, adeo ut caeteri quoque ejus socii a ludo abstinerent.*' Whether I shall have the like success I know not (for truly our sport is much like it, and unfit for serious spectators). However, I have spit-out your dirty shoon.

THE END.

NOTES AND ILLUSTRATIONS.

Origin of the Title of ' The Rehearsal Transpros'd.'

'BAYES ..... No man yet the sun e'er shone upon has parts sufficient to furnish out a stage, except it be with the help of these my Rules.

JOHNSON. What are those Rules, I pray?

BAYES. Why, Sir, my first Rule is the Rule of Transversion, or *Regula Duplex:* changing verse into prose, or prose into verse, *alternative* as you please.

SMITH. How's that, Sir, by a Rule, I pray?

BAYES. Why, thus, Sir; nothing more easie when understood: I take a book in my hand, either at home or elsewhere, for that's all one, if there be any wit in't, as there is no book but has some; I Transverse it; that is, if it be prose, put it into verse (but that takes up some time); if it be verse, put it into prose.

JOHNSON. Methinks, Mr. Bayes, that putting verse into prose should be call'd Transprosing.

BAYES. By my troth, a very good notion, and hereafter it shall be so.'

The Rehearsal: by George Villiers, second Duke of Buckingham, 1672. [Arber's reprint (1868), p. 31.]

Notwithstanding the title-page, and the reference (as *supra*), 'Transpros'd' is constantly miswritten 'Transpos'd'—in ignorance of Marvell's design and reference; kindred with Elkanah Settle's, when, daring to answer Dryden, he dubbed his satire 'Achitophel Transprosed,' and drew down on himself the merciless ridicule of 'glorious John' in the couplet:

'Instinct he follows, and no farther knows;
For to write verse with him is to *transprose.*'
Absalom and Achith. pt. ii. 443-4.

In the 4to, before title-page, by the kindness of Messrs. Longman and Co., is furnished a vignette of Marvell's residence, now the property of the present Lord Mayor of London (Waterlow). See Essay prefixed to vol. ii. for notices of the 'cottage,' from Howitt's 'Northern Heights of London.' G.

NOTES AND ILLUSTRATIONS ON THE REHEARSAL TRANSPROSED.

Part I.

Page 3, *Title-page.* See the original one, with other details, in our Essay on the Life and Writings of Marvell, vol. ii. (of Works)=vol. i. Prose.

Page 4, '*Advertisement.*' N. P. was Nathaniel Ponder, a somewhat notable publisher and bookseller. On the 'counterfeit impression' see Memorial-Introduction, vol. i. (Verse) p. liv., and Essay, as *supra*.

Page 5, '*Bishop Bramhall's Vindication.*' See title-page, &c., as *supra*.

Page 5, '*A Discourse,*' &c., '*A Defence,*' &c. See title-pages, &c., as *supra*. In both, Parker's term is 'Politie,' not 'Policy.'

Page 5, '*same wanton and incontinent Scribler.*' In first edition 'lewd' precedes 'wanton,' &c.

Page 5, '*But if this,*' &c. This quotation is on page 13 [unpaged], and is exact, only 'to conclude' follows 'But.' On Marvell's quotations and references to Parker's books, and Parker's to Marvell's, see our Essay, as *supra*.

Page 6, '*Amaryllis.*' The original printer has made a sad jumble of the verse here and onward (p. 85). The quotations are from Guarini's Pastor Fido (atto terzo, scena quarta), and as being in near context to each other may be now given in full and accurately :

> 'Se 'l peccar è sì dolce,
> E 'l non peccar sì necessario, o troppo
> Imperfetta natura,
> Che repugna a la legge ;
> O troppo dura legge,
> Che la natura offendi.

> Ma che? poco ama altrui, chi 'l morir teme.
> Piacesse pur al Ciel, Mirtillo mio,
> Che sol pena al peccar fosse la morte.
> Santissima onestà, che sola sei
> D' alma ben nata inviolabil Nume,' &c.

The lines on p. 85 are the closing ones, *supra*.

Page 6, '*Chi lava la testa*,' &c. An Italian proverb equivalent to our 'washing a blackamoor white.' The French form adds, 'Whoso washes an ass's head only loses his time and his soap,' and is translated by Cotgrave, 'In vaine one strives to make learned a sottish, or make honest a graceless person.'

Page 6, '*A Preface*,' &c. See title-page, &c., in Essay, as *supra*.

Page 7, '*a yellow coif and a bull's head*.' On 'coif' see ref. in Notes and Queries, 1st series, vi. 224, whence I take the following: 'Consult Du Cange, *v*. Cufa; Spelman, *v*. Birretum album, Coifa; Strutt, 237; Serjeant Wynne, 'Observations touching the Dignity of the Degree of Serjeant-at-Law, 1765.' In the 1689 text of 'Last Instructions to a Painter,' for 'wife' in line 181 we find 'coif;' and probably this was Marvell's word, albeit the later 'wife' may have carried within it some personal allusions to domestic spousal authority known at the time and characteristically worked in. See vol. i. pp. 260 and 296. Chorlton became Chief-justice of Chester (Wood, *s.n.*). '*bull's head*'='the curled tufts of hair on the forehead of a woman' (Halliwell's Dict. Arch. and Pr. *s.v.*).

Page 7, '*dwinled:*' probably a misprint for 'dwindled,' though not placed among the errata by Marvell.

Page 7, '*tickets for the Bear-garden*.' A greater than Parker was employed to design 'tickets' for such places—William Hogarth.

Pages 7 and 44, '*malapert*' = saucy, impudently forward. See Glossary to 'Jack Jugler' in our Fuller Worthies' Miscellanies, vol. iv. *s.v.*

Page 7, '*ought*'=owed; and so elsewhere in R. T. So too in King James's Basilikon Doron, *ad. lect.* (1603). I have filled it in onward.

Page 8, '*no more clerkship than to save from hanging*.' See a note on Benefit of Clergy in Stephen's Commentaries (5th ed.), 1863, iv. 524-5. It was not abolished until 7 and 8 George IV., c. 28. Illustrations of the curious subject in Brand (ed. Bohn, iii. 382); and see Halliwell, as before, *s.v.* 'Neck-verse.'

Page 8, '*conventicles*.' The Conventicle Act of Charles II.'s reign was passed in 1664. Every one remembers how nobly John Hales vindicated 'conventicles' so-called. See onward.

Page 8, '*elbow-grease.*' When the kitchen-maid works hard to scour and polish and 'tidy,' she is said to spend a good deal of 'elbow-grease' on her work—being bared and stripped, and like work as opposed to mere appearance of it.

Page 8, '*spunges.*' The reference is to the 'pads' by which the type was and still is inked.

Page 8, '*B. and L., the publick tooth-drawers*'=Licensers of the Press. L.=L'Estrange *the* notorious. B.=Sir John Berkenhead, Master of Faculties, is suggested by a correspondent.

Page 9, '*stigmatized* slaves'=marked (with a red-hot iron): Latin, from Gr. στίγμα.

Page 9, '*a bulky Dutchman.*' That is, Laurence Koster of Haarlem, 1438.

Page 9, '*wine press.*' Lessening their own habits, as it were, by comparison, the English constantly represented Mynheer Van Dunk's compatriots as swillers of strong liquor, &c. Cf. Marvell's Satire on Holland, ll. 7-8, 95-6 (vol. i. pp. 243, 246).

Page 9, '*J. O.*'=Dr. John Owen, *clarum et venerabile nomen.* See our Essay, as before, on his answers to Parker, &c.

Page 10, '*Malmsbury.*' Here and elsewhere Marvell refers to Hobbes; but in the present instance perhaps he intended not so much a gird at the philosopher as a wish that his opponent might have an unquiet rectory, where he could indulge in controversy—and be beaten. Warburton said the Philosopher of Malmsbury was the terror of that age: 'the press sweat (*i.e.* sweated) with controversy, and every young Church-militant would try his arms by thundering on Hobbes's steel-cap;' and Charles II. likened him to a bear, against whom the Church played its young dogs to exercise them.

Page 10, '*a female.*' Marvell recurs so often and so pointedly, not to say grossly, to this, that it cannot be doubted he refers to some scandalous report; nor in all his books does Parker attempt to contradict or in any way meet the charges.

Page 10, '*pink of courteste . . . bur of importunity.*' On the former phrase see N. and Q. 3d s. xi. 139, where is an excellent elucidation of Romeo and Juliet, act ii. sc. 4, 'Nay, I am the very *pink* of courtesy,' &c., with reference to Steevens on the place. The 'bur' is a common wild plant's fruit or seed-vessel, which sticks fast wherever it touches, as in fleece of sheep, &c.

Page 11, '*indecencies*'=unfitness, uncomeliness, and the like, as well shown in Hobbes's preface to Gondibert, quoted in part by Richardson, *s.v.*

Page 11, '*A. C.*'=A. Clark, Parker's printer. See title-pages, as before.

Page 11, '*James Collins,*' the publisher of Parker's 'Reproof to the Rehearsal Transprosed.' See title-page, &c., as before; and Part ii. of R. T.

Page 11, '*Forasmuch as,*' &c. Our punctuation would be comma [,] after 'all,' not period [.]; *i.e.* 'at all, forasmuch' &c.

Page 11, '*one of the ancient Sophists . . . . kill'd himself with declaiming while he had a bone in his throat.*' This is not mentioned in Philostrati Vitae Sophistarum; nor has it been traced anywhere, though able and willing helpers joined me in 'searching' for the anecdote. I suspect Marvell had been reading Schenck (Obs. l. 2, p. 202), who is quoted in that strange medley, 'Nathaniel Wanley's Wonders of the Little World, or a General History of Man' (1678, folio), in which in c. xxxvii. l. 1, 'Of the different and unusual ways by which some men have come to their deaths,' we thus read (¶ 18): 'Tarquinius Priscus, while he was at dinner, feeding upon fish, one of the fish-bones stuck so unfortunately cross his throat that (not being to be remov'd) he miserably dyed thereby on the same night.' We do not find this elsewhere of the old monarch; but neither do we of any Sophist.

Page 11, '*like Archimedes:*' one of the *memorabilia* of his Life (Plutarch).

Page 12, '*This is Bayes,*' &c. The words ''Tis no matter for the plot,' though given as from the Rehearsal, are not in the first ed. The next three quotations are collected from different parts: Act i. (Arber reprint, p. 29); i. (p. 37, ib.), where Bayes tries to explain what he would mean, but gets confused; and i. (p. 33, ib.). See others in the places; and our Essay, as before, for relation of Marvell's R. T. to Buckingham's play.

Pages 12-13, '*Prince Volscius.*' The quotations are from Rehearsal, as before (Arber's reprint, pp. 85, 87, 83).

Page 13, '*Davenant's Ephemerides.*' Davenant was ridiculed in the Rehearsal, and his 'Gondibert' in after-editions is burdened with vindicatory Notes and Replies to his many critics. Such tid-bits as in the text may be gathered from Davenant; and yet his 'Gondibert' and other poems have great things in them.

Page 13, '*pure Sidrophel.*' William Lilly the astrologer is satirised under this name in Pt. ii. of Hudibras.

Page 14, '*shall I, shall I's.*' The origin and original form of 'shilly-shally.'

Page 14, '*like Bayes, his prologue.*' I have here inadvertently passed the comma after his: 'his'='s only.

Page 14, '*headstall for a crooper.*' (Crooper=crupper= rump of a horse); implying one as fit for the contrary use as its own, and therefore worthless for either.

Page 14, '*push-pin with the Bishop*'=put-pin, a very silly sport, being nothing more than simply pushing one pin across another (Strutt's Sports). A poor description—but I can find nothing more, nor whether it is the same as 'heads and points' (Fr. *bechever*, which means lying head and feet, as at two ends of a bed). Stupid as the game was, it was a gambling game among pages and the like, as may be seen by the punning conceit onward, ' and are past such boye's-play as to stake their crowns against your pins' (p. 175). In Hausted's 'Rivall Friends' (1632) the game is introduced with no little sprightliness between Mistris Vrsely and Merda. I regret I have not space to spare for the scene (act ii. sc. 2). See also N. and Q. 3d s. iii. 153.

Page 14, '*procatarctical cause:*' a Grecism of Parker's coinage.

Page 14, '*'tis not discernible, as in some animals,*' &c. Have we here the first form of John Bright's famous Skye terrier? See our Essay, as before.

Page 16, '*Lacy's face.*' John Lacy, the most celebrated actor of that day. He played Bayes in the Rehearsal. See Arber's reprint, as before, pp. 17, 22, 23. In that terrible book, 'The Secret History of the Reigns of K. Charles II. and K. James II.' (1690) there is another reference to this actor; 'To shew that as he was a great lover of comedies and enterludes, so he could act his part with e're a *Moon* or *Lacy* of 'em all, there is a story,' &c. (p. 19).

Page 16, '*tuant:*' a Gallicism=killing, as now a 'killing bonnet.' Marvell takes it from the Rehearsal (Arber, p. 99). Captain Thompson misprints it 'taunt.'

Page 16, '*the Irrefragable Doctor:*' Alexander Hales, founder of school-divinity. On him see note in Grey's ed. of Hudibras, pt. i. c. i. 152:

> 'In school-divinity as able
> As he that hight Irrefragable.'

Page 16, '*Bishop Bramhall.*' See notice of this Bishop in our Essay, as before.

Page 17, '*lay'd not.*' This use of 'lay'd' may illuminate the ever-reviving controversy on Byron's 'there let him *lay*.'

Page 17, '*jump.*' As before 'Mr. Bayes and he do very much symbolize' (434, 444), from συμβάλλω=to throw together, so here 'jump' is used, albeit there is strong reason for believing that the word has nothing to do with 'jump' to leap, but is a variant of 'imp.' Leycester's Ghost (1641) has an odd use of 'jump;' *e.g.* 'For I was *iump* of Julious Cæsar's minde' (p. 27).

Page 17, '*mine own opinion.*' Cf. 'his own opinion was his law' (Henry VIII. iv. 2).

Page 18, '*Grand Cyrus and Cassandra.*' *Le Grand Cyrus* in ten volumes, by Mdle. de Scuderi, the model of the high-flown sentimental romances which were then most popular. Molière ridiculed her and her coterie in the Femmes Savantes and Précieuses Ridicules. *Cassandra*, another French romance of the same kind, Englished by Sir Charles Cotterell in 1653, in obedience, as would appear from the preface, to the wishes of Charles II. The other, 'Knight of the Sun,' still circulates as a cheap book. 'King Arthur'—given a fresh renown by our Tennyson.

Page 18, '*Munster.*' He as ally of England fruitlessly invaded the United Provinces in 1665, and left us in the lurch.

> 'Let Munster's prelate ever be accurst,
> In whom we seek the German faith in vain!'

Dryden, Annus Mirabilis, 37. See Christie's note on the place in his most admirable 'Globe' Dryden, p. 48.

Page 19, '*Tories.*' This now familiar name occurs frequently in the State Poems. It seems to be admitted that the term was applied by the Irish Protestants to Roman Catholics who had been outlawed or had joined outlaws and lived by robbery, and in Irish Acts they are named together with rapparees and robbers; and Malone says that the name was derived from 'toree,' give me=stand and deliver. Almost all state also that it was first applied to the Court party about 1680, and Swift in Examiner (43) distinctly says that the terms Whig and Tory are not much above thirty years old; but see Bailey's Dictionary, *s.v.* See too Roger North's Examen, p. 32.

Page 19, '*Down by his side,*' &c. I have not been able to

trace these lines; evidently some attempt, as it would seem, after the manner of Hudibras=the sword cracks those men that are shelled in steel. Unfortunately hyphened.

Page 19, '*fellow-Pendets.*' Query—pundits?

Page 19, '*Dancehment Kan.*' See *infra* in title-page of Legend of Captain Jones.

Page 20, '*elogies*'=eulogies—probably a misprint; or, as taken through the French, it has the French form of 'eulogy.'

Page 20, '*legend of Captain Jones.*' For an account of this 'Legend'—quoting the passage of Marvell's—see N. and Q. 1st s. xii. 30, 74; and for full details the following now rarely seen book, 'Legend of Capt. Jones, relating his Adventures at Sea, Combat with a mighty Bear, furious Battle with 36 Men, Sea-fight, Combate with Bahader Cham, a gyant of the race of Og, &c. 1671' (12mo).

Page 20, '*ingenious writer of the Friendly Debates.*' This was Simon Patrick, Bishop of Ely. He spent part of his early life (1642-4) at Hull with Mr. Foxley, 'an wholesale grocer, a great dealer, and a very rich man;' and where also he went to school. See his autobiography, Oxford, 1839; also the 'Friendly Debate' in his collected works by Taylor. Patrick's autograph remains in a book in the Bowl-alley-lane Chapel library, Hull. Patrick has a long letter to Parker at the close of the latter's 'Defence'—very fulsome. We had occasion to expose one of his many false charges in the 'Friendly Debate' in our edition of Dr. Sibbes, vol. i. pp. 290-92.

Page 21, '*Secundinus . . . as Josselin relates.*' Had Marvell been reading John Josselyn's quaint and credulous 'New England's Rarities discovered in Birds, Beasts, Fishes, Serpents, and Plants of that Country' (1672); or his 'Relation of Two Voyages to New England' (1674), into which, as erratically as Burton himself, the author introduces all manner of odd facts and references?

Page 21, '*another Odo.*' The warlike bishop of Bayeux, half-brother of William the Conqueror.

Page 22, '*Strafford . . . . undeservedly suffered.*' Thomas Wentworth, Earl of Strafford, b. 1593, d. May 12, 1641. A statesman of magnificent powers; but the 'undeservedly suffered' is said with characteristic irony.

Page 22, '*Usher:*' Abp. Ussher, b. 1580, d. March 21, 1656.

,, 22, '*Grub-street.*' See an article quoting Marvell in N. and Q. 2d s. ix. 163, 251; also *post*, 262, 305.

Page 22, '*blue and white aprons:*' 'blue,' as a cheap colour, was much used by the lower classes, and 'blue aprons' were worn by tradesmen, as still by butchers. The 'white' aprons were waiters or apron-men.

Page 22, '*tankard-bearers*'=water-carriers. 'The Lazzari are the scum of the Neapolitan people, being most of them porters, scavengers, and tankerd-bearers' (Howell's Massaniello, part ii. 1663, p. 115).

Page 23, '*Irish Rebellion and Massacre;*' i.e. in Ulster, &c., October 1641.

Page 23, '*St. Christopher.*' A legend universally circulated, the '*infant*' being the Lord Jesus. Sir Thomas Browne says the 'picture of S.C. is known unto children, common over all Europe, not only as a sign to houses,' &c. There is a huge painting of him, I remember, in Antwerp. See Book of Days, ii. 123.

Page 23, '*too liberal of the public;*' i.e. too liberal in behalf of or as representing the (Protestant) public? or is it too liberal of public property?

Page 25, '*Alexander's architect . . . . Athos.*' One of the myths associated with Alexander in all the Lives. Athos is better remembered in relation to Xerxes.

Page 25, '*dig through . . . . the Red Sea and the Mediterranean.*' The Suez Canal effected this in 1870.

Page 26, '*rebatirg.*' Italian *rebattire*, to beat back (or commercially, again, *i.e.* to take off discount); and from being constantly used with edge, to rebate the edge, the verb itself came to have the signification of the whole phrase, and to be used, as here, for blunt. Consult Christie's Dryden, as before, pp. 89-90; also our JOSEPH FLETCHER, pp. 9-11.

Page 26, '*conn'd him thanks.*' Halliwell, as before, gives 'con,' to return thanks. He is wrong, because the noun is required. To 'conn' is to 'know,' and in all the old English dictionaries is to know without book. Hence to 'conn thanks' is not to 'return thanks' by rote, or as lip-courtesy, but to do so as one truly beholden. In this way the phrase answers, as Skinner and Tyrwhitt have said, to χάριν οἶδα, χάριν γινώσκω, savoir (bon) gré and savoir mal gré. Coles and Bailey explain *con* by *ken*.

Page 26, '*Austin the Monk:*' one of the commonplaces of our ecclesiastical semi-mythical history.

NOTES AND ILLUSTRATIONS. 535

Page 28, '*the commissioners of Scotland about the late Union:*' see Marvell's Letters, *s.v.*

Page 29, '*conference at Worcester-house*' (*i.e.* at Clarendon's), 22d Oct. 1660.

Page 30, '*severity about dirt-baskets.*' Contemporary tracts are full of abuse of the magistracy for zeal in such trivialities (relatively), while neglecting weightier matters.

Page 31, '*frontire*'=frontier.

,, 32, '*Grotius . . . . De Groot.*' References to passages showing Grotius's gradual perversion towards Romanism are given in N. and Q. 2d s. xii. 28, 58. Dr. Johnson was instrumental in assisting a descendant of Grotius's named De Groot: see Boswell, *s.n.*

Page 33, '*a copy of his countenance.*' See illustrations of this saying collected in N. and Q. 3d s. viii. 30, 114; 4th s. i. 457, ii. 460, iv. 133 (an example from Hickeringill's reply to Marvell's R. T.); to which may be added Sidney's Arcadia, 1629, p. 1.

Page 33, '*Draw-can-sir.*' The fierce [mock] hero in the Rehearsal, who fights his mistress, snubs kings, baffles armies, and does what he will, without regard to good manners, justice, or numbers (Bayes, Reh. iv. 1, p. 95). The quotation just above this, 'Mr. Bayes prefers,' &c. is from the same (p. 96, Arber).

Page 34, '*simarre:*' another Gallicism=a long loose robe or gown. Cf. Christie's Dryden, p. 588. The garment worn by the condemned at an auto-da-fé was called samarra. See Note onward. There keeps ringing in my memory a legend of some king who swore that he would trim his robe with the beards of his opponent-kings.

Page 35, '*those two that clubb'd with Mahomet in making the Alchoran.*' 1. Abdiah Ben Salon, a Persian Jew, whose name was changed by Mahomet to Abdallah Ebn Salem, and whose assistance is denied in the Koran, c. xvi. 2. Sergius, an apostate (Nestorian) monk, afterwards called Bahira, or Omahera.

Page 35, '*travesteere*'—transition-form of ' travesty.'

,, 35, '*I intend not Huddibras.*' See Marvell's vindication of this tribute to Butler in Part ii. pp. 493-4. The neglected Poet doubtless read both. He died in 1680. 'Man of the other robe'=of another garb or style; or query—a layman, not a clergyman?

Page 35, '*whiflers*'=a trifler, one who says or does nothing of any value or moment (Dyche). In Lod. Barrey's 'Ram-Alley' (1636) we read of Throte the Lawyer that he was 'knowne but onely for a swaggering *whyfler*' (act ii. sc. 1).

Page 36, ' *as a modern lady* .... *be at the charge of translating his works into Latin.*' The famous Duchess of Newcastle—a dainty selection from whose Poems, along with some of her husband's, is recently issued by E. Jenkins, Esq.—did this, if I err not, either for her own or for her husband's writings.

Page 36, '*Arminius and Baudius.*' James Arminius, died 1609: Dominic Baudius, died 1613. See their Lives and Controversies, which would furnish abundant additions to D'Israeli's 'Quarrels of Authors.'

Page 36, '*Mr. L.*'=L'Estrange, as before.

,, 37, '*the comet:*' probably that of 1664, just before the great Plague of London. See Notes on Poems, vol. i. p. 73.

Page 39, '*Dodona's Grove:*' the title of one of Howell's celebrated books, and so a phrase that came apt to all.

Page 39, '*Mistress Mopsa herself.*' The Arcadia of Sidney has a Mopsa; but no doubt Marvell intended Shakespeare's Mopsa (Winter's Tale). With reference to the former, Sidney's 'Mopsa' in his poem on Philoclea shows he had humour. See our edition of his Poems.

Page 40, '*the Helvetian passage*'=the passage of the Helvetii mentioned in Cæsar de B. Gall. l. i. c. 6, &c.

Page 41, '*as good as a play.*' The saying has been attributed to Charles II. See N. and Q. 1st s. viii. 363.

Page 41, '*as the Moon serv'd the Earth in the Rehearsal.*' (Arber, as before, p. 127.)

Page 42, '*reasons grew as plentiful as blackberries.*' (1 Hen. IV. act ii. sc. 4.)

Page 42, '*city of roaring lions* .... *and lake*'—Romance reminiscences. So below, 'Lake perillous.'

Page 42, '*Millecantons*'=the results of a thousand cantons like those few of Switzerland.

Page 44, '*poultry of the village*'=that though the kite, as resembling a bird of prey, may frighten the village poultry, yet the boy flying it has no such intent, but only his own *amusement* with it, so &c.

Page 45, '*like a raging Indian* .... *runs a-mucke.*' By 'Indian' is meant 'Malay.' The phrase 'run a-muck' is used by Dryden. See an article on it in N. and Q. 3d s. viii. 89, and Christie's Dryden, as before, p. 281.

Page 45, '*Calvin .... spoke something contemptuously of our Liturgy.*' Probably Marvell had been reading the following (now) scarce book, 'The Judgment of Forraign Divines as well from Geneva as other parts, touching the Discipline, Liturgie, and Ceremonies of the Church of England. Whereunto is added a Letter from Mr. Iohn Calvin to Mr. Knox, concerning the English Commmon [sic] Prayer, after he had purused [sic] the same. Now published for Public Information and benefit. London, 1660' (4to). In the Letter to Knox these words occur: 'In the Liturgie of England I see that there were *many tolerable foolish things;* by these words I mean, that there was not the purity which was to be desired. These vices, though they could not at the first day be amended, yet seeing there was manifest impietie, they were for a season to be tolerated. Therefore it was lawful to begin of such rudiments or absedaries, but so that it behoved the learned, grave, and godly ministers of Christ to enterprize farther, and so set forth something more filed from rust and purer.' See Calvin's Letters, 22d January 1555.

Page 45, '*constant pissing-place.*' Cf. Horace, Ars Poetica, 471. See also Christie's Dryden, as before, p. 257 : 'The wanton boys would piss upon your grave.' In the scathing Elegy and Epitaph upon Marsh, 'one of the infamous common Informers' against the (Protestant) Nonconformists (1675), the latter thus begins:

'Stay, Reader! and piss here; for it is said
Under this dirt there's an Informer laid.'

Page 45, '*Pall-mall.*' See Brand's Pop. Antiq. (Bohn, ii. 434); N. and Q. 3d s. viii. 492; Book of Days, i. 464-6; Wheatley's Dict. Redup. Words, 67. The word occurs in K. James's Basilikon Doron (1603), 'palle maille, and such like other faire and pleasant field games,' p. 121. Roger North, in his Examen, spells it 'pezle mezle,' p. 53. Coles, *s.v.* gives 'Palemaille' or 'pell mell' (1696).

Page 45, '*arbalet*'=cross-bow: *courte-boule*—not mentioned in Strutt; but 'long bowls' was the name for the game where 'bowls' were rolled some twenty or thirty yards at nine pins, and courte-boule, *i.e.* short bowls, was, teste Cotgrave *s.v.*, the French term for our bowls.

Page 45, '*foot of St. Katherine.*' See 'The Dr. Farmer MS.' as edited by us for the Chetham Society, for a curious satirical poem under the heading of 'Katherine.'

Page 46, '*Hogsdon :*' query, a lunatic asylum or Bedlam in Hoxton? Thomas Heywood jests on this in the title of one of his plays, viz. 'The Wise Woman of Hogsdon, a Comedie' (1638).

Page 47, '*camarado,*' *i.e.* comrade. From Rehearsal (Arber, p. 115).

Page 48, '*domesticks.*' This agrees with Macaulay's summary: History of England, c. iii. See this illustrated in N. and Q. 1st s. i. 26, 104, 167, 222, 374; vi. 194, 274; vii. 191; also Randolph's Pedlar, 1668, p. 328: Oldham (edit. Bell), p. 224 n.

Page 49, '*tippet :*' a canonical part of clerical dress. It was an appendage to the hood, but the word also seems to have been used for the stole. See N. and Q. 3d s., v. 456; x. 129.

Page 49, '*Maudlin de la Croix.*' The addition to the Magdalen seems to refer to some church, statue, or painting.

Page 49, '*speculate his own baby*'=to view or see as in a mirror. See note in Poems, vol. i. p. 114, and Wither in N. and Q. 2d s. x. 205.

Page 50, '*broken looking-glasses.*' Dr. Donne quaintly uses the metaphor, vol. ii. p. 210 (our edition).

Page 50, '*center :*' the boast of Archimedes was, that if he had a fulcrum, or stand-point, he could move the world.

Page 50, '*tay, tay, tarree :*' the nonsense-chorus of various songs—not utterly died out.

Page 50, '*King's or the Duke's house*'=the theatres. So Ben Jonson, 'Nor leave my title-leaf on posts or walls.' These were the only two theatres permitted. The King's Theatre had been in Drury-lane till burnt down in January 1672; and the company then removed to the house in Lincoln's-inn-fields, which had been the Duke's House. The Duke of York's company had moved to Dorset-gardens. The King's Theatre was licensed after the Restoration to Thomas Killigrew, and the Duke's at the same time to Sir William Davenant, poet laureate.

Page 51, '*King of France that lost his wits.*' In 1392, not long after reaching his majority, Charles VI. of France was riding with several armed attendants through a forest, when a man of gigantic height and half naked rushed out of the wood, seized his bridle, and after crying out with a loud voice, 'O roi, n'avance pas, tu es trahi!' as suddenly disappeared. This threw the king into a profound reverie, during which his lance, borne by one of the two pages who were following him, struck against his companion's casque. Roused by the noise, and imagining that his life was attempted, Charles drew his sword, killed four of his attendants, and the rest took flight. Some hours after, he was found asleep at the foot of a tree; and when with difficulty they awoke him, he had lost his reason.

Page 51, '*surcingle* :' the girdle worn round the waist over the cassock.

Page 51, '*lycanthropy*.' See Dr. Pusey's 'Daniel' (1864; pp. 425-433), for a masterly dissertation on the whole subject; Baring-Gould's Book of Were-Wolves, *s.v.*; and N. and Q. 4th s. vi. 113.

Page 51, '*chaps*'=jaws.

„ 52, '*assigned. That*' &c. Our punctuation would be 'assigned, that' &c.

Page 52, '*words of Cabal* :' see Note on the Poems on 'Cabal,' vol. i. *s.v.* Probably the word is here used in reminiscence of the Jewish Cabbala. The form of the word 'cabal' then existed. Cotgrave has ' Cabale, *f.* The Jewes Caball; or a hidden science of divine mysteries, which the Rabbies affirme was revealed and delivered, together with the Law, unto Moses, and from him derived, by successive relation, unto posterity (yet is it, in truth, no better than a vaine rubble of their owne traditions' [to which Richardson, *s.v.* adds, apparently from another edition than ours] 'and a crew of rogues.' Cotgrave also gives ' Tenu secret comme Cabale,' ' concealed as a speciall mysterie;' and putting the two together, we get the meaning and origin of our later-age 'Cabal.'

Page 53, '*Bishop Prideaux* :' John of Worcester, died July 29, 1650. His fugitive Sermons are very notable.

Page 53, '*Dr. Heylin*.' The 'lying Peter' of Thomas Carlyle. He died May 8, 1662. He is often named by Marvell.

Page 53, '*Rationale, &c. . . . . Holiness of Lent*.' See note on page 167.

Page 53, ' *Mr. B.*'=Richard Baxter, as onward.

„ 54, '*bullice*,' or bullace=wild plums—not obsolete as a (humble) dish.

Page 54, ' *Art thou forlorn of God*,' &c. The authorship of these lines I have failed to trace.

Page 54, ' *Hebrew Jew*'=Hebrew of the Hebrews.

Page 55, '*pounds of his flesh.*' Merchant of Venice: Shylock.

Page 55, '*Guelphs and Ghibilines:*' the immortal feud of Italy.

Page 56, '*creep on his knees up the whole stairs*'—the famous penance at Rome, *the* crisis in Luther's life perhaps.

Page 56, '*coming.*' In Lod. Barrey's 'Ram Alley' (1636), Boutcher, to whom the Widow Taffeta had made advances, and was repulsed, is upbraided when on second-thoughts he returns and would pay his addresses to the (same) widow. Adriana, her maid, meets Boutcher with badinage, and among other things gives an excellent early example of this uncommon word:

> 'And why did you fall off
> When you perceived my mistris was so *comming*?
> D'you thinke she is still the same?'
> Act ii. sc. 1.

In As You like It (act iv. sc. 1), the disguised Rosalind says, 'But come, now I will be your Rosalind in a more *coming* on disposition, and ask me what you will, I will grant it.' Here =approachable, agreeing, agreeable, or yielding. The American hunter's phrase, to make an animal come, *i.e.* to kill it, may be a remnant of this sense of 'come,' or may be drawn from the fall of the animal from a tree or height. Dryden uses the word 'coming' thus:

> 'What if he taught our sex more cautious carriage,
> And not to be too *coming* before marriage?'
> Epilogue to Love Triumphant.

Page 56, '*Gonzales:*' the original I do not know, but De Foe wrote ' The strange Voyage and Adventures of Gonsales to the World in the Moon.' The genius of Poe has revived the fancy.

Page 57, '*verger*' = the rod-bearer in a cathedral (from 'virga').

Page 57, *run the ganteloop:*' probably a corruption from *gatloop*, still 'further corrupted into *gantlope* and *gauntlet*—a punishment where the offending soldier ran between two lines of men, each of whom struck him as he passed. Marvell's spelling (nearly) is found in Lord Shaftesbury's Diary, 'run the gantelope' (Christie's Life of S. i. 81, and note).

Page 58, '*chimnies.*' See notes in Poems, vol. i. pp. 308, 392. For derivation, see N. and Q. 3d s. vii. 374.

Page 58, '*rat-divines.*' This reminds us of the old controversy between Thomas Vaughan, brother of the Silurist, and

Dr. Henry More. One of the former's many queer title-pages is as follows: 'The Man-Mouse taken in a Trap, and tortur'd to death for gnawing the Margins of Eugenius Philalethes' (1650). See our edition of Henry Vaughan, vol. ii. pp. 295-368.

Page 58-9, '*a sow in Arcadia,*' &c. I know nothing more of this than what Butler says:

> 'A Saxon duke did grow so fat,
> That mice, as histories relate,
> Ate grots and labyrinths to dwell in
> His postique parts, without his feeling.'   Pt. ii. c. 1.

Page 59, '*Cris-cros row*'=the alphabet; either, says Nares, as some say, because a cross was prefixed to or put at the head of it; or, more likely, because it was from superstitious motives arranged cross-fashion as a charm.

Page 60, '*Mr. Bales:*' I have found nothing on this name, doubtless a local J.P.

Page 60, '*syderal*'=sidereal.

„ 61, '*blew-John:*' used in Parker's Reproof, p. 189, as follows: 'such small tap-lash and blew-John that he has wantonly squirted upon your venerable and immortal name.' The word seems to mean, by the analogy of the rest of Marvell's sentence, 'blue mould' or blue-vinney, as in cheese.

Page 62, '*from post to pillar,*' &c. I do not discern the difference: but as before, 'explicating a post or examining a pillar,' are sly quotations from Parker. The usual form is 'from pillar to post,' as in the Interlude of Appius and Virginia, by R. B. (1575); 'from pillar to poste poore Haphazard daily was toste' (sig. E).

Page 62, '*Fayal,*' one of the Azores, anciently the Isles of Fire, so called from their numerous volcanoes.

Page 62, '*glowing tobacco-pipes.*' One Richardson—he was noticed for the feats of the text in the Journal des Scavans for 1680, and Evelyn states what he saw at Lady Sutherland's. As it explains and corroborates all but the last phrase, it may be quoted: 'He devoured brimstone on glowing coals before us, chewing and swallowing them; he molted beer-glass and eat it quite up; then taking a live coal on his tongue, he put on it a raw oyster, the coal was blown with bellows till it flamed and sparkled in his mouth, and so remained till the oyster gaped and was quite boiled. Then he melted pitch and wax together with sulphur, which he drank down as it flamed. I saw it flaming in his mouth a good while. He also took up a thick piece of iron, such as laundresses use to put in their smoothing boxes: when it was fiery hot he held it between his teeth, then in his hand, and threw it about like a stone; but this I observed he cared not to do very long.'

Page 62, '*love your love with an J.*' 'You play at purposes, and love your loves with A's and B's.' Hudibras, pt. iii. c. i. 1005. The game is still known.

Page 63, '*aspick*'=asp or venomous serpent. So Shakespeare: 'this is an aspick's trail:' Ant. and Cleo. act v. sc. 2.

Page 63, '*spiders:*' believed (popularly) to be poisonous. See Denham's Sophy, act i. sc. ii.; Shakespeare's Winter's Tale, act ii. sc. 1; Lucas on Waters, ii. 68; Brand, as before, iii. 381.

Page 63, '*Tom Triplet:*' Dr. Thomas Triplet, canon of Durham, who lies in Westminster Abbey in a grave that was previously occupied by Davenant. Wood and Walker ('Sufferings of the Clergy,' pt. ii. p. 68) call him a Poet, 'a great wit, a good Grecian;' but his productions have never been collected, and I have been unable to trace them. He died in 1670. See Cosin's Correspondence (Surtees Soc.), pt. ii. for an incidental notice.

Page 63, '*Dr. Gill:*' head-master of St. Paul's School. Milton was one of his pupils. In Oldham (ed. Bell, 1854 p. 222 *s. n.*) we read,

> 'With birchen sceptre there command at will,
> Greater than Busby's self, or Doctor Gill.'

Page 64, '*Priscian.*' This celebrated grammarian is honoured in the proverb, 'To break Priscian's head'=to use bad grammar; as more lately Lindley Murray.

Page 64, '*jerking*'=thrusting with a jerk.

,, 64, '*poynant*'=poignant.

,, 64, '*peeks*'=piques, and so onward.

,, 65, '*Osbolston:*' Lambert O., or Osbaldeston, head-master of Westminster School, 1622; died 1659. He is celebrated by Fuller. In Nichols's Literary Anecdotes (viii.: additions to iii. p. 445-6) we read of another thus: 'he chastised pretty severely, though he never once in his life sent a boy home with anything like a piece of buckram attached to his posteriors, common as it was with those famous tutors Osbolston and Busby.'

Page 65, '*Dr. Busby.*' Of Dr. B. see an account, with portrait—a formidable face—in Nichols's Illustr. of Lit. History, iv. 395.

Page 65, '*censure*' = judgment — not (as now) necessarily condemnatory.

Page 66, Verses. See under Tom Triplet on p. 63.

,, 67, '*J. O. . . . . . former authority.*' Dr. John Owen had been Vice-chancellor of Oxford.

Page 67, '*spit thrice.*' On spitting three times as a charm among the Greeks, see much in Brand's Pop. Antiq. (Bohn, iii. 259 and n.): spitting was a sign of the greatest contempt. Cf. Deuteronomy xxv. 9; Job xxx. 10.

Page 67, '*camarades*' = comrades, as before.

,, 68, '*politick engine*'' = instrument.

,, 70, '*great minister of State :*' viz. Clarendon, who recommended, and, as some think, drew up, the Act of Conformity.

Pages 70-1, '*his quod scripsi scripsi.*' Parker so closes his 'Reproof'—and Pilate preceded him, St. John xix. 22.

Page 72, '*nonse*' = nonce.

,, 74, '*enabled*' = strengthened or increased the powers of the Prince.

Page 75, '*territories of Malmsbury :*' another hit at Hobbes, as onward a little, on Leviathan.

Page 75, '*Gondibert.*' Few moderns have any idea of the wealth of thought in this very remarkable Poem. Davenant's Dramatic Works have recently been worthily reprinted—and welcome; but his Poems are greater in every way. Archbishop Trench, in his 'Household Poetry,' does not over-estimate him.

Page 75, '*fetch*' = artifice, trick. So in Lear, 'mere *fetches*,' act ii. sc. 4.

Page 76, '*non obstante*'—a law phrase. See Cowell, *s.v.*

,, 76, '*jejunium Cecilianum.*' It was so called from Cecil, Lord Burghley—the Fasts being politic fasts for the encouragement of the seafaring population, with the clause spoken of introduced, to prevent the belief that it indicated a return to Romanism.

Page 77, '*lightly*' = commonly, usually; and so onward, p. 81.

Page 77, '*performed already*'—as by Dr. Owen and Baxter.

,, 78, '*ramp*' = to frisk or jump about [or ' up,' as here] : 'to play at all sorts of gambols, to play the hoiden' (Dyche). Ramp, as a substantive, was used as hoyden.

Page 80, '*prophane Ben Johnson :*' i.e. by quoting him in such a connection.

Page 80, '*Horace : Hunc male*,' &c. Sat. i. 20. It is 'Cui' in the original.

Page 81, '*concealed lands*.' In Elizabeth's time lands which should have fallen to the State on the sequestration of monasteries, &c., but which were taken by private individuals. The projectors, or 'concealers,' as they were then called, sought out such, and informed against the holders of these or of supposedly concealed lands. In Charles's time the same was done with reference to State lands given away or taken during the time of the Commonwealth.

Page 81, '*prolling*' = prowling for plunder, and hence to plunder.

Page 83, '*peach*'=tell upon, betray, as an informer; a slang term now.

Page 83, '*he cuts indeed*.' A horse 'cuts' when he strikes one foot against the other, and then not unfrequently 'falters' or comes down. I fancy the phrase, a man is cut, *i.e.* 'so drunk that he can neither stand nor go' (Dyche), is of the same origin.

Page 85, '*Amaryllis*.' See the original in note on page 6.

,, 85, '*moral poet*.' Juvenal, Sat. x. 365-6.

,, 86, '*Turk*.' I take the following from Davenant's play, 'House to let,' act i. sc. 1 :

> ' All the day old Fools of Bartholomew Fair
> Are come to hire our house. The German Fool
> Yan Boridge of Hamb'rough ; and numberless
> Jack-Puddings ; the new motion-men of Norwich,
> Op'ra Puppets ; the old Gentlewoman
> That professes the Galliard on the Rope ;
> *Another rare Turke that flies without wings.*'

This is said to have been added in 1663, and the first act could not have been written before the Restoration. From the quotation the Turk's performances seem to have been similar to those on the trapeze.

Page 88, '*the moralist :*' Juvenal, Sat. vi. 292. It is 'habes' for 'abest' in original.

Page 89, '*Sybarites :*' see, on the story, in Hudibras, pt. i. c. ii. 844 (Grey's notes).

Page 89, '*allay*'=alloy, as elsewhere. So Naunton's *Fragmenta Regalia* of Anne Bulleyn. See also Christie's Dryden, as before, pp. 231, 364, 466.

Page 90, '*Julian :*' the Apostate (so called). See all the Lives.

NOTES AND ILLUSTRATIONS. 545

Page 90, '*mure-up*'=wall-up.

,, 90, '*Bartlemew register.*' The enactments of the Act of Conformity of 1661 were made to come into force from St. Bartholomew's-day, the tithes being due at Michaelmas.

Page 90, '*March licenses:*' those issued under the Declaration of Indulgence of 15th March 1671-2.

Page 90, '*breaks no square:*' an old proverb. See N. and Q. 3d s. xii. 413, 487, 488-9.

Page 91, '*one neck:*' as Caligula wished the Romans to have had.

Page 91, '*set crosses:*' as in the Plagues.

,, 92, '*ciurma:*' Ital., a mob of canaille, but generally applied to the slaves of a galley, or to the mob of forçats and hired men that went to make up the rowing crew (Vanzon). Marvell —by its being contrasted with the rest named—clearly uses it in its more ordinary sense of galley-slaves, whether slaves or felons.

Page 93, '*Sir John Baptist Dutel.*' Doubtless the 'Captain Du Tell' mentioned by Pepys (13th June 1666) as a Frenchman patronised by the Duke of York; and again, 27th July 1666. The duke seems to have given him a command in the navy, from which he was removed by the Duke of Albemarle; whereupon the Duke of York took him into his service, as yeoman of the cellar and cupbearer. This gives point to Denham's satirical notice of him in 'Directions to a Painter:'

> 'Cashier the memory of Dutell, raised up
> To taste, instead of death, his highness' cup.'

He was, perhaps, subsequently knighted; or he may have had foreign knighthood.

Page 93, '*admire*'=wonder.

,, 93, '*deifie the divine after the ancient manner:*' query, by murdering and so making a spirit? See page 462 in confirmation.

Page 94, '*entremets:*' entromese=entremesse, Fr. entremets =the slighter dishes between courses.

Page 94, '*drivels*'=slavers.

,, 95, '*non legit:*' see note on page 8, on 'no more clerkship,' &c.

Page 95, '*Synesius:*' the Neo-Platonist (?); d. 431 (?); but where?

Page 95, '*those engines, whose very names,*' &c. I must refer the curious on these names to the old dictionaries, *s. v.*

Page 96, '*Macassar:*' one of two small tribes rather than nations, that occupy the southern peninsula of the island of Celebes.

Page 96, '*Push-pin divinity.*' See note on page 14.

,, 96, '*experiments*'=experiences.

,, 96, '*opiniastre*'=opinionative: a Gallicism=obstinate. See Christie's very valuable Life of Shaftesbury, ii. 145.

Page 96, '*imp*'=shoot. The question whether ivy is detrimental to buildings has been lately discussed in N. and Q. 4th s. vi. 131, 179, 243.

Page 97, '*disvalise:*' a Gallicism from *de va liser*.

,, 97, '*nodes*'=swellings on the bones; generally the result of the *morbus gallicus*.

Page 98, '*Scotland . . . Mas Johns restored :*' see N. and Q. 4th s. viii. 431.

Page 98, '*archbishop turn'd out of his see.*' This was Alexander Burnett, Archbishop of Glasgow, whom Lord Lauderdale obliged to surrender the office in December 1669. His successor was the ilustrious Leighton, who having resigned in 1674, Dr. Burnett was restored to his see by the King's letter and an Act of Privy Council in September 1674. In 1679 he was translated to the bishopric of St. Andrew's, where he died in 1684.

Page 99, '*when born, all the teeth:*' alluding to Richard III., who is said to have been born with teeth.

Page 99, '*criticisms*'=animadversions.

,, 100, '*desire Mr. Bays:*' query 'discern'? But does the following, in Dr. Donne's verse-letter to Woodward (st. 7), shed any light on the phrase (twice repeated)? He says,

'Seek we ourselves in ourselves,'

i. e. in our truer and better selves, or in that soul which is oneself. So perhaps Marvell is=to find the inner and truer Mr. B. in the looser Mr. B., or conversely.

Page 100, '*being old.*' I was inclined to fill-in 'being [of] old excellent;' and punctuated with a comma after 'old,' as a compromise; but closer scrutiny has convinced me that Marvell used 'old' here in the sense of continual, frequent, exceeding, which proves to be of not uncommon occurrence. Cf. the Merry Wives of Windsor (i. 4), 'here will be an old abusing of God's patience and the king's English;' and Macbeth (ii. 3), 'he should have old turning the key.' It is, of course, so used because old implies continuance, frequency, and perfection; just

NOTES AND ILLUSTRATIONS.   547

as in our phrases 'old saint' and 'old sinner.' So in George Chapman, &c.

Page 100, '*a great prelate:*' I cannot assign these words.

  „   101, '*look too't, I'll doo't :*' from the Rehearsal (Arber, p. 45).

Page 101, '*in querpo*'=divested of the outer looser garments, and leaving such only as fitted closely to the body, or 'cuerpo' (Spanish).

Page 104, '*one night hath made men gray:*' a long-lived and often-applied legend. Actual cases are not easily found.

Page 104, '*remonstrate to*'=to point back, and therefore to appeal to.

Page 106, '*Sardanapalus.*' See Byron's tragedy, and relative notes.

Page 106, '*Justine,*' the historian.

  „   107, '*to perish*'=desires should perish.

  „   109, '*money hath no ear-mark.*' I can only suppose the meaning is, nothing in it of mark (as of sheep), as belonging to fanatics, to distinguish it as theirs or from the opposite owners'. Or does he intend that fanatic money was not base or counterfeit, and had not been 'marked' by nailing to the counter or driving a nail through it? And therefore (continuing the allusion to the thief who 'distinguishes' between the fanatic and his wealth) the meaning is, No one can plead that in taking such money he was only performing the part of a good citizen and preventing harm to the Commonwealth?

Page 111, '*Jejunium Cæcilianum.*' See note on page 76.

  „   113, '*Sortes Virgilianæ.*' John Forster, in his Life of Dickens, gives the last example of this on the Author sitting down to write Dombey and Son. The book proved to be Sterne's Tristram Shandy, and the passage turned up and touched was singularly *apropos*. The biographer places in the margin *Sortes Shandyanæ*.

Page 114, '*quetch:*' Kersey, whose Dictionary contains a number of Suffolk words, gives 'quetch' as to budge or stir; and in the unexplained quotations in Halliwell (as before, *s. v.*) from Gosson's School of Abuse, 1579, it has this meaning: '. . . . The constables and officers of their parish watch them so narrowly that they dare not *queatch* to celebrate the Sabbath, flock to theatres,' &c. So in Prompt Parv. *Qvycchyñ* or Mevyñ. . . . Moveo, and in the Editor's note, are sufficient examples that it means as above, and to make a noise (as the result of stirring the lips). Marvell may have used it in this last sense, or he may have used it in Cotgrave's application of it: 'Il n'y a homme qui ose lever l'œil devant luy: Every one stands in wonderful awe of him; no man dare *quitch* or stir before him.' Cotgr. s. œil.

Page 115, '*lock :*' in sense of anything that stops, as of a door, stream, or the locking of wheels, or in our phrase of coming to a dead-lock.

Page 115, '*counters-scrap*'=counterscarp. Probably a printer's transposition and mere press error.

Page 116, '*augurate.*' We have 'prognosticate' in the following 'presage:' hence 'augurate'=the previous act of discerning by augury.

Page 117, '*scattering passages*'=present active for past passive in our present English. This may be found in Shakespeare and others, but here the use is stronger than usual. Perhaps by a wording which is most unusual with Marvell, he would imply that not only were there such sentences here and there, but that they were in themselves disjointed.

Page 117, '*Tiberius . . . his distracted letter to the Senate:*' a classical commonplace. (See Suetonius.)

Page 120, '*Tarlton.*' Dick Tarleton, the great mime and jester in Queen Elizabeth's days, whose homely comicality, says Fuller (*s. n.*), 'enabled him to cure his queen of melancholy better than all her physicians' (Book of Days, *s. n.*). The same sly use of Tarleton's name is made by Dr. Donne in his mock Catalogus Librorum: 'Tarltonus de privilegio Parliamenti.'

Page 120, '*niches are yet empty.*' In 1708 only seventeen of the twenty-four niches of the Royal Exchange had been filled up. The statues were those of our kings and queens; a list of them, with the inscriptions belonging to them, is given in Hatton's New View of London, 1708, ii. 615. Charles I. was placed next to James I. in 1683, being No. 5 on the north side.

Page 121, '*sleeps upon both ears*' sleep soundly, or take no heed or care for. A variant on Ter^{e}nce's 'in aurem utramvis dormire,' which is more literally translated by Massinger (The Guardian, ii. 2), 'Sleep you secure on either ear;' and by Ben Jonson (Oberon). The origin of the saying is probably this, that he who can sleep soundly and is free from cares and bodily ills, can throw himself down and go off in any position, while the poor sleeper kept from sleep by any of these causes can only sleep on his accustomed side, and then keep, as it were, one ear awake. Folk-lore has many parallels.

Page 122, '*salivation:*' we say sputtering or foaming.

„ 122, '*Thunder and Lightning,*' &c. From the Rehearsal (Arber, pp. 43-5).

Page 122, '*None accuses you, what you make sport with, of burning,*' &c. See Poems and related notes on 'burning ships at Chatham,' vol. i. p. 374, &c. This is an odd-sounding sentence, and reads as though there were some error; but the construction intended was probably, None accuses you of burning, &c. with what you make sport with, *i. e.* with those aforesaid sparkles of wit.

Page 123, '*St. Paul's . . . Diana's temple.*' Dr. Donne similarly combines the two. See our edition of DONNE, vol. ii. pp. 37, 40.

Page 124, '*Dr. Thorndike . . . . is lately dead.*' He died in 1672, as onward.

Pages 124-5, '*Appello Cæsarem,*' &c. The title of one of Mountagu's many ultra-royalist books. See our Essay on him and them; also our Memoir of Dr. Sibbes, in our edition of his works (7 vols. 8vo).

Page 126, '*Treatise of Schism,*' by John Hales: see our Essay on Life and Writings, as before.

Page 126, '*occasionally light*'=on occasion, accidentally. Light=lighted, as I have filled-in.

Page 131, '*putanism*'=the trade of a prostitute; or here rather—for he is speaking of vices attributed to the Romish clergy—trading in or affecting prostitutes, whoremongering; from French *putain.*

Page 132, '*adream'd.*' This sounds like that rustic northern phraseology which Marvell sometimes affected. 'I am adream'd' was used occasionally by Elizabethan writers for 'I dreamt,' &c. See Nares and Halliwell, *s. v.*

Page 132, '*moral satirist:*' Juvenal, vi.

„ 133, '*Well fare,*' &c. This is afterwards played on.

„ 133, '*assassinats*'=assassinations. It is used in the Rehearsal for an assassin; but it is put into the mouth of a strange-speaking (probably Irish) soldier.

Page 134, '*Evangelical Love,*' '*Church Peace and Unity.*' Well-known treatises by Richard Baxter. See our annotated list of his writings, *s.v.* (one vol. 8vo, 1871). Dr. John Owen also wrote on the same subjects. See his works by Dr. Goold, *s.v.*

Page 135, '*fat Sir John Falstaffe's singular dexterity in sinking:*' as in the Merry Wives of Windsor immortalised.

Page 135, '*Morality of the Lord's Day*.' Richard Baxter edited Dr. Thomas Young's treatise on this subject, and himself wrote on it. See Gilfillan's work on 'The Sabbath,' *s. n.*

Page 136, '*kept touch*'=kept agreement.

„ 137, '*collar of -nesses :*' pun upon collar of SS, worn by Knights of the Garter, the well-known Lancastrian livery collar, found on monumental effigies and the like of the 15th century. Antiquaries are not agreed as to the meaning of SS. See communications in N. and Q. 1st s. ii. *passim* (General Index, *s.v.*), Gentleman's Magazine for 1842, and recently in *Athenæum*.

Page 137, '*Dongioness, Innerness, and Cathness*.' The first is Dungeness, scene of the sinking of the 'Northfleet' so tragically, as I am working on these Notes; the second, query Inverness? the third, Caithness.

Page 139, '*make merry on the Sabbath day . . . with it.*' This reminds us of an old Scotchwoman, who, on her way to the 'kirk' [church], seeing a young man breaking the edge of a limestone rock by the wayside, asked what he was about? and receiving for curt answer that he was merely breaking a bit of stone, as she might see, received as retort, 'Ay, sir, and mair [more] than that, ye're *breaking* the Lord's-day,' to his confusion.

Page 140, '*Mambrino's helmet, and the ass's pannel,*' &c.: in Don Quixote.

Page 141, '*fanatical book of martyrs :*' the great book of John Foxe.

Page 141, '*Mr. Guichard*.' This is a singular misprint for [George] Wishart, one of the early martyrs of Scotland. Froude, in his first edition of the History, misplaced the 'burning' in Edinburgh instead of St. Andrew's. He promised to us he would correct the oversight.

Page 142, '*Campanella :*' an account of C.'s philosophy is given in Hallam's Lit. of Europe (ed. 1839, iii. 143-9).

Page 142, '*a modern author lately dead :*' I have failed to trace this author.

Page 143, '*downright lie :*' cf. 'lie circumstantial and the lie direct' (As You like It, act v. sc. 4). In Laman Blanchard's Essays is a charming paper on 'Black, Gray, and White Lies.'

Page 144, Lines: from Rehearsal (Arber, pp. 123, 5.)

„ 144, '*a rapper*'=a notorious or great lie, an oath, a thundering sort of speech (Dyche). Equal our present vulgarism 'whopper,' which is also applied to a great lie or anything great.

P. 144, '*clary*.' The words, 'drunk' and 'Heliogabalus' and 'his burning,' and its use with eggs, show that the herb clary was meant as a strong drink prepared from it, which, according to Kersey, went by the same name. Clary, besides clearing the eyes of specks, was, as implied by its name horminum, ὅρμινον, a herb *ad venerem excitans*, 'the seed or leaves being taken in wine.' 'It was also in much use with men or women that have weak backes to help to strengthen the reines.' It was put, it is said, into ale or beer to make it more heady and fit for drunkards, and was a restorative in general, and 'helpeth a cold stomacke oppressed with cold phlegme' (Parkinson's Herbal). From a passage in Beaumont and Fletcher (Chances, act iii. sc. 1) it would seem to have been used for that which in our text may be expressed in the word 'burning.'

Page 145, '*Doctor Baily's romance of the Wall-flower:*' the reference is to a very singular book, viz. 'Herba Parietis; or the Wall-flower as it grew out of the Stone-chamber belonging to Newgate. By Thomas Bayly, D.D. London, 1650' (folio), with frontispiece.

Page 145, '*Heliodorus:*' born at Emisa, he lived about the end of the fourth century under Theodosius and his sons. His romance is entitled Æthiopica, and sometimes Charicleia, from its relating the loves of Charicleia and Theagenes. He afterwards became Bishop of Trissa; but the story in the text is rejected by modern critics. Crashaw versified the introduction of the romance; see our ed. of his Poetry (vol. i. pp. 212-13). Some assign the origin of the Arcadia to it: see our edition of Sir Philip Sidney's Poetry.

Page 145, '*at the Nag's Head . . . the Cock:*' the former a standing ecclesiastico-historical legend, still gravely 'disputed,' of *in re* apostolical succession of Bishops; albeit, to the praise of his candour as a Roman Catholic, rejected by Canon Estcourt in his 'Anglican Ordinations Considered,' recently published. The 'Cock' and the 'Dog and Partridge' (onward a little) were celebrated inns, the 'Cock' figuring in many contemporary books.

Page 145, '*Cartwright:*' the actor who played Thunder in the Prologue and second King in Bayes' play. See Rehearsal, i. p. 43 and v. p. 11.

Page 146, '*whip a gig as boyes do*'=a top. See Halliwell, *s.v.*

Page 146, '*Sir Edmond* [Berry] *Godfrey :*' the magistrate who was so foully murdered on the 12th of October 1678. We have here a good example of how well known he was as a magistrate.

Page 146, '*stupendous :*' it is spelled 'stupendious ;' and words in ' ous' were then not unfrequently so spelled, though now it is only a vulgarism. ' Stupendous' is thus spelled by Denham :

> ' With such an easy and unforced ascent,
> That no stupendious precipice denies access.'   (Cooper's Hill.)

Naunton in Fragmenta Regalia has similarly ' dexteriously' (under ' Elizabeth'). See ' stupendious,' ' stupendiously ;' also pp. 475, 492. So too in Hausted's Rivall Friends (1632), ' robustious clowne' (act ii. sc. .5).

Page 147, '*run up to the wall by an angel :*' alluding to Balaam (Numbers xxii. 25).

Page 147, '*apparently*'=evidently, plainly.

,, 148, '*ratio ultima cleri :*' the legend ' Ultima ratio regum' was inscribed by Louis XIV. on his cannon. See on the origin of the phrase, N. and Q. 3d s. xii. 436 ; 4th s. i. 19.

Page 148, '*pudder*'=pother, bustle, or stir, disturbing fuss. Hickeringill in his reply to Marvell has ' putter' (p. 245).

Page 149, '*a pertinent passage in St. Austin.*' See the place given onward by Marvell (page 150).

Page 150, '*good Augustulus : Quum,*' &c. : the opening lines of Horace (Epist. ii. 1) addressed to Augustus. Marvell uses the diminutive in ridicule of Bayes, *i.e.* Parker.

Page 151, '*the Welch have a proverb,*' &c. It is as follows : ' Da yw'r main gyda'r Efengyl.'

Page 152, '*a Father's opinion.*' There was a keen thrust here, for (as onward) Parker's own ' father' had published books very antagonistic to the son's opinions.

Page 152, '*insults*'=triumphs, boasts, as elsewhere.

,, 152, '*mowsled*'=from 'moused,' like many frequentatives in *le*=to worry, as a cat does a mouse.

Page 153, '*a lock.*' See our note on page 115.

,, 153, '*Terra Incognita of Geneva.*' Marvell is never weary of girding at Parker's droll ignorance of the position of Geneva.

Page 153-4, '*Whitgift :*' born 1530, died 1604. His Works have been collected and published by the Parker Society (3 vols. 1851-3).

NOTES AND ILLUSTRATIONS.

Page 154, '*curtana:*' the name of the first royal sword of England for many centuries, specially of Edward the Confessor's sword, the emblem of mercy. See farther in N. and Q. 1st s. i. 364. So Dryden in his Hind and Panther :
> 'But when Curtana will not do the deed,
> You lay that pointless clergy-weapon by.' (Christie's ed.)

Page 154, '*Sir Salomon's sword; cock,*' &c. : the 'sword' of the Romances, with apparently a dim reminiscence of Solomon's in 1 Kings iii. 24. 'Cock' is used as in our cock-of-the-walk, queller or overcomer.

Page 154, '*dead-doing*'=death-dealing. So Spenser, 'hold your dead-doing hand' (F. Q. b. ii. c. iii. st. 8).

Page 154, '*Scanderbag.*' The 'a' is substituted for 'e' waggishly. It is used as a slang term of reproach in the play of 'Sir Martin Marall' (Dryden and Duke of Newcastle), 'Oh, scanderbag villanie!' An account of his sword, which by the proverb required his own arm to wield it, is given from 17th-century authors in N. and Q. 1st s. vii. 35, 143, 511. English writers had become acquainted with his fame through the 'History of Scanderbeg,' translated from the French : London, 1596, folio. See N. and Q. 3d s. i. 461.

Page 154, '*every mother's son.*' See Halliwell, as before, *s. v.* I add Mids.-Night's Dream, i. 2.

Page 155, '*a great prelate:*' viz. Bishop Cosin.

,, 155, '*the Roman emperour.*' Suetonius tells the story of the emperor Caligula, who, with all the parade of war, ordered his soldiers to gather seaside shells in their shields and helmets, and then built a high tower as the monument of his victory (iv. 46). See our Essay for Marvell's (alleged) translation of Suetonius.

Page 157, '*insana laurus.*' 'In the same tract [of Pontus] there is an hauen ennobled and renowned by the name of Amycus the King of the Bebrycians there slaine. His tombe from the very day of his sepulture hath been overshadowed with a bay-tree (planted there and then for that purpose), which the people of that country do call the raging or mad lawrell; for pluck but a branch or twig thereof, be it neuer so small, and carie it into a ship, all the mariners and passengers within will fall a brawling, and neuer agree vntill it be cast out and throwne away out of the vessell' (Holland's Pliny's N. H. l. xvi. c. 44).

Page 158, '*palliated*'=cloaked or shrouded (Latin *pallium*). See p. 403.

Page 158, '*colluded*'=entered into a play with. Our form is *collusion*.

Page 158, '*of Seven Sacraments.*' See note *ante*.

,, 159, '*Holiness of Lent.*' See note on page 167.

,, 159, '*Dr.* [Herbert] *Thorndike.*' Died 1672, as before.

,, 160, '*impertinence*'=want of pertinency, as 'impertinent' elsewhere in R. T. (p. 163).

Page 161, '*tap-lash*'=the muddy last runnings of a beer cask=tap-droppings, before. As 'tap' is also French, 'lash' may be the French lasche (lâche), slack, flagging, languishing, slow, or that which comes flaggingly from the tap. It is used by Parker in his Reproof, p. 189.

Page 163, '*Augustus Cæsar . . . used to fly from a new word.*' See on this more fully and playfully in Part II.

Page 163, '*homiousians* and *homoiousians:*' the terms on which the great Arian heresy turned. The Nicene Creed was framed by the Council of Nicea, A.D. 325, to oppose the heresy. Hence the origin of our phrase 'one jot,' *i.e.* one iota (ι); cf. St. Matthew v. 18.

Page 163, '*Languedoc.*' See an account of the Langue d'oil and Langue d'oi, the north and south dialects of France, in N. and Q. 2d s. xi. 186, 377 ; xii. 194.

Page 166, '*Worster-House*'=Worcester, as before.

,, 167, '*Rationale :*' doubtless Bishop Sparrow's 'Rationale upon the Book of Common Prayer,' first published in 1657, and of which there have been many editions. See more of it onward.

Page 167, '*good Archdeacon.*' See Richard James, D.D., on 2 Timothy iv. 13 (1625). Like other kindred things, this story has been told of many, and even in our own day.

Page 168, '*bran :*' perhaps from 'brand;' or more probably =the Latin phrase 'nostræ farinæ' (Persius, v. 115). Cf. Cornelianum Dolium, 1638, i. 2. See onward on Part II.

Page 168, '*Only what Bishop Bramhall saith of Grotius his defect in school-divinity.*' He frequently 'carps' at the great scholar, and especially as a theologian.

Page 172, '*Parliament of Poland will be their King's taylor*' =prescribe his dress.

Page 172, '*King of Spain, when upon a Progress . . . . pleased to ride with one leg naked,*' &c. The Biscayans, or Basques, have from time immemorial preserved their so-called Fueros or charters, and no king is recognised or was recognised

NOTES AND ILLUSTRATIONS. 555

who did not, under the sacred oak of Guernica, swear to respect and uphold these Fueros. Probably, therefore, the 'naked leg' symbolised the laying down of the royal authority on entering the territory for the first time, and so far as the Church was concerned no Castilian prelate would be acknowledged, the Pope being the only authority the Basque clergy recognised. It must be remembered that Marvell visited Spain. See our Essay, as before.

Page 172, '*bushel of fleas.*' See more on this in humorous enlargement in Part II.

Page 172, '*Queen being desired to give a town-seal.*' Ibid.

,, 173, '*Queen of Sweden . . . Io non voglio governar le bestie.*' Such an act (as *supra*) would not be unlikely in Christina of Sweden.

Page 173, '*revolt of Switzerland.*' As I write these Notes tidings reach that the Swiss *savans* have exploded the whole patriotic myths of Tell, Gesler, &c. Alas for the poetry of History!

Page 173, '*unhoopable*'=that cannot be hooped tight. See more on this word, with sarcastic illustrations, in Part II. p. 313, &c.

Page 175, '*against your pins.*' See note on page 14.

,, 177, '*Cæsar's bloody coat.*' See Shakespeare's Julius Cæsar, iii. 2.

Page 177, '*Thomas-à-Becket's bloody rochet:*' 'bloody' in the murder at the altar, Canterbury.

Page 177, '*scourges of Heaven*'=wars and plague.

,, 177, '*glorious father*'=Charles I. On which and like references, see our Essay, as before. See also page 211.

Page 178, ' 'Twas well replied of the Englishman in Edward the Fourth's time, to the Frenchman that ask'd him insulting, when they would see us there again? "When your sins are greater than ours."' A commonplace of history.

Page 179, '*Bold Betrice.*' This can scarcely be Shakespeare's Beatrice (Much Ado about Nothing).

Page 180, '*Robert Parker.*' See onward, on p. 281.

,, 180, 'Parker, *de Antiquitatibus Ecclesiæ Britannicæ.*' Of this work it is alleged only fifty copies at most were printed in 1572 (folio). See Bohn's Lowndes, *s. n.*

Page 183, '*swash-buckler and hectoring way.*' So Shakespeare's 'swashing blow' (Romeo and Juliet, i. 1); and 'Hector' all through Troilus and Cressida.

Page 183, '*gird.*' So in Shakespeare's King Henry IV. (part ii. act i. sc. 2).

Page 184, '*fetch.*' See note on page 75.

„ 184, '*brought up:*' perhaps a misprint for '*bought* up.'

„ 185, '*artificially*'=skilfully.

„ 185, '*Mountague's Essayes:*' sic. But as it was 'Mountagne's' in the first edition, probably Montagne's is a mere misprint for 'Montaigne,' the great, if erratic, essayist of France. But Walter Mountague's or Montagu's Essays equally answer the description. (Corrected in our 4to and 8vo as 'Mountagne' =Montaigne.)

Page 188, '*beat up the pulpit drums.*' So Hudibras, Part i. c. i. ll. 9-12 :

'When Gospel-trumpeter, surrounded
With long-eared rout, to battle sounded ;
And pulpit drum ecclesiastic
Was beat with fist instead of a stick.'

Page 190, '*that for a bandoleers even, from Keckerman.*' Bartholomäus Keckerman, a theologian of some mark in his day; died 25th Aug. 1609. Bandoleers=a large leathern belt, thrown over the right shoulder, and hanging under the left arm; worn by ancient musketeers for sustaining their fire-arms. See Ogilvie's Imperial Dictionary, *s. v.* 'Bandolier' is thus defined in Phillip's World of Words: 'Bandoleers or Bandeleers, little wooden cases covered with leather, each of them containing the charge of powder for a musket, of which every musketeer wears twelve, hanging on a shoulder-belt or collar.' The Puritans had Williams's 'picture cut in brass, attired in his episcopal robes, with his square cap upon his head, and bandileers about his neck, shouldering a musket upon one of his shoulders in one hand, and a rest in the other' (Heylin's Laud, 461). Cf. Wood's 'Life,' July 1, 1685, and Nares. Some may be seen at Windsor Castle, where they were placed by Prince Rupert (Evelyn, Aug. 28, 1670). From Professor Mayor's 'Matthew Robinson,' pp. 18-19.

Page 191, '*Un accident sinistre* . . . I know not whether 'twas Bassompierre or Abigné.' Baron François de Bassompierre, a general of France; born 1579, died 12th Oct. 1646. His Mémoires were published in 1665. 'Abigné'=Aubigné or D'Aubigné, *i. e.* Théodore Agrippa d'; died 29th April 1630.

Page 193, '*leasings*'=lyings or falsehoods. Yet, as the two, are often found together, there must have been a shade of difference between 'leasing' and 'lying.' See our notes to Enterlude of 'Quene Hester' (1561), in Fuller Worthies' Miscellanies, vol. iv.

Page 194, '*leystal*'=laystall, dung or refuse heap.

„ 194, '*sanbenitas*.' The san- or sam-benitas was a robe like a dalmatic, worn by sorcerers, heretics, and the like, when compelled by the Inquisition to walk in the procession of the auto-da-fè, as a punishment. It was made of a yellow stuff, with crosses of St. Andrew painted in red in front and behind. Those who were condemned to be burnt at the stake wore a scapulary called ' samara,' the ground of which was of a gray colour. A portrait of the wearer was depicted on both sides, placed on burning fire-brands, with ascending flames and surrounded by demons; his name and crime were inscribed beneath the picture. See Dellon's Inquisition at Goa (1684), transl. 1812, p. 101.

Page 195, '*Petra dedit Petro, Petrus diadema Rudolpho :*' an ecclesiastical commonplace.

Page 195, '*cokesing*.' I have placed coaxing in brackets; but it may be noted here that Marvell's spelling reveals the original meaning, viz. to make a cokes or ninny of one.

Page 197, '*Abbot, in the Narrative . . . concerning his disgrace at Court*.' See his 'Life' along with his brothers' (1791), and prefixed to the modern reprint of his 'Jonah.' His 'Narrative' is rarely to be met with. This venerable man was born 29th Oct. 1562, died 4th Aug. 1633.

Page 197, '*Laud . . . his learned book against Fisher :*' 'A Relation of the Conference betweene William Laud, then Lord Bishop of St. David's, and Mr. Fisher the Jesuite; with an Answer to such Exceptions as A. C. takes against it' (1639). In Laud's Works (6 vols. 8vo, 1847-9).

Page 198, '*play at picket . . . play pieces*.' The double sovereigns of 20 (Cotgrave). The person betted on his side that he might be able to look over his hand, and then betrayed it.

Page 199, '*rob . . . in the habit of a bishop*.' It will be remembered, that in our own time, at the opening of the Exhibition in the Crystal Palace, at least two pickpockets were arrested duly dressed as bishops.

Page 199, '*pickthankness*'=thanklessness. See Halliwell, *s. v.* 'pick-thank.'

Page 200, '*Naked Truth*.' These words came to figure largely in Marvell's after-writing in the same vein with the

Rehearsal Transpros'd, viz. in his defence of Bishop Croft. See our vol. iv.

Pages 200 and 204, '*Sibthorp.*' See Eachard's History of England, vol. ii. pp. 44, 126; folio, 1718, and our Essay, as before, on this notorious, rather than famous, divine and timeserver.

Page 201, '*marrying the Earl of D. to the Lady R.*'=the Earl of Devonshire to Lady Rich—alas, Sidney's Stella! See our edition of Sir Philip Sidney's Poems.

Page 201, '*Bishop Williams.*' The great Welshman immortalised in Hackett's folio; died 25th March 1650. Sibthorp betrayed his dinner table-talk.

Page 202, '*Dr. Harsnet.*' Samuel Harsnet, Archbishop of York; born 1561, died 25th May 1651.

Page 203, '*Seven Sacraments.*' By Bishop Cosin, as before, and onward.

Page 203, '*Dr. Woral.*' He still remains 'one Dr. Woral,' obscure. But Wood in his Fasti, under July 18, 1623 (i. 411), notes him as then created Doctor of Divinity. He was of Brasenose College, and his Christian name Thomas.

Page 203, '*Mountague's Arminian book.*' On Montague and his books, see our Life of Dr. Sibbes, prefixed to his Works (7 vols. 8vo); also our Essay on Marvell, as before.

Page 204, '*Dr. Manwaring.*' Roger Manwaring (sometimes Mainwaring), Bishop of St. David's. He died in 1653. See more on him in our Essay, as before.

Page 206, '*Jack Gentleman.*' There is a proverb, 'Jack will never be a gentleman.' Cf. Shakespeare's Richard III. (act i. sc. 3):

'Since every Jack became a gentleman,
There's many a gentle person made a Jack.'

Hickeringill (in Father Greybeard, p. 23) says the proverb was, 'Jack would be a gentleman, if he could speak French.' But Marvell may not refer to the proverb, for he seems rather to use it as=gentry.

Page 207, '*magnificate:*' apparently the revival of a word used by Marston.

Page 208, '*Barnevelt:*' *i.e.* I. van Olden Barneveldt, the grand Pensionary of Holland; executed 13th May 1619.

Page 212, '*Hell's broke loose.*' Marvell's reading was out-of-the-way, and he may have caught-up the title-page of 'Hell's broke Loose: the Life and Death of John Leyden' (1605), a

NOTES AND ILLUSTRATIONS.   559

quaint wild poem by an anonymous S. R. Probably it was from this the phrase got into currency. It occurs in Hausted's 'Rivall Friends' (1632), as follows :

' Fye, fye, Hell is broke loose upon me ; all her furies
Are come at once t' assault me.'   Act v. sc. 10.

Perhaps Marvell had this in memory. Another phrase in the ' Rivall Friends' occurs onward. See note on page 325.

Page 212, ' *The arms of the Church are prayers and tears :*' I think a reminiscence of St. Augustine, and much used by the mediæval preachers.

Page 213, ' *sea-marks*'=beacons placed so that a vessel may avoid shoals, sunken rocks, &c., *not* lighthouses. So Dryden of Cromwell :

' He private mark'd the faults of others' sway,
And set as sea-marks for himself to shun.'

Page 213, ' *bed-roll*'=bede-roll.

„ 214, ' *stigmatical.*'   See note on page 9.

„ 214, ' *schism.*'   Rebellion and Schism were added to the Litany in 1662.

Page 214, ' *drill'd.*' See on this word our HENRY VAUGHAN, *s. v.* Glossary.

Page 215, ' *one memorable day.*' The ejection of the Two Thousand in 1662, as see note on page 90.

Page 215, ' *ought*'=owed, as before.

„ 216, ' *a Rationale,*' &c., as before, p. 167.

„ 216, ' *a great Minister of State*'=Clarendon.

„ 217, ' *in a matter of divorce, wherein his Majesty desired that justice might be done,*' &c. The reference is probably to Lord Ross's bill to compel him to marry again, his wife being divorced from him by the Ecclesiastical Court. The king was very eager for the success of the bill, as it would make a precedent for himself if he could get a divorce from Queen Catherine for barrenness. All the bishops were against it, except Cosins, Wilkins, and perhaps Reynolds. See Bishop Burnet, i. 262 ; and Marvell's Letters of March 21, 1670.

Page 217, ' *trinkle*'=to endeavour to turn the opinion of another by unfair means (Eastern Counties, Halliwell, *s. v.*).

Page 220, ' *shoe wrings him*'=pinches.

„ 221, '*page.*' Roger Ascham says he heard the parents (gentle folks) of a little boy under five years of age laugh at their hopeful son on his being able to ' rap out so many vyle othes' (Scholemaster, 1570 : Arber, p. 57).

Page 223, 'a set of Elizabeth players, that in the country worn-out and over-acted . . . laid their wits together to make a new one of their own. No less man than Julius Cæsar was the argument; and one of the chief parts was Moses perswading Julius Cæsar,' &c. Erudite helpers have fruitlessly seconded my efforts to ferret-out such a play.

Page 224, '*pork.*' See this drolly enlarged on in Part II. pp. 491-2.

Page 224, '*King Phys and King Ush of Brantford.*' Cf. the Rehearsal (Arber, p. 97), with whom the playwright is said by Mr. Smith to be a 'little too familiar.'

Page 224, '*five-mile act :*' passed in the parliament at Oxford (during the plague of London, 1665), which made it penal for any Nonconformist minister who had not taken the oath of non-resistance to teach in a school, or go within five miles of any city, borough or corporate town, where he had taught or preached since the Act of Uniformity. Many of the largest and most influential Nonconformist congregations now existing originated in this infamous 'Five-mile Act;' and what was intended for opprobrium has been transfigured into honour.

Page 225, '*Bishop Davenant.*' Not, of course, the venerable Bishop Davenant (died 1641), but as sarcastically applied to Sir William Davenant, whose 'Gondibert' we have had already occasion to notice, albeit Marvell evidently disliked the man. See our Essay for a singular hidden reference to him, which baffled us before in its place in the Poems. The present quotations are from c. vi.

Page 226, '*Astragen.*' This is another satirical 'gird' at Sir William D'Avenant: Lord Astragon the wise and wealthy—a character in Gondibert—who in a triangular building did dedicate three fanes 'to days of praise, of penitence, and pray'r' (Gondibert, as *supra*).

Page 226, '*hum and buz :*' from the Rehearsal, where Love, in form of a humble-bee, says, 'I will . . . both hum and buz before your eye.'

Page 227, '*Aretine, the libertine Poet.*' The author of this supposititious epitaph has not come down. Peter Aretino is intended.

NOTES AND ILLUSTRATIONS.

Part II.

Page 233, '*kind of child :*' viz. a mouse—the old fable of the mountain in labour.

Page 234, '*Plutarch, indeed, gives us the minutes,*' &c. See 'Lives' under Alexander the Great.

Page 234, '*the Dutch historian Aytzema,*' &c. Leo Aitzema, the historian of the United Provinces, died at the Hague in 1669. He 'glorifies' the House of 'Orange.'

Page 235, '*an At-all of so many capacities*'=one who endeavours to be a Jack of all knowledge. Probably Marvell had in his memory Sir Positive At-all of Shadwell's play—a caricature of Sir Robert Howard, who is referred to as Sir Positive in 'Farther Instructions to a Painter.' See our vol. i. 324, l. 48, and relative note.

Page 235, '*Had he acted Pyramus,*' &c.=Bottom in Mids.-Night's Dream.

Page 235, '*Nero . . . considerable a fidler :*' a common-place of his 'Life.' See Suetonius, *s.n.*

Page 235, '*sneeze . . . salute.*' It was (and yet is in some places) the custom to say to a person sneezing, 'God bless you!' or some similar exclamation. See Brand's Pop. Antiq. (Bohn, iii. 124-5); N. and Q. 1st s. x. xi. &c. *s.v.*

Page 236, '*Mufti and the Mulla :*' Mufti=high-priest or chief ecclesiastical dignitary among the Mohammedans. Mulla =Mollah or Moolahs, principal judges of Mohammedan law in fourteen principal places in the Turkish empire.

Page 236, '*Agra :*' Marvell is here a little behindhand. Agra was the capital of the Mogul empire till 1647, when Shah Jehan, father of Aurunzzebe, who was reigning 1671, removed to Delhi.

Page 237, '*faults :*' the first editions of the Authorised Version were very faulty in their printers' errors.

Page 238, '*Abelteria*'=ἀβελτερία, stupidity.

„ 239, '*accost :*' Cotgrave gives the French *accoster* not merely as meaning accost in our sense of the term, but, as its derivation implies, to join side by side. So Fuller W. Derbyshire (Richardson, *s.v.*), 'Lapland hath since been often surrounded (so much as *accosts* the sea) by the English.' In an old play 'accord' is distinctly used for 'kiss;' and it is probably used in the same sense in Twelfth Night, for Sir Andrew had already spoken to Maria, and Sir Toby explains it by 'front her, *board her*, woo her, assail her,' where Shakespeare shows his knowledge of the etymology of ' accord' by the word ' board' (T. N. i. 1). The word must have been new, or there would have been no point in making the provincial, or it may be Scotch, Sir Andrew fall into so stupid a blunder.

Page 239, ' *Tentamina*,' &c. See our Essay for notice of Parker's Writings.

Page 239, ' *ranks it among his colours*'=colorable or probable reasons. But see Bacon, *s.v.*

Page 240, ' *Stilpo . . . Theodorus.*' See Cicero *de Fato*, c. 5 ; and Diog. Laert. ii. 116, &c.

Page 240, ' *the rest of the clergymen's wives were but dishclouts*' = vulgar and menial. Shakespeare has ' Romeo's a *dishclout* to him' (iii. 5).

Page 240, ' *Sir John Hinton :*' one of this name died in 1682.

,, 240, ' *Dr. Chamberlain*' = Edward Chamberlayne, F.R.S. LL.D.

Page 240, ' *Dr. Harvye's egg-shell :*' alluding to Dr. Harvey's ' Omne vivum ex ovo.'

Page 242, ' *pick-a-pack*'=over-riding him, and governing him as the Old Man of the Sea did Sinbad, the man being the slave, as when the old peasant in the fable carried his ass. Cf. Wheatley's Dict. Redup. Words, *s.v.*; and Hudibras, pt. i. c. 2, l. 71.

Page 242, ' *curate of Ikham with his maid*,' &c. : a piece of scandal Parker never gainsays.

Page 243, ' *his whole Tridentine portmantle of polity :*' Tridentinus belongs to Tridentum or Trent, the city of the Council : ' portmantle'=portmanteau now.

Page 243, ' *windows :*' alluding to the Cornelianum dolium, or main remedy for the *morbus gallicus*.

Pages 244 and 248, ' *Hicringill.*' As before, Marvell refers to the author of ' Gregory Greybeard.' See our Essay on the various Answers to the R. T.

Page 246, ' *elephant upon a guinny :*' referring to the small figure of the elephant which appears under the effigies of Charles on his sovereigns.

Page 246, ' *prayed betwixt the teeth :*' I apprehend that this does not mean so much ' cursed,' as might be imagined from what goes before, but ' prayed' for them with lip-prayers (though having rancour in his heart). Cf. Shakespeare, Ant. of Augustus :

'When the best hint was given him, he not took't,
 Or did it from his teeth ;'

and the cognate phrases quoted on the passage, which show that it meant for 'appearance' sake only,' and consequently on some occasions 'for pretence,' or deceitfully.

Page 246, '*coife :*' see note in Part i. page 7.

,, 247, '*Tartars . . . phthiriases*'=the morbus pedicularis, of which Sylla the Dictator died (Pliny, N. H. l. 26, c. 13), and of which it has been supposed Herod Agrippa (Acts xii. 27), Herod the Great (Josephus, Wars of the Jews, l. i. c. 33), and Antiochus Epiphanes (2 Macc. ix. 9) also died. Phterophagi= louse-eaters. 'Tartarians . . . one of them eateth the lyce from another's head, sayinge, Thus will wee doe to our enemyes' (A brief Collection . . of straunge and memorable Things gathered out of the Cosmographie of Seb. Munster, Lond. 1574, p. 72).

Page 247, '*tribute of fleas :*' see Part i. p. 172.

,, '*Beggars-bush.*' 'This is the way to Beggers-bush.' 'It is spoken of such who use dissolute and unprovident courses which tend to poverty. Beggers-bush being a tree notoriously known, on the left hand of the London-road from Huntington to Caxton.' Ray's Proverbs, p. 244, ed. 1768 (Dyce's Beaumont and Fletcher, Beggar's Bush, ix. 18).

Page 249, '*brass-coppers*'=debased money.

,, 249, '*Energumeni :*' those supposed to be possessed with devils and under care of exorcists. They were allowed to be present at the Church service, but were not admitted to baptism or the Lord's table.

Page 252, '*deodands.*' See Note on Poems, Works, vol. i. pp. 57-8.

Page 253, '*prick-ears*'=erect (or erected) ears, as of a hare listening; perhaps with a sub-thought here of a donkey's while braying. Bailey, *s.v.*, from Grew, says, 'a greyhound hath pricked ears.' So in 'Return from Pernassus' (1606), 'prick-eard curres' (act ii. sc. 5), in a quaint enumeration of 'dogs.'

Page 253, '*after-meath*'=after-math, the second growth of a meadow in one season, also called eatage, addish, fog, &c. Scoticè, 'fug' is=moss.

Page 255, '*vaccated*'=made void.

,, 255, '*Tithes.*' Was it the law that he could recover treble for tithes withheld?

Page 257, '*prædicari*'=preachers. So we have 'predication=preaching, as in the Enterlude of Hester (1561).

Page 257, '*chase the blown deer*'=the deer long-chased and his 'wind' almost gone. It can hardly be=diseased or tainted, as if fly-blown.

Page 258, '*recollection*'=re-gathering or bringing together. See Poems, vol. i. p. 305.

Page 258, '*degrades :*' alluding to the ceremony of unfrocking, by which an ecclesiastic was degraded to a laic before being handed over to the punishment of the secular arm.

Page 260, '*liquors . . . turn eager :*' French aigre, sour.

,, 262, '*Theology went on mumminy*' = masking: so 'mummery.'

Page 262, '*a sort of Divines*'=a sect, party. So Dryden:
'A sort of doves were housed too near their hall.'
Hind and P. (Christie's Dryden), iii. 946, and relative note, p. 275.

Page 263, '*nursery . . . Killigrew's patent.*' Killigrew's patent for the King's Theatre was granted in July 1660. The King's company acted at first in Vere-street, Lincoln's-inn-fields, and removed in April 1663 to a new house in Drury-lane. About the same time that Killigrew had a patent in the King's company Sir William Davenant had a second for the Duke's Theatre. In July 1663 a license was granted to Thomas Killigrew and Sir William Davenant together ' to erect a third playhouse, as a *nursery* for training actors for the other two already allowed to them' (Mrs. Everett Green's Calendar of Domestic State Papers, 1663-4, p. 214). See Dryden's lines on the Nursery in MacFlecknoe, 74 et seq. There is an allusion to the Nursery in the Rehearsal, act. ii. sc. 2. (Cf. Arber's reprint and note, p. 13.) Oldham, in Spencer's Ghost on Settle, also thus passingly refers to it:

'Then slighted by the very Nursery.'

Page 264, '*the nation of the Bravos and Filoux.*' As bravo is Ital. and filou French, Marvell uses 'nation' figuratively and much as the French *gens*.

Page 265, '*buttering one book upon another.*' Query=sandwiching?

Page 265, '*letters of mart :*' now of 'marque.'

,, 265, '*Sir John Falstaff :*' as in the 'Merry Wives of Windsor.'

Page 265, '*Bricolle*'=a snare for wild beasts. Bricile and Bricolle: a side-stroke at tennis or banking of bowls, from one of the latter of which apparently comes the phrase 'Il m'a joué d'une bricole;' he hath plaid me sore or foul play, offered me hard or odde measure; dealt extremely or cunningly with me; also he hath deceived or disappointed me (Cotgrave).

Page 266, '*Onias the son of Simeon the Just . . . officiating in a woman's zone*,' &c. See Josephus, Ant. xii. 4; and Macc. in Apocrypha.

Page 267, '*Lucretius . . . Divum hominumque voluptas*' (i. 1).
,, 269, '*so near his form*'=lair or seat of a hare.
,, 269, '*sent out a general siquis*.' A law phrase; see Cowell. Wither headed one of his tractates a *Si Quis*.

Page 270, '*voiced*'=proclaimed.
,, 270, '*donative*.' See Poems, vol. i. p. 116.
,, 270, '*since the day of St. Bartholomew*'=when the two thousand were 'ejected.'

Page 270, '*Surrogate . . . Paritor:*' familiar ecclesiastical officers.

Page 271, '*orifacture*'=soap-bubbles made with the mouth, not the hand.

Page 274, '*clancular contrivance:*' fr. clancularius, secret, concealed.

Page 275, '*got a sixiesme du valet in his hand . . . to make a quatorze*'=a sequence of six from the knave reckoning for ten, quatorze = the four kings, queens, or tens reckoning as fourteen countings in the game of piquet. Marvell says he is resigned, because if, as above, the adversary can count thirty and the other nothing, the thirty counts as ninety, the game being 101.

Page 275, '*Gregory Greybeard*.' See note on page 244.
,, 275, '*like the Smectymnus:*' a commonplace of history; a word formed from the initials of the names of the several writers, as follows: S[tephen] M[arshall], E[dmund] C[alamy], T[homas] Y[oung], M[atthew] N[ewcomen], and W[illiam] S[purstowe].

Page 275, '*whom to slayle*'—as recorded by Shakespeare in the cases of King Henry IV. at Shrewsbury (1 K. H. IV. v. 3) and Henry VII. at Bosworth, where the number agrees with that of the six Scaramuccios:

'*Rich* I think there be six Richmonds in the field :
Five have I slain to-day instead of him.' Rich. III. v. 5.

Page 276, '*the two learned brothers of St. Marthe.*' Query =Martha? Mary of Bethany *contemplativæ vitæ figura*.

Page 277, '*Dr. Donne's Progress of the Soul.*' See our ed. of the Complete Poems of Dr. Donne, vol. i. pp. 65-96.

Page 280, '*Henry Parker, a Carmelite Friar.*' Author of Diues et Pauper; printed by Pynson, 1493 (folio). See Anth. a-Wood, Athenæ Oxon. *s.n.*

Page 281, '*Robert Parker.*' See an account of him in Brook's Puritans, *s.n.*

Page 281, '*Humfrey Parker.*' See our Essay, as before, on him and his books.

Pages 281-2, '*Martin Parker's ballads :*' the prelate's poet. For account of him consult N. and Q. 2d s. x. 212. The following bookling by him is noticeable: 'Nightingale warbling forth her own Disaster; or the Rape of Philomela, newly written in English Verse' (1632).

Page 282, '*signature :*' *id est*, the markings or resemblance which prove the lineage. This, as a frequent law, is being re-established, and connects itself with a similar law in Parthenogenesis.

Page 282, '*the Duke of Muscovy . . . declared war against Poland.*' Our own age has found Russia and Austria 'persecuting' not the poets of Poland only, but all free-speaking authors. The particular poet referred to is unknown, as well as the particular Duke of Muscovy.

Page 282, '*Saffron Hill and Pye Corner.*' *Saffron-hill* is north of Holborn, a poor district, and out of the City jurisdiction; two reasons, perhaps, why it was a ballad-singers' and ballad-hawkers' haunt. *Pye-corner:* Giltspur-street is famous as one of the limits of the great fire, which, in popular phrase, began in Pudding-lane and ended at Pye-corner. Cf. Chettle's Kind-Hart's Dream, under Anthony.

Page 284, '*the Lords . . . Capel, Holland, and Hamilton :*' sad commonplaces of history, not calling for annotation here; but see Lady Theresa Lewis' 'Lives of the Friends and Contemporaries of Lord Chancellor Clarendon' (1852).

Page 284, '*picking the teeth*'=after performing some base and servile offices.

Page 285, '*mantlings and atchievements of the family :*' heraldic terms in living use still. Mantlings=drapery of a coat of arms; atchievements=family actions of note worked into the shields of arms or escutcheons.

Page 285, '*more graves than all the rest in his porridge.*' Halliwell gives ' the refuse at the bottom of the melting pot in making tallow candles. Pressed into oblong cakes, it is boiled in water as food for dogs.' Junius gives ' greaves, the juice of boiled or roast meat remaining in the dish after the meat is cut in pieces.' The word is clearly connected with ' gravy' and the fatty composition used in graving a ship; and Junius's words confirm an impression that I have met with the word used in a kitchen and not merely in a tallow-chandler's sense.

Page 286, ' *Muleasses king of Tunis.*' This can scarcely be a reference to Mason's play of Muleases.

Page 287, '*dissipation*'=dispersion.

,, 289, '*Dr. Bathurst :*' i.e. Ralph Bathurst, dean of Wells, a poet and man of science; died, in a ' good old age,' 14th June 1704.

Page 290, '*unlucky*'=in not being in his full wits.

,, 291, ' *stuck his groat in Lambeth wainscot.*' I cannot interpret this odd saying, unless ' wainscot' be a misprint for ' waistcoat' (=dress), which it could scarcely be. It seems a slang phrase whose allusive meaning has passed away. Could it be some old custom on taking possession, or perhaps of becoming a dependent of the lord or possessor?

Page 291, ' *agoe*'=agone. According to Halliwell it is still Somerset for gone or passed, and was so used of old as in his examples *s.v.* Marvell evidently uses the word and phrase colloquially, and in the derivative sense in which we say a thing is gone or done for, the ' Tout est perdu,' of the old song.

Page 291, ' *stirrops himself*'=sits up in his stirrups, vaunts himself as a rider who does this; but I have not met with the phrase elsewhere.

Page 294, ' *the third crambe of the same purulent matter*' = a play at short verses, in which the word is given to the parties contending who can find most rhymes to it. It is also used, says Halliwell, by Dekker as a drinking term (and if so, perhaps by Jonson). Here and in a similar usage by Glanville quoted in Richardson, but not explained by him, it would seem to mean what a crambo verse more frequently was—a foolish or common thing or saying.

Page 294, ' *William the Conqueror.*' So in all the Lives of him, if mythical.

Page 295, '*imp'd*'=helped. See our Fuller Worthies' Library, often, for this word (Glossaries), and N. and Q. *s.v.*; also Christie's Dryden, as before, p. 63.

Page 295, '*eagle.*' Byron used the simile pathetically of Henry Kirke White in his 'English Bards and Scotch Reviewers.'

Page 297, '*icterus, a bird good against jaundice.*' 'A bird there is called in the Greeke Icterus, of the yellow colour which the feathers carry, which if one that hath the jaundise do but look vpon, he or she shall presently be cured thereof, but the poore bird is sure to die for it. I suppose that this is the same bird which in Latin is called Galgulus.' P. Holland's Pliny, N. H. l. 30, c. 11.

Page 298, '*reincamerate*'=to re-add some land-right or revenue to the Pope (incameration : Dyche).

Page 299, '*sounds another trumpet than that in Sheere-lane,*' &c. See a notice of Sheer-lane in N. and Q. 3d s. x. 371, 424.

Page 300, '*his ancient palace of Bridewell.*' See Cunningham's London, *s.v.*

Page 306, '*we-ship :*' Thompson has the bad misprint of 'worship.'

Page 306, '*Will he not sound a trumpet,*' &c. Such is the legendary account of a court-custom of the Emperor of China.

Page 309, '*Cardinal Antonio's suffrage.*' Antonio Perrenot de Granvelle was first minister of Charles V. and Philip II. He was execrated in Flanders for his administration during the time of Margaret of Parma; afterwards became Viceroy of Naples. Born 1517, died 1586. See Motley, Rise of D. Rep. vol. i. *s.n.*

Page 309, '*Mr. Baxter baptized in blood.*' See our Essay on this notorious incident in literature.

Page 310, '*abrenunciate*'=absolutely renounce; abrenunciation=absolute denial.

Page 310, '*rotundity and cadence :*' from *ore rotundo.*

,, 311, '*adlubescence*'=pleasantness or pleasuring.

,, 313, '*unhoopable.*' See note in Pt. i. page 173.

,, 313, '*an empty cask :*' a sea-tradition.

,, 313, *harping-iron*'=harpoon. Hull was our chief port in connection with the whale-fishery in the 17th-18th century.

Page 313, '*moyles*'=toils, labours.

,, 313, '*Claudius . . . edict De bene picandis doliis.*' Suetonius, *s.n.*; a classical commonplace.

Page 314, '*Cornelius his tub*' = the sweating-tub of the

physician of that name, used in the disease to which Marvell so often refers.

Page 314, ' *Cardinal Cusanus :*' probably Cardinal Nicholas de Cusa (1401), whose writings did not uphold all the traditionary history of the Papacy.

Page 314, ' *rectifies*'=becomes straighter.

,, 315, ' *Du Foy.*' See N. and Q. 2d s. xii. 250.

,, 316, ' *send to Co'chester*' = Hickeringill. See our Essay as in note on page 244.

Page 319, ' *thumming the busk :*' see Halliwell under ' busk.' In Hausted's ' Rivall Friends' (1632) we have, ' What, must we stand thrumming of cats all day ?' (act iv. sc. 9.)

Page 319, ' *chronology*,' &c. The great scholar's ' De Temp.' &c. suggesting the allusion.

Page 321, ' *ears . . . glow.*' It is an abiding superstition, that when a person's right ear burns, some one is speaking well of him; the left the contrary. Many parallels in Folk-lore.

Page 321, '*running away like Evagrius*'=of Pontus, born about 345, died about 399 ; besides a remarkable running away from sin in early life, when an ascetic he fled from Theophilus, patriarch of Alexandria, for the reasons stated in the text.

Page 321, ' *like Ammonius, cut off*,' &c.=the Monk fl. 372. He accompanied Athanasius to Rome, and when the Arian persecution broke out, he retired first to Palestine and then to Egypt.

Page 323, ' *another Oliver, a barber, discharged under Lewis the Eleventh*' = Oliver le Dain, barber, adviser, and agent of Louis XI. ; but I know not the homely employment intended.

Page 323, ' *snickering*'=snicker or snigger, to laugh in one's sleeve, or to half-laugh contemptuously.

Page 323, ' *colosseros.*' As may be gathered from Marvell's suggestion as to his ' girdle,' Parker was corpulent : hence he coins the comparative ' bigger Colossus.' Alluding to the frequency of the terms brazen-brow, &c., Marvell says brass upon brass is false heraldry, salt upon salt (wit upon wit is not).

Page 324, '*As Cicero said, Multa quidem,*' &c. Cf. Cicero's De Divinatione, b. i. c. 54.

Page 325, ' *Dr. Tomkins.*' He is incidentally mentioned in Wood's Fasti, ii. 256, 266, 336, in 1663 and 1673. He was Chancellor of the church of Exeter.

Page 325, ' *say-masters of orthodoxy*' = assay - master, an officer of the Mint.

Page 332, '*Father's 'nown son:*' 'nown' and the like was common contemporary slang, and even as early as Henry VIII. See Jack Jugeler, an Interlude, in our Miscellanies, vol. iv. p. 505. As stated in note on p. 212, Marvell may here have remembered Hausted's 'Rivall Friends,' act v. sc. 4, 'Why, Merda, you'll come when your nowne father calls.' So 'nuncle' for 'uncle,' as in Lear (frequently).

Page 332, '1650.' The following are two out of a multitude of tractates elucidatory of this reference: 1. 'Arguments and Reasons to prove the inconvenience and unlawfulness of taking the New Engagement, modestly propounded to all persons concerned.' 1650, 4to. 2. 'Conscience Puzzled about subscribing the New Engagement in the Solution of this Quære, whether a Man that hath taken the Oaths of Allegiance and Supremacy, the Protestation and Covenant, may, upon the Alteration of the Government from a Monarchy into a Free State, subscribe the Engagement "to be true and faithfull to the Commonwealth of England as it is now established, without King and House of Lords."' 1650, 4to.

Page 336, '*inclinable*' = somewhat inclined — a noticeable form.

Page 337, '*achronismes:*' query, a misprint for 'anachronisms,' or a variant? 'Anachronism' would seem to have been a new word, as it does not occur in Cotgrave, or Florio, or Minsheu or his guide Holyoke, or Bullinger.

Page 337, '*great eater of Kent*' = Nicholas Wood, celebrated by Taylor the Water-Poet. See N. and Q. 2d s. ii. 33; also Hone's Every-day Book, *s.n.*

Page 340, '*Mr. Hobbs:*' another reference to Hobbes of Malmesbury.

Page 342, '*Nero . . . . . Caligula . . . . . one neck:*' another commonplace. Suetonius, *s.n.*

Page 343, '*derived upon:*' a sort of abbreviation of the Latin phrase, 'derivare suam culpam (vel crimen) in aliquem' (Cic.), to throw his own fault on another.

Page 346, '*ensigns of all the gods*' = claimed to represent all.

,, 347, '*a poictrell:*' Fr. poictrell and 'poitril' = a horse's breastplate or breast-leathers.

Page 348, Couplet. Rehearsal, iv. i. p. 103.

,, 349, '*Prote Ennoia*' = πρώτη ἔννοια.

,, 350, '*Mr. Lee of Ickham.*' A curate in the service of Parker, of whom the less said the better.

NOTES AND ILLUSTRATIONS. 571

Page 350, '*Don Sebastian.*' The reference is to the false Sebastian, whose case excited great discussion, and whose peculiarities of body resembled those of the true, much more than a cut on the head and a mark over the right eye, though these were among them.

Page 350, '*Pseudo-Nero . . . . Perkin-Caligula.*' Marvell anticipates Carlyle in his apt coinage of nicknames. 'Perkin' is of course Perkyn Warbeck.

Page 350, '*adiatrepsia*'=ἀδιατρεψία. See Suetonius, iv. 29.

„ 352, '*Vicar of Brackley . . . Dr. Sibthorpe :*' see Essay, as before.

Page 353, '*pinne-paper :*' would seem to be a remembrancing paper of heads of discourse, pinned where the speaker could glance at it.

Page 353, '*flower of your brann.*' See note on Part i. page 168. Here and there=one of the same meal, or same leaven or batch. See p. 488.

Page 354, '*ex tripode*'=oracularly.

„ 355, *Couplet:* Rehearsal, iv. i. (Arber, p. 103).

„ 359, '*Uilenspiegled :*' see N. and Q. *s.v.* Eulenspiegle and Owleglass.

Page 359, '*without weights leap plum* [b].' It is a common belief that a man can jump better with stones or weights in his hands.

Page 361, '*depositum.*' See Chitty on Contracts.

„ 362, '*Callimelanos :*' of calomel; another of Marvell's too frequent allusions to m. gallicus.

Page 363, '*Rogation week perambulate.*' See note on Poems, vol. i. p. 225.

Page 364, '*a Chaucer's word . . . . Mr. Limitour*'=a friar licensed to beg within a certain district.

Page 364, '*gravitate and levitate*'=heavy and light.

„ 365, '*halcyon holidayes . . . a brumal quiet*'=peaceful, as in Spring.

Page 367, '*good memories.*' 'Liars should have good memories' (proverb).

Page 371, '*allay*'=alloy or mixture, as before. See our Glossarial Index in vol. iv.

Page 371, '*punctual*'=exact.

„ 372, '*hare their people*'=hunt and frighten them, as hares are.

Page 373, '*extorted :*' not necessarily by force=pressed out.

But see Enterlude of Hester (1561), as before, for a capital example of ' extort' in its primary sense.

Page 374, ' *knits*'=collects, gathers together.
,, 376, ' *benevolous*'=benevolent, full of good will.
,, 377, ' *counterparts*'=counterfoils, duplicates.
,, 379, ' *brabbles*=trifling discussions. So p. 476.
,, 380, ' *inable*'=make able, strengthen.
,, 382, ' *tumultuate*'=to raise a tumult; *i.e.* rise as an ocean in tumult, there being a kind of passivity in the word.

Page 384, ' *Mosarabe ceremonies.*' Spanish Christians who lived under the Arab rule were called ' Mosarabes' — ' quasi mixti Arabibus'—because Musa in Arabic signifies a Christian, or because = Mixtarabes ; or, as others say, from Muza, an Arab ruler in Spain. Their ' office' retained the name of Mosarabes, and was used to the time of Alphonsus VI., when it was changed by Gregory VII. It is, however, still used in six parishes in Toledo, and in the chapel of Fr. Franc Ximenes in the cathedral, and on certain days in the chapel Doctoris Talıbricensis in Salamanca. It is described by Eupenius Roblesius, whose account is given in the Biblioth. Patrum, tom. vi.; Du Cange, *s.v.* See Richard Carpenter's The Pragmatical Jesuit New Leven'd, *n.d.*, but acted between May 1660 and March 1662, in introduction of act iv., for curious notices of Spanish-church ' customs,' which may have suggested Marvell's allusion.

Page 387, ' *As the fool thinks,*' &c. An old proverb is, ' As the bell tinks, so the fool thinks.'

Page 393, ' *subalternals*'=subalterns, unusual or unique.
,, 393, ' *hoch-hoch*'=hodge-podge. In the ' Return from Pernassus' (1606) we have the definition of it : ' *Rec.* That's plaine in Littleton, for if that fee-simple and the fee-taile be put together, it is called hotch potch: now this word hotch potch in English is a pudding, for in such a pudding is not commonly one thing only, but one thing with another. *Amor.* I thinke I do remember this also at a meeting in our Temple: so then this hotch potch seemes a terme of similitude.' Act iv. sc. 2. See Wheatley, as before, *s.v.* pp. 45, 47 ; and N. and Q. *s.v.* recently.

Page 396, ' *cart-wheels . . . buries in flannel.*' In many old church-registers I have come on records of burials in flannel, according to the law for encouragement of its manufacture. ' Carts' were taxed according to the breadth and number of their wheels.

NOTES AND ILLUSTRATIONS. 573

Page 396, '*damnation*.' An example of the use of the word in its strong sense, and which being still retained in our English Bible, gives a needlessly terrible significance to certain passages, as 1 Corinthians xi.

Page 397, '*like that Italian . . . kill their bodies and damn their souls*.' Iago does this twice in the killing of Roderigo and in the ensnaring of Othello:

'Will you, I pray, demand that demi-devil
Why he hath thus ensnared my soul and body?'   Act v. sc 2.

But does Marvell refer to him or to some historical person? He was a reader of Shakespeare.

Page 397, '*speak to the quick :*' a cognate phrase with our 'cut to the quick,' or speak sharply and home.

Page 400, '*capable*'=able to understand.

„   400, '*danger*.' I have filled-in here ['be in'], otherwise it is an odd phrase.

Page 402, '*a new law . . a halter*,' &c.: as the Spartans did.

„   403, '*palliate*.' See note on page 158. Here=disguise with.

Page 404, '*jealous*'='I very much suspect:' preserved in our colloquialism 'I jealous=I suspect.'

Page 406, '*sossiego*'=ceremonious complements . . . gravitie in manners (Florio: old Italian); or qu. Spanish for 'calmness'? (*sosiego*).

Page 406, '*Mr. Johnson*' of The Rehearsal, as before.

„   408, '*Hooker*.' It is pleasant to meet with such high praise as Marvell's of the serene-souled High-Churchman.

Page 409, '*bulbeggers*'=bugbears, probably a corruption of bug-beggar.

Page 409, '*casual theology*'=casuistical.

Page 412, '*key-cold*' (see N. and Q. xi. 171, xii. 148, and Halliwell)=cold as a piece of iron; and as a key was generally at hand, to put down one's back when the nose bled, therefore 'key-cold.'

Page 412, '*scatches*.' To 'skatch' a wheel is to stop the wheel, as of a cart or wagon, by putting a stone or block before it (Bailey). But while this yields a meaning in the text as =Parker can go over all without stumbling or meeting with a hindrance, probably 'skatches' here is from the Fr. *échasses* =stilts to put the feet in for walking over dirty places (Webster, *s.v.*).

Page 413, '*Dr. Grigg*.' '1664, 30 Sep. Thomas Grigg, A.M.

col. ad eccles. S. Andreae Undershaft, per resigno. John Pritchett' (Wood and Newcourt, *s.n.*).

Page 413, '*inch of candle.*' From the London Gazette, No. 2006, 1684, I cull this: 'In Greek Street near King Square, at a great House built for a Tavern, will be exposed to Sale by *Inch of Candle*, several rich cabinets, &c.' Similar notices are in Spectator, 17th May 1712. See N. and Q. 3d s. iii. 49.

Page 414, '*Ad insigne pelicani.*' See note on this in the Poems, Works, vol. i. p. 235.

Page 414, '*meet full bob*' = meet full stroke, run up against; bob = stroke. In Lod. Barrey's 'Ram Alley' (1636) we have 'bob'd:'

> 'Throte thou art *bob'd*, although thou boughtest the heire,
> Yet——' Act iv. sc. 1.

Page 414, '*Buckworth's lozenges.*' 'Those so famous Lozenges or Pectorals, approved for the cure of consumptions, coughs, catarrhs, asthmas, hoarseness, and all other diseases incident to the lungs, and a sovereign antidote against the Plague and all other contagious diseases and obstructions of the stomach, are made by Mr. Theophilus Buckworth, at his House on Mile-end Green.' . . . 'Quantities of them sealed up with his coat-of-arms' were sold at the shops of six different booksellers in London. See the advertisement (of 14 lines) in the Mercurius Politicus, No. 611, March 8-15, 1660, p. 1167.

Page 415, '*rebate.*' See our JOSEPH FLETCHER, *s.v.* = beat back.

,, 416, '*Dr. Bathurst,*' as before, p. 289.

,, 416, '*syderatus*' = planet-struck.

,, 417, '*pegging out.*' Does this refer to the explanation given by some to Genesis xl. 13, 19? or, is it from that boys' game where, by casting your peg-top, you try to peg your adversary's top out of the ring?

Pages 418, 451, '*Sir Francis Vere, he would for certain have spit in your mouth.*' Perhaps the best example of this proverbial mode of expressing likeness is in the Holy and Profane State, in which, speaking of the gallow-clappers sent to the Plantations, it is said: 'It was rather bitterly than falsely spoken concerning one of our western plantations, consisting most of dissolute people, that it was very like unto England, as being *spit out of the very mouth* of it.' Vere, one of the Worthies of England, needs not annotation.

Page 418, '*a heathen poet*' = Horace in the Ode parodied by

Marvell. See Poems, Works, vol. i.; also another reference to this on p. 466.

Page 418, '*Mr. Croxton.*' See N. and Q. 2d s. xii. 192, for notice of a Rev. James Croxton.

Page 419, '*cock-a-hoop.*' See Todd and Nares. Three derivatives are possible—to set the cock of the barrel or the hoop; to sit like a boisterous reveller athwart the barrel Bacchus-fashion; and cock-a-whoop. Whatever the original, it was probably taken as derivable from either cock-a-whoop or one of the others, at the pleasure of the user.

Page 420, '*Pinners-Hall*' = Pinmakers' Hall became a great central meeting-place of the Independents, and is associated with courses of theological lectures.

Page 421, '*Salvator Winter.*' No doubt one of the numerous leaders of the numerous sects of those times. In Rogers' 'Life and Opinions of a Fifth Monarchy Man,' we read, 'In 1651 one Church in Dublin chose J. Rogers . . . . and another chose *Mr. Winter;*' both, says Col. Hewson, 'godly men' (p. 29). Perhaps Marvell dubbed him waggishly ' Salvator.' I think I have seen old title-pages bearing his name.

Page 420, '*puff-paste*' = pastry (light).

„ 421, '*Don Belianis . . . grand Cyrus . . . Cleopatra:*' romances so named. The first, Don Belianis (of Greece), is often quoted in Don Quixote.

Page 425, '*glandula pinealis:*' medical-anatomical designation, not calling for annotation here, save that it was formerly believed to be the seat of the soul.

Page 427, '*Flaccus Illyricus,*' *i. e.* Flacius Illyricus, being the Latinised form of Francowitz Mathias Flach, a German Protestant divine of note, friend of Luther, opponent of Melancthon ; died 11th March 1575.

Page 428, '*mobled up.*' Cf. 'mobled Queen Hecuba,' in Hamlet, where the commentators do not seem to have perceived that Polonius approved of the epithet, because it described her as one who being suddenly aroused had thrown something around her head.

Page 429, '*brangle*' = brawl.

„ 429, '*white aprons.*' See note on page 22 and on page 139.

Page 431, '*inabled :*' see note on p. 74.

„ 432, '*good memories*' = liars, as before, p. 367.

„ 437, '*Gondomar . . . Rawleigh.*' The former, the Spanish ambassador to James I., the bitter enemy of the illustrious Raleigh. See Edwards' Raleigh, *s.n.*

Page 438, '*clutter*' = to collect together, as a hen her chickens.

Page 440, '*conne.*' See note in Part i. p. 26. I add here the following from Professor Mayor's 'Nicholas Ferrar' (1855), p. 116: 'He would con them no thanks.' So, 'Frend Hoggarde, *I cun you thanke*, that you have learned somewhat at Father Latimer's Sermons,' &c. Crowley (1548).

Page 440, '*propriery.*' Is this a misprint for 'propriety,' or a word coined after the fashion of 'impery'? (p. 464.)

Page 421, '*Balderdash*' (see N. and Q. 1st s. viii. 342; 2d s. v. 32) = 'a rude mixture, or mingle-mangle; a paltry confused discourse:' Kersey. Balderdash, *v.* to adulterate, spoil or mix a good and bad commodity together; also anything done confusedly and without judgment:' Dyche. See Ben Jonson, The New Inn, act i. sc. 1; also D'Israeli's Amenities of Literature, i. 2.

Page 444, '*malapert*,' as before, note on page 7.

„ 445, '*finding his son returned.*' These words seem to have slipped out of their own place. I have been unable to find the book 'Caesares Juliani,' whereby to put right.

Page 447, '*rake-shame.*' One who is a shame and scorn, cognate with rake-hell, and both are probably derived from 'reake,' which see note, p. 455.

Page 447, '*dearest cuzzes*' = coz's.

„ 448, '*unanimating :*' 'unanimate' = unanimous, or the agreeing in one mind.

Page 451, '*Cardinal Granwell*,' or Granvelle. See note on p. 309.

Page 451, '*Mazarines on your table*' = small dishes to be set in the middle of a larger dish for the setting out of ragoos or fricassees. Also a sort of small tarts filled with sweetmeats.' Kersey and Dyche. Query, called after the Cardinal? or a diminutive of mazer, a large bowl? Cole gives 'mazerar = drinking-cup.'

Page 451, '*spit out of his mouth :*' a colloquialism for being like. See note on p. 418.

Page 452, '*The great Galilean.*' Julian is 'said' to have exclaimed, 'Ah, Galilean, thou hast conquered!'

Page 452, '*knick-knacks.*' See Wheatley, Dict. of Redup. Words, p. 59.

NOTES AND ILLUSTRATIONS.

Page 452, '*betwixt you*' = your two wits are not to be compared except one with the other.

Page 452, '*chaw'd bullets:*' bitten to make them jagged, and so inflict a worse wound. It was the custom for musketeers to carry the bullets for immediate use in their mouths: hence, when they, on a capitulation, marched out with the honours of war, they did so 'drums beating, flags flying, and a bullet in mouth,' as though unconquered except by famine or the like.

Page 454, '*bell in Spain*.' See our Essay for notice of Marvell's visit to Spain and his reminiscences thereof.

Page 454, '*Stentoro-phonick*' = speaking-trumpet?

„ 455, '*I doubt*' = I suspect.

„ 455, '*reake*.' 'Dégonder, to lift off the hinges; ils commencent à se dégonder: they begin to lash or flie out, to revell it or play reakes; they begin very much to disorder themselves.' Cotgrave.

Page 457, '*Elizabeth Hampton:*' a patron-friend of Parker in his Nonconformist days. See our Essay thereon.

Page 458, *Lines*. Author remains still unknown.

„ 459, '*Pinne-makers Hall*' = Pinners' Hall, a great meeting-place of Nonconformists, as before.

Page 459, '*Aberford in Yorkshire:*' birth-place of Parker. See Drunken Barnaby's Journeys, pt. i.; Wheater's Sherburn and Cawood, 1865, p. 177.

Page 460, '*is proclaim'd*.' I have ventured to correct an error of number ('are' for 'is'), either of printer or author, owing to the preceding 'lines.'

Page 460, '*bear-ward*' = keeper of bears.

„ 461, '*in opposition:*' *i.e.* through your opposition to.

„ 462, '*pelt*'=pet and fume. Still used in the phrase 'a pelting rage.'

Page 462, '*Cæcilian figs . . . . il fico*.' The former refers to an epigram in Martial (l. i.), in which he speaks of Cæcilianus as having a skin-disease, ficus or sychosis (σύκωσις). For the rest, see Nares, *s.v.* Connecting, however, the biting of the thumb, as (meo judicio) we ought, with the other gesticulation, I am disposed to believe that both had their origin in the barbarous custom of mutilating the dead, when, in derision, genitalia abscissa labiis cadaveris interponebantur. On this supposition, *ficus* would require to be used in a sense derived from Genesis c. iii.; just as *fica* in Italian has from the same

VOL. III. 4 *e*

cause that double sense of ficus et mulieris pudenda, which may perhaps have given the hint to the barbarity of Barbarossa. Finally, we read, 'he had a fig given him to intoxicate his brains.' James Howell's Massaniello, pt. ii. 1663, p. 13.

Page 464, '*no more promise*' = no greater promise.

,, 464, '*impery*' = empire, government.

Page 466, '*Baldwin's Garden . . . Three Crane Court . . . Bond's Stables and the Pall Mall*.' All more or less disreputable places. See all the Histories of London, as Allen, Cunningham, &c.

Page 466, '*Horace's of Augustus*.' See Poems, vol. i. p. 402: see also before, p. 418.

Pages 466-7, '*impoysoned with the Sacrament . . . . sirname from the font, Constantius Capronymus . . . . Wenceslaus . . . . Andronicus Comnenus . . . . . or . . . . . an ecclesiastick :*' commonplaces of ecclesiastical (mythical) history.

Page 468, '*Dutch oath :*' Sacrament, a common Dutch oath.

Page 469, '*bustle*' = thrust forward, as in a crowd.

,, 470-1, '*Stillingfleet*.' He died 27th March 1699.

,, 471, '*groons . . . a Latine classical saying :*' 'groons' = grounds, the settling or dregs of drink.

Page 471, '*rosial :*' unusual, if not unique word.

,, 473, '*In laudem*,' &c.: alluding to 'Great Tom' of Oxford. See Dugdale's Monasticon, *s.v.*

Page 474, '*Sanford*,' *i.e.* Sandford.

,, 476, '*brabble*' = disputation or contention, as before, p. 379.

Page 482, '*cross and pile*.' See note on Poems, Works, vol. i. p. 225.

Page 483, '*all the fleece :*' fleece. The proverb runs of his Satanic Majesty's mistaking a pig for a sheep when he tried to shear it: 'All cry and no wool here.'

Page 484, '*Moses and Julius Cæsar*,' as before. The Enterlude of 'Hester' (1561) introduces the wars of France and Scotland. See our Fuller Worthies' Miscellanies, vol. iv.

Page 484, '*Culina*.' The tributes to Calvin might easily be extended a thousand-fold. A recent and very weighty one will be found in Dr. Perrowne's Preface to his masterly Commentary on the Psalms, 2 vols. 8vo.

Page 484, '*Hooker*,' as before. See our Essay hereon.

NOTES AND ILLUSTRATIONS.   579

Page 488, '*bran*,' as before. See notes on pp. 168, 355. Here=one of the same meal, or same leaven or batch.

Page 488, '*in her quinto Eliz.*'=Jejunium Cæcilianum, as before.

Page 491, '*Philemon Holland :*' the quaint old translator of various of the classics, as Pliny.

Page 493, '*bouleverse so :*' one of Marvell's French words.

„ 493-4, '*Hudibras*.' See our Essay, as before, on these allusions to Butler. See also note on p. 35.

Page 495, '*Ruac Hakodesh is but a Bath col*.' Marvell jests at Parker's learning by quoting the simplest Hebrew possible —very slyly too.

Pages 498-500, '*J. M.*' On this profoundly interesting Defence of Milton see our Essay.

Page 499, '*huffing*'=puffing out, swaggering.

„ 501, '*Manwaring*,' as before.

„ 502, '*Worcester House*,' as before. See p. 166.

„ 503, '*Recorder of London*.' Sir John Howell, who had been Deputy Recorder, became Recorder of London in 1668, and held the office until 1676, when he resigned. He was knighted 29th July 1668, and died about 1683.

Page 504, '*quag yourself*'=plunge in a 'quag' mire.

„ 504, '*mine host in France*,'—common to the Jestbooks. Query—vend le? Misprinted 'venie,' in the errata it is asked to be corrected into 'renie.'

Page 504, '*Play of Moses and Julius Cæsar*,' as before, note on p. 484, &c.

Page 505, '*rules*.' Rehearsal, act i. p. 31, Arber: see the passage *in extenso* on p. 526.

Page 506, '*Lord Falkland*.' See our collection of Falkland's Poems, with Introduction and Notes, in our Fuller Worthies' Miscellanies, vol. iii.; also Lady Theresa Lewis, as before.

Page 506, '*Polydore Virgil*'=Vergil; died 1555.

„ 507, '*growns .... taplash*.' See notes on pp. 161, 471.

Page 507, '*smutty :*' an earlier use of the word in this sense than any given by Richardson, *s.v.*

Page 508, '*scumming you*'=to take off the scum: cognate with but stronger than skimming.

Page 510, '*Oliver*' [*Cromwell*]. See Carlyle and all the 'Lives.'

Page 511, '*Fifth-monarchy men . . . . Vennor:*' one of the *fantastiques* of ecclesiastical heresy; a commonplace of Church-history. Yet were some of the men very noble and 'believing.'

Page 511, '*in deck*'=a card not played out, but kept in the deck or pack.

Page 511, '*orbicular*'=spoken *ore rotundo.*

,, 512, '*suborn'd suggestion*' = prompting : 'suborned suggesters' (Richardson, *s.v.* from Beaumont and Fletcher, but Dyce has not recorded it).

Page 513, '*miserere, or iliac passion :*' miserere mei, or Domine, miserere mei: an obstruction &c. of the intestines, in which there is vomiting of fæces. Iliac passion is one of various names. See the Breviarie of Health, p. 35, by A. Bond.

Page 514, '*period*'=end.

,, 516, '*grannamish:*' an unusual word, allusive to 'grandame' (?).

Page 516, '*canterburing.*' Now 'cantering'—a memorial word of the easy pace used in the Canterbury Pilgrimage.

Page 521, '*experiment*'=experience.

,, 521, '*rub . . . bias . . . cast :*' terms of play in games of bowls = an unevenness of surface or other impediments.

Page 521, '*fly :*' an old trick played on an absent-minded philosopher.

Page 522, '*Walloons at Canterbury.*' See Agnew's Huguenots, and Smiles's, *s.v.*

Page 522, '*deigned :*' misprinted 'designed'—unless = intended ?

Page 523, '*one of the Pope's . . . indignation for his peacock.*' This turns up in many old books, but always anonymously.

Page 523, '*blatant and latrant :*' the latter an unusual word.

,, 523, '*savage Javoes*' = natives of Java. As I write this, tidings reach of Holland's being called on to put forth all her strength to quell disturbances in the same regions. Thus does History, as Biography, go on repeating itself. G.